ConUNdrum

ConUNdrum

The Limits of the United Nations and the Search for Alternatives

Edited by
Brett D. Schaefer

Published in cooperation with the
Heritage Foundation

ROWMAN & LITTLEFIELD PUBLISHERS, INC.
Lanham • Boulder • New York • Toronto • Plymouth, UK

Published by Rowman & Littlefield Publishers, Inc.
A wholly owned subsidary of The Rowman & Littlefield Publishing Group, Inc.
4501 Forbes Boulevard, Suite 200, Lanham, Maryland 20706
http://www.rowmanlittlefield.com

Estover Road, Plymouth PL6 7PY, United Kingdom

Copyright © 2009 by The Heritage Foundation

Published in cooperation with the Heritage Foundation.

Published in association with the literary agency of Alive Communications, Inc.,
7680 Godard Street, Suite 200, Colorado Springs, Colorado, 80920
www.alivecommunication.com.

British Library Cataloguing in Publication Information Available

Library of Congress Cataloging-in-Publication Data

ConUNdrum : the limits of the United Nations and the search for alternatives /
edited by Brett D. Schaefer.
    p.   cm.
  Includes bibliographical references and index.
  ISBN 978-1-4422-0006-7 (cloth : alk. paper)—ISBN 978-1-4422-0008-1
(electronic)
    1. United Nations—Evaluation. I. Schaefer, Brett D.
  JZ4984.5.C665   2009
  341.23—dc22

                                                                    2009019874

∞ ™ The paper used in this publication meets the minimum requirements
of American National Standard for Information Sciences—Permanence of
Paper for Printed Library Materials, ANSI/NISO Z39.48-1992.

Printed in the United States of America

Contents

Acknowledgments

I would like thank Dr. Edwin Feulner, Dr. Kim Holmes, Dr. Nile Gardiner, and my other colleagues at The Heritage Foundation who supported and encouraged me in organizing and editing this book. Additional thanks must go to the chapter authors, whose professionalism and expertise made the process a pleasure. The book would not have been possible without their patience and perseverance. Special thanks must also go to Rebecca Hagelin and Genevieve Wood, who guided the book through the publishing and marketing process; Janice A. Smith, who read all the chapters and provided me with exceptionally valuable comments and suggestions; Jon Rodeback, whose diligence in copyediting consumed many hours beyond closing time; and Ambassador Terry Miller, Steven Groves, and others who were kind enough to offer thoughts and suggestions throughout the process. The final product is a tribute to all their hard work.

List of Acronyms

ACABQ	United Nations Advisory Committee on Administrative and Budgetary Questions
AFRICOM	U.S. Africa Command
AIDS	acquired immunodeficiency syndrome
AMFm	Affordable Medicines Facility for Malaria
AU	African Union
CAT	Convention against Torture and Other Cruel, Inhuman or Degrading Treatment or Punishment
CBD	United Nations Convention on Biological Diversity
CDC	Centers for Disease Control and Prevention (U.S.)
CDP	Clean Development Partnership
CEDAW	Convention on the Elimination of All Forms of Discrimination against Women
CERD	Committee on the Elimination of Racial Discrimination
CESCR	Committee on Economic, Social and Cultural Rights
CHR	Commission on Human Rights
CITES	Convention on International Trade in Endangered Species of Wild Fauna and Flora
CRC	Convention on the Rights of the Child
CRPD	Convention on the Rights of Persons with Disabilities
CRR	Center for Reproductive Rights
CTBT	Comprehensive Nuclear Test Ban Treaty
DDA	Department for Disarmament Affairs
DPI	United Nations Department of Public Information
DPT3	three-dose childhood diphtheria, pertussis, and tetanus vaccine
DRC	Democratic Republic of the Congo
ECOSOC	United Nations Economic and Social Council

ECOWAS	Economic Community of West African States
EU	European Union
FAO	Food and Agriculture Organization of the United Nations
FARDC	Forces Armées de la République Démocratique du Congo
FDA	U.S. Food and Drug Administration
FDLR	Democratic Forces for the Liberation of Rwanda
FoE	Friends of the Earth
FY	fiscal year
G-77	Group of 77
GATT	General Agreement on Tariffs and Trade
GAVI	Global Alliance for Vaccines and Immunization
GDP	gross domestic product
GEF	Global Environment Facility
GHG	greenhouse gas
GONGO	government-operated (or government-organized) NGO
GPOI	Global Peace Operations Initiative
GM	genetically modified
GSP	Generalized System of Preferences
HIV	human immunodeficiency virus
HRC	Human Rights Council
IAEA	International Atomic Energy Agency
ICC	International Criminal Court
ICCPR	International Covenant on Civil and Political Rights
ICERD	International Convention on the Elimination of All Forms of Racial Discrimination
ICESCR	International Covenant on Economic, Social and Cultural Rights
ICJ	International Court of Justice (or World Court)
ICTR	International Criminal Tribunal for Rwanda
ICTY	International Criminal Tribunal for the former Yugoslavia
IFPRI	International Food Policy Research Institute
ILO	International Labor Organization
IMF	International Monetary Fund
IMT	International Military Tribunal
IPCC	Intergovernmental Panel on Climate Change
ITC	International Trade Center
ITO	International Trade Organization
IUCN	International Union for Conservation of Nature
MDG	Millennium Development Goal
MFN	most favored nation
MIM	Multilateral Initiative on Malaria
MONUC	United Nations Organization Mission in the Democratic Republic of the Congo

MOST	Management of Social Transformation
MVA	manual vacuum aspirator
NAM	Non-Aligned Movement
NATO	North Atlantic Treaty Organization
NGO	nongovernmental organization
NPT	Treaty on the Non-Proliferation of Nuclear Weapons
OECD	Organisation for Economic Co-operation and Development
OHCHR	Office of the High Commissioner for Human Rights
OIC	Organization of the Islamic Conference
OIOS	Office of Internal Oversight Services
OMB	U.S. Office of Management and Budget
PAROS	prevention of an arms race in outer space
PCIJ	Permanent Court of International Justice
PEPFAR	U.S. President's Emergency Plan for AIDS Relief
POPs	Stockholm Convention on Persistent Organic Pollutants
PRC	People's Republic of China
PSI	Proliferation Security Initiative
ROC	Republic of China on Taiwan
SARS	severe acute respiratory syndrome
SIGN	Safe Injections Global Network
SMEs	small and medium enterprises
TDR	Special Program for Research and Training in Tropical Diseases
TRNC	Turkish Republic of Northern Cyprus
UDHR	Universal Declaration of Human Rights
UNAIDS	United Nations Joint Program on HIV/AIDS
UNAMA	United Nations Assistance Mission in Afghanistan
UNAMIR	United Nations Assistance Mission in Rwanda
UNCDF	United Nations Capital Development Fund
UNCED	United Nations Conferences on Environment and Development
UNCSD	United Nations Commission on Sustainable Development
UNCTAD	United Nations Conference on Trade and Development
UNDG	United Nations Development Group
UNDP	United Nations Development Program
UNDPKO	United Nations Department of Peacekeeping Operations
UNEP	United Nations Environment Program
UNEPS	United Nations Emergency Peace Service
UNESCO	United Nations Educational, Scientific and Cultural Organization
UNFCCC	United Nations Framework Convention on Climate Change
UNFICYP	United Nations Force in Cyprus
UNFPA	United Nations Population Fund

UNICEF	United Nations Children's Fund
UNIDO	United Nations Industrial Development Organization
UNIFEM	United Nations Development Fund for Women
UNIFIL	United Nations Interim Force in Lebanon
UNMOGIP	United Nations Military Observer Group in India and Pakistan
UNSAS	United Nations Stand-by Arrangements System
UNTSO	United Nations Truce Supervision Organization
UPR	Universal Periodic Review
USAID	U.S. Agency for International Development
WEOG	Western European and Others Group
WFP	World Food Program
WHO	World Health Organization
WHOPES	WHO Pesticides Evaluation Scheme
WIPO	World Intellectual Property Organization
WTO	World Trade Organization
WWF	World Wide Fund for Nature (World Wildlife Fund)

Foreword

The Key to Changing the United Nations System

Ambassador John R. Bolton

There has perhaps been more commentary in the United States that is critical of the United Nations in recent years than in any comparable period. There are many reasons for the growth of this criticism: the Security Council's failure to take its own resolutions seriously in case after case, especially in the face of Saddam Hussein's defiance; the Oil-for-Food scandal; the endless efforts in one policy area after another to "norm" the United States into compliance with a liberal agenda that could not achieve a majority within our own democratic system; and international officials who seem to think that U.N. member governments work for them and not the other way around.

Whatever the reasons, and they are many, the growing criticism has legitimately raised the attendant question: what do you plan to do about it? This volume is a significant step toward answering that question, covering as it does the broadest range of U.N. activities. The succeeding chapters are rich with ideas and suggestions for "change," the political flavor of the day, thus in themselves giving the lie to the idea that there is no alternative to the United Nations as we know it.

This foreword attempts to set the stage for the creative analyses and proposals that follow by briefly describing the sad, and largely unsuccessful, history of U.N. reform efforts in the past thirty years and by then explaining revolutionary change that might actually produce a different result: moving toward voluntary funding of the U.N. and its activities. In addition, it provides complementary information about the culture of the U.N. organization and its member states that any subsequent American reform efforts, in whatever substantive policy area, will have to take into account. The high-minded won't like reading these pages, but it will do them a world of good.

THE SOURCE OF THE PROBLEM

Core funding for most U.N. agencies ("regular budgets") and nearly all peacekeeping activities typically comes from "assessed," or "mandatory," contributions, a system under which members' shares are calculated on the basis of a so-called capacity to pay formula that is adjusted periodically to take changes in per capita gross national income and other factors into account.[1] Significantly, however, decisions on budgets and programs by the General Assembly and the governing bodies of the galaxy of U.N. special-ized agencies are made on the basis of one-country, one-vote no matter what share of the assessments any member government pays.[2] Not surpris-ingly, governments that pay comparatively low assessments but receive comparatively high benefits have combined repeatedly to create and fund programs that inure to their benefit.

Under this system, the United States was "assessed" 22 percent of U.N. "regular" budgets in 2007 and just over 26 percent in the case of peacekeep-ing.[3] Each of the U.N.'s 191 other member governments pays a far lower rate of assessment than the United States. Japan was the second-largest con-tributor to the U.N. regular budget in 2007, paying 16.6 percent, followed

---

1. There are significant problems with the "capacity to pay" concept, the calcula-tion of which rests on prevailing exchange rates rather than, for example, "purchas-ing power parity" calculations, and involves various adjustments ("the scale of limits") that have been injected into the calculations over the years. So heated and so complex are the debates over this formula that the periodic reviews of the meth-odology of its calculation conducted in 2006 could not reach agreement on any-thing other than extending the long-standing existing methodology despite its widespread flaws.

2. Article 18, Section 1, of the U.N. Charter provides that "each member of the General Assembly shall have one vote." Section 2 provides that "budgetary ques-tions" are among those considered to be "important," thus requiring "a two-thirds majority of the members present and voting." Article 17, Section 2, of the Charter provides that "the expenses of the Organization shall be borne by the Members as apportioned by the General Assembly."

3. The five permanent members of the Security Council pay larger assessments for peacekeeping because of the political circumstances after the 1973 Arab–Israeli war. Contrary to the prevailing mythology, there is nothing inevitable about this extra obligation for the permanent members. U.N. General Assembly, "Scale of Assessments for the Apportionment of the Expenses of United Nations Peacekeep-ing Operations," A/61/139/Add.1, December 27, 2006, 2–8.

by Germany at 8.6 percent. Permanent U.N. Security Council member Britain was the fourth-largest contributor at 6.6 percent, followed by fellow European permanent Security Council member France at 6.3 percent. The other two permanent members of the Security Council, China and Russia, paid 2.7 percent and 1.2 percent, respectively. Thus, the United States paid more in regular budget assessments than the combined totals of the other four permanent members of the Security Council.

The lowest-paying fifty-four U.N. member governments that were assessed 0.001 percent for the regular budget in 2007, in the aggregate, pay a whopping 0.054 percent of the total U.N. regular budget. The 128 least assessed governments combined pay less than 1 percent of the budget. By contrast, the seventeen countries that each pay annual, regular-budget assessments of over 1 percent contributed, in the aggregate, 86.5 percent of the U.N.'s regular budget in 2007. Yet under U.N. rules each of those countries has equal say in adopting the budget. That means that two-thirds of the General Assembly membership (128 out of 192 total member states) that pays, in the aggregate, less than 5 percent of the amount that the U.S. alone is assessed, can under U.N. rules approve the U.N. budget over the objections of the United States and the sixteen other countries that foot over 86 percent of the bill. Thus, despite the U.N. Charter's requirement that budgetary questions must be decided by a two-thirds majority of the U.N. General Assembly,[4] in practice the two-thirds provision has provided little practical protection to the largest contributors.

Instead, the system of assessed contributions, combined with one-country, one-vote decision making, has created a kind of "entitlement mentality" within the U.N. system over the years as governments and Secretariats routinely expect that budgets will be funded without regard to agency performance, effectiveness, transparency, or accountability.

The U.N.'s strongest supporters often chide its critics for blaming the Secretariat or the U.N. itself for its failures rather than blaming the member governments—a criticism that is often richly deserved. In the matter of U.N. reform, this analysis is true in spades, and even support from former secretary-general Kofi Annan was not enough to persuade Non-Aligned Movement (NAM) and Group of 77 (G-77) countries to go along with his reform proposals. But the real failure was not the unwillingness of the Third World to try to fix them, but the failure of will among many of the U.N.'s largest contributing countries to support the reform effort.

Of course, the NAM and G-77 should have seen that their real long-term self-interest would lie in a more effective United Nations, a point that the United States has made time and again. Unfortunately, the Third World view was largely "if it ain't broke, don't fix it," which certainly suited their

---

4. See note 2 above.

short-term interest. More mystifying was the unwillingness of many Western nations to stand firm for reform—not just on financing issues, but on so many others as well—despite their own manifest interest in keeping U.N. costs under control and justifying to their public, as we in the United States have to do, and legitimately so, that U.N. assessments were actually being used for worthwhile purposes.

Here is where the great divide between the United States, Japan, Australia, Canada, and a few others on the one hand and most of the member states of the European Union (EU) on the other was most clearly exposed. Many diplomats from countries with relatively large assessed contributions simply did not care as much about reform as their public rhetoric, and that of their political masters back in their capitals, suggested. Perhaps because the actual size of their assessed contributions was nowhere near as high as those for the United States, or perhaps because the U.N. contributions could be sold to the leftward side of their political spectrums as helping the developing countries, or perhaps because they were more concerned about measuring inputs to the U.N. system than they were about measuring outputs, their commitment to reform usually failed in the crunch.

In fact, because of their domestic government decision-making mechanisms, almost all EU members, as a purely practical matter, simply do not have the burden of justifying the rate or the amount of U.N. assessments as much as do the United States and a small number of others. In substantial measure, domestic political support for the U.N. in EU countries, often generated by government-funded "nongovernmental organizations" (a true oxymoron if ever there was one), takes criticism of the U.N. off the table in their internal budget deliberations. EU governments simply point to the amount of their respective assessments, explain that payment is "mandatory" under international law, and have their parliamentary majorities approve whatever the amount is.

Indeed, very few U.N. member governments actually scrutinize agency budgets intensively, and only a handful actually have more than one or two full-time civil servants for whom U.N.-system budget issues are their assigned responsibility. Most U.N. ambassadors, not to mention foreign ministers, disdain to engage in "bean counting," thus ensuring that budget issues do not receive anything like adequate attention. Inevitably, this lack of member-government oversight, combined with the theory and practice of assessed contributions, leads to inefficiency and, too often, corruption in the implementation of U.N. programs, especially in the area of procurement. Moreover, since the bulk of U.N. funding in, for example, the Secretariat in New York goes for salaries and related expenses, positions in the Secretariat are highly prized by diplomats and politicians from many member governments, forming, over the years, yet another kind of entitlement.

More skeptical Americans (and a few others, as noted above) actually want to know whether their tax dollars are being used effectively, so there is a true cultural gap across the Atlantic. There are, of course, skeptical Europeans who also like to think their tax dollars are well spent, and there are Americans who disdain to question U.N. assessments, but the cultural gap is nonetheless real.

Thus it is, in the real moments of decision at the U.N., often late at night when the media have departed or in closed sessions where they were never permitted entry, that the Europeans break ranks on reform and budget issues. Shrinking from open voting, devoted to the concept of "consensus" that provides cover for the timid and almost guarantees the triumph of the lowest common denominator, time and time again, EU governments support "compromises" with the NAM and the G-77 that generally look like Third World victories to naive, straw-in-their-hair Americans.

The resulting ineffectiveness, fraud, and mismanagement have led to increased attention in the United States by the public and by policymakers, and episodic efforts to address those failings through various reform efforts. Three examples illustrate different tactics, but similar results.

WITHHOLDINGS AND THE "CONSENSUS-BASED BUDGET"

In the 1980s, faced with repeated U.S. losses in the General Assembly on program and budget issues and general anti-Americanism within the U.N. system, reflected in vote after vote, the U.S. Congress revolted against the "mandatory" nature of assessed contributions and began to withhold substantial amounts of funding from the U.N. system. Congress had previously withheld limited amounts of assessments, targeted at particular U.N. programs or practices (such as those intended to aid the Palestine Liberation Organization, or PLO), but the across-the-board withholdings of the mid-1980s represented large cuts in the congressional appropriations accounts for international organizations and, after several years of withholdings, amounted to substantial sums.

Congress tried other approaches as well, such as the Kassebaum-Solomon Amendment, which called for the U.N. either to adopt a system of "weighted voting" based on assessment levels rather than one-country, one-vote or to see even steeper cuts in American contributions. At the same time, the Reagan administration announced that the United States (later joined by the United Kingdom and Singapore) was withdrawing from the United Nations Educational, Scientific and Cultural Organization (UNESCO), effective December 31, 1984, largely because of gross mismanagement and the politicization of the agency's supposedly educational programs. The three withdrawals from UNESCO meant the loss of almost one-third of the total assessments from member governments (the U.S. share at that point being 25 percent).

These losses—and the potential that more were coming—caused a major trauma in the U.N. system. The entitlement system seemed broken, and indeed it was. By withholding substantial sums of money and actually withdrawing from a U.N. specialized agency, the Reagan administration and Congress had demonstrated that American patience was not unlimited. Although the United States received strong international criticism for what many foreign governments saw as an excessively blunt response, in the United States, the moves generated wide bipartisan support.

For instance, Congress adopted the Kassebaum-Solomon Amendment to the Department of State Authorization Act for 1986 and 1987, which withheld 20 percent of U.S. assessed contributions to the U.N. regular budget and specialized agencies until weighted voting on budgetary matters was adopted. To turn the U.S. spigots back on, if for no other reason, the U.N. and its specialized agencies moved toward "consensus-based budgeting," a system under which all budget decisions were to be taken unanimously (the proper definition of "consensus"). Under such a system, it was argued, the United States in effect would have a veto over budgets, programs, and assessments that it did not like, since it could withhold its support for such measures and thus "block consensus." Thus protected against being routinely outvoted, or so it was argued, the U.S. could resist mismanagement, fraud and abuse, bloated budgets, and unproductive programs. Moreover, the major contributors, worried now—finally—about the reliability of the U.S. assessed contribution and working through their loose association, known as the Geneva Group, developed a position known as Zero Real Growth in U.N. budgets, a technique for measuring budgets to eliminate the seemingly inevitable upward creep in U.N. budget levels.

At the end of the Reagan administration and into the new Bush administration, convinced that things had really changed at the United Nations, and in large part to take advantage of "new thinking" in Soviet foreign policy, the United States began a program to repay the arrearages that had accumulated over the 1980s. The consensus-based budgeting was deemed an acceptable compromise and President Ronald Reagan exercised his waiver under Kassebaum-Solomon so that the United States could pay its assessment in full. In the early 1990s, the Kassebaum-Solomon legislation was not reauthorized, thereby removing the financial consequences of failing to adhere to the consensus-based budgeting agreement. As events transpired in the U.N. system, however, consensus-based budgeting did not live up to expectations. The United States and its program and budget priorities remained highly isolated within the U.N., and time and time again, U.N. budget meetings would find only the U.S. delegation "blocking" a consensus.

Invariably, however, the United States would give in, agreeing to join the consensus rather than remain isolated, thus revealing a key cultural flaw in American diplomacy and the central weakness of consensus-based budgeting: American diplomats—and, to be fair, those of many other countries—fear being "isolated."

It is not good form in diplomatic circles to be "isolated," even if that means following instructions from your government and adhering to positions your government believes to be in its interest. Other diplomats, friend and foe alike, harp on your "isolated" position, on how out of step you are, and on how late in the evening it's getting, how many spouses and dinner parties are being stood up, or how many weekend plans are being frustrated. Even though the overwhelming loss of a General Assembly vote is tangible evidence of isolation, being almost the only country to refuse to join a "consensus" is a near relation. Other delegations—not just those from the G-77 and the NAM, but particularly those from the EU—prey on the fear of "isolation."

In short, being "isolated" is no fun for diplomats and they strenuously avoid it. Only rarely did the United States stand against the risk of being isolated, whether on budget or policy issues or at their intersection. One important example—and a lesson about life in the U.N.—took place during the PLO's 1989–1990 campaign to gain admission as a "state" to U.N. specialized agencies.[5] Faced with the near certainty that the PLO would succeed in becoming a member of its first target agency, the World Health Organization (WHO), Secretary of State James A. Baker III in effect threatened that the United States would withhold U.S. assessments from any agency that enhanced the status of the PLO in any way, thus preventing the PLO from creating new "facts on the ground" in the Middle East through the pretense of being recognized as a "state" within the U.N. system. The threat to defund was, of course, not as profound as withdrawing from UNESCO, but it demonstrated that the U.S. executive branch, as well as Congress, was fully capable of exercising financial leverage within the United Nations when it served American interests to do so.

The critical point, however, is that the protection supposedly afforded to the United States by the requirement of a consensus on budget and program issues broke down in practical terms. The U.N. resumed making decisions on expenditures without adequate attention to U.S. positions and interests, and Congress again reacted, especially in light of the huge growth in peacekeeping budgets in the 1990s and the failures of many U.N. mis-

---

5. The governing documents of most U.N. agencies limit membership to "states," so what the PLO was trying to do was to transform itself into a "state" in the eyes of the U.N. system and then use this new "fact" in its negotiations with Israel.

sions.[6] Peacekeeping had, in any event, never really been subject to the concept of Zero Real Growth, which had always been most applicable only to core agency administrative budgets, and a spike in peacekeeping operations drove budgets sharply higher. Congress responded in the mid-1990s with another wave of general withholdings across the U.N. system that once again placed its entitlement mentality in jeopardy. This time, the U.N. response was a reduction in the level of U.S. assessments, down from 25 percent to 22 percent for general budgets and from approximately 31 percent to 27 percent in peacekeeping.

The reduction in the U.S. assessment and the commensurate increase in the assessment rates for a number of other countries to offset the U.S. reductions mollified congressional critics in the short term by reducing upward budget pressures on the U.S. even though it did not actually reduce the U.N. budget. But the reduced assessments did not address the central underlying problem that the United States faced: a continuing decline in its influence. The "consensus" system continued, reflected in continued defeats and concessions by the United States.

Ironically, it was during the administration of George W. Bush that the policy of seeking Zero Real Growth or even Zero Nominal Growth in U.N. budgets broke down. Following the successful initial operations in Afghanistan and Iraq, the United States sought greater U.N. involvement in rebuilding those states and establishing democracies. The United States preferred that these operations be special political missions funded through the regular budget at a lower cost to the United States than if they were peacekeeping missions (22 percent versus over 26 percent). Many U.N. member states, which resented President George W. Bush's decision to sidestep official U.N. approval of the Iraq war, insisted that funding for these missions be in addition to existing budgetary commitments and resisted U.S. efforts to cut other parts of the regular budget to fund them. The falling U.S. dollar also led to increased operational costs for the U.N. that were built into the U.N. budget increases. For all these reasons, the United States agreed to increase the budget.

In Bush's second term, budget restraint at the U.N. all but disappeared. The administration acquiesced to U.N. budget increases for which a Clinton administration would have been pilloried, and this acquiescence encouraged even higher budgets. In December 2007, the General Assembly voted 142 to 1 to approve a 2008–2009 biennium budget that is projected to reach $5.2 billion, a 25 percent increase over the previous budget; the United States cast the sole "no" vote. This outcome marked the formal demise of the "consensus" voting process on U.N. budgets, a two-decade tradition that had given each country a "veto" on budget matters—further

---

6. See, generally, Frederick H. Fleitz Jr., *Peacekeeping Fiascoes of the 1990s: Causes, Solutions and U.S. Interests* (Westport, CT: Praeger, 2002).

demonstrating that U.N. promises regarding reform are meaningless unless backstopped by the threat of U.S. financial withholdings.

THE "OIL-FOR-FOOD" SCANDAL

Enormous amounts of once-hidden information have come to light because of the exhaustive report on the Oil-for-Food Program prepared by Paul Volcker, former chairman of the Federal Reserve Board; the investigative reporting of journalists including Claudia Rosett and Eric Shawn;[7] and congressional investigations led by Senator Norm Coleman (R-MN), Congressman Chris Shays (R-CT), and now-deceased congressman Henry Hyde (R-IL), formerly chairman of the House International Relations Committee. Saddam Hussein's perversion of what was supposed to be a humanitarian assistance program for the Iraqi people into an instrument for reinforcing his Ba'ath regime's power, the level of corruption exposed within the U.N. system and among governments and businesses gorging on Oil-for-Food revenues, and the inattention of the U.N. Secretariat and members of the Security Council stunned many in the United States.

One of Paul Volcker's most important contributions in uncovering the morass within the Oil-for-Food Program was his penetrating insight that its many problems were not unique to the program. To the contrary, Oil-for-Food emerged out of the existing U.N. system, relying on existing U.N. procedures and regulations, employing many longtime U.N. employees in senior positions, and following well-trodden U.N. pathways in its operations, including an appalling lack of oversight from top Secretariat officials, including former secretary-general Kofi Annan.

Ineluctably, therefore, Volcker concluded that the prescription for avoiding future Oil-for-Food scandals was basic reform of the United Nations itself—a conclusion quite surprising to top U.N. management at the time, which had hoped that Volcker's report would confine the attention of the press and member governments to the now-defunct Oil-for-Food Program. Faced instead with a repudiation of the culture of inattention to effectiveness and lack of management oversight that had grown right alongside the entitlement mentality in the U.N. system, even top U.N. management officials recognized that they had to do something to stop the coruscating stream of criticism they now faced, especially in the United States.

Volcker himself recommended a number of reforms, largely calling for greater accountability, stricter auditing procedures with outside oversight, and management techniques that are second nature to publicly held corpo-

---

7. See, generally, Eric Shawn, *The U.N. Exposed: How the United Nations Sabotages America's Security and Fails the World* (New York: Sentinel/Penguin Group, 2006).

rations in the United States and around the world and accepted practice among most Western governments. Only at the U.N. could Volcker's suggestions be treated as revolutionary or threatening. Indeed, the U.S. program of reform was far broader, although Volcker's proposals were certainly first steps that were worth supporting, but only with the expectation that more sweeping changes had to follow.

What finally emerged after a long, confused, and inconclusive struggle in the U.N. General Assembly, however, were "reforms" that only barely increased the levels of accountability and oversight rather than the kinds of changes that were truly needed to change the underlying culture of the organization. Related efforts to bring the U.N.'s budget under control through review and reform of the countless "mandates," or programs of work created for the Secretariat over the years by the General Assembly and other U.N. bodies, similarly went essentially nowhere.

Broader reforms were often buried in the assembly's Fifth Committee, which almost all diplomats in New York recognize as essentially the graveyard of reform efforts. Of course, one reason the nearly impenetrable deliberations of the Fifth Committee had evolved over decades the way they had was that ambassadorial-level personnel from major contributing countries, especially those of the European Union, rarely graced the committee's deliberations with their attention or their presence. The United States and Japan, as the U.N.'s two largest contributors, have, over many years, been exceptions to this tendency, but their efforts alone rarely sufficed.

By leaving the committee's responsibilities to working-level "experts" for so long, the ambassadors demonstrated how little they cared about its work or its decisions. As one Latin American ambassador said to me with no trace of irony, "It's only money." By contrast, the ambassadors and experts from the developing countries of the Non-Aligned Movement and the Group of 77 became truly proficient in the arcane ways of the Fifth Committee, which they had largely helped shape over the years to protect favorite programs and staff positions in the Secretariat. Thus, after one of the most extensive reform efforts in recent U.N. history, the progress made was limited.

THE HUMAN RIGHTS COUNCIL

The U.N. Commission on Human Rights (CHR) for many years had been a target for U.N. reformers because of its prominence as a refuge for human rights violators, which used their membership to protect themselves against real human rights scrutiny. Moreover, the CHR was a hotbed of anti-American and anti-Israeli activity, as well as a locus for international leftist interest groups to pursue their own agendas, such as opposition to the death penalty. Over the years, the United States had strongly resisted the outrages annually perpetrated in the Commission on Human Rights, starting with President Reagan's decision to appoint a refugee from Fidel Castro's tyranny, Armando Valladares, as the U.S. representative to the CHR. Eventually, even Kofi Annan called for eliminating the CHR in order to remove its continuing stain on the U.N.'s reputation and for replacing it with a body that would actually promote human rights internationally rather than serve as a propaganda vehicle for authoritarian regimes.

To that end, the United States, the EU, and several other key U.N. members laboriously constructed the elements for a new Human Rights Council (HRC) that would avoid the errors of the commission it was to replace. Through a series of procedural devices (smaller membership, flat ineligibility for human rights violators, election by a two-thirds majority of the General Assembly rather than a simple majority, etc.) operating in tandem, the reformers believed that a new body could actually be constructed that would function differently from the existing CHR.

Unfortunately, faced with determined opposition from Russia, China, and the NAM, the Europeans step-by-step backed away from almost all the procedural reforms that had been proposed, either watering them down or dropping them entirely. No one concession or compromise in the draft resolution creating the new HRC was dispositive, but the cumulative effect of the European retreat was to guarantee that the new body would be composed pretty much as its predecessor had been and would therefore behave in pretty much the same way.

I knew that all hope had to be abandoned when the Europeans gave up a provision in the draft resolution that would have barred from HRC membership any nation under Security Council sanctions for gross abuses of human rights or support for international terrorism. What was the NAM argument against this provision that collapsed the Europeans? The provision was unfair because no permanent member of the Security Council would ever be under sanctions, and therefore, no other countries should be precluded from HRC membership simply because they were not a permanent council member.

I knew the game was up at that point, and, in truth, so did the Europeans. I concluded that the United States should vote against creating the new Human Rights Council, arguing within the State Department that bringing into existence a new body that was no better than the existing Commission on Human Rights would doom real reform for as far as the eye could see. The only hope was to keep the existing CHR in operation for one more year to remind everyone just how bad it was and then try in the following year (so I argued internally) to stiffen European spines to the point where we could take a real run at reform.

That argument was persuasive inside the U.S. government, and we decided to vote "no." Somewhat more obliquely made to the Europeans, however, the argument failed, because they were more determined to declare victory in a "reform" effort than they were to acknowledge that they had been collectively outnegotiated by the NAM. Indeed, the Europeans not only argued that we should vote in favor of the new HRC, but also urged that we seek election to the first session of that body and try to do there precisely what we had failed to do in the General Assembly authorizing resolution.

By the close of the negotiations on the draft resolution, the Europeans had turned from trying to fix the resolution to doing anything they could to get the United States to support it, despite its contents, and to commit to run for election. They knew full well that if the United States stood apart from the new HRC, it would delegitimize the body, at least in U.S. eyes and quite likely more broadly. It was with this background in mind that I said to the press that the United States did not intend to put lipstick on a caterpillar and call it a butterfly.

The Europeans proceeded to do just that, and the new HRC was created by an overwhelming vote in the General Assembly, with the United States and three other close allies well and truly isolated. Although I cannot prove it after the fact, I believe that the only thing that might have saved the new HRC from infamy would have been a U.S. pledge to withhold financial support from the new body. So eager were the Europeans to have the United States support it and seek to join it, to have our presence give their retreat protective coloration if nothing else, that the threat to withhold funding might, in and of itself, have been such a shock to their sensibilities that it might have brought them back to reality. This was the technique that worked for Secretary of State Baker when he used the threat to withhold American contributions from the World Health Organization or other agencies that admitted the PLO as a member government in 1989–1990, and it might well have worked again.

Given the alignment of views within the U.S. Department of State, however, withholding funds, or even threatening to do so, was never a possibility. As a result, we now have a body that even the *New York Times* and the *Washington Post* agree is as bad as or even worse than its predecessor.

THE NEED TO MOVE TO
VOLUNTARY FUNDING

Each of the above examples demonstrates the importance of moving to voluntary contributions and using the withholding of U.S. assessed contributions as a means of achieving that objective. Dogged efforts to reform the U.N. have stalled or ended inconclusively despite years of struggle: consensus-based budgeting has failed; Zero Nominal (or even Real) Growth is dead as a policy; U.N. budgets are once again climbing at an alarming rate; high-profile examples of the need for increased oversight and accountability, such as the Oil-for-Food scandal, have resulted in few substantial improvements; and a widely supported effort to improve the key U.N. body overseeing human rights resulted in a new body that arguably is worse than its predecessor.

We have essentially reached the end of the line of decades of effort at marginal or incremental reform of the U.N. system. Every time some small progress is made, a new or different abuse is uncovered. As we work to resolve the serious issues raised by the Oil-for-Food scandal, we uncover "Cash for Kim" cash flows from U.N. agencies or programs that have allowed North Korea's dictatorial Kim Jong Il regime to channel resources intended for humanitarian purposes to help keep itself in power. Procedural fixes have not worked, costs continue to climb, and the role and influence of the United States continue to diminish.

The accumulated evidence of decades points unarguably to the conclusion that only a major shift in attitudes within the U.N. system can lay the basis for sustained improvements in U.N. performance, accountability, and transparency. That shift must entail breaking the grip of the one-country, one-vote decision-making system in the U.N. and simultaneously breaking the entitlement mentality that has long pervaded the system. There is only one reform that can accomplish these objectives, and that entails shifting from today's predominant financing system, which relies on assessed contributions to defray the costs of U.N. agency budgets, to voluntary contributions. Transparency alone cannot succeed, even though the United States, supported by only a few other U.N. members, has continued to work to bring greater transparency to the U.N. system.[8]

Moving to voluntary funding would end the practice of the U.N.'s charging the member states for the expenses of the U.N. and its activities. Member states would instead determine for themselves how much they provide to the United Nations and, importantly, the specific tasks and activities that those contributions would support. The shift toward a voluntary payment system would impose a stronger market incentive for U.N. programs and activities to meet their goals and justify continued funding. After all, if an activity, program, or office could not demonstrate its effectiveness, member states would be reluctant to continue to support it.

Contrary to the claims of those who oppose moving toward voluntary funding, such a system would not necessarily threaten U.N. activities. Many independent U.N.-affiliated funds, programs, and specialized agencies cur-

---

8. For example, see Colum Lynch, "U.S. Officials Divulge Reports on Confidential U.N. Audits," *Washington Post*, February 12, 2008, A10.

rently work well relying on voluntary funding. Such funding has remained fairly stable from year to year with donor nations consistently and reliably providing money for activities that they support. Indeed, in many cases, voluntary funding has increased sharply. Almost without exception, only voluntarily funded activities that fail to meet donor expectations of performance experience reductions in funding levels. This type of financial accountability is precisely what is needed at the U.N.

No one can doubt that such a shift would require even more Herculean efforts than the reform movements that have gone before and that it would encounter equal if not greater opposition, both from U.N. member governments and from the Secretariat. The difference is that—instead of relying on ponderous efforts within the U.N. system that produce minimal or no results—this reform could be initiated by the United States, acting on its own through the congressional appropriations process, and the rest of the U.N. system could then react.

Even a serious and extensive discussion of shifting to voluntary contributions would have a profound impact across the U.N. system, and this impact can be only beneficial. As with the broad withholdings of the 1980s and 1990s, more targeted efforts such as those against PLO-related activities, the withdrawal from UNESCO, and the threat to defund WHO, anything that so dramatically threatens the status quo has the potential to produce a cultural revolution in the U.N. system. Moreover, seeking to establish a system of voluntary contributions would be no more difficult, and may perhaps be even more popular, than the system of weighted U.N. voting contemplated by the Kassebaum-Solomon Amendment of the 1980s, which would have required amending the U.N. Charter rather than simply having the General Assembly exercise its powers under Article 17.[9]

The concept that switching to voluntary contributions would have an important positive impact rests in part on the evidence provided by several decades of operations by U.N. agencies and programs that have largely been so funded. The World Food Program, the U.N. High Commissioner for Refugees, the U.N. Joint Program on HIV/AIDS (UNAIDS), and other voluntarily funded programs have typically been more responsive to major contributors, more effective in their work, and more transparent than those funded by assessed contributions. Their leaderships have typically recog-

---

9. See note 2 above. An alternative that would have the benefit of not requiring an amendment to the Charter would involve the General Assembly's adopting an additional requirement through a resolution that the budget must have support from member states paying at least two-thirds of the budget in addition to the Charter's requirement that it be supported by two-thirds of the member states. In essence, this would create a double hurdle for budget approval and protect the interests of large contributors to the U.N. budget.

nized that, lacking an "entitlement" to assessed contributions, they have to demonstrate their utility on a continuing basis or will find donors taking their scarce resources to other agencies and programs that the donors deem more effective.

Not surprisingly, therefore, it is the pressure of budgets constantly at risk that drives agency managements to superior performance, much as competition in private enterprise drives the necessity to measure outputs and not just inputs. Voluntary funding is not the only important factor, of course, as even some agencies so funded, such as the U.N. Development Program (UNDP), have often proven to be as uncooperative and intransigent as agencies funded through assessments.

Nonetheless, voluntary funding is at least a necessary if not a sufficient condition for the profound improvements we should insist on. The general pattern is clear, and much of the analysis in the following chapters examines ways in which the question of voluntary funding and related initiatives can be implemented across the U.N. system. Many other improvements are needed, to be sure, but the advent of voluntary funding would unquestionably enhance the role and impact of U.S. views and interests. We are concerned here not with creating simply a Platonically "better" United Nations, but with creating one that more closely advances the interests of the United States. For, surely, if the U.N. cannot be used more frequently as an effective instrument of American foreign policy, its long-term prospects for success are minimal at best.

Some will respond that such an unambiguous assertion of U.S. national interests will simply encourage other nations to do the same and leave the U.N. open to often-conflicting national agendas. Those who know the U.N. well, of course, know that this is already the case and that too often it is the U.S. agenda that does not prevail. If U.S. efforts to move to voluntary funding should spur other nations to increase their own funding as a way to retain or enhance their level of influence, so be it. Let those who prefer to channel funds through U.N. programs they see as desirable do so without limit, and let them have influence accordingly. And let those less impressed with this or that U.N. agency take their money elsewhere in the U.N. system or out of it entirely.

Some will argue that withholding assessed contributions violates our obligations under the U.N. Charter, and thus international law, crying out, *"Pacta sunt servanda"* ("agreements must be observed"). These claims are false. For one thing, compliance with the U.N. Charter has been a sometime thing for almost all the members throughout its history, and this irregularity hardly gives force to the idea that we are required to pay for programs being repeatedly voted on by Charter violators. Indeed, if legal doctrines matter here, the one that matters most significantly is *rebus sic stantibus,* the doctrine that changed facts and circumstances render a treaty nonobligatory.

Moreover, and more practically, the level of assessments is an inherently political decision and can be resisted as a matter of legitimate political disagreement. Suppose, for example, that an overwhelming U.N. majority, desiring to express its displeasure at the U.S.-led overthrow of Saddam Hussein without express Security Council authorization, decided to make the U.S. assessment 99 percent. There is nothing in the U.N. Charter to prevent the other U.N. members from doing this. Would anyone in the U.S. Congress seriously argue that we were legally obligated to pay such an assessment?

At its base, this is not a question of law, but a question of political conflict among U.N. member states. Undoubtedly, if the United States were to resume the withholding of assessed contributions—in our third great wave of such withholdings—there would be a political uproar in the General Assembly, and the eventual outcome would be decided in a political fashion, which is exactly the way it should be.

As this book was being written, Congress and the Bush administration decided to withhold the proportionate American share of HRC funding from the overall U.S. assessment for the U.N. Such a withholding is a relatively small (in Washington terms) amount of money, perhaps $2 million–$3 million, but the decision to withhold sent a powerful political signal throughout the U.N. system.

First, it showed that the United States, if sufficiently motivated, will withhold assessed contributions, certainly with respect to programs with little or no support in our country.

Second, it signaled to other illegitimate and unproductive U.N. programs that they could be next.

Third, and most significantly, it signaled to the entire U.N. universe of agencies, funds, and programs that the prospect of broader, across-the-board withholdings was back on the table.

While broad-based financial withholding has little support on the left, it is a powerful tool to leverage reform in the United Nations. The Obama administration and the Democratic majorities in Congress should consider their options carefully before deciding to oppose withholding on principle. Those committed to multilateral action through the U.N. have the most to lose from an ineffective, unresponsive, and unaccountable United Nations.

The purpose of this volume is to look forward on a U.N. systemwide basis. The authors certainly do not have lockstep views on the subjects they cover. They do, however, provide an array of fresh ideas and new thinking on the U.N., presenting analyses and ideas that all should welcome, from those who are skeptical that any reforms can truly succeed at the U.N. to the U.N.'s strongest advocates.

Indeed, it is the latter who should pay the closest attention.

Introduction

Edwin J. Feulner

The United States belongs to dozens of multilateral organizations covering virtually every international policy issue imaginable. They include large, well-known organizations such as the World Trade Organization and the North Atlantic Treaty Organization. They also include tiny organizations such as the International Seed Testing Association and the International Bureau of Weights and Measures, which are largely overlooked by all but a few dedicated experts and bureaucrats charged with overseeing them. While all these international organizations have their discrete purposes and problems, none have embodied the hopes and aspirations of so many or been fraught with as much controversy and disappointment as the United Nations and its affiliated bodies.

The establishment of the United Nations was largely an American-led effort to create an organization to replace the defunct League of Nations. In fact, "United Nations" was first suggested by President Franklin D. Roosevelt in the 1942 "Declaration by the United Nations"[1] to identify the Allied nations that opposed the Axis powers during World War II. The term was then adopted as the name of the League's successor in subsequent meetings that culminated in the 1945 United Nations Conference on International Organization to draft the U.N. Charter in San Francisco.

The founders of the United Nations had a clear vision of its roles and responsibilities as a facilitator of cooperative action among sovereign nations to prevent a repetition of the twin scourges of global conflict and

---

1. "Declaration by the United Nations," January 1, 1942, at www.ibiblio.org/pha/policy/1942/420101a.html (accessed January 30, 2009).

1

economic depression. The 1945 Charter of the United Nations establishes four purposes for the organization:

1. To maintain international peace and security, and to that end: to take effective collective measures for the prevention and removal of threats to the peace . . .
2. To develop friendly relations among nations based on respect for the principle of equal rights and self-determination of peoples . . .
3. To achieve international cooperation in solving international problems of an economic, social, cultural, or humanitarian character, and in promoting and encouraging respect for human rights and for fundamental freedoms . . .
4. To be a centre for harmonizing the actions of nations in the attainment of these common ends[2]

The past sixty years have seen the U.N. struggle to meet these expectations. For instance, there have been hundreds of wars since 1945 resulting in millions of deaths. Despite its charge to undertake collective means for maintaining international peace and security, the U.N. has played a negligible role, authorizing the use of force in response to aggression only in the cases of North Korea's invasion of South Korea in 1950 and Iraq's invasion of Kuwait in 1991. Similarly, the U.N. counts notorious human rights violators and repressive governments among its membership despite the organization's call to respect human rights and self-determination.

Failure to meet its core purposes has not curbed expansion of the organization. In addition to the core United Nations headquartered in New York, which includes the Security Council, the General Assembly, and the Secretariat, the U.N. system includes dozens of affiliated funds, programs, offices, commissions, and other bodies dedicated to various international concerns ranging from economic development to health concerns to environmental problems to human rights. Some of these organizations actually predate the U.N. and were placed under the U.N. umbrella for convenience. Others have been established since the United Nations was created.

Only rarely were these organizations and mandates established in the context of a thorough examination of the existing system and with a deliberate design to fill specific gaps between the existing jurisdictions and authorities of other U.N. bodies. Today's United Nations is the result of decades of poorly considered mandates, duplicative responsibilities without clear lines of responsibility, insufficient transparency and accountability, and bureaucratic mission creep and institutional overreach. Lack of

---

2. Charter of the United Nations, art. 1, pars. 1–4.

reform has resulted in a bureaucratic, costly, and cumbersome U.N. system that is often incapable of fulfilling the responsibilities placed on it.

The paucity of reform is not for a lack of trying. The past six decades have seen dozens of initiatives from governments, think tanks, foundations, and panels of experts aimed at reforming the U.N. to make it more effective in meeting its responsibilities. Although reform efforts have occasionally succeeded, they have fallen short of the steps necessary to address the core problems that continue to plague the organization.

The Heritage Foundation has been a key contributor to these reform efforts. In recognition of the increasing importance of the United Nations in the ideological battles of the Cold War, in 1982 Heritage established the United Nations Assessment Project to study and provide recommendations to the U.S. government on its policy positions vis-à-vis the United Nations. Over the past twenty-five years, Heritage has published numerous studies focused on assessing the work of the U.N. and its related bodies. This work has contributed to exposing mismanagement in the U.N. system and has helped to improve the effectiveness and focus of those bodies.

Perhaps the most ambitious effort by the U.N. Assessment Project was a book entitled *A World Without a U.N.: What Would Happen if the United Nations Shut Down*, published in 1984. It asked ten distinguished scholars whether the world would be worse, better, or unchanged if the U.N. closed its doors. In nine chapters, the authors discussed U.N. contributions to economic development, health, environment, education, the world food supply, human rights, disarmament, and peacekeeping and its function as "the world's safety value." What did they conclude? In the words of the book's editor, Burton Yale Pines:

> How would a world without a U.N. look? For one thing, it would remain a world filled with multilateral bodies. The United Nations did not create the multilateralism typified by the World Health Organization, International Labor Organization and International Telecommunications Union and the U.N. is not required for the continuation of such multilateralism. . . .
>
> This all could function as well as it now does without the U.N.'s costly Secretariat, its cronyism, legions of bureaucrats, its high salaries and lavish perquisites and its anti-Western ideology. After existing for four decades, the U.N. cannot complain that it has not been given a fair chance. It now is the U.N. which has the burden of proving that it warrants continued support and confidence. This proof must rest on the factual record of the U.N.'s performance— not simply on good intentions and the rhetoric of idealism. An examination of this record will reveal that a world without the U.N. would be a better world.[3]

---

3. Burton Yale Pines, *A World Without a U.N.: What Would Happen If the U.N. Shut Down* (Washington, DC: Heritage Foundation, 1984), xviii–xix.

On the twenty-fifth anniversary of *A World Without a U.N.* one must assume that the authors would be gravely disappointed. The U.N. remains fundamentally unchanged from the severely flawed organization of 1984. Issues are distorted to exaggerate the priorities of influential actors, technical issues are politicized, conflicts are often exacerbated and perpetuated, and repressive nations continue to find unwarranted solace and stature. Yet the U.N. continues, largely invulnerable to reform, with an ever-increasing budget and an ever-growing portfolio of responsibilities.

In many ways, this volume is the successor to *A World Without a U.N.* in that it seeks to take a fresh look at the U.N. system to determine what it does well and what it does not. It too assembles experts and asks them to assess U.N. performance in a variety of international policy areas: multilateral diplomacy; international law; disarmament; peacekeeping and conflict resolution; economic development; trade; the environment; human rights; economic, social, and cultural rights; and health.

Considering the lack of U.N. reform, it is not surprising that topics such as disarmament, economic development, environment, health, human rights, and peacekeeping and conflict resolution were also discussed in the earlier book. However, radical changes in the world in the intervening years have led these authors to discuss new problems unexplored by the previous authors or to review old problems in a new light.

One dramatic example illustrates how an ongoing concern has taken on additional weight since 1984. In 1984, the total U.N. peacekeeping budget of $141 million[4] provided for five missions and about twelve thousand personnel.[5] Today, the U.N.'s Department of Peacekeeping Operations directs and supports eighteen current peace operations involving more than 112,000 personnel and an annual budget of more than $7 billion.[6] Some problems that may have been minor concerns two decades ago have since exploded in relevance, along with the size, scope, and expense of U.N. peacekeeping.

Along with problems that have festered for decades is a host of new concerns. An increasing number of international declarations, conventions, and treaties has expanded the scope of international law in a manner that

---

4. Michael Renner, "Peacekeeping Operations Expenditures: 1947–2005," Global Policy Forum, at www.globalpolicy.org/finance/tables/pko/expend.htm (accessed January 30, 2009).

5. See Brett D. Schaefer, "Time for a New United Nations Peacekeeping Organization," Heritage Foundation *Backgrounder*, no. 2006 (February 13, 2007), at www.heritage.org/Research/InternationalOrganizations/bg2006.cfm.

6. U.N. Department of Public Information, "United Nations Peacekeeping Operations," December 31, 2008, at www.un.org/Depts/dpko/dpko/bnote.htm (accessed January 30, 2009).

would have been unimaginable only twenty years ago. Nonstate actors operating through advocacy groups and nongovernmental organizations, virtually unknown at the U.N. in the early 1980s, now exert influence over U.N. deliberations and activities on a level that is sometimes nearly on par with sovereign states.

The end of the Cold War also radically altered the U.N. landscape, paving the way for new ambitions as the member states assigned new tasks to the U.N. under the mistaken belief that its inadequacies were a reflection of Cold War impediments and blockages. Instead, new divisions arose. Old alliances between the U.S. and the Western world have weakened without the Soviet threat, and differing national priorities have taken precedence. Developing countries have banded together to use their numerical advantage to focus the U.N. on their priorities. Sadly, reforming the U.N. to make it more effective was not among these priorities.

In short, while many of the issues raised in *A World Without a U.N.* remain relevant, we believe that taking a new look at the U.N. system is essential. Despite the flaws and weaknesses of the U.N. system, policymakers in the United States and other nations reflexively turn to the U.N. as a convenient forum in which to discuss and resolve international concerns or to undertake collective action. The need to work with other nations through multilateral organizations or in less formal ways to address international issues will not disappear in the future.

However, this does not necessarily mean that the current U.N. system is the best option. With the vast scope of U.N. activities in mind, The Heritage Foundation asked fifteen distinguished experts to assess the role of the United Nations in specific policy arenas and to evaluate the effectiveness of the U.N. in addressing its overarching objectives and goals. To aid policymakers, these assessments are accompanied by specific principles to guide decisions on how and when they should encourage U.N. intervention and recommendations on how to fix the current system.

In nearly every case, the authors identify a number of areas where the U.N. was already making or could make a positive contribution. However, as Kim Holmes notes in his chapter, the trick is to know when working through the United Nations is likely to yield a successful or useful outcome and when to explore other options.

Some authors conclude that the U.N. contribution, in part if not the entire scope of its activities, is uniquely valuable and cannot be replaced by anything less than a multilateral organization with universal membership. For instance, on health matters, Roger Bate and Karen Porter suggest that the World Health Organization restrict its activities, but that its universal character is critical to fulfilling its mandate.

In some instances, the authors conclude that the U.N. would be better served by taking a backseat to other efforts. Christopher Horner, for instance, argues that former U.S. president George W. Bush's Clean Development Partnership initiative is superior to the U.N.'s Kyoto Process as a means for addressing global warming because the former is far less vulnerable to manipulation by third parties and more likely to achieve its objectives.

Other authors offer a more specific set of policy recommendations. For example, Greg Mills and Terence McNamee lay out a strategy for improving U.N. peacekeeping. Yet "where direct U.N. involvement is not possible or is not feasible," they recommend using coalitions of the willing or regional organizations. Daniella Markheim recommends a dramatic streamlining of United Nations bodies engaged in trade-related matters in favor of the U.N. Conference on Trade and Development, provided that it restricts its activities to supporting the World Trade Organization and advising developing nations on how to more smoothly integrate into the global economy through market liberalization. Terry Miller concurs, noting that the U.N.'s adherence to flawed economic theories has done untold harm by constraining economic growth and development.

Some authors conclude that the U.N. is actually an impediment to achieving its overarching goal. Brett Schaefer and Steven Groves conclude that the United Nations, because of its universal membership, is fundamentally incapable of being an effective advocate for fundamental human rights, and they point to the failings of the U.N. Commission on Human Rights and the Human Rights Council as evidence. They recommend establishing an alternative human rights body with restricted membership that can serve as an effective international proponent and arbiter of fundamental human rights. Baker Spring similarly sees U.N. efforts in arms control and disarmament as largely counterproductive and recommends focusing those efforts through states that have a direct, vested interest in effective and verifiable agreements.

Lee Casey and David Rivkin offer an excellent set of principles for dealing with international legal bodies and instruments without unduly compromising U.S. sovereignty and its right to defend its interests. Susan Yoshihara illustrates the existing and potential consequences of failing to adhere to these principles in the face of efforts to impose social, economic, and cultural rights through United Nations bodies, conferences, and treaties.

As demonstrated by the current financial crisis, the world is becoming smaller and more closely linked by the day. While it is not certain that the world would be better off without the United Nations, there is little doubt that the world deserves a better U.N. than the one we have today. Certainly, even a world without the U.N. would not be without multilateral organizations. U.S. policymakers need a vision for what types of organizations would best serve American interests on the international stage.

The authors in this book offer a rethinking of the United Nations and its role in the international system. As Ambassador John Bolton notes in the foreword, this book provides an "array of fresh ideas and new thinking on the U.N., presenting analyses and ideas that all should welcome, from those who are skeptical that any reforms can truly succeed at the U.N. to the U.N.'s strongest advocates." Indeed, the U.N.'s strongest advocates should pay the closest attention to the authors' ideas. An effective United Nations, even if smaller and less overtly powerful, is far more likely to remain relevant and fulfill its vital missions.

I commend all the distinguished scholars who contributed to this study. Their contributions will provide a valuable resource for policymakers seeking to focus the United Nations on its core missions and responsibilities. This task serves the interests of the United States and every nation that contributes to the United Nations and seeks to work through it to address international concerns.

1

Smart Multilateralism

When and When Not to
Rely on the United Nations

Kim R. Holmes

Multilateralism is not an end in itself. It is one of many foreign policy tools, admittedly a very important one, in the diplomatic kit. Basically a dialogue among nations that hope to work out common approaches to common concerns, multilateralism complements the enormous amount of bilateral diplomacy that thousands of government officials conduct every day to promote and protect their nations' interests and priorities.

The need for multilateralism is obvious. Nations share concerns about many problems and issues for which coordinated efforts could be mutually beneficial. Yet only rarely do all governments agree on the nature of a problem and the means to address it. At times, negotiations result in a less-than-perfect, but still acceptable, course of action. Disagreements can also lead to no action or the use of force or other confrontational measures. One of the purposes of multilateralism is to minimize the number and intensity of such confrontations. The process itself, however, is fraught with political challenges that can undermine potential solutions and even lead to other problems.

For the United States, multilateralism faces its greatest challenge at the United Nations, where U.S. diplomats seek cooperative action among member nations on serious international problems. Therein lies the tension. The United Nations is first and foremost a political body made up of 192 states that rarely agree on any one issue. Even fundamental issues, such as protecting and observing human rights, a key purpose of the U.N. that all member states pledge to uphold when they join it, have become matters of intense debate.

A key reason for this difficulty is the fact that the voices and votes of totalitarian and authoritarian regimes have equal weight to those of free nations at the U.N. The all-too-frequent clash of worldviews between liberty and authoritarian socialism has stymied multilateralism more than facilitated it, frequently leading to institutional paralysis when a unified response to grave threats to peace and security or human rights and fundamental freedoms was needed. U.S. secretary of state John Foster Dulles, who attended the San Francisco meetings that established the U.N., acknowledged this Achilles' heel in 1954 when he told reporters: "The United Nations was not set up to be a reformatory. It was assumed that you would be good before you got in and not that being in would make you good."[1]

Fifty-five years later, the ideological fray at the U.N. has turned the terms "democracy" and "freedom" on their heads. Autocracies that deny democratic liberties at home are all too keen to call the Security Council "undemocratic" because in their view not every region, country, or bloc is sufficiently represented. During my time at the State Department, I was told repeatedly by other diplomats at the U.N. that the very concept of "freedom" is taboo because the term is "too ideologically charged." In this environment, how can the United States or any freedom-loving country advance the purposes set forth in the U.N. Charter, including "encouraging respect for human rights and for fundamental freedoms for all,"[2] when the word "freedom" itself is considered too controversial?

More money will not do it. No other nation contributes more to the U.N.'s regular budget, its peacekeeping budget, or the budgets of its myriad affiliated organizations and activities than the United States. America has continued its generous support even though Americans increasingly view the U.N. as inefficient and ineffective at best and fraudulent, wasteful, anti-American, and beyond reform at worst.[3]

If the United States is to advance its many interests in the world, it needs to pursue multilateral diplomacy in a smarter, more pragmatic manner. This is especially true when Washington is considering actions taken through the United Nations. A decision to engage multilaterally should meet two criteria: First, it should be in America's interests, and second, it

---

1. "The Great Wall," *Time*, July 19, 1954, at www.time.com/time/magazine/article/0,9171,857449,00.html (accessed January 28, 2009).

2. Charter of the United Nations, art. 1, par. 3.

3. Lydia Saad, "Americans' Opinion of U.N. at Record Low," Gallup, March 6, 2008, at www.gallup.com/poll/104806/Americans-Opinion-UN-Record-Low.aspx (accessed January 28, 2009).

will serve to advance liberty. Unless the United States can achieve both these ends acting within the U.N. system, it should find ways to work around it.

Such "smart multilateralism" is not easy, particularly in multilateral settings. It requires politically savvy leaders who can overcome decades-old bureaucratic inertia at the State Department and in international organizations. It requires the political will and diplomatic skill of people who are dedicated to advancing U.S. interests in difficult environments, especially where progress will likely be slow and incremental. It requires a belief in the cause of liberty, gleaned from a thorough study of our nation's history and the U.S. Constitution, and a deep appreciation for the values and principles that have made America great.

Smart multilateralism requires a fundamental awareness of the strengths and weaknesses, capabilities and failings, of the U.N. and other multilateral negotiating forums, so that the United States does not overreach. Perhaps the most critical decision is whether or not to take a matter to the U.N. in the first place. It would be better to restrict U.S. engagement at the U.N. to situations in which success is possible or engagement will strengthen America's influence and reputation. Selective engagement increases the potential for success, and success breeds success. When America is perceived to be a skillful and judicious multilateral player, it finds it easier to press its case. Smart multilateralism thus requires well-formulated and clear policy positions and a willingness to hold countries accountable when their votes do not align with our interests.

Finally, smart multilateralism is not the same thing as "smart power," a term that Secretary of State Hillary Clinton has used. Suzanne Nossell, a former diplomat at the U.S. Mission to the U.N. in New York, coined that term in 2004 and described it in an article in *Foreign Affairs*.[4] Smart power is seen as a takeoff of "soft power," which suggests that America's leaders downplay the nation's military might as well as its historic role in establishing an international system based on the values of liberty and democracy, and de-emphasize its immense economic and military ("hard") power. Smart power seeks to persuade other countries from a position of assumed equality among nations. This assumption has become the Achilles' heel of the U.N. system and other Cold War–era organizations. Smart multilateralism does not make that same mistake.

---

4. Suzanne Nossel, "Smart Power," *Foreign Affairs* 83, no. 2 (March/April 2004): 131–42.

CHALLENGES TO EFFECTIVE
U.S. MULTILATERALISM

The United States belongs to dozens of multilateral organizations, from large and well-known organizations such as NATO, the World Trade Organization (WTO), and the International Monetary Fund to relatively small niche organizations such as the Universal Postal Union and the International Bureau of Weights and Measures. The 2009 congressional budget justification[5] for the U.S. Department of State included line items for U.S. contributions to some fifty distinct international organizations and budgets.[6] The United Nations and its affiliated bodies receive the lion's share of these contributions.

While the World Bank and International Monetary Fund weight voting based on contributions, most international organizations subscribe to the notion of the equality of nations' votes. With a few exceptions such as Taiwan,[7] all nations—no matter how small or large, free or repressed, rich or poor—have a seat at the U.N. table. Every nation's vote is equal, despite great differences in geographic size, population, military or economic power, and financial contributions.

This one-country, one-vote principle makes the U.N. an extremely difficult venue in which to wage successful multilateral diplomacy. In this envi-

---

5. U.S. Department of State, *Congressional Budget Justification, Fiscal Year 2009*, 619–20, at www.state.gov/documents/organization/100326.pdf (accessed January 28, 2009).

6. Some of these organizations include only a few dozen member states. Others, such as the Organization of American States, are regionally oriented. About one-third of these budget line items go to organizations directly affiliated with the U.N.

7. The Republic of China (ROC) was a founding member of the U.N. and a permanent member of the Security Council at its creation. When the Communist Party of China seized power over mainland China in 1949, it established the People's Republic of China (PRC). The ROC government fled to the island of Taiwan, but continued to represent the entirety of China in the U.N. until October 25, 1971, when the General Assembly recognized the PRC as the "the only lawful representatives of China to the United Nations." U.N. General Assembly, "Restoration of the Lawful Rights of the People's Republic of China in the United Nations," Resolution 2758, October 25, 1971. Only the PRC's opposition bars Taiwan from U.N. membership. Taiwan fulfills all the requirements of a nation-state in that its government exercises control over its territory and population and it has a defined territory. Using the U.N. principle of universal membership, the autonomous government of Taiwan is certainly as qualified for membership as failed states such as Somalia. In some ways, such as the fact that Taiwan is a democracy that respects the right of its 23 million citizens (a larger population than more than half of all current U.N. member states) to choose their own government, it is more worthy of membership than many current U.N. members.

ronment, multilateralism becomes a double-edged sword. It can sometimes speed up global responses to global problems, as with the avian flu outbreak and the Asian tsunami. At other times, it can slow or prevent timely responses, as with halting Iran's nuclear weapons program and stopping genocide in Darfur. Too often, multilateralism at the U.N. is the political means by which other countries and regional blocs constrain or block action. Groups of small nations can join together to outvote the great powers on key issues, and this situation can often lead to bizarre outcomes and compromises. Even seemingly noncontroversial issues, such as improving auditing of U.N. expenditures, require days of skillful, almost nonstop negotiations.

The U.N. is simply too poorly primed for American multilateralism. It is a vast labyrinth of agencies, offices, committees, commissions, programs, and funds, often with overlapping and duplicative missions.[8] Lines of accountability and responsibility for specific issues or efforts are complex, confused, and often indecipherable. For example, dozens of U.N. bodies focus on development, the environment, and children's and women's issues. Coordination is minimal. Reliable means to assess the effectiveness of the bodies' independent activities is practically nonexistent.

Although institutional fiefdoms and bureaucratic interests strongly influence the formulation of U.N. policy, programs, and resolutions, the most powerful actors remain the member states. Each tries to persuade the U.N. as an institution to advocate and adopt its positions on the matters most important to it. The chaos of conflicting priorities rarely results in consensus for decisive action. The most common result is inaction or a lowest-common-denominator outcome.

Too often, the United States also finds that other countries' positions on an issue have been predetermined in their regional or political groupings. These groupings include the European Union; the G-77, or Group of 77 (which is really a caucus of some 130 countries, including China, Iran, and Cuba); the Non-Aligned Movement (NAM); the African Union (AU); the Arab League; and the Organization of the Islamic Conference (OIC). Some countries participate in several of these blocs. Added to this mix is heavy lobbying by "civil society" special interest groups, especially on contentious causes, which helps to explain why the United States faces an uphill battle in successfully husbanding any policy proposal through the U.N. system. Perhaps the most stunning example came under President Bill Clinton, when the United States was trying to negotiate changes to the Rome Statute, which established the International Criminal Court (ICC), so that the

---

8. See U.N. Department of Public Information, "The United Nations System," December 2007, at www.un.org/aboutun/chart_en.pdf (accessed January 28, 2009).

United States could sign it. Intense lobbying by nongovernmental organizations at the proceedings culminated in dramatic cheering when 120 countries voted in favor of the statute despite U.S. objections.[9]

Of course, the most difficult forum for negotiating multilateral solutions is the Security Council, where the most serious security matters are raised and the greatest failures of multilateralism have occurred. During the Cold War, the Soviet Union largely shut down the council with its veto. As a result, the United States conducted most of its international affairs outside of the U.N., yet very few complaints of unilateralism were heard. That changed when the Soviet Union dissolved, and the hope was that the U.N. would at last become a force for good in the world. Instead, new rivalries have emerged that undermine its effectiveness.

Perhaps the most frustrating development for U.S. multilateralism at the U.N. in the post–Cold War era has been the inability of the United States to develop a shared position with some of its best friends in Europe. Often, the allies say that they cannot negotiate with the United States until the European Union has taken a "common European position." Yet after that common position has been adopted, individual European countries claim far less flexibility to negotiate.

The EU also has been known to strong-arm its allies as well as its member states to oppose U.S. positions. For example, on the issue of genocide in Darfur, I witnessed the EU's most visible leaders pressing the United States to accept the ICC as the international judicial authority to try war crimes committed in Sudan, rather than setting up an ad hoc tribunal. Furthermore, they leaned on Romania to go along with their position, even threatening Romania with punitive action if it did not.

Countries hostile to the United States and to economic and political freedoms can and do take full advantage of this crack in the West's once-unified front. Sometimes, though, the United States is its own worst enemy. Intense

---

9. President Clinton eventually signed the Rome Statute on December 31, 2000. He had refused to sign the treaty for the previous eighteen months because, in his words, it had "significant flaws" that threatened legitimate activities of the U.S. military and the rights of Americans. After attempts to change the objectionable parts of the statute proved ineffective, the Bush administration sent a letter to the U.N. secretary-general declaring that "the United States has no legal obligations arising from its signature" of the Rome Statute—in essence "unsigning" the treaty. See press statement, "International Criminal Court: Letter to UN Secretary General Kofi Annan," U.S. Department of State, May 6, 2002, at http://2001-2009.state.gov/r/pa/prs/ps/2002/9968.htm (accessed January 28, 2009). For more on the NGO involvement in this decision and others, see David Davenport, "The New Diplomacy," *Policy Review*, no. 116 (December 2002/January 2003), at www.hoover.org/publications/policyreview/3458466.html (accessed January 28, 2009).

interagency discussions must take place before the State Department sends out any instruction cable to its negotiators at the U.N. and diplomats in capitals. Such delays can be costly because they give other countries time to sway votes against the U.S. position, leaving U.S. negotiators with little time to convince others to change their minds.

For U.S. negotiators, this process can blur not only the clarity of purpose, but also policy objectives. Even after the State Department, Defense Department, and National Security Council hammer out a policy, U.S. diplomats are sometimes simply unable to advance it. Many who are fairly new to the negotiations must deal with counterparts from other countries who have worked the same issue in international settings for years. Some U.S. diplomats would rather settle for consensus than work for an outcome in which the U.S. will be isolated and which places America alongside pariah states such as Zimbabwe or Sudan, even if those countries voted with the United States for starkly different reasons.

Principled foreign policy may put the United States in just such a predicament, but U.S. diplomats should know that Americans expect them to hold the line. Americans need confidence in both the policies we promote as well as the people we send to argue for them.

American diplomats who are new to the multilateral game also need to know that the United States has offered sound policy prescriptions more often than not. We have offered ways to address climate change that are economically sound. We have advanced proven market solutions to poverty and disease and promoted effective methods to counter terrorism without violating civil liberties. Every new class of U.S. diplomats should know enough about these issues and America's track record to argue for them forcefully. Cabled instructions are rarely sufficient to equip diplomats with all the background necessary to defend a controversial or complex policy.

Above all, diplomats must do a better job linking U.S. proposals to the defense of liberty. Too often, U.S. diplomacy has been devoid of American philosophical content, as though our diplomats are ashamed of the blessings that liberty has delivered. Smart multilateralism should explicitly link the spread of liberty with the policy outcomes that we advocate.

THE NEED FOR SMART MULTILATERALISM AT THE U.N.

Clearly, with global terrorism and nuclear proliferation abounding, the United States cannot abandon multilateral forums. Americans understand this. Surveys show that most Americans appreciate the value of having a forum like the U.N. where all the world's nations talk. They just want it to do a far better job and not to work against the United States or freedom in general.

The trick is to know the objective and how best to achieve that goal. For instance, at times, U.N. peacekeeping operations may be necessary and even effective, but whenever these missions are being deliberated, smart multilateralism means U.S. negotiators must ensure the mandates spell out the specific parameters for success. If the United States believes a U.N. mission may not be optimal, then it should unashamedly promote alternatives, such as the international coalition that is helping Iraq become a stable democracy in the Middle East. To do this effectively, the United States must conduct sufficient advance work to inform its decision on whether to take an issue to the U.N. or to pursue an alternative. This must happen before urgency on the ground removes that option and the United States is forced either to veto a resolution or to walk away from a consensus because the legal or policy outcome is unacceptable.

Smart multilateralism always will require hard decisions and hard-nosed determination. Sometimes the United States will need to ask for help, which is a vulnerable negotiating position even when we are protecting others' interests. Yet we must never be so desperate for help that we start cutting bargains on issues of lesser importance to us. The United States also must resist tempering its decisions by how much criticism they might provoke. We will never please everyone; we should prepare for and expect criticism. Our diplomats and policymakers should be strategic, respectful, and consistent in their negotiations. Our allies eventually will see that we are serious and that what they do and say in multilateral forums matters very much to us.

Our diplomats will also need to find ways to overcome the tyranny of the voting blocs that I mentioned earlier. It is a problem that even President Ronald Reagan felt called to address in his remarks to the U.N. General Assembly in 1983:

> The founders of the United Nations expected that member nations would behave and vote as individuals after they had weighed the merits of an issue— rather like a great, global town meeting. The emergence of blocs and the polarization of the United Nations undermine all that this organization initially valued.[10]

Frequently, some of our oldest allies have collaborated to push through policies at the U.N. that would force America to become more like them, such as progressive social policies that give over more sovereignty to supra-

---

10. Ronald Reagan, address to the U.N. General Assembly, September 26, 1983, at www.reagan.utexas.edu/archives/speeches/1983/92683a.htm (accessed January 28, 2009).

national, but unaccountable institutions. In their eyes, the United States is on the wrong side of history when it comes to the International Criminal Court, Guantánamo Bay, the death penalty, global warming, and gender quotas. The United States would do well to remind the Europeans that we find some of their policies equally objectionable, such as their draconian immigration policies, discrimination against minorities, and disregard for trafficking in persons while promoting the legalized sex trade that contributes to it.

For Europeans, achieving consensus can trump the substance of a resolution or document, but that is not the case with America. Substance matters. Our negotiators should take a note from the Europeans' diplomatic manual and push back on their issues if they push back on ours. After all, European leaders followed this tactic in 2007 at the Bali summit on climate change, threatening to boycott President George W. Bush's later conference on climate in Washington, D.C. Some even hinted that they might quit the G-8 if he went ahead with it. The United States need not go that far, but neither should we be any less committed to our interests. With developing countries, the key is to let them know that supporting U.S. positions provides certain benefits and that opposing them imposes some costs. The United States must become more adept at creating incentives that encourage more countries to support its policy priorities at the U.N.

As my colleagues Brett Schaefer and Anthony Kim have suggested, one way is to link U.S. aid to a country's voting practices at the U.N.[11] Congress has mandated an annual report delineating how countries voted each year on issues of concern to the United States. Yet too little has been done with that valuable information. Countries that work against U.S. interests on critical matters should not be rewarded for their opposition, least of all with Americans' hard-earned tax dollars. There should be consequences. At the very least, the United States should always make clear to its friends and allies that its willingness to work with them on soft issues they find important, such as climate change, will be directly related to their willingness to cooperate with us on the hard issues important to us, such as fighting terrorism and the proliferation of nuclear weapons. Washington has too often refrained from this kind of hard bargaining at the U.N. because the United States is already doing so much around the world. But these good deeds actually generate the goodwill that is the legal tender of multilateralism. America should not refrain from spending it when necessary.

Critically, the United States must become better at recognizing and

---

11. Brett D. Schaefer and Anthony B. Kim, "How Do U.S. Foreign Aid Recipients Vote at the U.N.? Against the U.S.," Heritage Foundation *Backgrounder*, no. 2171 (August 18, 2008), at www.heritage.org/Research/InternationalOrganizations/bg 2171.cfm.

blocking efforts at the U.N. that run counter to U.S. interests or undermine its efforts and priorities. "Reforming" the Security Council by enlarging it or giving more of its members a veto is a case in point. Such reform would damage the council's effectiveness, not improve it. Those who seek to expand the council claim that many countries feel the Security Council no longer reflects modern power realities. While the five permanent members of the council are a reflection of the power realities in 1945, the founders of the U.N. understood that permanent membership and the veto were bargaining chips to secure the commitment of the victors of World War II. If they were to be held responsible for securing peace in the world, they would need a veto over Security Council decisions that may not be in their best interests.

This formula admittedly makes working through the council difficult, but adding more permanent seats and veto-wielding members would only compound the problem. The proposals to increase the size of the Security Council (from the current fifteen countries to twenty-five or twenty-six) so it better reflects today's power realities would at best be a temporary solution, lasting only until those power realities shifted. The problem is that few countries will willingly relinquish a permanent seat they hold when power realities change yet again.

Increasing the size of the Security Council poses other practical problems. The council has a well-earned reputation for inaction and paralysis in major crises. Its members differ greatly on serious matters, such as how to deal with Iran, Sudan, and terrorism. Bringing more decision makers to the table will make reaching consensus on issues even more unlikely. A larger council will merely increase competing interests, leading to more gridlock and diluting the influence of the United States and its best allies. From a purely parochial point of view, enlarging the council will not necessarily bring in more countries that support the United States on key issues.[12] It certainly would not have changed the outcome over Iraq.

In the end, enlarging the Security Council will likely result in the United States and other powers looking for more ways to work around the Security Council rather than through it. The only measure that could facilitate more frequent consensus in the council would be to enforce the U.N. Charter's own standard of membership, so that all the nations seated at the council table share the same basic values and commitment to freedom, security, and sovereignty.

Whether in the Security Council or any other U.N. body, smart multilateralism will require American diplomats who understand that success is not

---

12. Nile Gardiner and Brett D. Schaefer, "U.N. Security Council Expansion Is Not in the U.S. Interest," Heritage Foundation *Backgrounder*, no. 1876 (August 18, 2005), at www.heritage.org/Research/InternationalOrganizations/bg1876.cfm.

always determined by winning a vote. Sometimes, standing on principle, even if it means losing a vote, will be necessary, and it can lead to subsequent victories. That was the case with a vote the United States called in the now defunct Commission on Human Rights after Libya, which was under Security Council sanctions, was permitted to assume the chair of the commission by regional group rotation. The United States lost the vote, but Libya's chairmanship served as the penultimate embarrassment for the commission and ultimately led to the effort to replace it with the U.N. Human Rights Council.

Such smart multilateralism is a strategy that needs to be employed in every international forum. We will not be credible as a multilateral player if we do not stand firmly on principle and are not clear about what winning or losing a decision means.

Being effective in negotiations is about competence, not bullying or arrogance. France was not labeled a bully when it sabotaged America's effort to obtain Security Council support for the campaign in Iraq. The U.K. was not accused of arrogance when it forced the United States to retreat on an ICC resolution for Darfur. China, Russia, and other countries drive hard bargains to support their own interests without fear of being labeled bullies. Even small countries such as Cuba press unashamedly for their interests. The United States should do the same. Of course, America can and should be sensitive to others' interests, but we should be no less forthright in asserting our own. We need not bow to every demand simply because we want the United States to appear to be more multilateral.

A key component of a smart multilateral strategy must include continuing to push for reform at the U.N. When the decision is made to go through the U.N., the United States obviously would like the U.N. to implement and manage the endeavor responsibly and efficiently, and it would like measures included in the mandates to ensure transparency and accountability. The current U.N. system falls far short of that standard, as the well-publicized scandals involving the Iraq Oil-for-Food Program and corruption in U.N. procurement demonstrate. Pushing for reform, however, will require the commitment of both Congress and the executive branch.

Granted, the United States and like-minded countries have provoked a few reforms in recent years, such as the creation of the U.N. Ethics Office and adoption of whistle-blower protections. Yet progress has faltered even in these areas. The U.N. Development Program has rejected implementing standard U.N. rules and protections for whistle-blowers as well as the authority of the U.N. Ethics Office, thereby weakening these reforms. The Office of Internal Oversight Services (OIOS), the U.N.'s quasi inspector general, is not fully independent from the agencies it investigates, raising questions about its objectivity. The Procurement Task Force was eliminated despite uncovering over $600 million in contracts tainted by fraud and mismanagement.[13] Senior U.N. officials have refused to file financial disclosure statements, even after U.N. secretary-general Ban Ki-moon asked them to follow his lead. U.N. organizations refuse to give the member states that fund them unrestricted access to their internal documents and audits, even when U.N. and independent investigations confirm extensive evidence of mismanagement, as was the case with UNDP programs and activities in North Korea.[14]

Former Federal Reserve chairman Paul Volcker, who was tasked with leading the U.N. investigation into the Oil-for-Food scandal, concluded that reform was not only necessary, but critical to the future of the organization. He told an audience at DePauw University in 2005:

> The simple fact is that the cheating, the corruption, the absence of disciplined administration has cost the United Nations grievously. Its competence [and] its honesty has been called into question. As a result, its credibility is undermined. And, if its competence and its credibility is undermined, so inevitably is any sense of its legitimacy.[15]

History has shown that some of the surest ways to provoke U.N. reform are for the United States to threaten to leave, to actually withdraw, or to make its contributions to an organization contingent on specific changes. President Reagan withdrew the United States from the United Nations Educational, Scientific and Cultural Organization (UNESCO) in 1984 because it had become the playground of socialists pushing policies that were anathema to free societies. Reforms came slowly after that, but they did come. In 2003, the United States rejoined UNESCO after President George

---

13. Steve Stecklow, "U.N. Allows Its Antifraud Task Force to Dissolve," *The Wall Street Journal*, January 8, 2009, at http://online.wsj.com/article/SB123138018 217563187.html?mod=googlenews_wsj; and Colum Lynch, "U.N. Cites $20 Million in Fraud," *Washington Post*, October 21, 2008, A13, at www.washingtonpost .com/wp-dyn/content/article/2008/10/20/AR200810 2003277.html (accessed January 28, 2009).

14. See U.N. Development Program, External Independent Investigative Review Panel, *Confidential Report on United Nations Development Programme Activities in the Democratic People's Republic of Korea, 1999–2007*, May 31, 2008, at www.undp .org/dprk/docs/EIIRP_Final_Report_31%20May.pdf (accessed January 28, 2009), and Permanent Subcommittee on Investigations, Committee on Homeland Security and Governmental Affairs, U.S. Senate, *United Nations Development Program: A Case Study of North Korea*, January 23, 2008, at www.undp.org/dprk/docs/UNDP-senate -report.pdf (accessed January 28, 2009).

15. DePauw University, Office of Media Relations, "United Nations 'Urgently Needs Reform,' Paul Volcker Says in Opening Session of DePauw Discourse 2005," September 15, 2005, at www.depauw.edu/news/index.asp?id=16262 (accessed January 28, 2009).

W. Bush concluded that it had reformed sufficiently. The OIOS was established only after Congress passed legislation in 1993 withholding 10 percent of America's regular budget assessment until the U.N. established "an independent office with responsibilities and powers substantially similar to offices of Inspectors General authorized by the Inspector General Act of 1978."[16] Similarly, the Helms-Biden United Nations Reform Act of 1999 made payment of U.S. arrears to the U.N. contingent on reforms, including reducing the U.S. assessment for the U.N. regular budget from 25 percent to 22 percent.

Short of withholdings or withdrawal, the United States has to work within the many U.N. bodies to rein in runaway budgets and seek more equitable assessments. This is usually a losing battle. According to a 2006 report by the U.S. Office of Management and Budget (OMB), the United States contributed $5.3 billion to the U.N. in 2005[17]—a 30 percent increase over the $4.1 billion contributed in 2004. Yet the United States exercises minimal influence over how those resources are spent. Budgetary decisions require the approval of two-thirds of the General Assembly (128 countries). Coincidentally, the 128 least assessed countries pay a combined total of about 1 percent of the regular U.N. budget and less than one-third of 1 percent of its peacekeeping budget. In contrast, the United States pays 22 percent of the U.N. regular budget and about 26 percent of the peacekeeping budget, yet it has only one vote.

These two key U.N. budgets are growing rapidly. The U.N. regular budget has increased by an average of 17 percent annually over the past five years and by 193 percent since the 1998–1999 biennial budget, according to the U.S. Mission to the U.N. The U.S. Mission projected the 2008–2009 biennial budget will exceed $5.2 billion. This represents a 25 percent increase over the final 2006–2007 biennial budget and, in dollar terms, the largest increase in the regular budget in U.N. history.[18] The projected budget for U.N. peacekeeping operations was $7.4 billion for the twelve months from

---

16. Marjorie Ann Browne and Kennon H. Nakamura, "United Nations System Funding: Congressional Issues," Congressional Research Service *Report for Congress*, updated November 13, 2008, p. 33, at http://assets.opencrs.com/rpts/RL33611 _20081113.pdf (accessed January 28, 2009).

17. Tom Coburn, "U.S. Contributions to the U.N. System Are Over $5.3 Billion," August 1, 2006, at http://coburn.senate.gov/ffm/index.cfm?FuseAction = Oversight Action.View&ContentRecord_id = cb1276da-802a-23ad-4f6e-9b71d30d4064 (accessed January 28, 2009).

18. Press release, "Statement by Ambassador Mark D. Wallace, U.S. Representative for UN Management and Reform, on the 2008/2009 U.N. Budget," U.S. Mission to the United Nations, December 11, 2007, at www.usunnewyork.usmission .gov/press_releases/20071211_367.html (accessed January 28, 2009).

July 2008 through June 2009.[19] This is a 10 percent increase over the previous budget and a nearly threefold increase since 2003. It makes the annual peacekeeping budget triple the size of the annualized U.N. regular biennial 2008–2009 budget that covers the operations of the rest of the U.N. Secretariat.

The United States has been unable to prevent budget growth through diplomacy alone. In fact, the U.N. passed the largest budget increase in its history over the objections of the United States in December 2007.[20] That decision to overrule the United States broke a twenty-year tradition of consensus-based budget decisions. It was ushered in with a standing ovation by other member states.

Quite simply, there is a free-rider problem caused by the one-country, one-vote system. The countries that contribute very little to the U.N. budgets, yet receive the most in terms of U.N. services, can as a bloc drive the financial and programmatic decisions. Because they pay little into the U.N. budget, they are less concerned about waste or mismanagement than about protecting their disproportionate returns.

However, not just these countries favor the status quo. Other countries that make significant contributions also choose not to champion budgetary restraint or management reform in order to gain support for their own policy priorities.[21] In the first Bush term, France repeatedly blocked U.S. efforts in the Geneva Group General—a group made up of countries that each contribute more than 1 percent of the U.N. budget—to bring a common tough position on budgetary restraint and reform to U.N. budget negotiations.[22]

---

19. U.N. Department of Public Information, "Budget Committee Takes Up $7.4 Billion Proposal for 2008/09 Peacekeeping, Board of Auditors Report on 2006/07 Peacekeeping Financial Statements," GA/AB/ 3846, May 8, 2008, at www.un.org/News/Press/docs/2008/gaab3846.doc.htm (accessed January 28, 2009).

20. U.N. Department of Public Information, "Fifth Committee Recommends 2008–2009 Budget of $4.17 Billion, as It Concludes Work for Main Part of Current Session," GA/AB/3835, December 21, 2007, at www.un.org/News/Press/docs/2007/gaab3835.doc.htm (accessed January 28, 2009).

21. Brett D. Schaefer, "The U.S. Should Oppose the Largest Budget Increase in U.N. History," Heritage Foundation *WebMemo*, no. 1741 (December 13, 2007), at www.heritage.org/Research/InternationalOrganizations/wm1741.cfm.

22. According to a presentation given to a U.N. agency, the Geneva Group General was "established in 1964 of those like-minded countries contributing more than 1% to the UN system. Membership includes Australia, Belgium, Canada, France, Germany, Italy, Japan, Netherlands, Spain, Sweden, Russia, Switzerland, UK and USA." U.N. Chief Executives Board, "IT/MIS Recommendations of the Geneva Group General," modified February 27, 2006, at http://ict.unsystemceb.org/reports/200503/item5 (accessed January 28, 2009).

Counteracting the free-rider and clientitis problems that the current system of assessed funding creates requires a new approach. It may require moving more organizations to weighted voting by which the nations that pay most of the bills have more control over programming decisions. This system has worked for the Universal Postal Union and other U.N.-affiliated organizations. Alternatively, more U.N. agencies could be moved to voluntary funding, as Ambassador John Bolton recommends in the foreword. Both approaches will require smart multilateralism to build the case that this kind of change would help to increase accountability and effectiveness in the U.N. system.

WHEN THE U.N. SYSTEM FAILS

America's success in reshaping the international system to better advance freedom, security, and human rights ultimately will depend on how well its leaders implement smart multilateralism. International political, legal, and economic institutions should be transformed in ways that do not equate free and democratic nations with tyrannical and failed states. The U.S. Senate should continue its decades-long record of not ratifying the two dozen or so problematic treaties that it has determined pose problems for U.S. sovereignty, the Constitution, and our system of federalism.[23] America will need to strengthen its security alliances and resist new interpretations of international law that are inconsistent with its interests and founding principles. It will need to create new partnerships when needed and undertake an aggressive strategy of smart multilateralism in America's interest.

A blueprint for this strategy must start with U.N. reform. As many of the authors in this book point out, America's great financial leverage could be better used to convince the U.N. to reform more rapidly. Whatever the mechanism—targeted withholdings of U.S. contributions to programs that are ineffective, insufficient, wasteful, or fraudulent; moving more programs and activities to voluntary funding; or securing weighted voting—the result would be greater accountability, transparency, and oversight of a system riddled with abuse. As Ambassador Bolton rightly observes, even the mere

---

23. Treaties in this category include several sitting in the Senate Foreign Relations Committee since 1949, such as the Law of the Sea Treaty, the Comprehensive Test Ban Treaty, and the International Covenant on Economic, Social and Cultural Rights. The president should request that the Senate send them all back for a fresh review, and resubmit only those that do not threaten U.S. sovereignty or undermine the Constitution. In a dangerous world, the president needs all the flexibility that he can garner to decide what is best for America.

discussion of these steps can provoke member states to do the right thing. Other ideas for reforming the U.N. are presented throughout this volume.

Even when the U.N. is unwilling, incapable, or poorly positioned to respond to a crisis or critical global problem, the United States should not stop trying to improve the outcomes. Nor should the United States and its friends shy away from seeking creative work-arounds. Some issues are simply ill suited to the highly politicized and universal nature of the United Nations. President Clinton made such a determination about the Balkans crisis, and President George W. Bush made similar determinations. For example, when the Security Council proved unable to deal with the issue of illicit trafficking of weapons of mass destruction, most notably by the A. Q. Khan network run by the head of Pakistan's nuclear program, President Bush created the Proliferation Security Initiative (PSI). Over ninety countries have conducted training exercises with the United States and signed agreements allowing inspectors to board their ships to find and interdict illicit weapons and technologies transported by sea. Successful interdictions are on record. The best the Security Council could do was to adopt its first nonproliferation resolution, which endorses and encourages PSI-type activities outside the U.N. system.[24] The United States and Russia cosponsored the resolution.

In another notable work-around, President George W. Bush put up the very first pledge of $200 million to start a global fund to provide effective medicines to people and communities hard hit by HIV/AIDS and other potential pandemics. The U.N. General Assembly unanimously endorsed the concept a month later in June 2001, and in 2002, the Global Fund to Fight AIDS, Tuberculosis and Malaria was established. Today, it is an active partnership of governments, civil society, the private sector, and communities. To encourage other countries to participate, Congress enacted legislation that limits U.S. donations to 33 percent of total donations. The fund has committed more than $11 billion to finance "aggressive interventions" in 136 countries, and the U.S. share has exceeded $3.3 billion. Other examples of work-arounds included hosting the Annapolis Conference to reinvigorate work on a two-state solution for the Israelis and Palestinians.

IMPLEMENTING SMART MULTILATERALISM

Smart multilateralism focuses on using the best options to achieve the best results. The more options that are available, the better, especially when going through the U.N. would result in nominal or no action. The United States should lead an effort to create additional alternative structures and

---

24. U.N. Security Council Resolution 1540, S/RES/1540, April 28, 2004.

programs through which the free world can target its resources more directly to solve the world's thorny problems. To this end, the United States should:

Create alternative security structures

Recent events such as Iran's defiance of the U.N. regarding its nuclear weapons program, North Korea's nuclear weapons and ballistic missile tests, China's use of a ground-based missile to destroy a satellite in space, and Russia's invasion of Georgia highlight how ill equipped the U.N. is to respond to the world's security crises. In the more than sixty years since the U.N. was created, there have been over three hundred wars resulting in over 22 million deaths. Yet during that time, the U.N. authorized military action to counter aggression just twice: in response to the North Korean invasion of South Korea in 1950 and to the Iraqi invasion of Kuwait in 1990. At other times, U.N. peacekeepers have stood aside and failed to prevent despicable acts, including the genocide in Rwanda. In the Democratic Republic of Congo and other countries, U.N. peacekeepers have abused or raped the very people whom they were supposed to protect.

With the growing threat that a rogue regime or terrorists will obtain weapons of mass destruction, Washington simply cannot afford to rely on the U.N. for the security of the free world. America must strengthen its alliances and pursue alternative arrangements with new allies that better enable it to respond to today's challenges. Topping the list should be developing a new, more flexible security arrangement, a truly global alliance that would include only those states deeply committed to liberty. Free nations have far more in common than what divides them politically, militarily, or geographically. NATO is simply too slow, too divided, and too parochial to become that institution.

Countries committed to freedom should create a "global freedom coalition," a flexible platform that enables them to collaborate more closely to counter terrorism, proliferation of weapons of mass destruction, trafficking in persons, international crime, and other threats that the U.N. and other organizations and security alliances are unable to address.[25] It should be a voluntary association made up of nations from around the world that believe that security and liberty are inextricably linked and that broader multilateral security cooperation is necessary. The options for closer coop-

---

25. For more on this idea, see Kim R. Holmes, "Time for 'Global Freedom Coalition,'" *Washington Times*, September 11, 2008, A4. See also Kim R. Holmes, "Time for a New International Game Plan," Heritage Foundation *Backgrounder*, no. 2231 (January 22, 2009), at www.heritage.org/Research/InternationalOrganizations/bg 2231.cfm.

eration include coordinated sanctions, increased intelligence sharing, better-integrated law enforcement, and joint military training and exercises. The successful Proliferation Security Initiative proves that such multilateral coordination is not only possible, but a productive option. The Global Freedom Coalition could eventually consider drawing that successful initiative into its global strategy.

The only requirements for membership in the coalition should be a demonstrated commitment to freedom at home and abroad, a willingness and readiness to take immediate action in the face of a threat, and an ability to contribute meaningfully to the coalition's activities. States that are committed to its objectives but still transitioning to greater liberalization should also be involved in some fashion, much as our Cold War alliances included Portugal even when it was not yet fully democratic.

Create an alternative to better promote human rights

The United States should launch a Liberty Forum for Human Rights.[26] The "new" U.N. Human Rights Council has not been an improvement over the disbanded U.N. Commission on Human Rights. In its first three years, it failed to hold most of the world's worst human rights abusers accountable. The world and especially the oppressed people in places such as Sudan, Burma, Cuba, Iran, and China need a legitimate standard-bearer for human rights, one with members that truly respect liberty and the rule of law and are willing to seek new ways to advance them.

A Liberty Forum would give them a platform from which to highlight the critical linkages between human rights and security and between economic freedom and political freedom. It would be a place where emerging democracies could go to gain better understanding of the proper role of the sovereign state in upholding individual liberties and equality before the law, and guidance on ways to improve their human rights. Its members that sit on U.N. bodies such as the Human Rights Council could advance the Liberty Forum's agenda in those bodies and support each other's candidacies for important leadership positions. To be successful, such an entity should have strict membership rules and a clear strategy to coordinate their activities.

Transform the Community of Democracies

Washington should also undertake a new campaign to transform the Community of Democracies, a Clinton-era initiative ostensibly dedicated

---

26. Kim R. Holmes, *Liberty's Best Hope: American Leadership for the 21st Century* (Washington, DC: Heritage Foundation, 2008), and Kim R. Holmes, "Liberty Forum Better than U.N. Rights Council," *Washington Times*, December 29, 2008, A4. See also the chapter by Brett Schaefer and Steven Groves in this volume.

to promoting democracy. Regrettably, it has accepted a number of members and observer states that are not true democracies, such as Egypt and Russia. Having such countries at the table confuses the true meaning of democracy, makes speaking and acting with one voice difficult, and gives political cover to those clamping down on freedom.

Membership in the Community of Democracies should be a high honor and privilege. Only countries designated as "free" in Freedom House's annual *Freedom in the World* survey or a similar independent evaluation deserve seats at its ministerial meetings. Less-free nations could be observers if they are making positive improvements toward freedom and not backsliding. Members should strive to more closely coordinate activities that advance democracy, such as organizing election monitors and promoting freedom of the press, the rule of law, property rights, and economic freedom. Such a revamped Community of Democracies could contribute to and reinforce the efforts of the U.N. Democracy Fund to give democracy promotion and democratic values a more central role in the U.N.'s work.

Revamp the international economic system

The current global economic crisis has highlighted the need for America to take the lead in revamping the international economic system. The world's international financial and economic institutions are antiquated. Radical anti-American and anti-free-trade leaders in Russia, Venezuela, and other countries are calling for a new international economic system based on increased regulation and the redistribution of wealth. If the United States does not step up and use this opportunity to lead the world down the proven path to economic freedom and prosperity, such harmful proposals will fill the void.

The United Nations, which claims in its Charter the goal of improving living standards and freedom around the world, has spent billions of donor dollars over the years to foster development without achieving that goal. On this point, Ambassador Terry Miller's argument in this volume is right: The failure may be because the U.N. "eschews the proven development strategies of classic liberal economics" and instead promotes "aid-focused plans that almost certainly do more harm than good because they emphasize and enhance the role of government and central planning."

For fifteen years, the *Index of Economic Freedom*,[27] published by The Heritage Foundation and the *Wall Street Journal*, has tracked economic policies

---

27. Terry Miller and Kim R. Holmes, *2009 Index of Economic Freedom* (Washington, D.C.: Heritage Foundation and Dow Jones & Company, Inc., 2009), at www.heritage.org/index (accessed January 29, 2009).

in nations around the world. It provides conclusive evidence that economic freedom, as expressed in market-based policies bolstered by the rule of law, provides the surest path to real development and prosperity. The U.S. Millennium Challenge Account has demonstrated how linking aid to sound economic policies can bring about lasting change that helps people pull themselves out of poverty.

The world needs a new approach to development and the global economy. It needs a new way to explain the benefits of trade liberalization for poor people around the world. The time has come to create a new venue where countries that believe in economic freedom can freely discuss what works and what does not and where they can develop collaborative responses to the latest stresses on the global economy. The White House could take the initiative on this, but it might be better if the president asked Australia or another key economic ally to take the lead in establishing a Global Economic Freedom Forum.[28] The goal would be a venue where leaders of the fifteen or twenty freest economies could work together to set common trade agendas and issue joint statements highlighting how they each have benefited from such policies as lowering taxes, eliminating subsidies, reducing regulation, improving property rights, liberalizing investment laws, and signing trade agreements.

The first summit should be hosted in Washington, D.C., and the more diverse the geographic representation of countries is, the better. Bahrain, Chile, Ireland, Mauritius, and Singapore could bring as much to the discussion as Canada, the U.K., and Australia. The initial group of countries could eventually become a steering committee that determines the agenda of future forum summits. For example, each summit could include sessions led by countries that have shown particular leadership in specific issues such as reducing agricultural subsidies or protecting intellectual property rights. Larger meetings could be held to include countries that do some things well, but fall short in other areas. Undoubtedly, as the forum's prestige grows, its policies could be echoed in the G-8 and WTO and could even become the basis for a U.N. caucus on economic freedom.

CONCLUSION

The executive branch and Congress should consider all the recommendations in this book and unveil a new strategy for revamping the international system to better respond to tomorrow's challenges. Employing smart multilateralism will be key, but it will not be a panacea. As Ambassador Jeane J. Kirkpatrick so aptly described in 2002:

---

28. Holmes, *Liberty's Best Hope*.

Multilateral decision making increases the cultural, political, and geographical distance between those who choose decision makers, those who make decisions, and those affected by these decisions. Abstract relations cannot produce the same solidarity among people as common identifications, education, and experience. The democratic institutions that make and keep decision makers representative and accountable are national. . . .

The officials of multilateral organizations are not elected by a popular vote. Often they are not even chosen by elected officials. Multilateral institutions do not merely add another layer of bureaucracy between rule makers and those who live under their rules; these institutions create wholly new jurisdictions that do not coincide with existing institutions—based on nation-states—that provide democratic accountability. Voters can rarely "throw the rascals out" when the rascals hail from 200 countries scattered around the globe.[29]

Multilateralism in liberty's best interests will always face uphill battles, but America has faced immense odds in the international realm many times before. When its decisions have stood firmly on principle and its dedication to liberty and the ingenuity of its people have been unleashed, it has prevailed. The challenges we face compel the United States to employ smart multilateralism in every venue, but especially at the United Nations, where the decisions often have the greatest or most destructive impact on people and on liberty itself.

ACKNOWLEDGMENTS

I would like to thank Janice A. Smith of The Heritage Foundation for her invaluable assistance in researching and writing this chapter. I would also like to thank the editor, Brett D. Schaefer, for his input and review.

---

29. Jeane J. Kirkpatrick, "The Shackles of Consensus," *Foreign Policy* (September/October 2002): 37.

2

Making Law

The United Nations' Role in Formulating and Enforcing International Law

Lee A. Casey and David B. Rivkin Jr.

The United Nations is many things, but despite all its standing bodies and prognosticating committees, it is not an international legislature that passes laws binding on all the people of the world. The United Nations has no formal authority to establish or impose law internationally. The U.N. Charter is not a global constitution. The U.N. General Assembly is in no sense a legislature, and the Security Council is a political, not judicial, body. The International Court of Justice (ICJ), or World Court, is best understood as an arbitral panel with a limited jurisdiction and no actual enforcement authority.

Today, as for several centuries past, international law is made by states—either in the form of treaties or as customary rules developed over time that states feel compelled to obey. Nevertheless, the actual process of international lawmaking is a fluid one, and the U.N.'s principal bodies—particularly the ICJ, General Assembly, and Security Council—profoundly influence the development and direction of international law.

American policymakers have by turns viewed the U.N.'s "lawmaking" role as a good and bad thing, usually depending on the impact any particular U.N. effort has on U.S. interests and foreign policy goals at the time. Over the long term, however, the growing influence that U.N. bodies exercise over the development, interpretation, and implementation of international law should be of great concern to the United States. Governments, nongovernmental organizations, and international bodies have increasingly undercut traditional notions of sovereignty by promoting an institutional vision that claims for various international organizations—whether established U.N. bodies such as the ICJ or newly created "courts" such as the International Criminal Court and the Security Council's ad hoc criminal tribunals—the right (even a right superior to that of states) to interpret and apply international law. However, American democracy is founded on those very notions of sovereignty, which guarantee the United States' right to govern itself through its own constitutional institutions.

DEVELOPING A LAW OF NATIONS

Some tension has always existed between the concepts of an "international law" and representative democracy. In a representative democracy, the power to make positive law is exercised by an elected and accountable legislature, with varying degrees of participation by national executives and courts. This was of little consequence throughout much of the early modern period, both because there were few representative democracies as currently understood and because international law was not viewed as positive law that could be made.

Beginning with the breakdown of medieval universalism in religion and politics (in theory at least) during the Renaissance and Reformation, international law as we know it began to take shape. This "law of nations" remained grounded in widely accepted notions of natural law. The title of Emmerich de Vattel's influential mid-eighteenth-century treatise—"The Law of Nations or Principles of the Law of Nature Applied to the Conduct and Affairs of Nations and Sovereigns"—explains the system concisely and had an important effect on the framers of the U.S. Constitution.

Natural law bound sovereigns and subjects alike, and its legitimacy was taken for granted. These were the rules set down by nature, or by nature's God, to govern human affairs. Man could not make or alter such rules. He could only—perhaps—conceive or discover a more accurate understanding of them.

At least, that was the theory. In practice, new rules were necessarily adopted over time because society and international relationships were changing. This was especially the case in the mid-seventeenth century with the final recognition of the modern state system, in which each sovereign and independent nation was legally equal to all other such sovereign and independent nations. The critical event is traditionally identified as the 1648 Peace of Westphalia, which ended the Thirty Years' War in Germany and Holland's eighty-year war of independence from Spain. In particular, the relevant treaties recognized that the various German states could have their own foreign policies, separate and apart from that of the Holy Roman Emperor.

Of course, despite the supposedly "natural" basis of international law, there were arguments over its content and meaning, as there are today. Then as now, it was important for states to justify their acts and policies by reference to legal rules, whether local, national, international, or divine. For example, in the 1660s, King Louis XIV justified an aggressive war along what is now France's border with Belgium by referring to local inheritance laws that favored his Spanish Hapsburg wife's claims over those of her younger half brother, the king of Spain. The most clearly defined rules were those governing diplomatic intercourse and, at least to some extent, warfare.

In general, international law did not attempt to define the relationship of individual citizens to their own government. It was genuinely a law of nations, and there were relatively few international rules that states could not ignore (derogate from) in the right circumstances. Indeed, in this important formative period of international law, the whole system became increasingly consensual. Over time, new rules were developed and old ones were affirmed or discarded based on the actual practice and behavior of states. Yet states that refused to recognize a particular norm as it emerged were not bound by it. Rules were also increasingly recognized by treaty, although such agreements tended to be bilateral between two states and therefore were not binding on others.

As a result, this system of international law—binding in principle, but actually applicable only to states and grounded in their practice and consent—did not prevent the establishment of the United States as a republic of increasingly democratic bent, in a world dominated by more or less authoritarian monarchies. Indeed, the Constitution's framers embraced the law of nations, adopting language that gives Congress the power "to define and punish Piracies and Felonies committed on the high Seas, and Offenses against the Law of Nations" and making "all Treaties made, or which shall be made, under the Authority of the United States" the supreme law of the land.[1] These provisions are highly important because, among other things, they reveal the framers' understanding that the United States would be subject to international norms, especially the rule requiring states to keep their treaties (*pacta sunt servanda*), and that it was the right and obligation of the American government to recognize and define those obligations for itself. Thus, as James Madison explained in the Federalist Papers, most states had defined piracies and other international law offenses themselves and "neither the common, nor the statute law of [Great Britain] or any other nation

---

1. U.S. Constitution, art. 1, sec. 8, cl. 10, and art. 6, cl. 2.

ought to be a standard for the [judicial] proceedings of this [nation], unless previously made its own by legislative adoption."[2]

Indeed, this right to define, interpret, and apply international law on a national basis has been and remains the key component in reconciling an ever-expanding set of international law norms with the sovereign right of states to govern their own affairs. There is no international "supreme court" or other body with the inherent competence to say authoritatively what international law means generally or in any particular case. All states, large and small, are equal in law and have an equal right to identify and interpret their own international law obligations. States may be subjected to international judicial or legislative authority only through their own consent. In reforming the U.N.'s lawmaking role, the United States can accomplish much by forcefully and consistently opposing efforts to change this fundamental principle.

LEGISLATING INTERNATIONAL LAW

This is critical because, while all the basic rules outlined above are still the backbone of international law, they are very much under pressure. Efforts to create a more "legislative" international law system, based on compulsion rather than the consent of states, grew exponentially after the world wars of the twentieth century. This is especially true in the human rights area, where a series of multilateral conventions—most drafted under the U.N.'s aegis—have attempted to establish binding and often nonderogable legal norms that must be applied both domestically and internationally. Although these treaties have adopted many provisions that are consistent with American values, this has not always been the case. Perhaps more to the point, to the extent that they legislate rights or obligations applicable to individuals through the system of international negotiation, accountability becomes more and more remote, undercutting the fundamental principle that the people can legitimately be governed only by their own consent as may be expressed through their own elected representatives.

Of course, in the United States, treaties have a democratic character. They are ratified only after two-thirds of the Senate has approved. Moreover, unless the treaty is self-executing, its provisions can be enforced in American courts only after Congress enacts implementing legislation through the normal legislative process. A self-executing treaty is one in which "existing law is adequate to enable the United States to carry out its obligations."[3] To

---

2. James Madison, *The Federalist*, no. 42.

3. American Law Institute, *Restatement, Third, of the Foreign Relations Law of the United States*, sec. 111(3)(4), comment h (1987).

the extent that a treaty would achieve a result that otherwise "lies within the exclusive law-making power of Congress under the Constitution,"[4] it is non-self-executing and cannot be given effect by American courts without implementing legislation. This is especially the case when an agreement would require federal funding, because only Congress can appropriate funds.

This includes the U.N. Charter. The Charter is a treaty and to the extent it requires the United States to make certain contributions to fund U.N. operations, Congress does not violate the Constitution when and if it fails to make good on those obligations. However, depending on the circumstances, a failure in this regard may put the United States in violation of its international obligations.

This is the case even though treaties are the supreme law of the land. In fact, although treaties have equal dignity with federal statutes, like statutes they remain subject at all times to the Constitution itself and can neither amend that document nor prevail over its provisions in federal or state court. A statute enacted after a treaty is ratified that is inconsistent with the treaty will prevail over the treaty, although this may put the United States in violation of its international legal obligations.

From a "democracy deficit" perspective, the real problem with treaties—especially modern, multilateral rights conventions—is that they are often used as "evidence" of emerging or established customary international law norms, which might bind the United States regardless of whether it has consented to the treaty in question. Strictly speaking, such claims are highly dubious from an international law perspective, because even consent by every nation does not transform a particular agreement into an international statute or custom. As noted, there is no international legislative authority, and every treaty is subject to interpretation and application by each state party. By contrast, customary rules are exactly that—norms based on long and consistent practice over time that states consider to be legally binding and, most importantly, behave as if they were legally binding. Nevertheless, for the very reason that international law is made (or explicated) through such informal processes, such arguments continue and often are given great weight, especially in the courts.

THE ICJ: A QUESTION OF "RESPECTFUL CONSIDERATION"

International judicial authority, including the right to interpret and enforce international legal norms through binding orders and even coercion, is a

---

4. American Law Institute, *Restatement*, sec. 111(3)(4), comment h (1987).

very new phenomenon. The traditional international system, which is grounded in the legal equality of states, vested in each independent sovereign the right to interpret its own international law obligations. This right was and is tempered by an overarching requirement that states act in good faith in interpreting their treaties and, by extension, international custom and practice. Nevertheless, no supranational authority has the right or power to interpret international law authoritatively for states.

Unsurprisingly, before the twentieth century, international judicial tribunals were not a regular part of the international system. In the form of the *Alabama* Claims Commission involving the United States and Great Britain, the nineteenth century had seen an especially significant attempt to resolve a bilateral dispute between states through international arbitration. Pursuant to an 1871 Anglo–American treaty, the *Alabama* claims were adjudicated by a five-member international body sitting in Geneva, Switzerland. These claims involved depredations by Confederate raiders, including the notorious CSS *Alabama*, against U.S. shipping during the American Civil War. These raiders had been built and/or provisioned in British ports, violating Britain's international obligations as a neutral in the conflict.[5]

However, the first permanent international court with a general jurisdiction, the Permanent Court of International Justice (PCIJ), was not established until 1921–1922. Headquartered in The Hague, the PCIJ was closely linked to the League of Nations, having been formed pursuant to the Covenant of the League of Nations. Despite its relative novelty, the PCIJ was very much part of the traditional state system. Its jurisdiction or competence extended only to states and other internationally recognized entities. Individuals and nonstate corporate entities could not be parties before the court.[6] Moreover, its decisions were not enforceable through any coercive means or mechanisms. The same is true of today's International Court of Justice (ICJ), the PCIJ's successor.

The ICJ is the United Nations' "principal judicial organ." Although all U.N. member states are also parties to the ICJ's statute, the court's actual authority—its jurisdiction or competence in any given case—depends on the type of consent given by the states involved. Thus, states that have accepted the court's compulsory jurisdiction are subject to suit by other states that have also accepted compulsory jurisdiction. States that have not

---

5. Earlier efforts at international arbitration or mediation tended toward the unrealistic, obviously political, or absurd, such as the Hapsburg emperor Joseph II's unsuccessful efforts to submit the underlying issues of the American War for Independence to his mediation. T. C. W. Blanning, *Joseph II* (London: Longman, 1994), 137.

6. For example, see Statute of the Permanent Court of International Justice, art. 34, and Statute of the International Court of Justice, art. 34.

accepted the ICJ's compulsory jurisdiction or have withdrawn from it, such as the United States, are subject to the court's authority only in cases in which they specifically consent or their consent is contained in another treaty. Although the ICJ lacks coercive authority over states—it can only refer a state's failure or refusal to comply with its judgments to the Security Council—its decisions are viewed internationally with much respect. That being the case, the ICJ has seen a number of efforts to use its processes as political tools against the United States.

Nicaragua v. United States

The first instance of a foreign government's attempting to use the ICJ to undermine American foreign policy grew out of U.S. efforts to thwart Soviet expansion in Central and South America. Nicaraguan dictator Anastasio Somoza was overthrown in 1979 and was ultimately replaced by the communist Sandinista government, led by Daniel Ortega. Neighboring El Salvador and other Central American republics were also targeted for subversion during this period. In 1980 under President Jimmy Carter, the United States began to provide economic and limited military support to the Salvadoran government. The Reagan administration expanded this support and provided assistance to the Nicaraguan Contras, the Sandinistas' noncommunist opponents. In addition to training and financial support, the CIA led an effort to interfere with Soviet and Cuban shipments to the Sandinistas by mining Nicaragua's harbors. In response, the Sandinista government sued the United States in the ICJ, claiming that Washington had violated customary international law rules against interfering in another state's domestic affairs.

The Reagan administration challenged the court's jurisdiction to hear the case because Nicaragua had not properly recognized the ICJ's compulsory jurisdiction or undertaken obligations reciprocal to those of the United States. However, the ICJ rejected this argument, and the United States thereafter refused to participate in the proceedings, which it considered politically motivated and beyond the ICJ's legitimate authority. As the State Department explained at the time:

> The conflict in Central America, therefore, is not a narrow legal dispute; it is an inherently political problem that is not appropriate for judicial resolution. The conflict will be solved only by political and diplomatic means—not through a judicial tribunal. The ICJ was never intended to resolve issues of collective security and self-defense and is patently unsuited for such a role. Unlike domestic courts, the World Court has jurisdiction only to the extent that nation-states have consented to it. When the United States accepted the Court's compulsory jurisdiction in 1946, it certainly never conceived of such a role for the Court in such controversies. Nicaragua's suit against the United

States—which includes an absurd demand for hundreds of millions of dollars in reparations—is a blatant misuse of the Court for political and propaganda purposes.

As one of the foremost supporters of the ICJ, the United States is one of only 44 of 159 member states of the United Nations that have accepted the Court's compulsory jurisdiction at all. Furthermore, the vast majority of these 44 states have attached to their acceptance reservations that substantially limit its scope. Along with the United Kingdom, the United States is one of only two permanent members of the UN Security Council that have accepted that jurisdiction. And of the 16 judges now claiming to sit in judgment on the United States in this case, 11 are from countries that do not accept the Court's compulsory jurisdiction.

Few if any other countries in the world would have appeared at all in a case such as this which they considered to be improperly brought. Nevertheless, out of its traditional respect for the rule of law, the United States has participated fully in the Court's proceedings thus far, to present its view that the Court does not have jurisdiction or competence in this case.[7]

The ICJ issued its judgment against the United States in 1986.[8] It ruled, among other things, that the United States was liable to pay compensation to Nicaragua because it had violated Nicaragua's sovereignty and improperly interfered in that country's internal affairs through its actions supporting the Contras. The United States refused to recognize the judgment and paid no reparations. Efforts to enforce the decision were effectively blocked in the Security Council, and the United States withdrew from the ICJ's compulsory jurisdiction in 1986.

Whether the ICJ's ruling and the American withdrawal had any real impact on America's foreign policy or international standing is debatable. As noted in the State Department's statement, the United States had been unusual in accepting the ICJ's compulsory jurisdiction in the first instance—it was one of only two permanent members of the Security Council to have done so. However, the United States is still subject to the court's authority in individual cases based on treaties that provide for ICJ dispute resolution mechanisms or in cases of specific consent. In more recent years, other states have attempted to use the ICJ to affect American domestic affairs, particularly the United States' refusal to abolish the death penalty. To date, however, the U.S. Supreme Court has rebuffed these efforts.

---

7. U.S. Department of State, "U.S. Withdrawal from the Proceedings Initiated by Nicaragua in the ICJ—International Court of Justice—Transcript," *Bulletin*, January 18, 1985, at http://findarticles.com/p/articles/mi_m1079/is_v85/ai_3659121 (accessed October 2, 2008).

8. See *Case Concerning the Military and Paramilitary Activities in and Against Nicaragua (Merits)*, June 27, 1986.

The Effect of ICJ Rulings on American Courts

The U.S. Supreme Court has consistently and correctly held that ICJ decisions are not automatically binding on American courts: "Nothing in the structure or purpose of the ICJ suggests that its interpretations were intended to be conclusive on our courts."[9] Those decisions are entitled to no more than "respectful consideration" by American judges interpreting international norms and do not have precedential effect. Even so, the ICJ was the focus of efforts by Germany and Mexico to upset otherwise lawful capital convictions of their nationals in the United States. The jurisdictional basis was U.S. accession to the Vienna Convention on Consular Relations (Vienna Consular Convention) and its relevant protocols.

Under Article 36 of the Vienna Convention, foreign citizens arrested in the United States are entitled to seek assistance from their own country's resident diplomats. This provision guarantees the consular officials of one state party access to any of their nationals who may be detained by another state party in its territory. In addition, if the local consul so requests, a state party must notify the consul whenever one of the consul's nationals is detained and must forward any request for consular assistance made by an individual detainee. Detainees must also be informed of their rights under this provision. The treaty has been widely adopted, and the United States ratified it in 1969. In fact, this critical provision permits U.S. State Department officials to visit Americans who are arrested overseas. The Vienna Consular Convention is a highly important international agreement.

However, the decentralized nature of the American judicial system in which state and local authorities handle most criminal prosecutions has sometimes made implementing this treaty in the United States difficult. Foreign nationals detained in the United States have not always been informed that consular services are available to them. This is especially the case when a detainee's foreign nationality is not readily apparent. However, because American due process requirements are so stringent, the courts rarely consider that a defendant's case has been prejudiced by a lack of consular assistance. As the Supreme Court explained:

> A foreign national detained on suspicion of crime, like anyone else in our country, enjoys under our system the protections of the Due Process Clause. Among other things, he is entitled to an attorney, and is protected against compelled self-incrimination. . . . Article 36 adds little to these "legal options."[10]

Nevertheless, Article 36 binds the United States, and both Germany and Mexico have sued the United States in the ICJ, alleging violations of Article

---

9. *Sanchez-Llamas v. Oregon*, 126 S.Ct. 2669, 2684–2685 (2006).

10. *Sanchez-Llamas v. Oregon*, 126 S.Ct. 2669, 2684–2685 (2006).

36 in the death sentences imposed on their nationals by American courts. Germany was first to bring an ICJ action in 1999, seeking a stay-of-execution order for Walter LaGrand, a German national convicted by the state of Arizona.

Walter LaGrand and his brother Karl were born in Germany, but were raised in the United States. They retained their German citizenship. In 1982, the LaGrand brothers killed a man during an attempted bank robbery and were convicted of capital murder in Arizona. Neither man had been promptly informed that he could contact the German consulate pursuant to Article 36, although Arizona later conceded that it knew the LaGrands were foreign citizens. Both sought to attack their state sentences based on this failure. However, the issue was not raised in a timely manner during their criminal proceedings, and under generally applicable procedural default rules, this point was not subject to further review in the federal courts. It certainly was not a basis for overturning their convictions, and both men were executed in 1999.

Responding to Germany's petition, the ICJ initially indicated "provisional measures" against the United States, stating that the U.S. government should take action to prevent Walter LaGrand's execution before the court could hear the case. (Karl LaGrand had been executed a few days before Germany filed its initial ICJ application.) The State Department concluded that this order was not binding on the United States (the ICJ statute does not give it the "equitable" power to issue injunctions or stays), and the U.S. Supreme Court declined to intervene.[11] Walter LaGrand was executed, and Germany then modified its ICJ application to demand both a determination that the United States had violated its international obligations and an order granting it reparations.

In 2001, the ICJ ruled that the United States had indeed violated its international obligations to the LaGrand brothers individually by not informing them of their right to seek consular assistance under Article 36 and its international obligations to Germany by depriving Germany of the right to offer that assistance in a timely fashion.[12] The court found that, if German nationals are sentenced to "severe penalties" in the United States without the benefit of Article 36, the United States by a means of its own choosing should allow review and reconsideration of the convictions.

Mexico raised the same issue in 2003, also initiating ICJ proceedings against the United States. This case sought provisional measures and a judgment that the capital convictions and sentences of more than fifty Mexican nationals (some of whom were also American citizens) in the United States

---

11. *Federal Republic of Germany v. United States*, 526 U.S. 111 (1999).

12. See *Germany v. United States of America*, Judgment of 27 June 2001 (June 27, 2001).

should be annulled. The ICJ refused to go that far, but it did conclude that the United States had violated its Vienna Consular Convention obligations in most of the identified cases and adjudged that the United States "shall provide, by means of its own choosing, review and reconsideration of the conviction and sentence, so as to allow full weight to be given to the violation of the rights set forth in the Convention."[13] This was to be accomplished without regard to the procedural default rules applicable to other cases in American courts.

This ruling, which the United States accepted as binding, raised an immediate problem for then president George W. Bush. The Mexican nationals at issue were held by the states and were not federal prisoners held under federal laws. Neither state governments in general, nor state courts in particular, are ordinarily subject to the president's direction. Nevertheless, the president undertook to implement the ICJ's judgment by issuing a memorandum to the U.S. attorney general. Relying on his constitutional authority as chief executive, President Bush determined that the United States would "discharge its international obligations under the" ICJ's Avena Decision "by having State courts give effect to the decision in accordance with general principles of comity in cases filed by the 51 Mexican nationals addressed in that decision."[14] Jose Ernesto Medellin, who was one of the fifty-one named Mexican nationals and had been convicted of capital murder in Texas for the gang rape and murder of two teenaged girls, sought state court review of his conviction under the president's memorandum.

The Texas courts denied that review based on the very procedural default grounds that the ICJ had rejected. The Supreme Court agreed to hear the case to decide two critical questions: (1) whether the ICJ's judgment was directly enforceable in American courts without further action by Congress, and (2) whether the president's memorandum could require the states to review these cases without regard to their regular, procedural default rules. In 2008, the court ruled that the ICJ's decisions were not directly enforceable in American courts and that the president's memorandum was insufficient—as exceeding his constitutional power—to require state courts to review convictions without regard to their ordinary procedural rules. The court's reasoning in the landmark *Medellin v. Texas* decision[15] was joined by seven of nine justices and deserves careful examination because it settles

---

13. *Case Concerning Avena and Other Mexican Nationals (Mexico v. United States of America), Summary of Judgement of 31 March 2004* (March 31, 2004).

14. George W. Bush, "Memorandum for the Attorney General: Compliance with the Decision of the International Court of Justice in Avena," the White House, February 28, 2005, at www.whitehouse.gov/news/releases/2005/02/20050228-18.html (accessed October 2, 2008).

15. 128 S. Ct. 1346 (2008) (June 1, 2009).

any question of the ICJ's ability to affect rights or obligations directly through the American judicial system.

Medellin v. Texas: ICJ Judgments Are Not Self-Executing

Chief Justice John Roberts, writing for the Supreme Court's majority, accepted that "the ICJ's judgment in *Avena* creates an international law obligation on the part of the United States."[16] At the same time, however, that obligation is not automatically applicable as a rule of decision in American courts—that is, it is not "self-executing." As the court had previously concluded in *Sanchez-Llamas v. Oregon*, neither the ICJ's statute nor the Vienna Convention's Optional Protocol (which gave the ICJ jurisdiction in this case) is considered to be enforceable federal law without some additional, affirmative legislative action by Congress. This is an important distinction, because the U.S. Constitution's supremacy clause makes treaties along with federal statutes and the Constitution itself the "supreme law of the land."[17] Self-executing treaties must be directly applied by the courts, federal or state, regardless of whether Congress has enacted a law to that effect.

In general, a treaty is considered self-executing only if it "operates of itself without the aid of any legislative provision."[18] Examples of such agreements include commercial treaties that directly guarantee individual rights to conduct certain types of business activity or agreements that permit foreign nationals to inherit property in the United States because these treaties are clear and complete in themselves and, having been approved according to constitutional procedures, require no additional action to enable their implementation or their enforcement directly by the courts.[19]

The Supreme Court has not decided whether Article 36 of the Vienna Convention itself is self-executing.[20] The question in *Medellin* was whether the ICJ's judgment was self-executing, and the court decisively said that it was not. This was both because the U.N. Charter's plain language provided merely that U.N. members "undertake to comply" with ICJ decisions and because the only sanction for noncompliance is a report to the Security Council. Of course, the United States would be in a position to veto any enforcement measures that the Security Council may try to adopt—a point both the president and Senate understood when the Charter was approved and ratified.[21] Thus, absent a change in the relevant treaty language or con-

---

16. *Medellin v. Texas*, Slip Op. at p. 27.

17. U.S. Constitution, art. 6, cl. 2.

18. U. S. Constitution, p. 8.

19. See, generally, American Law Institute, *Restatement, Third, of the Foreign Relations Law of the United States*, sec. 111(3)(4), comment h and rept. note 5 (1987).

20. *Medellin*, Slip Op., p. 10, note 4.

21. *Medellin*, p. 13.

gressional implementing legislation, ICJ judgments are not directly enforceable against individual citizens or the government in American courts.[22]

However, in the course of its opinion, the Supreme Court did suggest that in the future the United States could agree to a self-executing treaty that would create domestic rights or obligations, directly enforceable by the federal and state courts, in the form of a foreign tribunal's decision. This issue was not actually before the court in *Medellin* because the relevant treaties were not self-executing, so the court's speculation on this point was nonbinding obiter dictum. Nevertheless, it is important to note that any such agreement to be bound by the rulings of a non-American court would be subject to the Constitution's other provisions. As the court reaffirmed in *Medellin*, "If the treaty is to be self-executing in this respect, the Senate must consent to the treaty by the requisite two-thirds vote . . . consistent with all other constitutional restraints."[23]

For the time being, therefore, ICJ decisions are not directly binding on American courts. However, they do stand as internationally recognized statements indicating whether the United States and other countries have complied with their international obligations, and they are often cited as evidence of what international law requires. In this regard, they can be especially powerful and persuasive (even if not binding) in common law jurisdictions like the United States, where lawyers and judges are trained to seek authoritative statements of what the law is, or shall be, in judicial opinions and judgments.

THE GENERAL ASSEMBLY

The General Assembly consists of all U.N. member states. It is predominantly an advisory body, entitled in most circumstances to discuss issues of international cooperation and to make recommendations to the Security Council. Its most important actual authority is the consideration and approval of the U.N.'s annual budget. The General Assembly also presides

---

22. The court also ruled that the president did not have the authority, acting without Congress, to transform an ICJ decision into a self-executing international obligation. It reasoned that the president cannot, on his own authority, transform a non-self-executing treaty into a self-executing one. Such an action would effectively be legislative action that is constitutionally reserved for both Congress and the president through the ordinary lawmaking process. As chief executive and the nation's sole organ in foreign relations, the president can take action to implement a non-self-executing treaty. He simply cannot, on his own authority, give that treaty domestic effect by unilaterally declaring it binding on the courts. *Medellin*, Slip Op., pp. 27–37.

23. *Medellin*, Slip Op., pp. 30–31.

over a vast array of subsidiary organs, such as the U.N. Human Rights Council, the International Law Commission, and the U.N. Disarmament Commission. These bodies enjoy largely advisory authority but over time have played a critical role in U.N. efforts to develop or drive international law in particular directions.

The General Assembly's principal influence on the development and direction of international law is through its sponsorship of various multilateral conventions. In particular, since the U.N.'s founding, the General Assembly has promoted a series of human rights treaties, including the International Covenant on Civil and Political Rights (ICCPR); the International Covenant on Economic, Social and Cultural Rights (ICESCR); the Convention on the Rights of the Child (CRC); the Convention Against Torture and Other Cruel, Inhuman or Degrading Treatment or Punishment (CAT); the International Convention on the Elimination of All Forms of Racial Discrimination (ICERD); and the Convention on the Elimination of All Forms of Discrimination against Women (CEDAW). These instruments are widely accepted, and some are justly viewed as having advanced the cause of international human rights.

However, these agreements also purport to regulate the basic relationship between states and their own people—matters traditionally beyond the scope of international law. Although the treaties recognize rights that are considered universal in the American legal and political tradition—such as the rights to life, liberty, and property—many also contain provisions recognizing "rights" that in the United States would more properly be viewed as matters of social or economic policy. For example, the ICESCR would require states to guarantee the "rights" to "social security, including social insurance"; "an adequate standard of living"; and "the enjoyment of the highest attainable standard of physical and mental health," among other things. Not surprisingly, therefore, the United States has ratified only the ICCPR, the CAT, and the ICERD.

Nevertheless, the treaties rejected by the United States still influence international law and American law. Once articulated on the international level in a multilateral convention or even in documents of a far lesser dignity, such as conference statements or nonbinding resolutions of U.N. bodies, these "emerging norms" are regularly cited to condemn inconsistent American practices. In this connection, the CRC is a particularly interesting case study.

The CRC was drafted under U.N. auspices in the late 1970s. The General Assembly adopted the convention's text in 1989, and every nation-state has ratified the treaty with the exception of the United States and Somalia. In this area, American exceptionalism—always difficult for non-Americans to understand—is based on the treaty's many provisions that, if implemented, would intrude deeply into issues that have traditionally been reserved to the police powers of the several states or to the sound discretion of individual parents. Examples of the treaty's injunctions include:

- Children have a right to freedom of expression, including the "freedom to seek, receive and impart information and ideas of all kinds, regardless of frontiers, either orally, in writing or in the form of art, or through any other media of the child's choice."[24]
- Children have a right to "freedom of association and to freedom of peaceful assembly."[25]
- Children have a right to education, which must be directed toward "development of the child's personality, talents and mental and physical abilities to their fullest potential," the development "of respect for human rights and fundamental freedoms, and for the principles enshrined in the Charter of the United Nations," and the development of respect for the "natural environment," among other things.[26]
- Children have a right to "rest and leisure, to engage in play and recreational activities appropriate to the age of the child and to participate freely in cultural life and the arts."[27]

Although the treaty also forbids (or requires state parties to forbid) various forms of exploitation of children, the average American can be forgiven for wondering why issues of juvenile education, freedom of expression, and opportunities for play are the proper subjects of international concern, much less of the negotiation and adoption of a multilateral convention on the subject. The United States has, in fact, acceded to the CRC's optional protocols—additional treaties open for signature that forbid the use of child soldiers, trafficking in children, child prostitution, and child pornography. The CRC can be counted as an instance in which the very serious protocols should be the convention and the convention itself should be the optional protocols.

As is the case with many U.N. human rights treaties, including the ICCPR and CAT, the CRC also established a standing committee to monitor implementation. The Committee on the Rights of the Child meets annually and, among other activities, issues interpretations of the convention's human rights provisions. Although these interpretations are not binding in the sense of judicial determinations, they nevertheless have an important impact in any debate over what the treaty means and how the states parties must implement it. They are also critical to any debate over whether the

---

24. Convention on the Rights of the Child, art. 13(1).
25. Convention on the Rights of the Child, art. 15(1).
26. Convention on the Rights of the Child, art 29.
27. Convention on the Rights of the Child, art. 31.

United States should accede to this treaty because they provide an open window into the views of the treaty's supporters and of the body that monitors its implementation. In this connection, the committee provides a useful example:

> A shift away from traditional beliefs that regard early childhood mainly as a period for the socialization of the immature human being towards mature adult status is required. The Convention requires that children, including the very youngest children, be respected as persons in their own right. Young children should be recognized as active members of families, communities and societies, with their own concerns, interests and points of view.[28]

However, the U.S. refusal to ratify the CRC has not prevented courts from using it as a statement of international norms, if not customary law. For example, the U.S. Supreme Court cited it in *Roper v. Simmons*,[29] in which the court concluded that the death penalty could not constitutionally be applied to "juvenile offenders" in the United States. As part of its rationale why imposing capital punishment on adults for offenses committed under the age of eighteen violated the Eighth Amendment's injunction against cruel or unusual punishments, the court applied its established "evolving standards of decency" test. It noted that the CRC "which every country in the world has ratified save for the United States and Somalia, contains an express prohibition on capital punishment for crimes committed by juveniles under 18."[30]

This is a classic example of how treaties and the norms they adopt may find their way into American law regardless of whether the United States has accepted or ratified those agreements. In this instance, U.S. courts used the CRC's provisions to "confirm" a conclusion by referencing international opinion. This also shows how the current U.N. system can effectively "make" law even in the absence of any formal legislative authority.

THE INTERNATIONAL CRIMINAL COURT: BRAVE NEW WORLDS

In addition to promoting an international standard for domestic legal norms, the U.N. has also supported the creation of courts that can reach the

28. U.N. Committee on the Rights of the Child, "Implementing Child Rights in Early Childhood: General Comment No. 7 (2005)," CRC/C/GC/7/Rev.1, September 20, 2006, pp. 2–3, at www2.ohchr.org/english/bodies/crc/docs/GC7.Rev.1 _en.doc (accessed October 2, 2008).

29. 543 U.S. 551 (2005).

30. 543 U.S. 551, p. 576.

individual citizens of states, including government officials. Significantly, in determining that the ICJ's judgments are not self-executing, the Supreme Court noted in *Medellin v. Texas* that the ICJ only has authority to hear disputes between states. It has no jurisdiction over individuals and cannot, therefore, act directly on individual rights and obligations.[31] This is not the case with the International Criminal Court (ICC), the most important new international legal institution. Even though the United States has refused to become part of the ICC system—largely because of potential for the court to be misused as a political tool—the court's broad jurisdictional claims have substantially complicated America's relationship to the U.N. and some of its most important allies.[32]

The ICC represents a fundamental break with the past. It has jurisdiction over individuals, including elected or appointed government officials, and its judgments may be directly enforced against them, regardless of their own national constitutions or court systems. Unlike the ICJ, the ICC has the very real potential to shape the policies of its member states in the substantive areas where it operates. These include the core issues of when states can lawfully resort to armed force, how that force may be applied, and whether particular actions constitute the very serious international offenses of war crimes, crimes against humanity, or genocide.

Established in 2002 after sixty countries ratified the 1998 Rome Statute of the International Criminal Court, the ICC is not a U.N. entity, strictly speaking. It is an independent treaty body controlled—at least in theory—by the states that have ratified the Rome Statute and accepted the court's authority. However, the ICC is subject to the U.N. Security Council's direction in certain key respects, based on the terms of the Rome Statute, and it was very much the product of a concerted U.N. effort. Beginning in the late 1940s, the General Assembly's International Law Commission was tasked to articulate the legal principles recognized by the post–World War II military tribunals and to prepare a draft statute establishing a permanent international criminal court. After various fits and starts, the General

---

31. 543 U.S. 551, pp. 15–16.

32. This point was proven recently when the ICC prosecutor brought charges against Sudan's President Omar Hassan Ahmed al-Bashir. Although al-Bashir may be responsible for the crimes committed by Sudanese government surrogates in the Darfur region, indicting him during the conflict has made a settlement more difficult. Reaching a settlement is the only option because neither the U.N. nor any state has shown itself willing to provide sufficient military support and protection for Darfur's suffering people. The ICC prosecutor has effectively elbowed his way into the negotiating room and, as a practical matter, no agreement can now be reached without his approval as long as al-Bashir is in power.

Assembly proposed a diplomatic conference to consider and adopt an ICC statute in 1998.[33]

As an institution, the ICC is divided into three parts: the bench of judges, the prosecutor's office, and the registrar. In addition, the Rome Statute provides for an assembly of state parties that, in addition to electing the court's judges and prosecutor, determines the court's budget and oversees its administration. The judges are empowered to settle any dispute over the court's "judicial functions." These functions include determining whether a member state has been unwilling or unable to investigate and prosecute its own citizens for offenses otherwise within the court's jurisdiction—a necessary predicate to most ICC prosecutions. This is the principle of "complementarity," which is supposed to limit the court's power and avoid its political abuse.

However, complementarity applies only if the state in question handles the particular case at issue in a manner consistent with the ICC's understanding of the applicable legal norms. If the court concludes that a state has been unwilling or unable to prosecute one of its citizens or government officials because it does not consider the questioned conduct unlawful, based on its own interpretation of the relevant international legal requirements, the court can proceed with an investigation. Some state parties, such as Australia, have attempted to avoid this eventuality by noting an "understanding" as part of their Rome Statute ratifications that the ICC will interpret the relevant law consistent with their own views. This is an intriguing approach, but it is far from clear that it will succeed.

The ability both to interpret the law and effectively to force member states to adopt its view gives the ICC unprecedented power. For the first time, a permanent international institution is entitled to determine the legal obligations of states and their individual citizens and to criminally punish those individual citizens—even if its understanding of the law radically differs from the relevant state's position. Moreover, the ICC's judges are not otherwise subject to the supervision or control of the states parties, except in matters of personal corruption. Thus, when the ICC determines what international law requires in any of its areas of competence, this is arguably the final word.

The United States has rightly refused to become a part of the ICC system. President Bill Clinton signed the Rome Statute in late 2000, but recommended against its ratification, and President George W. Bush withdrew the Clinton signature in 2002. However, the court claims jurisdiction over the citizens of nonmember states in certain circumstances, such as an offense that allegedly occurred on the territory of a state party. This claim is incon-

---

33. See M. Cherif Bassiouni, ed., *The Statute of the International Criminal Court: A Documentary History* (Greenburgh, NY: Transnational Publishers, 1999), 10–18.

sistent with the rule of traditional international law that treaties, such as the Rome Statute, cannot bind states that have not agreed to be so affected. As a result, the United States has had to obtain a series of U.N. Security Council resolutions making clear that its citizens are not subject to ICC jurisdiction so that American forces could participate in various U.N. missions without fear of being targeted by the ICC.

In addition, the United States has entered into a series of Article 98 agreements. These agreements are designed to take advantage of Article 98 of the Rome Statute, which prevents the ICC from proceeding with requests for surrender or assistance if this would require a state party to violate its other international law or treaty obligations. Despite the claims of ICC supporters, these agreements are not efforts to obtain exemption from international law, but simply to protect Americans from the power of an international institution that their country has not consented to obey. These agreements effectively reserve to the United States its established right as an independent sovereign to ultimately determine the scope and meaning of its own international law obligations.

Not surprisingly, adherence to the ICC has become a litmus test for those who wish to fundamentally change the nature of sovereignty, as a means of moving power from states to some type of not very well-defined "international community." This is especially true of the European Union, which insists that aspiring member states ratify the Rome Statute and has opposed U.S. efforts to remain out of the ICC regime through the use of Article 98 agreements. Because the court has jurisdiction over individuals, it is uniquely well placed to force adoption of its own views on an international basis—views that its supporters naively assume will always be Western or "progressive" in nature. The ICC will continue to be a significant concern for American policymakers attempting to pursue national or global interests based on views of international law that differ from those of the ICC.

THE SECURITY COUNCIL: AD HOC COURTS

The Security Council is the most powerful U.N. body. Under Chapter 7 of the Charter, it is empowered to "determine the existence of any threat to the peace, breach of the peace, or act of aggression and shall make recommendations, or decide what measures shall be taken . . . to maintain or restore international peace and security."[34] These measures can include economic or diplomatic sanctions or the use of armed force. Although the Security Council has no independent military force at its disposal, its deci-

---

34. Charter of the United Nations, art. 39.

sions are considered binding on the U.N. membership, which may act individually or collectively to carry out the council's determinations.[35]

Under the guise of exercising its Chapter 7 authority, the Security Council has created a series of ad hoc international criminal courts. It has vested these bodies with the authority to investigate, prosecute, try, and punish various offenses, including genocide, war crimes, crimes against humanity, and grave breaches of the Geneva Conventions. To date, the most important of these courts have been the International Criminal Tribunal for the former Yugoslavia (ICTY), established in 1993, and the International Criminal Tribunal for Rwanda (ICTR), established in 1994. Courts have also been established for Cambodia and Sierra Leone by agreements between those states and the U.N.

Over the past fifteen years, both the ICTY and ICTR have had successes. Numerous trials have been conducted (although often over very extended periods of time—a pattern that has been repeated in the ICC), and many individuals responsible for serious offenses in the former Yugoslavia and Rwanda have been judged and punished. However, the tribunals' legitimacy as judicial institutions remains questionable. Neither the international community in general nor the United Nations in particular has any inherent judicial power, which is an attribute of sovereignty. Of course, states can vest an international or supranational court with judicial power as long as it is consistent with their own individual constitutions and otherwise respects applicable international law rules. The ICC is an example of this type of delegation to the extent that it limits itself to investigating, prosecuting, and trying the citizens of its member states.

However, the Security Council imposed the U.N. ad hoc courts. To the extent that these ad hoc tribunals exercised any lawful judicial authority, it must be found in a delegation from the U.N. member states, but the source of that delegation is very unclear. It certainly is not expressed in the U.N. Charter, which speaks in terms of military, economic, and diplomatic measures. Rather, it must be inferred from the general agreement of U.N. members to "give the United Nations every assistance in any action it takes in accordance with the present Charter" and the requirement that member states "shall join in affording mutual assistance in carrying out the measures decided upon by the Security Council."[36]

The U.N. courts themselves have not given a satisfactory answer to the question of the ultimate source of their legal power. The leading case remains the ICTY's decision in *Prosecutor v. Tadic* (1995), in which the tribunal's appeals chamber sidestepped the issue entirely. In response to the

---

35. "Members of the United Nations agree to accept and carry out the decisions of the Security Council." Charter of the United Nations, art. 25.

36. Charter of the United Nations, arts. 2.5 and 49.

argument that the Security Council cannot delegate judicial powers it does not have, the court merely asserted that the Security Council had not delegated judicial power to the ICTY. It had created the tribunal "as an instrument for the exercise of its own principal function of maintenance of peace and security, i.e., as a measure contributing to the restoration and maintenance of peace in the former Yugoslavia."[37] Yet this merely states the obvious and does not answer the question about the source of the the ICTY's and ICTR's judicial power.

Here, the Security Council's ad hoc tribunals must be distinguished from the International Military Tribunal (IMT), which tried the top Nazi leaders at Nuremberg and to which the U.N. courts are often compared. The IMT clearly identified the source of its legitimate judicial power as the Allied powers that established the court and were exercising the sovereign rights of Germany. Upon the Third Reich's unconditional surrender, German sovereignty was at the Allies' disposal. As the IMT explained,

> The jurisdiction of the Tribunal is defined in the [London] Agreement [of August 8, 1945] and Charter [of the International Military Tribunal], and the crimes coming within the jurisdiction of the Tribunal, for which there shall be individual responsibility, are set out in Article 6. The law of the Charter is decisive, and binding upon the Tribunal.
>
> The making of the Charter was the exercise of the sovereign legislative power by the countries to which the German Reich unconditionally surrendered; and the undoubted right of these countries to legislate for the occupied territories has been recognised by the civilised world. The Charter is not an arbitrary exercise of power on the part of the victorious nations, but in the view of the Tribunal, as will be shown, it is the expression of international law existing at the time of its creation; and to that extent is itself a contribution to international law.
>
> The Signatory Powers created this Tribunal, defined the law it was to administer, and made regulations for the proper conduct of the Trial. In doing so, they have done together what any one of them might have done singly; for it is not to be doubted that any nation has the right thus to set up special courts to administer law. With regard to the constitution of the court, all that the defendants are entitled to ask is to receive a fair trial on the facts and law.[38]

Neither the U.N. Security Council nor the ICTY exercised any such authority over the territories of the former Yugoslavia or Rwanda. As a

---

37. *Prosecutor v. Tadic*, October 2, 1995, par. 38, at www.un.org/icty/tadic/appeal/decision-e/51002.htm (accessed October 2, 2008).

38. Office of the U.S. Chief Counsel for Prosecution of Axis Criminality, *Nazi Conspiracy and Aggression: Opinion and Judgment* (Washington, DC: U.S. Government Printing Office, 1947), 48, at www.loc.gov/rr/frd/Military_Law/pdf/NT_Nazi-opinion-judgment. pdf (accessed October 2, 2008).

result, the power of the ad hoc tribunals must be viewed as a species of political, not judicial, authority. This has obvious and important implications for the "precedential value" of their decisions in individual cases.

In any case, that value is open to question based on the Security Council's actions in establishing the courts. The secretary-general's report presented in accordance with Security Council Resolution 808[39] made clear that by creating the ICTY, "the Security Council would not be creating or purporting to 'legislate' [international humanitarian] law. Rather, the International Tribunal would have the task of applying existing international humanitarian law."[40] The Security Council later approved this report in Resolution 827, which founded the ICTY.

Nevertheless, the various judgments of the ICTY and ICTR are regularly referenced in the academic literature, have been cited by U.S. courts,[41] and frequently appear in debates over the content and meaning of international law. This is to be expected given the relatively fluid nature of the "evidence" of international law. The "sources" of that law are clear: international agreements and customary practices that are accepted by states as legally binding. The actual practice of states in interpreting and applying treaties and customary rules is critical to determining what international law requires in any particular situation. However, in determining what that practice may be, several sources are generally accepted, including the judgments of international and national tribunals, statements by states, and the writings of international law scholars and publicists.

None of these sources are determinative, but all are entitled to be given due weight and consideration. The "works of jurists and commentators" are consulted "not for the speculations of their authors concerning what the law ought to be, but for trustworthy evidence of what the law really is."[42] However, in practice at least, there is little formal hierarchy among these sources, with the decisions of inferior national courts, national supreme courts, international tribunals, and commentators being freely cited, discussed, and relied on.

Nevertheless, the decisions of courts—regardless of whether they are regularly constituted courts of law exercising legitimate judicial power or political expedients following a "judicial" model—tend to have greater impact

---

39. In Resolution 808, the Security Council determined to establish "an international tribunal . . . for the prosecution of persons responsible for serious violations of international humanitarian law committed in the territory of the former Yugoslavia since 1991." U.N. Security Council Resolution 808, February 22, 1993.

40. U.N. Secretary-General, report on the former Yugoslavia, S/25704, May 3, 1993, par. 29.

41. See, for example, *Hamdan v. Rumsfeld*, 126 S.Ct. 2749, 2785 (2006).

42. *The Paquete Habana*, 175 U.S. 677, 700 (1900).

on those schooled in the common law. This is because civil law jurisdictions, at least formally, do not follow a system of precedent and stare decisis in which judicial precedents are expected to control the outcome of future cases. Therefore, the rulings of the U.N. ad hoc tribunals can be expected to substantially affect the course of international law over time, despite the uncertain legitimacy of their parentage.

THE FUTURE

In all these ways, the United Nations has had and will continue to have a profound impact on international law. In truth, the United States can do little about that and, an even greater truth, may not wish to. U.S. presidents—Democrat and Republican, liberal and conservative—have used the U.N. system to promote their own visions of the international order and national interest, and they will continue to do so. The 2008 presidential candidates indicated that they too would like to work with and through the United Nations system, and there is little doubt that the U.N. has been useful to the United States over the years. However, engagement with the U.N. has costs as well as benefits. The United States can clearly maximize the return on its multilateral investments over the long term if it remains true to certain fundamentals:

- The United States should maintain and refuse to compromise the basic rule that every sovereign state is equally entitled to determine for itself the content and meaning of international law, including and especially the extent to which individual countries must comply with the judgments of international courts and tribunals. International law requires states to act in good faith, but all states are equal in law, and none is inherently competent to judge another.
- The United States should not consent to any permanent international jurisdiction, either in the form of an international tribunal or claims by other states to exercise a "universal" jurisdiction that operates directly on American citizens as individuals. States can and do properly exercise various forms of jurisdiction over their own citizens and the individual citizens of other states, but accepting a generalized right to enforce international norms would undercut the states' right and ability to protect their own citizens and govern themselves.
- In this connection, the United States should maintain the traditional international immunities of government officials. This does not mean that officials are or should be above the law or exempt from its strictures. It does mean that neither international nor national courts can

try to punish individual officials for their official actions without their own state's consent and waiver of immunity. Those unique situations in which the trial and punishment of government officials by some "international community" may be justified should be treated as exceptions to the rule and be limited to instances in which consent to this action is given by the state in question.

- On a regular basis, the United States should formally reaffirm that it is not bound by international agreements that it has not ratified and that it will not accept customary rules that are otherwise inconsistent with its constitution, laws, and legal traditions.
- As a general rule, the United States should follow a policy of negotiating and ratifying only non-self-executing international agreements, so that these agreements cannot be enforced by American courts without previous congressional action.
- Congress should reaffirm, through its constitutional power to establish the jurisdiction of the federal courts, that binding judicial rules of decision cannot be drawn from international tribunal precedents.
- The executive branch should adopt a regular policy of "unsigning" treaties that have not been ratified after a reasonable period, especially when there appears to be little chance that the Senate will approve the particular instrument in the foreseeable future. This is important because the 1969 Vienna Convention on the Law of Treaties provides that such signatures are binding to the extent that a state that has signed but not yet ratified a treaty may not take action to defeat the treaty's object or purpose. The United States has not ratified the Vienna Convention, and the binding nature of this particular provision as customary international law is dubious. Nevertheless, an argument can certainly be made that signed but unratified treaties limit U.S. action on the international level. Therefore, if there is no reasonable prospect that a signed treaty will be ratified, the American signature should be formally withdrawn to avoid any such implications.
- The United States should actively seek out opportunities to address international issues through "coalitions of the willing," reaffirming that the U.N. is only a treaty organization and that it is not the exclusive means by which global problems can or should be solved. It must make clear, and seek the agreement of other states, that working through the United Nations is only one means of legitimating foreign policy decisions. States have the right—even under the U.N. Charter—to pursue their security and other interests individually or through regional groupings. They also have the right to act in concert with "values" coalitions—democracies willing to challenge the growth and expansion of nondemocratic systems—or on their own when necessary or appropriate.

CONCLUSION

The United States has been a steadfast proponent of international law since declaring its independence from Great Britain in 1776. At that time, as recited in the Declaration of Independence itself, the newly united American states assumed "among the Powers of the Earth, the separate and equal Station to which the Laws of Nature and of Nature's God entitle them."[43] That separate and equal station, guaranteed by the natural law of nations, meant that the United States could establish and govern itself, even in a world in which its representative institutions were truly exceptional. Principles of national sovereignty and a consent-based approach to changing international law norms were central to the traditional Westphalian system in which the United States and its unique American experiment flourished.

American democracy is threatened by efforts to change these most basic precepts and to develop a new international order in which states and/or their individual officials and citizens are subordinate to supranational institutions. If the United States can be bound by norms to which it has not agreed or that are otherwise inconsistent with its own constitutional institutions and values, its government no longer can be said to derive its "just Powers from the Consent of the Governed."[44] Consequently, to be true to its unique heritage and identity, the United States can and must oppose any effort to establish international lawmaking authorities. This is especially true with entities such as the International Criminal Court, which could claim authority to interpret the international legal obligations of Americans and their government. The United Nations is not such a body, but it could eventually become one. Even today, the U.N.'s profound influence on the direction and development of international law is an obvious and growing fact of global life.

The United States need not, and emphatically should not, withdraw from the United Nations or the international scene. Yet these troubling developments must be recognized and confronted. The United States must make clear in all its international dealings and particularly in its interactions with the U.N. bureaucracy and other member states that it respects the law of nations, but that it also continues to reserve to itself the right to interpret and apply that law on its own account. It must act consistently with this position in the formulation and implementation of American foreign policy and should urge other states to maintain the same position.

This does not mean that it cannot or should not openly and zealously disagree with the legal views and positions of other states when appropriate. Nor does it mean that the United States should never take account

---

43. Declaration of Independence, par. 1 (1776).
44. Declaration of Independence, par. 2.

of those views in determining whether its own position on a particular issue may be incorrect or otherwise flawed. It must simply maintain consistently that as a sovereign it is not subject to the judgment of any other sovereign or group of sovereigns unless it has itself consented to be so bound.

Because international norms are developed by the actions of states, how the United States behaves in this regard is critical. By suggesting that the views of the international community relative to the force and meaning of international norms is binding on states, particularly by acting as if this were the case either in managing its own affairs or in interacting with other countries and international institutions, the United States could over time erode the basis of its own independence and democratic system. This can be avoided with vigilance and consistency. Otherwise, the power to create new international norms will continue to drift toward undemocratic, non-state groupings and institutions.

3

Mission Improbable

International Interventions, the United Nations, and the Challenge of Conflict Resolution

Greg Mills and Terence McNamee

"Conflict resolution" is one of the most common buzzwords at the United Nations, European Union, and other leading multinational institutions involved in preventive diplomacy and peacebuilding. Yet only a handful of successes have resulted from decades of involvement by the international organization set up to ensure peace and resolve conflict. U.N.-mandated missions in Afghanistan (2006), Georgia (1994), and Darfur (2007) have not prevented new violence or conflict. Peace seems distant in the Democratic Republic of the Congo (1999) and Lebanon (1978). In extended peacekeeping operations in the Middle East (1948), Cyprus (1964), Kashmir (1949), and Western Sahara (1991), the U.N. may have actually prolonged the disputes by providing an excuse for the parties to delay negotiations or refuse to compromise on entrenched demands.[1]

Then again, perhaps we should not be surprised that the international

---

1. Brett D. Schaefer, "United Nations Peacekeeping: Challenges and Opportunities," testimony before the Subcommittee on International Operations and Organizations, Democracy and Human Rights, Committee on Foreign Relations, U.S. Senate, July 23, 2008, pp. 7–8, at http://foreign.senate.gov/testimony/2008/Schaefer Testimony080723pp.pdf (accessed October 3, 2008).

community rarely seems to measure up to its lofty aims: Seldom is conflict ever *resolved*. The abatement of armed conflict within states or between them is a process—uneven, complex, and nearly always reversible. Each of the three stages of peace operations—peacemaking, peacekeeping, and peacebuilding—involves distinct, difficult challenges. The job is not over when the guns fall silent and CNN coverage ends, that is, after the peacemaking stage. On the contrary, in most cases this is when the toughest work begins—keeping the hard-won peace and encouraging sustainable stability and long-term economic growth and prosperity. Research shows that more than half of all postconflict states slide back into war within a decade of a peace settlement.[2]

South Africa is widely regarded internationally as *the* modern exemplar of successful conflict resolution. In part this explains why the outbreak of xenophobic attacks in Johannesburg and other urban areas in 2008 proved so shocking to the outside world, but people living there found it much less so. Since the end of apartheid, the country has struggled to keep a lid on myriad political and socioeconomic problems, not least of which is rampant violent crime. South Africa is a potent reminder that building peace—with or without the help of outsiders—takes generations, not just months or years.

For all their society's problems, South Africans are at least able to devise solutions based on what *they* think will work best for them. A great failing of much interstate and intrastate conflict resolution of the past fifty years is that local actors have not "owned" the peacebuilding[3] processes in their

---

2. See Paul Collier, "Development and Conflict," Oxford University, Department of Economics, Center for the Study of African Economies, October 1, 2004, at www.un.org/esa/documents/Development.and.Conflict2.pdf (October 3, 2008).

3. There are two contrasting views of "peacebuilding." The United Nations defines peacebuilding as efforts at capacity building, reconciliation, and societal transformation. In this view, it is a long-term process that occurs after violent conflict has slowed or stopped. As of July 2008, the U.N. categorized only its missions in Sierra Leone and Burundi as peacebuilding missions. The broader definition adopted in this chapter recognizes that peacebuilding efforts must sometimes be undertaken while conflict is ongoing, as in Afghanistan. It reflects most closely the U.K. Ministry of Defence definition, which describes peacebuilding as political, economic, social, and military measures designed to strengthen political settlements, in order to redress the causes of conflict. Peacebuilding is thus synonymous with "stabilization," the aim being to support countries emerging from conflict by preventing or reducing violence; protecting people and key institutions; promoting political processes, which lead to greater stability; and preparing for longer-term, nonviolent politics and development. See U.K. Mission to the U.N., "Peacebuilding," 2007, at http://ukun.fco.gov.uk/en/uk-at-un/thematic-issues/post_conflicts/peacebuilding (accessed November 29, 2008).

own countries. The international community, particularly the United Nations, has often developed and sustained solutions that express the political will of its most powerful members and its own bureaucratic interests rather than those of the parties to a conflict.

What the U.N. and the ever-increasing number of international organizations operating in unstable states from Afghanistan to the Democratic Republic of the Congo (DRC) should be doing is devising better ways to address the sources of conflict; to mitigate, manage, and contain it; and to provide a space for locals to work toward enduring solutions. This requires a more realistic approach to peacebuilding based on intensive assessments of the unique dynamics on the ground, not generalized assumptions and templates imported from other cases. The tendency to paper over the cracks and impose an ultimately unworkable solution has often had devastating consequences for affected populations. Above all, our approach to peacebuilding must be sensitive to the oft-neglected fact that sometimes getting involved only makes matters worse.

This chapter first examines why international bodies, especially the United Nations, engaged in peace operations today suffer a credibility gap, notably in Africa. This is followed by a summary of U.N. involvement in peacekeeping and peacebuilding, focusing on some of the key challenges identified in the 2000 Report of the Panel on United Nations Peacekeeping Operations, more commonly known as the "Brahimi Report" after Lakhdar Brahimi, the chairman of the report's authoring panel.[4] Explored next are three case studies that reveal the depth of these challenges. The final section suggests a number of measures to improve the effectiveness of international diplomatic and peacebuilding efforts.

CREDIBILITY GAP

Since the United Nations was founded in 1945, no event has damaged perceptions of the organization, and peacekeeping in general, more than the Rwandan genocide. On April 7, 1994, some 2,538 troops and personnel of the United Nations Assistance Mission in Rwanda (UNAMIR) were on the ground. The mission was instituted by the U.N. to aid the implementation of the Arusha Accords, signed seven months earlier, to end the civil war in Rwanda. Yet when the premeditated killing of the country's minority Tutsi population by Hutu extremists commenced on April 7, the U.N. balked. The U.N. Department of Peacekeeping Operations (UNDPKO) refused to

---

4. U.N. General Assembly and U.N. Security Council, "Report of the Panel on United Nations Peace Operations," A/55/305 and S/2000/809, August 21, 2000, at www.un.org/peace/reports/peace_operations (accessed October 3, 2008).

authorize U.N. peacekeepers to seize weapons caches prior to the genocide or to take stout action to protect civilians once the killings began. Indeed, two weeks into the slaughter, the U.N. Security Council passed a resolution stating that it was "appalled" at the large scale of violence in Rwanda,[5] but at the same meeting voted to reduce UNAMIR to just 270 volunteer personnel and to limit its mandate. Over the next 100 days some 800,000 Rwandans, mostly Tutsis and moderate Hutus, were slaughtered.[6]

The U.N. catastrophe in Rwanda was not the fault of the UNAMIR force. Indeed, Force Commander Lieutenant General Romeo Dallaire and his undermanned and largely abandoned (by U.N. headquarters in New York) force had saved thousands of lives before being pulled out. It was the fault of a more fundamental failure of the entire U.N. system. The mission's vague mandate was unclear about the use of force, particularly in defense of civilians. As the genocide unfolded, the major U.N. powers dithered. They prevented any strengthening of UNAMIR's mandate and delayed contributing personnel until the killings had largely ended.

On the tenth anniversary of the genocide, former U.N. secretary-general Kofi Annan, who was assistant secretary-general of the Department of Peacekeeping Operations at the time of the genocide, remarked:

> The genocide in Rwanda should never, ever have happened. . . .
>
> If the international community had acted promptly and with determination, it could have stopped most of the killing. But the political will was not there, nor were the troops.
>
> If the United Nations, government officials, the international media and other observers had paid more attention to the gathering signs of disaster, and taken timely action, it might have been averted. . . .
>
> . . . I realized after the genocide that there was more that I could and should have done to sound the alarm and rally support.[7]

UNAMIR's mandate extended past the overthrow of the government by the Tutsi-dominated Rwandan Patriotic Front in mid-July 1994 and into the Great Lakes refugee crisis. The camps that sprang up in the wake of the genocide, particularly around Goma in eastern Zaire (now the Democratic Republic of the Congo, or DRC), housed around 1.5 million Rwandans, creating enormous health and security challenges. Among its inhabitants

---

5. U.N. Security Council, S/RES/921, April 21, 1994.

6. Anthony Goodman, "Annan Asks Probe of UN Response to Rwanda Genocide," Reuters, March 22, 1999, at www.globalpolicy.org/security/issues/rwanda7 .htm (accessed October 3, 2008).

7. Kofi Annan, remarks at the Memorial Conference on the Rwanda Genocide, Office of the U.N. Secretary-General, March 26, 2004, at www.un.org/News/Press/ docs/2004/sgsm9223.doc.htm (accessed October 3, 2008).

were remnants of the *génocidaires* who continued to terrorize and attack Congolese citizens and Rwandan refugees in the Congo and occasionally launch raids into Rwanda. In effect the camps turned into international humanitarian protectorates for some of the worst perpetrators of the violence. With the new Rwandan government insisting that UNAMIR had failed in its priority mission, the U.N. withdrew its mandate in March 1996. After Mobutu Sese Seko was removed from power in Zaire a few months later, most of the refugees returned home under Rwandan auspices, against the advice of the U.N. That a decade later U.N. forces are reeling from another major setback in eastern DRC while Rwanda is stable, democratic, and vigorously engaged in a national reconciliation process with little substantive contribution from the U.N. is perhaps the greatest indictment of the organization's sorry record in the country.

Darfur offers a second illustration of the U.N.'s credibility gap. In April 2008, the U.N. issued a report claiming that more civilians (some 300,000) had been killed in Darfur than originally estimated.[8] Despite key players in the international community describing the conflict, accurately or not, as "genocide," China repeatedly stymied attempts to deploy a U.N.-mandated peacekeeping force by threatening to veto any such Security Council resolution. China was abetted by resistance from the Sudanese government, backed by African and Middle Eastern countries, to having non-African peacekeepers participate in the mission. Nor was the West eager to risk blood and treasure to save the Sudanese from one another. Hence, an African Union (AU) force was deployed and later expanded by the Security Council into a hybrid AU/U.N. peacekeeping operation with an authorized strength of some 31,000 uniformed and civilian personnel.[9] The force is still not fully manned and lacks the equipment and mandate to adequately protect itself, much less innocent civilians, against marauding militia forces. The perception of a U.N. standing by while "another Rwanda" unfolds has already crystallized in some quarters.

The crisis in Zimbabwe provides another resonant image of U.N. weakness—some would argue unwitting complicity—in the face of mass suffering and political repression. Overwhelming evidence suggests that President Robert Mugabe and his supporters manipulated the March 2008 election to force a runoff with Morgan Tsvangirai's Movement for Democratic Change. Tsvangirai eventually withdrew from the runoff due to a government-led campaign of violence and intimidation against him and his

8. BBC News, "Darfur Deaths 'Could Be 300,000,'" April 23, 2008, at http://news.bbc.co.uk/2/hi/africa/7361979.stm (accessed November 29, 2008).

9. U.N. Security Council, S/RES/1769, July 31, 2007, and U.N. Department of Peacekeeping Operations, "UNAMID: African Union/United Nations Hybrid Operation in Darfur," at www.un.org/Depts/dpko/missions/unamid (accessed October 3, 2008).

supporters. The subsequent U.N. Security Council session on Africa produced voluble admonitions, but essentially refused to hold President
Mugabe to account, with Russia and China even preventing any tightening
of sanctions. This placed President Mugabe in a position of strength in
postelection negotiations over a power-sharing arrangement. Meanwhile,
the involvement of U.N. humanitarian agencies, however well intentioned,
in feeding Mugabe's population was effectively helping to keep the octoge-
narian in power by removing—or at least distorting—the link of responsibility between him and his people. Instead of devising policies to feed his
people, Mugabe could manipulate the humanitarian relief to his political
advantage, knowing that the international agencies would step into the
void.

The failings of U.N. peacekeeping are more than political. U.N. peacekeeping, as with other parts of the U.N. system, have proven vulnerable
to mismanagement, corruption, and misconduct. A U.N. Office of Internal
Oversight Services (OIOS) audit of $1 billion in U.N. peacekeeping pro-
curement contracts over a six-year period found that at least $265 million
of these contracts was subject to waste, fraud, or corruption.[10] A 2007 report
on the audit of the U.N. mission in Sudan revealed that tens of millions of
dollars had been lost to mismanagement and waste, and the audit found
substantial indications of fraud and corruption.[11]

Furthermore, in recent years, U.N. personnel have committed a disturbing number of crimes, ranging from smuggling to rape and forced prostitution of women and young girls. The most notorious of these reports
involved peacekeepers with the U.N. Mission in the Democratic Republic
of the Congo having sex with underage girls, soliciting prostitutes, trading
arms for gold, and disregarding their mandate to disarm militia groups.
Worse, evidence provided by the BBC indicates that the U.N. covered up
wrongdoing by its peacekeepers in the DRC.[12] However, wrongdoing by

---

10. U.N. Security Council, "Peacekeeping Procurement Audit Found Mismanagement, Risk of Financial Loss, Security Council Told in Briefing by Chief of Staff,"
SC/8645, February 22, 2006, at www.un.org/News/Press/docs/2006/sc8645.doc
.htm (accessed October 3, 2008). The OIOS serves as the U.N.'s quasi inspector
general.

11. Colum Lynch, "Audit of U.N.'s Sudan Mission Finds Tens of Millions in
Waste," *Washington Post*, February 10, 2008, A16, at www.washingtonpost.com/
wp-dyn/content/article/2008/02/09/AR200802 0902427.html (accessed October 3,
2008).

12. BBC News, "UN Troops 'Armed DR Congo Rebels,'" April 28, 2008, at http://
news.bbc.co.uk/2/hi/africa/7365283.stm (accessed October 3, 2008), and Joe
Bavier, "UN Ignored Peacekeeper Abuses in Congo, Group Says," May 2, 2008, at
www.reuters.com/article/featuredCrisis/idUSN02278304 (accessed October 3,
2008).

U.N. peacekeepers is not restricted to the DRC. Allegations and confirmed incidents of sexual exploitation and abuse by U.N. peacekeepers have occurred in Bosnia, Burundi, Cambodia, Guinea, Haiti, Kosovo, Liberia, Sierra Leone, and Sudan.[13] Far too often, the U.N. has been unable or unwilling to hold its personnel and peacekeepers accountable for their misconduct.

This links to a final image of today's U.N., which is not as vivid as UNAMIR or Darfur, but is no less insidious. Among the largest warehouses in the Kenyan port of Mombassa are those operated for the U.N.'s World Food Program. Humanitarian grain shipments destined for South Sudan, Uganda, Congo, and elsewhere in the region account for 10 percent (some 1.5 million tons) of the port's throughput. For the port and the truckers, if not those managing such largesse, humanitarian aid has become a business, which comes with its own set of incentives and pressures—good and bad. Yet the implications of these shipments are seldom considered, especially for the conflict systems that give rise to such shortages.

Of course, these examples only begin to tell the story of U.N. involvement in peacebuilding. Individual U.N. personnel do remarkable work in the nineteen operations overseen by the UNDPKO (sixteen peacekeeping missions and three political or peacebuilding operations) as of July 31, 2008, and in other unstable regions of the world.[14] Their efforts come with a sacrifice: Nearly 2,500 staff from more than 100 countries have been killed while serving on U.N. missions. In countless ways the organization has supported processes of reconciliation, justice, and democratization. The mere presence of the U.N. has doubtless steered belligerents away from war in a number of postconflict states. Its—at best—meager record in *resolving* conflicts may say more about the inherent intractability of certain conflicts than about any particular failings of senior U.N. decision makers.

The U.N. system, however, requires surgery. Sir Jeremy Greenstock, former British ambassador to the U.N. and the U.K.'s first special representative to post-Saddam Iraq, recently observed that we are "faced with a world that is changing so fast that the institutions of the post–Cold War era are

---

13. See Kate Holt and Sarah Hughes, "UN Staff Accused of Raping Children in Sudan," *Daily Telegraph*, January 4, 2007, at www.telegraph.co.uk/news/worldnews/ 1538476/UN-staff-accused-of-raping-children-in-Sudan.html (accessed October 3, 2008); Kate Holt and Sarah Hughes, "Sex and the UN: When Peacemakers Become Predators," *Independent*, January 11, 2005, at www.independent.co.uk/news/world/ africa/sex-and-the-un-when-peacemakers-become-predators-486170.html (accessed October 3, 2008); and Colum Lynch, "UN Faces More Accusations of Sexual Misconduct," *Washington Post*, March 13, 2005, A22, at www.washingtonpost.com/ wp-dyn/articles/A30286-2005Mar12.html (accessed October 3, 2008).

14. U.N. Department of Public Information, Peace and Security Section, "United Nations Peacekeeping Operations," *Background Note*, July 31, 2008, at www.un.org/ Depts/dpko/dpko/bnote.htm (accessed October 3, 2008).

manifestly insufficient." National governments continually call for action and reform, but nevertheless "do not invest money, effort and political capital in a truly effective United Nations. Sovereign imperatives and short-term pressures are too strong for that."[15]

This situation helps to explain why the system functions increasingly more like an industry than a mechanism for building peace, staffed by service providers for whom the service is the end rather than the means to facilitate political settlements and stability. This is not to argue that every U.N. mission or international assistance effort should be of finite duration. Indeed, there is a strong case that only planning and preparing for longer-term commitments will improve effectiveness.

The problem instead is institutional. The system incentivizes the creation of projects and spending money (outputs), but not necessarily results (outcomes). For instance, in Afghanistan, the U.N. and countless foreign aid organizations have spent billions of dollars on projects, which in itself provides a measure of justification for their continued presence in the country. New schools, rebuilt clinics, power-generating facilities, and the like can meaningfully improve the lives of conflict-affected populations, but all too often they are either not linked into a wider conflict management strategy or left to atrophy once the publicity photo has been taken.

A recent BBC report suggests that approximately two-thirds of all aid money bypasses the Afghan government, and about 40 percent is spent in *donor* countries. A former head of office with United Nations Assistance Mission in Afghanistan (UNAMA) interviewed by the authors could not cite a single substantive UNAMA achievement in his province during a yearlong tenure.[16] Failure to focus aid and to prioritize aims is not an exclusively U.N. problem, but a failing across the whole international peace-building landscape. What is sorely lacking are means to audit effectiveness.

The problem is also diagnostic. Do the facts on the ground suggest that U.N. support is likely to be efficacious, and if so, in which specific areas? Or is involvement driven by the need "to do something"—and as much of it as parties to a conflict will permit? No question is more fundamental to the future of peacebuilding.

U.N. PEACE OPERATIONS AND
THE BRAHIMI REPORT

The U.N. Charter gives the U.N. Security Council the power and responsibility to take collective action to maintain international peace and security.

15. Jeremy Greenstock, review of *New World Disorder: The UN after the Cold War—An Insider's View*, by David Hannay, *RUSI Journal* 153, no. 4 (August 2008): 80.

16. UNAMA official interviewed by the authors in London, December 2007.

Although the term is not found in the U.N. Charter, peacekeeping is defined by the United Nations as "a way to help countries torn by conflict create conditions for sustainable peace."[17] The Security Council must authorize all U.N. peacekeeping missions. In effect, this stipulation ensures that approval is based less on the potential efficacy of a U.N. force deployment than on whether a proposed mission might advance or threaten core interests of the five permanent members.

As of July 31, 2008, there have been 63 U.N. peacekeeping missions. Since 1948, 130 nations have contributed an estimated 1 million military and civilian personnel to U.N. operations.[18] The 60 years of peacekeeping operations from 1948 to 2008 cost an estimated $54 billion. In the 19 peacekeeping, peacebuilding, and political operations overseen by UNDPKO as of August 31, 2008, 119 countries contributed 82,230 uniformed personnel (military and police).[19] To put these numbers in perspective, the uniformed personnel deployed for U.N. operations at that time exceeded the uniformed personnel deployed by any single nation, except the United States. In addition to military and police personnel, 5,188 international civilian personnel, 1,981 U.N. volunteers, and 12,477 local civilian personnel were working in missions overseen by UNDPKO.[20] At the end of August 2008, a total of 109,831 personnel were involved in U.N. peacekeeping, political, or peacebuilding operations overseen by UNDPKO.

The U.N. peacekeeping budget has increased to reflect the size and complexity of these operations. The approved U.N. peacekeeping budget for July 2007 through June 2008 was approximately $6.8 billion. The projected peacekeeping budget for the 2008–2009 fiscal year is $7.4 billion—a 10 percent increase over the 2007–2008 budget and nearly a threefold increase

---

17. "Dag Hammarskjöld, the second U.N. Secretary-General, referred to it as belonging to 'Chapter Six and a Half' of the Charter, placing it between traditional methods of resolving disputes peacefully, such as negotiation and mediation under Chapter VI, and more forceful action as authorized under Chapter VII." U.N. Department of Peacekeeping Operations, "United Nations Peacekeeping," at www.un.org/Depts/dpko/dpko (accessed October 3, 2008).

18. U.N. Department of Public Information, "United Nations Peacekeeping Operations." The U.N. offers contributing nations some $1,000 per soldier per month, plus equipment, which can provide a significant source of revenue for the armies of developing countries. Notably, only about 4.5 percent of the troops and civilian police deployed in U.N. peacekeeping missions come from the European Union, and less than 1 percent come from the United States.

19. U.N. Department of Public Information, "United Nations Peacekeeping Operations."

20. U.N. Department of Public Information, "United Nations Peacekeeping Operations."

in budget and personnel since 2003.[21] The U.N. peacekeeping budget is now triple the size of the annualized U.N. regular biennial 2008–2009 budget. The United States was assessed approximately 26 percent of the U.N. peacekeeping budget for 2008—more than all the other permanent members combined.[22]

> Japan and Germany, even though they are not permanent members of the Security Council, rank second and third in assessments at 16.6 percent and 8.6 percent, respectively.
> Based on the UN's [$7.4 billion] budget projection for peacekeeping, the U.S. will be asked to pay over $1.9 billion for UN peacekeeping activities. . . . The 30-plus countries assessed the lowest rate of 0.0001 percent of the peace-keeping budget for 2008–2009 will be assessed $7,352 based on that projection.[23]

Historically, Africa has been the focus of U.N. peacekeeping operations, accounting for more than 40 percent of all U.N. operations, past and present. As of July 31, 2008, nine of the nineteen U.N. operations overseen by UNDPKO are in Africa, four are in Asia, three in the Middle East, two in Europe, and one in Latin America. The focus on Africa reflects the prevalence of conflict on the continent, but it also reveals the attenuation of interest among the major powers in African security over the past two decades.[24] Paradoxically, this has made approval of Africa-based missions more likely. Indeed, in many ways Africa has "emerged as the laboratory for the experimentation" of "all types of peacekeeping concepts and operational innovations."[25]

The U.N. Charter stipulates that all U.N. member states should make available to the Security Council the necessary armed forces and facilities to maintain peace and security worldwide. However, this requirement is seldom observed, and the U.N. struggles at times to wheedle enough troops and equipment from member states to fulfill mission requirements. As of May 31, 2008, the top ten contributors of uniformed personnel to U.N.

---

21. Harvey Morris, "UN Peacekeeping in Line of Fire," *Financial Times*, May 20, 2008, at www.ft.com/cms/s/0/67ae1fe4-23ac-11dd-b214-000077b07658.html (accessed October 3, 2008).

22. China is assessed 3.15 percent; France, 7.4 percent; Russia, 1.4 percent; and the U.K., 7.8 percent. U.N. General Assembly, "Scale Implementation of General Assembly Resolutions 55/235 and 55/236," A/61/139/Add.1, December 27, 2006.

23. Schaefer, "United Nations Peacekeeping: Challenges and Opportunities," 3.

24. The establishment of the U.S. Africa Command (AFRICOM) in October 2008 could be cited as indicative of a contrary trend.

25. See David Francis, "Peacekeeping in Africa," in *Major Powers and Peacekeeping: Perspectives, Priorities and Challenges of Military Intervention*, ed. Rachel E. Utley (London: Ashgate, 2005).

operations are nearly all developing countries: Pakistan (10,623), Bangladesh (9,037), India (8,862), Nigeria (5,218), Nepal (3,711), Ghana (3,239), Jordan (3,017), Rwanda (3,001), Italy (2,864), and Uruguay (2,617).[26] Although the United States and other developed countries regularly provide lift and logistical support for U.N. operations, they are generally reluctant to participate directly. The five permanent members jointly contributed less than 6 percent of U.N. uniformed personnel on May 31, 2008. A number of reasons account for this situation, including the fact that major contributors use U.N. participation as a form of training and income,[27] while most developed countries fail to recoup their costs when they contribute uniformed personnel to U.N. peacekeeping operations.

The first U.N. peacekeeping mission, the United Nations Truce Supervision Organization (UNTSO), was launched in 1948 to monitor the ceasefire between Arab states and the newly created state of Israel. The second peacekeeping operation, the United Nations Military Observer Group in India and Pakistan (UNMOGIP), was approved the next year. The 1950–1953 Korean War soon followed, with the United States leading a U.N. force to resist North Korean aggression. However, Cold War tensions along with the bitter lesson of the first Congo peacekeeping operation[28] led the U.N. Security Council to approve few peacekeeping operations in the first forty-five years of the organization's existence. Between 1945 and 1990, the

---

26. U.N. Department of Peacekeeping Operations, "Contributions to United Nations Peacekeeping Operations," May 31, 2008, at www.un.org/Depts/dpko/dpko/contributors/2008/may08_1.pdf (accessed October 3, 2008).

27. "The UN pays the governments of troop contributing countries $1,110 per soldier each month of deployment." This amount is far greater than what most developing nations pay their troops participating in the missions. United Nations Foundation, "Season of the Blue Helmets," *UNF Insights*, no. 4, at www.globalproblems-globalsolutions-files.org / unf_website / PDF / unf_insights_issue_4_season_bluehelmets.pdf (accessed October 3, 2008).

28. The U.N. entered into peace enforcement in the Congo (1960–1964), where U.N. peacekeepers confronted a mutiny by armed forces against the government and sought to maintain the Congo's territorial integrity and prevent civil war after the province of Katanga seceded. According to a RAND study, "UN achievements in the Congo came at considerable cost in men lost, money spent, and controversy raised. . . . As a result of these costs and controversies, neither the United Nations' leadership nor its member nations were eager to repeat the experience. For the next 25 years the United Nations restricted its military interventions to interpositional peacekeeping, policing ceasefires, and patrolling disengagement zones in circumstances where all parties invited its presence and armed force was to be used by UN troops only in self-defense." James Dobbins, Seth G. Jones, Keith Crane, Andrew Rathmell, Brett Steele, Richard Teltschik, and Anga Timilsina, *The UN's Role in Nation-Building: From the Congo to Iraq* (RAND Corporation, 2005), xvi, at www.rand.org/pubs/monographs/2005/RAND_MG304.pdf (accessed October 3, 2008).

Security Council established only eighteen peace operations, despite a multitude of conflicts during that period that threatened international peace and security to greater or lesser degrees.

The end of the Cold War precipitated a dramatic shift in U.N. and multilateral peacekeeping. The U.N. Security Council has approved over forty new peace operations since 1990. The UNDPKO was created in 1992 to support the increased demand for larger and more complex missions, often to help implement comprehensive peace agreements in intrastate conflicts. Furthermore, peacekeeping came to involve more and more nonmilitary elements that ensured the proper functioning of civic functions, such as elections, as part of a wider strategy of peacebuilding. Under the strain of increasing peacekeeping operations and evidence of mismanagement, the U.N. recently divided UNDPKO into the Department of Peacekeeping Operations to conduct the missions and the Department of Field Support to handle logistics and procurement.

Of course, the nature of armed conflict has changed over the past fifty years, especially since the end of the Cold War. Conflict has occurred with greater frequency *within* rather than *between* states, partly as a function of wars of liberation in the 1950s, 1960s, and 1970s. However, these wars also drew in whole regions, as people moved unchallenged across borders as refugees and insurgents. Increasingly, such wars have involved civilians. By some estimates around 90 percent of war-related deaths in 1989 were civilian.[29] The ensuing humanitarian imperative to intervene has been highlighted by the role of the internationalized media, otherwise known as the "CNN effect." Yet, wars within states have generally proven much more difficult to stop than those between countries, especially where state structures are fragile or have collapsed.

Historically, four stages in international peacekeeping efforts can be discerned:

- **The Cold War period.** The period from 1946 to 1988 was defined by Cold War distrust, vetoes, and interests. From the mid-1970s to the mid-1980s, only one new mission was established, UNIFIL in Lebanon. In 1987, the United Nations had just five active peacekeeping missions, involving 10,000 personnel and costing $233 million annually. At this time, the Soviet Union, cognizant of its waning power, proposed strengthening the U.N.'s intervention capacity to include "a reserve of military observers and armed forces of the U.N. with countries allocating part of their forces on a standby basis for peacekeeping

29. See Anatol Rapoport, "The Twelve Most Unfortunate Countries in the World," *Peace Magazine* 7, no. 1 (January–February 1991): 25, at http://archive .peacemagazine.org/v07n1p25.htm (accessed October 3, 2008).

duties. Designated units would be mobilised for peacekeeping service on demand."[30]

- **Expansion.** From 1989 to 1993, demand for blue helmets accelerated, no longer constrained by Cold War politics. In 1992, the then secretary-general Boutros Boutros Ghali issued his report "An Agenda for Peace,"[31] in which he envisaged a renaissance of the U.N.'s capacities following the end of the Cold War. Notably, he outlined the sequence of steps—and consequent actions—of preventive diplomacy including preventive deployment, peacekeeping, peacemaking, and peace enforcement. Boutros Ghali's plan called for member nations to maintain forces permanently assigned to the U.N. on standby at high readiness to be available for interventions. In the same year UNDPKO's establishment provided a specific arm within the U.N. staff to take forward and realize his vision. By 1995, the U.N. was involved in seventeen peacekeeping missions with 75,000 troops at an annual cost of $3.6 billion, but Boutros Ghali's plan was shelved.[32]
- **Contraction.** This period commenced with the failure of the U.S.-led Operation Restore Hope in Somalia. The signal event was the Black Hawk Down operation in Mogadishu on October 3, 1993, in which eighteen American soldiers were killed. Much of the debate in the 1990s, framed by the experience of Rwanda and the Balkans, centered on rules of engagement and the suitability of authorizing deployments under Chapter 6 (U.N. forces as largely passive monitors) and Chapter 7 (U.N. forces in a peace enforcement capacity).
- **Resurgence.** The current stage has focused more on self-help peacekeeping missions, especially in Africa, and on devising new principles to confront the myriad challenges of peacebuilding, which most significantly found expression in the Brahimi Report. It commenced with the Nigerian-led ECOMOG operation in Liberia in the mid-1990s. In December 2005 the U.N. Peacebuilding Commission was established to extend the period of international attention on postconflict countries, among other things. By 2008, the annual cost of U.N. peacekeeping operations had reached $6.8 billion.

The Brahimi Report identified a number of proposals for improving external assistance to conflict resolution:

---

30. Michael Codner, "The Development of a Permanent United Nations Military Intervention Capability: Some Practical Considerations," *RUSI Journal* 153, no. 3 (2008).

31. U.N. Security Council, "An Agenda for Peace: Preventive Diplomacy, Peacemaking and Peace-Keeping," A/47/277 and S/24111, June 17, 1992, at www .un.org/Docs/SG/agpeace.html (accessed October 3, 2008).

32. Codner, "Development of a Permanent United Nations Military Intervention Capability."

- The need for mandates to specify an operation's authority to use force. This means bigger forces, better equipped, and more costly, but able to be a credible deterrent. In particular, U.N. forces for complex operations should have intelligence and other capabilities necessary to mount an effective defense against violent opposition.
- The importance of creating security at a local level by combining policing efforts with programs of national reconciliation, disarmament, demobilization, and reintegration.
- The importance of adapting peace operations to the information age. Missions require a substantive, global peace-operations extranet, through which missions can access databases, analyses, and lessons learned, among other things.
- The existence of wide disparities in staff quality and the need to address them by improving workloads and conditions.[33]

The Brahimi Report reflected a growing awareness, drawn from experiences as diverse as those in South Africa and East Timor, that new tools are required to mitigate and manage conflict. Indeed, the panel endorsed the secretary-general's recommendations on conflict prevention contained in the *Millennium Report* and in his remarks before the Security Council's second open meeting on conflict prevention in July 2000.[34] Most notably, this was an appeal to "all who are engaged in conflict prevention and development—the United Nations, the Bretton Woods institutions, governments and civil society organizations—[to] address these challenges in a more integrated fashion."[35]

The central problem highlighted in the Brahimi Report—developing more effective means to tackle the causes of conflicts—remains unresolved. Because U.N. mandates are political agreements, borne of uneasy compromises between adversaries with contrasting and sometimes incompatible interests, this is no small challenge. Yet we do not have to reinvent the wheel. Within the Brahimi Report and the lessons emerging from key U.N. missions is the foundation of a new approach to peacebuilding. Three cases—Cyprus, Lebanon, and the Democratic Republic of the Congo—illustrate in stark terms the broad challenge of conflict resolution, and how the U.N. has responded in each.

---

33. See U.N. General Assembly and U.N. Security Council, "Report of the Panel on United Nations Peace Operations."

34. Kofi A. Annan, *We the Peoples: The Role of the United Nations in the 21st Century* (U.N. Department of Public Information, 2000), at www.un.org/millennium/sg/report/full.htm (accessed December 1, 2008), and Kofi A. Annan, address to the U.N. Security Council, SG/SM/7491, July 20, 2000, at www.un.org/News/Press/docs/2000/20000720.sgsm7491.doc.html (December 1, 2008).

35. See U.N. General Assembly and U.N. Security Council, "Report of the Panel on United Nations Peace Operations."

Cyprus

Cyprus became independent in 1960 with a constitution that was intended to balance the interests of its Greek Cypriot and Turkish Cypriot communities, but a series of constitutional crises and outbreaks of inter-communal violence led to the establishment of the United Nations Force in Cyprus (UNFICYP) in 1964.[36] Forty-five years later, UNFICYP is still in Cyprus, supervising a cease-fire and maintaining a buffer zone between Turkish and Turkish Cypriot forces in the north and Greek Cypriot forces in the south.[37]

Today this buffer zone is policed by 915 U.N. personnel.[38] UNFICYP's original 1964 mandate called for it to use its best efforts to prevent a recurrence of fighting, to contribute to the maintenance and restoration of law and order, and to contribute to a return to normal conditions. Subsequent resolutions expanded UNFICYP's mandate, but the original aims of 1964 still pertain and are reaffirmed twice yearly following biannual reports of the secretary-general to the Security Council. UNFICYP deals with about 1,000 incidents each year, ranging from name-calling to unauthorized use of firearms. It also assists both communities on matters of mutual interest, such as electricity and water supply across the lines and some minor humanitarian work.

Yet it is the presence of a corps of 30,000 Turkish troops, not the U.N., that is keeping the peace on the island. In July 1974, Turkey launched an invasion—universally referred to in the north as the "intervention"—to safeguard Ankara's interests, protect the island's Turkish Cypriot population, and prevent the Greek Cypriot authorities from declaring *enosis* (union) with Greece. In the operation, Turkey seized two-fifths of the island, and ethnic cleansing resulted in thousands of deaths on both sides. In 1983, the Turkish side became nominally independent as the Turkish Republic of Northern Cyprus (TRNC), but the rest of the international community, except for Ankara, recognizes the Greek Cypriot government in the south as the only legitimate government of Cyprus. Since the invasion, numerous (mainly U.N.-led) attempts to "solve" the Cyprus conflict and

---

36. U.N. Security Council Resolution 186, March 4, 1964.

37. This section is based partly on a research trip to Cyprus taken in May 2008. For a view that is broadly sympathetic to the Greek Cypriot position, see Claire Palley, *An International Relations Debacle: The UN Secretary-General's Mission of Good Offices in Cyprus 1999–2004* (Oxford: Hart Publishing, 2005).

38. This includes 846 troops and 69 police, who are supported by 38 international civilian personnel and 108 local civilian staff. U.N. Peacekeeping Force in Cyprus, "Facts and Figures," at www.un.org/Depts/dpko/missions/unficyp/facts .html (accessed November 29, 2008).

reunify the island have failed.[39] Indeed so enmeshed is the U.N. in Cyprus's crisis-ridden past that it may now be part of the problem, part of the crisis furniture that does more to obstruct than to facilitate resolution.

The genesis of the most recent U.N. initiative was the G-8 Summit in 1999, at which the United States and the U.K., self-appointed arbiters of Cyprus's future, called on the secretary-general, Kofi Annan, to establish a new process of dialogue between the island's two communities with a view to a final settlement. Over the next five years, no fewer than five iterations of the "Annan plan" emerged. Annan V, a 9,000-page tome, was put to a referendum on both sides in April 2004. It stipulated the establishment of a new, bizonal entity, each with sovereign powers in its own territory, except for foreign affairs, finance, and a supreme court, which would be vested in a federal authority composed of Greeks, Turks, and foreigners. The more contentious elements of Annan V related to territory, confiscated property (arising from the 1974 war), and military force on the island. The plan would "solve the Cyprus problem, once and for all," proclaimed the secretary-general. The plan received the support of nearly two-thirds of Turkish Cypriots, but was rejected by more than three-quarters of Greek Cypriots, who generally believed that it gave too many concessions to Ankara.

A week after the referendum and following years of adroit diplomacy by the Greek Cypriot government, Cyprus entered the European Union, triggering an economic boom in the south. Membership has in effect given Cyprus "what the whole UN process was designed to avert"[40]—a veto over Turkish entry into the EU, which Cyprus could conceivably use to compel Ankara to withdraw its troops and settlers from the north.

The collapse of the Annan plan owes as much to major power stratagems as to internal island politics. Its rationale, argues UCLA history professor Perry Anderson, "lay outside Cyprus itself, the interests of whose communi-

---

39. The origins of the current impasse date back over a century, when the island was acquired by Britain from the Ottoman Empire and over time became a Mediterranean stronghold of the British Empire. The political will of its Greek and Turkish communities was neglected or manipulated in the service of Britain's strategic Cold War interests. The eventual compromise, the constitution of Zurich, that ended the anticolonial struggle and granted Cyprus quasi independence gave Britain sovereign military bases on the island—little "Gibraltars," as Macmillan put it. To this day, the bases provide Britain (and the United States) with a vital logistics and signals capacity in the wider region. However, the constitution also created unworkable political, military, and judicial structures, which fomented enmity and gave rise to the formation of irregular forces on both sides.

40. Perry Anderson, "The Divisions of Cyprus," *London Review of Books*, April 24, 2008, at www.lrb.co.uk/v30/n08/ande01_.html (accessed October 3, 2008).

ties were never more than ancillary in its calculus."[41] The Anglo–American desire to keep Turkey safely within the West's orbit and retain military enclaves on the island might have made sense to London and Washington on geopolitical grounds, but it distorted the negotiating process and effectively precluded any sustainable compact. As ever in conflict resolution, settlements imposed by external actors have a poor track record.

Rauf Denktas, who has been on the political scene in the north since the end of World War II, stepped down as president of the TRNC in 2005. He is the thread of continuity on the Turkish Cypriot side, but his unwillingness to compromise on a number of touchstone issues earned him a reputation for obduracy among Greeks and foreign diplomats. "They wrote intransigence on my forehead," Denktas concedes, "and it has never left me."[42]

Denktas is far from sanguine about the future. "Not in my lifetime," he says, "will there be a settlement since there is not the correct diagnosis of the problem. No one has diagnosed the problem as one party trying to take over the island."[43] He fears that the new generations in the south have little at stake in compromise and that their view of Turks is guided by polemics and mythology about the differences between the Turkish and Greek islanders rather than by reality.

The former president is not alone. Senior Turkish officials point to a lack of direct interest on the Greek side. Apart from reclaiming their territories such as the abandoned hotels and apartments on the beach strip of Famugusta in the southeast, the Greeks, now happily ensconced in the EU, have little incentive to settle. Turk Cypriots had hoped that EU membership would be the catalyst for solving this problem.

Given their long history of failed negotiations and discord, it is legitimate to ask whether the two communities, about 250,000 Turks and 800,000 Greeks, really want a settlement, or if the current modus vivendi is enough. It is equally valid to ask what price Washington and London would be willing to pay for a settlement. Not the bases, it would seem.

To some extent Cyprus is a great peace pantomime, the conflict backdrop frozen in place and the participants acting in the wings. It costs the U.N. about $50 million annually.[44] To the Turkish military, which ultimately calls the shots on questions of TRNC security, UNFICYP is essentially irrelevant. For the Greeks in the south, it provides "a second deterrent" against Turkey, an adversary that Greek Cypriot officials believe "can't be trusted."

---

41. Anderson, "Divisions."
42. Rauf Denktas, interview with the authors, May 29, 2008.
43. Denktas, interview.
44. Including voluntary contributions of one third from (Greek) Cyprus and $6.5 million from Greece.

At the time of writing, the stage was being set for launching yet another negotiation process. Driven by moderate leaders on both sides, this latest round of talks suggests that there is at last common ground across the ethnic divide and a realization that the answer to Cyprus's problem lies within the island, not in New York, Washington, or London. The lessening of physical partition, started by Denktas in 2003 and continued by his successor Mehmet Talat, seems increasingly like a harbinger of deeper cooperation between north and south. The opening up of crossing points reached a symbolic milestone in April 2008 with the opening of the Ledra Street crossing in the heart of old Nicosia. If foreigners are to assist in opening up another, wider discussion of the communities' future, they must not place the interests of Cypriots second.

Lebanon

For a country divided more or less equally among Shia, Sunni, and Christian, and home to some of the more radical expressions of these faiths, Lebanon is remarkably resilient. Indeed, by 2005, things in Lebanon appeared to be going well. The Israeli army, which invaded in 1982 to fight Palestinian fighters (or Fedayeen), had departed. The country's economy, built on banking and tourism and devastated by the bitter fifteen-year civil war that started in 1975, was picking up. Beirut was perceived by some to be on the cusp of recapturing its former glory as the "Paris of the Middle East," a sun-drenched Mediterranean tourist spot frequented by the beautiful set with a new downtown precinct remodeled in this imagination.

All this changed with the car bomb that killed Prime Minister Rafiq Hariri on February 14, 2005, as he passed through the city center that he had been instrumental in reviving. Backed by Saudi money, the Sunni prime minister had spent his way to power. The 1,200 kilograms of explosive were intended not only to kill him, but to send a message to others to not upset the regional and internal status quo.

Hariri's death was not an aberration, but rather a reflection of deep-rooted problems that the thirty-year U.N. presence has failed to resolve. The troops of the U.N. Interim Force in Lebanon (UNIFIL) have been based in the country since 1978 to separate Israeli military forces from their Palestinian and Lebanese adversaries and to confirm the Israeli withdrawal from Lebanon. U.N. Security Council Resolution 425 tasked the force with "restoring international peace and security" and "assisting the Government of Lebanon in ensuring the return of its effective authority in the area."

UNIFIL failed in its original mission. In the period up to 2006 it did not stop Hezbollah, the most significant Shia political and paramilitary organization, and other groups from using the Lebanese territory to raid and launch rockets at Israel. While the 12,500 U.N. military personnel[45] have constrained the open flaunting of weaponry by Hezbollah cadres since the last round of Israeli–Hezbollah fighting in 2006, they have specifically not been tasked with disarming the group. As such Hezbollah has moved some of its forces north of the strategic Litani River, gaining greater strategic depth and ensuring that the expanded UNIFIL presence acts as a (putative) buffer to prevent any Israeli assault. Meanwhile, Israel continues to conduct regular counteroperations in Lebanese air space, citing UNIFIL's failure to disarm Hezbollah and prevent its incursions and attacks on Israelis. The May 2008 armed takeover of West Beirut by Hezbollah and the lack of response by the Lebanese Armed Forces confirmed that Hezbollah had reached a modus vivendi with UNIFIL south of the Litani. At the same time, the presence of UNIFIL was irrelevant to Hezbollah's freedom of movement and activity elsewhere in the country. The current force—notable for the involvement of Spain, Italy, Germany, and France—is viewed as more important for tying these influential states to the politics of Lebanon than for its military presence. With armor and nine patrol vessels, it is configured for war, not peace, but it has neither the mandate nor will to effect real change. With over thirty participating countries suffering from the chronic lack of a common language and with the majority of the population of the south believing UNIFIL's mandate is to protect Israel, UNIFIL has a credibility problem and is anything but an "Interim Force in Lebanon."

The problem in Lebanon is more profound than any deal making or U.N. force can solve. It goes to the heart of reconfiguring the state and its role in Lebanon's multisectarian and multiethnic society.

The first challenge is dealing with the various traditional regional influences such as Lebanon's more powerful neighbors Israel and Syria, the second of which sees Lebanon as little more than its own proxy. Iran has also played a growing role in Lebanon's internal affairs by helping to create and strongly supporting Hezbollah. Not only are the state and the spoils divided between competing groups according to a prearranged formula, but there is now a more fundamental cleavage: Lebanese are caught between maintaining allegiance to the state and allegiance to the more narrowly defined interests of their ethnic or sectarian groups. Many Lebanese Shia give greater loyalty to Hezbollah and its vision of a global *ummah* (Islamic community) under the political and spiritual leadership of Iran's supreme leader, according to the doctrine of *vilayat al-faqih* (the rule of the Jurisprudent). With Shia birthrates above the national average, religion and demographics plus Iranian weapons and money and Syrian backing are proving to be a winning formula.

---

45. U.N. Interim Force in Lebanon, "Facts and Figures," at www.un.org/Depts/dpko/missions/unifil/facts.html (accessed October 3, 2008).

In November 2007, the last Lebanese president finished his second term and handed authority to Prime Minister Fouad Siniora, an ally of Hariri who sought to strengthen Lebanese independence against Syria. This exacerbated the political impasse caused when the Syrian-supported opposition's cabinet ministers left the government at the end of 2006. The opposition conditioned the rehabilitation of political and economic life on a new power-sharing deal, thus leaving the country without a functioning executive or parliament for more than eighteen months.

On May 9, 2008, Hezbollah and Amal Shia militants with their Syrian Socialist Nationalist Party colleagues temporarily took over West Beirut until they secured the deal that they wanted. The new power-sharing deal permits eleven out of thirty seats for the opposition in a government of national unity, enabling it to veto decisions with the "blocking third." This ensures that no Lebanese cabinet can attempt to move against Hezbollah's interests.

Lebanon's parliamentary system of confessionalism was established in an attempt to fairly represent the demographic distribution in the governing body, reserving high-ranking positions for members of specific religious groups. The president is by law a Maronite Christian, the prime minister a Sunni Muslim, the deputy prime minister an Orthodox Christian, the speaker of parliament a Shia Muslim, and so on. The 128 parliamentary seats are divided equally between Muslims and Christians. The Ta'if Accord, which ended the 1975–1990 civil war, adjusted the ratio from 6:5 in favor of Christians to equal representation to followers of the two religions.

Lebanese politics have been controlled by elites, functioning more as an oligarchy than a democracy. The country is dotted with political posters of assassinated family political scions. Between 1942 and 1980 just four families supplied the prime minister.[46] The state has deliberately been kept weak in support of this system. Unable to raise taxes, it is heavily indebted to the amount of $43 billion. The key political players cannot agree on how or even whether to fix the state, since many do not want an effective state. Hezbollah is providing its own schools, security, health care, and social networks. It does not need the state; rather, it requires a space free from state interference to do its own thing.

Political and religious tensions reflect the crisis of national identity in which many Christians prefer not to see themselves as Arabs, but of Phoenician stock. This identity crisis is complicated by the presence of 450,000 Palestinian refugees, who comprise 10 percent of Lebanon's population. Denied Lebanese citizenship and corralled into camps of desperate poverty, most would likely have nowhere to go even if the Israel–Palestine problems were settled because they are descendants of the 1948 generation whose

---

46. We are grateful to Alistair Harris for this observation.

land is unlikely to be given back in any settlement. Not a homogenous community, they have brought their own struggles to Lebanon.

Lebanon was once the archetype of a secular state, successfully accommodating eighteen different religious sects. Today the trajectories of the various groups, especially Hezbollah and the Shia, are taking them in different, increasingly violent directions. It appears that outsiders, including the U.N., can do little about this.

Democratic Republic of the Congo

Congo was the first major U.N. peacekeeping mission in Africa, and today, nearly fifty years later, it is the organization's largest and most expensive. Formerly Zaire, now the Democratic Republic of the Congo, it retains the legal personality of a state internationally, but scarcely functions like one. It has been at war with itself in one form or another since independence. For at least a century, external attempts ranging from King Leopold's brutal fiefdom to the softer approach of the U.N. Organization Mission in the Democratic Republic of the Congo (MONUC) to make it work as a single entity have failed. Indeed, outsiders keep doing much the same thing over and over again, with the same dismal results. Congo has a habit of corrupting the best of intentions.[47]

The brutal history of colonial exploitation was followed by independence on June 30, 1960. Six months after independence, four different regimes existed in the Congo: the central government in Léopoldville (Kinshasa) under Kasa-Vubu supported by Mobutu (as the army chief of staff), Moise Tshombe's government at Elisabethville (Lubumbashi) in Katanga, the "Diamond State" of Albert Kalonji in south Kasai, and the Lumumbist government in the east based at Stanleyville (Kisangani). Each relied on foreign patrons and troops to keep order.

All these "governments" failed to establish a stable civilian governing structure. In the midst of attempts by the mineral-rich southern Katangese province and eastern Kivu and Orientale provinces to secede, various coalition governments collapsed. An estimated one million people died in the five years of turbulent politics between independence and November 24, 1965, when General Joseph-Desire Mobutu staged his coup d'état.

Former Kinshasa CIA station chief Larry Devlin describes Mobutu as a "political genius," albeit an "economic spastic."[48] President Mobutu survived three decades through a combination of brutal repression including

---

47. This section is based partly on interviews conducted in the Congo and Rwanda between January and June 2008.

48. Larry Devlin, *Chief of Station, Congo: A Memoir of 1960–67* (New York: Public Affairs, 2007), 265.

public hangings of opponents, regular rotations of ministers (more than fifty full cabinet changes in three decades), huge inflows of foreign aid (an estimated $9 billion during the Mobutu years), nationalization of foreign interests including the rich copper and cobalt mines, development of a personality cult, and perfection of patronage politics including the management of state interests by political cronies. Many Congolese say that "of all the bad governments we had, the Belgian colonists are still the best."[49]

By the mid-1990s, annual per capita income had dropped to just over $100, two-thirds of preindependence levels.[50] Inflation reached 10,000 percent, and the currency—printed in 5-million-denomination notes—was virtually worthless. Copper production fell from 450,000 tons during the 1970s to 30,000 tons, and cobalt production fell sixfold over the same period.[51] Today per capita income loiters around $120 in spite of the country's abundant mineral wealth. Described by one World Bank official as a "virtual geological scandal," the DRC includes two-thirds of the world's cobalt supplies and huge reserves of copper, colombite-tantalite (or coltan), gold, and diamonds. The Congo is perhaps Africa's richest territory in natural resources, but its people remain among the poorest in the world.

Mobutu was evicted from power in May 1997 by a foreign invasion led by Rwanda, which originally intervened to deal with the remaining *génocidaires* located just across the border in Congo's eastern Kivu provinces. Since then, Congo has suffered more or less continuous civil war. Congo desperately lacks security, infrastructure, and investment. The Congolese have responded by asking the international community to provide security.

International efforts culminated in an elaborate and expensive peace process, of which the centerpiece was a negotiation jamboree at South Africa's Sun City holiday resort in April 2002. The resultant October 2006 multiparty elections, the first in the country's history, cost an estimated $1 billion. Yet the country remains fractured and beset by violence with large swaths of the country beyond the influence or control of the government.

Today, more than nineteen thousand U.N. military and civilian peacekeepers are stationed in the DRC at an annual cost of $1.15 billion. The U.N. Security Council established MONUC in 1999 to facilitate the implementation of the Lusaka Accord signed in 1999. Its mandate calls for monitoring and implementing the cease-fire agreement; disarming, demobilizing, repatriating, resettling, and reintegrating; and facilitating the tran-

---

49. According to a senior regional official in Bukavu interviewed by the authors.

50. Phillip Garner, "Congo and Korea: A Case Study in Divergence," Brigham Young University, March 23, 2006, at http://ssrn.com/abstract=889724 (January 5, 2009).

51. Martin Meredith, *The State of Africa: A History of Fifty Years of Independence* (London: Free Press, 2005), 392.

sition toward the organization of credible elections. The Security Council has authorized MONUC under Chapter 7 of the U.N. Charter to "use all means deemed necessary, within the limits of its capacities and in the areas of deployment of its armed units, to protect civilians under imminent threat of physical violence; and to contribute to the improvement of the security conditions."[52]

Still, this has not brought peace or stability. The North and South Kivu provinces in eastern Congo, which border on Rwanda, Burundi, and Uganda, remain violent. Rebel Tutsi general Laurent Nkunda waged war in the area more or less continuously since 1998. Attempts to defeat the Tutsi general failed badly in 2007. Even with U.N. logistical support, Kinshasa's 20,000 Forces Armées de la République Démocratique du Congo (FARDC) troops deployed in North Kivu failed to defeat Nkunda's much smaller force. Then, in late August 2008, General Nkunda launched another offensive, citing continuing violence by Hutu rebels against the region's Tutsi minority. During the last quarter of 2008, hundreds of thousands of people, many of whom were already internally displaced and living in temporary camps, were forced to flee the fighting. All sides were accused of massacres against civilians, General Nkunda threatened to overthrow Kabila's government by force, and the U.N. force failed to keep the peace.

Nkunda's fight was principally not against the government, but against the Interahamwe militia and other *génocidaires* still in the Congo. These forces are now grouped into the roughly 8,000-strong Democratic Forces for the Liberation of Rwanda (FDLR), which is intent on destabilizing Rwanda and launching attacks against Nkunda's Tutsi brethren.

Without the U.N. "the place would go nuts," as one World Bank expert put it.[53] Yet in the long term, the West's overall formula of assisting Kinshasa with security by providing U.N. troops, trying to improve governance with aid and advice, and supporting humanitarian delivery through nongovernmental agencies will not work to Congo's benefit.

Indeed, the U.N. perpetuates the fallacy of the single Congolese state. Willing or not, U.N. troops cannot deliver security, for example, by acting decisively against the FDLR. They lack the special skills, fighting intent, numbers, and mandate to do so. The Pakistani brigade in the southeast must cover a vast impenetrable territory with just one soldier per fifty-five square miles. The absence of roads and denseness of forests means that they must be ferried by helicopter for distances as short as 12.5 miles. It also remains difficult, as former MONUC commander Major General Patrick Cammaert wrote recently, to obtain reliable intelligence for "operations as

---

52. U.N. Mission in DR Congo, "Mandate," at www.monuc.org/news.aspx?news ID = 11529 (accessed December 1, 2008).

53. World Bank official, interviewed by authors, Kigali, Rwanda, June 2008.

the UN has no budget to pay informants and notoriously lacks technical capability to intercept communications between opposing groups and forces, as well as the equipment to carry out aerial surveillance."[54]

In early 2009, Rwanda surprised international observers by detaining Nkunda and placing him under house arrest in Rwanda, while the Congolese and Rwandan armies launched a month-long joint offensive— Operation *Umoja Wetu* (loosely translated, "our unity")—against the FDLR. According to initial assessments of the operation conducted in its immediate aftermath, about "70 per cent" of the mission was accomplished; the FDLR's capacity was reduced but not destroyed.[55]

It is unclear whether another joint Rwandan-Congolese operation in the Kivus is likely, and it would be premature to conclude that *Umoja Wetu* represents a new regional approach to tackling security problems in the Great Lakes. In the end, there is little prospect of any sustainable improvement in the situation if the Congolese government cannot establish better governance, crack down on corruption, promote and foster ethnic reconciliation within the country, and integrate and strengthen the FARDC. Indeed, the FARDC has *itself* become a major source of insecurity. As James Putzel argues, "There is no functioning chain of command, no doctrine, no discipline and soldiers remain without pay. . . . Neither their political nor military leaders are held to account." The path to security must begin, he adds, "with the consolidation of a functional and socially accountable national army in the DRC."[56]

Like his assassinated father, Laurent-Désiré, Joseph Kabila relied on allies to come to power, including the FDLR, which was equipped and supported by the capital to fight the various Mai-Mai militias for Kinshasa. Even today they are kept as a "FARDC reserve." According to U.N. officers, this cooperation continues, with the FDLR and FARDC staying in the same villages and extorting taxes together from the civilian population. The 100,000-strong FARDC is composed of Mobutu's former army, the Rwanda-assembled groups post-Mobutu, Mai Mai militia, and "other bandits, cannibals, and thugs."[57] However, it was constructed not to fight, but to make the elections possible.

54. Patrick C. Cammaert, "A Peacekeeping Commander's Perspective: From Headquarters and the Field," *RUSI Journal* 153, no. 3 (June 2008).

55. The authors' interview with Rwandan Brigadier General Frank Rusagara, London, March 20, 2009.

56. James Putzel, in press release, "International Community Risks Prolonging Crisis in Eastern DRC," London School of Economics, November 3, 2008, p. 1, at www.crisisstates.com / download / others / DRC%20Press%20Release%203%20No vember%20final.pdf (accessed January 5, 2009).

57. Senior expert in the Democratic Republic of Congo, interviewed by the authors, Kigali, Rwanda, June 2008.

The Congo's 66 million people display a seemingly endless capacity to tolerate suffering. Sexual violence against women by armed men is endemic; villagers are attacked, beaten, and displaced; and their houses are burned and their crops stolen.[58]

Kabila's election victory was facilitated through grants from the European Union and others. Yet less than a year later in September 2007, the young president granted the Chinese the right to exploit $80 billion worth of minerals in exchange for $5 billion of roads.

These "new colonialists" are unlikely to bring the stability through governance most Congolese long for. No governance systems or safeguards are in place to control what the rulers are doing or might be taking, and the promised delivery of infrastructure is already behind expectations.

The answer to the puzzle is not to expect the Congo to operate as a traditional state, with Kinshasa controlling things from the center. Mobutu's solution was essentially to run the country by running it down, using state resources to fund patronage, and keeping it dislocated by never building the infrastructure and other services that would have enabled it to communicate over its vast expanse. The same mentality pervades today. Kinshasa still sees anything that goes on in the periphery as a threat to its authority and has continuously undermined attempts at development in the provinces. As such, President Kabila's decision to cooperate with Rwanda in Operation *Umoja Wetu* might be a tactical ploy rather than a genuine strategic shift in thinking: his interests are served by keeping the FDLR and rebel armies alive because strong, stable, and united Kivus could pose a threat to his centralized rule.

Disarmament, pacification, demobilization, and repatriation/reintegration programs could help to dilute the security threat to the civilian population. However, this will require holding Kabila to task over the FDLR, removing the fig leaf of respectability hiding his indecision and weakness in filling the vacuum with U.N. troops. It will also require fundamental, root-and-branch reform, with decentralization at its core.

For decades the West has framed the Congo problem in simplistic terms. It has defaulted to the position of bolstering central rule in Kinshasa and investing hugely in elections because, perhaps understandably, the complexity of attempting another approach was too daunting. If Congo's vast territory can be governed by one state—still an open question—the international community will need to take innovative and bold steps, rather than continue to recycle old ideas that have never worked.

---

58. Tragically, U.N. peacekeepers have been accused of sexually abusing women and children, arming militias, and smuggling gold and ivory. In addition to the horrible mistreatment of those under U.N. protection, such crimes undermine the credibility of U.N. peace operations.

Multidimensional Challenges

The conflicts in Cyprus, Lebanon, and the DRC are not unique in their complexity and apparent intractability. Other significant missions not examined in this chapter operate in more favorable circumstances (e.g., in Liberia, the excellent and visionary leadership of President Ellen Johnson-Sirleaf) and afford U.N. forces and international assistance a fighting chance in helping to resolve conflict. The utility of these three cases rests in the multidimensionality of the challenges that they present—from the military and political to the economic and infrastructural and from the ethno-religious and human rights to administration and public information.

The Brahimi Report elegantly spoke to the need for all the components to work in an integrated manner in future U.N. missions. The final section of this chapter suggests some ways to improve the effectiveness of international interventions. It draws in part on the authors' participation in a recent series of meetings designed to establish a new set of principles and guidelines for international peacebuilding missions. The consensus of these meetings was articulated in the Tswalu Protocol in early 2008.[59]

OPTIONS FOR BUILDING PEACE

International intervention represents a failure of conflict prevention. Peacekeepers would not be in Lebanon, Cyprus, or the DRC if those countries had managed to resolve peacefully the issues that gave rise to armed conflict. For situations like these, the international community confronts a difficult decision: sit idly by while a crisis descends into chaos or widespread violence, or call on nations to support an intervention in which they may have little direct interest. This should lead to a careful assessment and discussion of what, if any, action is appropriate or feasible. Regrettably, all too often, the international community has reflexively decided to "do something" rather than to do the right thing.

A number of lessons that can be drawn from sixty years of U.N. peacekeeping:

---

59. The Tswalu Process that generated the Tswalu Protocol was comprised of three formal meetings held at Lake Kivu in Rwanda, on July 21–22, 2007; the Tswalu Kalahari Reserve, South Africa, on November 29–December 1, 2007; and the African Union headquarters in Addis Ababa, Ethiopia, on March 15–16, 2008. See Brenthurst Foundation, "Tswalu Protocol," at www.thebrenthurstfoundation.org/prog_tswalu.htm (accessed October 3, 2008).

Lesson #1: Prevention is more cost effective than peacekeeping

The persistent failure to find permanent solutions in Lebanon, Cyprus, and the DRC illustrates the importance of preventive involvement before a deteriorating situation becomes a crisis or conflict. The U.S. military refers to such initiatives as "Phase Zero Operations," which involve deploying specialists in conflict mitigation (e.g., from the U.S. Agency for International Development or the U.S. State Department) to forestall the need for future "phases" that would be activated in a buildup to war.

Lesson #2: Be careful to "do no harm"

A staggering array of organizations and businesses are driven by powerful institutional and financial incentives to *create* opportunities to assist countries in crisis or perpetuate the status quo. In a very real sense, these organizations and businesses thrive and profit from poor or absent governance in the countries beset by instability or violence. They step into the gap to provide services and governance where it is lacking on the ground, but in so doing, they remove incentives for indigenous institutions to develop. Thus, they set the stage for perpetuation or later resurgence of conflict.

The Security Council and the organizations involved in the peacekeeping business do not ask trenchantly enough, "Will we do more harm than good by becoming involved?" This question is as applicable to the external mediation efforts in Cyprus as to certain humanitarian agencies derided as "non-Somali warlords" in Somalia. In recent years, outsiders have exacerbated and prolonged more conflicts than they have brought to an end.

There are certainly strong arguments for international action against Sudan, but the clamor for intervention in Darfur doubtlessly arises more from an instinctive desire to "do something" than a nuanced understanding of the dynamics fueling the violence, which is necessary for effective action.

However, this is not to say we must accept the provocative entreaty of the American strategic thinker Edward Luttwak that we should "just give war a chance" and not interfere.[60] In some cases, waiting for the violence to exhaust itself will prove too unpalatable. Hopefully, we would not balk at intervening in another Rwanda. However, not every situation is ripe for a peacekeeping operation, holds the potential of degenerating into genocide or further violence, or requires a U.N.-led operation. Determining when U.N. action is appropriate is critical to ensuring that an operation will not inadvertently prolong or exacerbate the conflict.

---

60. See Edward N. Luttwak, "Give War a Chance," *Foreign Affairs* 78, no. 4 (July/August 1999).

Lesson #3: Clearly identify the purpose and goals of the operation and set the mandate and metrics for success accordingly

While international responses to armed conflict and state failure are invariably more ad hoc—due to the urgency of most interventions—than we would wish, future peacebuilders could refer to a number of choices and guidelines in the planning stages and after forces are deployed to help to offset the inherent limitations of peace operations. This is not to argue for a one-size-fits-all approach. That method's poor record, especially in Africa, speaks for itself. Rather, the point is that, when planning for an intervention, the unique context and details of a particular crisis can be placed in a framework or set of principles derived from past experience. A number of checks on foreign involvement should, if applied, enhance the prospects for successful external engagement in conflicts.

The first check involves assessing the range of available options. At one end of the spectrum is Luttwak's injunction: the circumstances of the conflict may be such that outside intervention would likely make matters worse than if the conflict were left alone. A lot of evidence suggests that Somalia fits in this category. Only in time will we be able to assess whether the current U.N. operation in the DRC defies the historical record of external involvement in the country by *not* contributing to its problems. There should be a realization that war may be a stage to peace itself and that ultimately a military solution may be the only plausible option (e.g., with the FDLR in the Congo).

Closer to the center of the spectrum is the option of "freezing" the conflict. The external response to the conflict in Cyprus is a textbook example. The "hot" war had to be halted by foreign powers (led by the U.K.) because violence between Turks and Greeks threatened to break apart NATO and harm their strategic interests in the region. Yet there was no realistic prospect of their settling the dispute. The U.N. presence contributed to the prevention of armed conflict after the 1974 invasion. The progress being made today to find a lasting solution is not due to U.N. or major power involvement, but to the efforts of internal actors.

A third option for international intervention is to actively encourage a negotiated settlement through various forms of external pressure and inducements, top-level informal negotiations (so-called Track 1.5 processes), and contacts within the respective civil societies. This option may be exercised in conjunction with or without a deployed peacekeeping force. Efforts to resolve the Cyprus conflict have no doubt been hindered by the absence of contact between the respective civil societies. Until recent internal changes, such as the opening up of crossing points between north and south and the issuance of Cyprus passports to Turkish Cypriots born in the south, the two communities were completely shut off from each other, except for interaction between their political leaders. In Lebanon, outsiders have played an especially pernicious role owing to their strong vested interests in seeing one side—Christian, Shia, or Sunni—in the conflict emerge as the strongest.

Finally, at the other end of the spectrum of international intervention is comprehensive and direct involvement, such as in Afghanistan today, but which we are not likely to see in any of the three cases examined here. By its nature, this type of intervention *demands* that foreigners become part of the problem, but also, hopefully, part of its solution.

Inherent in each of these four broad options is a certain level of responsibility. It is vital for the external actors to decide beforehand if they can live with it.

Lesson #4: Realize that peacekeeping is likely to be a lengthy endeavor

The international community, justifiably in many instances, is fixated on the need to establish an exit strategy for U.N. missions. In part this derives from experiences such as Cyprus and Lebanon, where no end is in sight to the costly U.N. presence, even as its contribution to the resolution of the crisis steadily wanes. The experiences in Lebanon, Cyprus, and the DRC also highlight why taking a long view is essential. Outbreaks of violence along with modest and slow results should be expected. These cases also highlight the myriad ways in which international actions can complicate the search for long-term peace.

The decision to intervene is a serious one likely to involve more resources, time, planning, and personnel than is initially apparent. Caution is advised before assuming what will likely be an open-ended commitment. There is a strong argument that a Security Council that limits itself to operations that are likely to succeed will help more people than a more active, but less prudent, institution. Taking account of these complexities, the international community may reasonably exercise the option not to intervene even where significant loss of life has occurred or is threatened.

A key difficulty for governments that contribute to U.N. or other international peace operations is convincing their electorates that the commitment is worthwhile and that some nations need assistance in finding the means to resolve their conflicts. Undoubtedly, there will be instances in which nations can and should participate in missions tangential to their interests. However, popular support for such operations is likely to be weak, lacking endurance, and vulnerable to the problems outlined in the three case studies.

Once approved, the U.N. Security Council must seriously undertake its periodic review and renewal of peace operations. Missions must be regularly reviewed to determine whether they are contributing positively to resolving military and/or political conflicts or are simply continuing out of inertia and habit. UNTSO and UNMOGIP were established in 1948 and 1949, respectively, and continue today. After six decades of intransigence, these missions are ripe for a thorough review of whether they are achieving their intended purposes or should be phased out or terminated. The U.N. Security Council gives these and other missions frequent scrutiny when they come due for renewal, but political considerations often overrule a frank assessment that would result in ending or transforming a mission because of current events or the mission's marginal or counterproductive contributions.[61]

Yet a prudent examination of a mission's value and contribution to resolving a conflict must not devolve into a precipitous or unwise retreat. Recent experience suggests that an excessive focus on the exit strategy can succor the spoilers who are bent on undermining peace and hamstring the international response. Thus, when deciding to intervene, the U.N. and other external actors need to think less in the planning stages about "how to get out" and more about "how to stay" and the mission's precise objectives against which to measure success because no outside involvement will

---

61. Former U.S. assistant secretary of state for international organization affairs Kim R. Holmes described how the U.S. State Department evaluated proposals for new U.N. peacekeeping operations or renewals of existing operations: "While the Security Council is hammering out the details of a peacekeeping resolution, member states work with the UN to figure out what that mission will require. We consider causes, regional equities, resources, the need for military forces and civilian police, the involvement of rule of law and human rights experts, reconstruction needs, and more. From the outset, we work to ensure each mission is right-sized, has a clear mandate, can deploy promptly, and has a clear exit strategy. This was particularly the case in getting peacekeepers into Haiti and expanding the mission in the Congo to target the main area of instability, the African Great Lakes region. . . . We are cautious because, historically, UN missions are not as effective at peace enforcement, when offensive military action is needed to end the conflict, as they are at maintaining ceasefires and supporting peace agreements. But our focused analysis has helped the UN close down most of the peacekeeping missions begun during the early 1990s, once their jobs were done. It is helping member states look for possible reductions in some long-standing missions, and press the UN to right-size or close other missions as they complete their mandates." Regrettably, this type of analysis in the context of Security Council authorization of U.N. peacekeeping operations appears to be the exception rather than the rule. Kim R. Holmes, "Statement Urging Congress to Fund Fully President's 2006 Budget Request for the UN," statement before the Subcommittee on Science, State, Justice, and Commerce, and Related Agencies, Committee on Appropriations, U.S. House of Representatives, April 21, 2005, at www.state.gov/p/io/rls/rm/45037.htm (accessed November 29, 2008).

succeed without a long-term commitment and a clear purpose. An exit strategy should still be considered and incorporated into the planning—every mission needs to contemplate the possibility of failure or redeployment after success—but once the Security Council approves a mission, the focus should be on achieving a successful mission and the means for achieving that success.

Lesson #5: Do not let an ideal outcome undermine an acceptable outcome

There must be a *real* basis for a settlement for any international response, particularly a U.N. mission, to be effective. Typically, that means that all or most parties to the conflict have tired of fighting and are ready for a solution. In practice, however, that is rarely the case. Outsiders invariably become engaged when the time is not right, when the situation is messy and ambiguous, and each party seeks to exploit foreign involvement to further its own aims. Making settlements stick is never easy. In the long run, the outcome depends not on the U.N. or any external entity, but on factors such as job creation, securing the rule of law, and providing basic services over which outsiders have little control. Often, their deterioration provoked conflict in the first place.

Increasingly, democratic elections are viewed as essential to this settlement process. This is true in many cases—perhaps none more so than South Africa's landmark vote in 1994. In the DRC, the 2006 elections served as a focal point for the various parties' energies, which might otherwise have been directed toward violence. It remains to be seen whether the local elections scheduled for 2008 and 2009 will have the same effect. However, elections produce winners and losers. Held too early, they can legitimize divisions within society. Conducted poorly, they can spark further conflict. In this regard the overriding objective of any international assistance should be to establish representative governance. In some circumstances this might require "power sharing" arrangements rather than a Western-style vote.

Lesson #6: Be flexible and consider options to maximize the likelihood of success

Once a mission's strategy and purpose are decided, those contemplating an intervention should consider the most effective and appropriate vehicle for undertaking the operation. An intervention should never be conducted simply to "do something" or because it can be done, but neither should a vital or necessary intervention be avoided or blocked due to an obsessive focus on operating through one channel. In some cases, this channel will be the U.N. In other cases, perhaps those situations requiring robust military action, or when U.N. action is blocked by a veto in the Security Council, nations willing to act will find it necessary or useful to organize around an ad hoc coalition or regional organization. Flexibility based on likelihood of success is critical.

Studies by Rand[62] and others have made the case that U.N. peacekeeping is a bargain for countries like the United States and the U.K., which would have to spend much more to send their own troops to perform similar operations. Sending a U.N. peacekeeping force is less costly than sending a U.S. or NATO force, but true value is not simply determined by cost. Other factors must be accounted.

The argument that U.N. peacekeeping is a bargain assumes that peacekeeping operations would be conducted regardless of circumstances. This is not necessarily the case. On the contrary, the very fact that the U.N. is being asked to conduct the peacekeeping operation implies that the issue is not a top-tier priority for the major powers and that, absent the U.N., they would likely not intervene. Thus, U.N. operations may be an additional cost for countries such as the United States that pay the lion's share of the U.N. peacekeeping budget, albeit a cost that could help to resolve a conflict.

While U.N. peacekeepers are generally less costly, in many ways "you get what you pay for." Assessments of a number of missions have revealed that U.N. peacekeepers are often poorly trained and equipped, ill coordinated, unprepared for combat, and undisciplined, as demonstrated by charges of corruption and rape against U.N. troops.

The U.N. lacks transparency and accountability in many areas, including peacekeeping operations. A 2006 audit by the U.N. Office of Internal Oversight Services concluded that at least $265 million of $1 billion in UNDPKO procurement contracts over six years was subject to waste, fraud, or abuse.[63] The U.N. also has limited options for holding peacekeepers accountable for their crimes because the standard memorandum of understanding between the U.N. and a troop-contributing country grants the contributing country jurisdiction over its military members participating in U.N. operations. Little is done if these countries fail to investigate, try, and punish those guilty of such crimes.

The objectives of U.N. peacekeeping operations have too often been poorly defined and the operations lack the means and mandate to fulfill

---

62. James Dobbins, "A Comparative Evaluation of United Nations Peacekeeping," testimony before the Committee on Foreign Affairs, U.S. House of Representatives, June 13, 2007, at www.rand.org/pubs/testimonies/2007/RAND_CT284.pdf (accessed November 29, 2008).

63. U.N. Security Council, "Peacekeeping Procurement Audit Found Mismanagement."

their objectives. Similarly, the bureaucratic nature of the U.N. can lead to indecision, paralysis, and infighting that can undermine the mission, such as happened in Rwanda and Somalia.

These factors combine to foment U.N. peacekeeping failures. This is not to say that U.N. peacekeeping operations are without worth. On the contrary, they can be extremely effective, as in Cambodia and Mozambique in the 1990s. Yet the weaknesses of U.N. operations must be acknowledged and taken into account to achieve similar successes in the future. When tempted to intervene in conflicts, the U.N. particularly needs to observe the Brahimi Report's central admonition:

> The United Nations does not wage war. Where enforcement action is required, it has consistently been entrusted to coalitions of willing States, with the authorization of the Security Council, acting under Chapter VII of the Charter.[64]

Where direct U.N. involvement is not possible or is not feasible, the Security Council should encourage regional organizations—such as NATO, the Economic Community of West African States (ECOWAS), and the African Union (AU)—or "coalitions of the willing" to undertake peacekeeping or peace enforcement tasks. As with U.N. operations, these operations have their strengths and flaws. Principal among the flaws is that, by their nature, they can elicit objections simply by not being a U.N. operation and lacking the "international legitimacy" conferred by a blue helmet. This objection is often nonsense. The AU mission in Darfur was ineffective, but not illegitimate. Nor would the NATO mission in Afghanistan lack legitimacy without a U.N. blessing.

The legitimacy of a conflict or intervention is based on its intent and implementation, not the color of helmets worn by its troops. Indeed, non-U.N. operations can often be more effective in warfighting and peacemaking by virtue of having clear chains of command, robust rules of engagement, proper training, proper equipment and support, and rapid deployment capabilities. That said, when political circumstances in the Security Council permit, non-U.N. interventions can avoid numerous problems if they are sanctioned by the U.N.

The key purpose of peacekeeping should be to facilitate conditions for resolving a conflict. The vehicle for pursuing this goal may vary widely. Adhering to one option or course of action can doom a peacekeeping mission before the first troops are deployed.

---

64. U.N. General Assembly and U.N. Security Council, "Report of the Panel on United Nations Peace Operations."

Lesson #7: Reform U.N. peacekeeping to improve accountability

The U.N. peacekeeping apparatus is poorly designed and constructed for peacekeeping operations. The U.N. Security Council approves missions, assigns their objectives, and reviews their operations. Yet the U.N. Secretariat, an organization not designed for such operations, carries out the missions. This has resulted in significant waste and inefficiency in peacekeeping operations. Relying on contributions from member countries has also led to a breakdown in accountability for U.N. peacekeepers that has tarnished their reputation. Some critical changes should be considered, including:

- Providing UNDPKO with the means to handle increased peace operations demands and plan for future operations more effectively. This requires more direct involvement of the Security Council and more resources for staff, supplies, and training. A core professional military staff must be maintained and utilized, but the UNDPKO should also be granted greater latitude to accept gratis military and other seconded professionals to meet exceptional demands on U.N. peace operations.[65] This would readily provide the expertise and experience needed to efficiently and realistically assess the requirements of mandates under consideration, including troop numbers, equipment, timelines, and rules of engagement. If necessary to circumvent existing rules prohibiting such flexibility in the U.N. Secretariat, the U.N. mem-

---

65. According to the secretary-general, "Gratis personnel were not regulated until the adoption by the General Assembly of resolutions 51/243 and 52/234, in which the Assembly placed strict conditions on the acceptance of type II gratis personnel. Among the conditions set out in administrative instruction ST/AI/1999/6, is the requirement that type II gratis personnel be accepted on an exceptional basis only and for the following purposes: (a) to provide expertise not available within the Organization for very specialized functions or (b) to provide temporary and urgent assistance in the case of new and/or expanded mandates of the Organization." U.N. General Assembly, "Gratis Personnel Provided by Governments and Other Entities," A/61/257/Add.1, August 9, 2006, at www.centerforunreform.org/system/files/A.61.257.Add.1.pdf (accessed November 29, 2008). The restrictions on gratis personnel were adopted at the behest of the Group of 77 developing nations, which thought that their nationals were not being given equal opportunity to fill U.N. positions because their governments could not afford to provide staff gratis. A possible solution could be to allow the countries to receive credit toward their assessed dues equivalent to the estimated salaries of gratis personnel. See "U.N. Gratis Personnel System Is Undemocratic, Says G-77 Chairman," *Journal of the Group of 77* 10, no. 1/2 (January/February 1997), at www.g77.org/nc/journal/janfeb97/6.htm (accessed November 29, 2008).

bership should consider establishing an independent peacekeeping organization.[66]

- Implementing mandatory, uniform standards of conduct for civilian and military personnel participating in U.N. peace operations. To end sexual exploitation, abuse, and other misconduct by peacekeepers, the U.N. must do more than adopt a U.N. code of conduct, issue manuals, and send abusers home. It must demand that member states commit to investigating, trying, and punishing their personnel in cases of misconduct. Investigators focused on peacekeeping operations must be hired, empowered to command full cooperation from mission personnel, and granted access to witnesses, records, and sites where alleged crimes occurred so that trials can proceed. Equally important, the U.N. must be more willing to hold member countries to these standards. States that fail to fulfill their commitments to discipline their troops should be barred from providing troops for peace operations.

- Improving oversight by establishing an independent U.N. inspector general dedicated to peace operations. Recent examples of fraud, mismanagement, and misconduct in U.N. peacekeeping operations amply illustrate the need for more transparency, rigorous accountability, and independent oversight accompanied by robust investigatory capabilities and a reliable system of internal justice. Now that the U.N. peacekeeping budget is triple the size of the regular U.N. budget, the U.N. should establish an independent inspector general to investigate and oversee alleged misconduct by U.N. peacekeepers and fraud and mismanagement in peacekeeping procurement.

- Exploring options for increasing the availability of peacekeepers for U.N. missions. The U.N. does not possess its own armed forces and is entirely dependent on member states to donate troops and other personnel to fulfill peace operation mandates.[67] The system is admittedly ad hoc and plagued by delays, inadequately trained personnel, insufficient military and civilian staff, inadequate planning, logistical gaps,

---

66. For one proposal, see Brett D. Schaefer, "Time for a New United Nations Peacekeeping Organization," Heritage Foundation *Backgrounder*, no. 2006 (February 13, 2007), at www.heritage.org/Research/InternationalOrganizations/bg2006.cfm.

67. The State Department budget includes a request for $106 million for the Global Peace Operations Initiative (GPOI) in fiscal year (FY) 2009, up from $81 million in FY 2007. Most GPOI funding, including the African Contingency Operations Training and Assistance program, goes to Africa-related programs. According to the budget, "Funding in FY 2009 is intended to train over 15,000 peacekeeping troops to reach the initiative goal of 75,000 peacekeeping troops trained worldwide." See U.S. Department of State, *Congressional Budget Justification: Foreign Operations, Fiscal Year 2009*, p. 113, at www.state.gov/documents/organization/101368.pdf (accessed November 29, 2008).

and inadequate or nonfunctional equipment.[68] This has led to calls for the U.N. to have its own forces to intervene more rapidly and decisively, such as a 2006 conference at the University of Castilla-La Mancha, which advocated a permanent U.N. Emergency Peace Service (UNEPS) with up to 15,000 personnel based at a number of designated locations and able to "quell an emergency within 48 hours after United Nations authorization."[69] In response, the U.N. has established a Standby Arrangements System (UNSAS) through which member states commit to preparing and maintaining military troops, specialized personnel, services, material, and equipment on standby in their home countries for deployment on U.N. peace operations.[70] The clamor for a legionary force reflects the fact that in times of violent crisis the U.N. Security Council typically cannot secure agreement on a course of action until the worst of the fighting is over. However, this delay is more often a political problem within the Security Council than one of insufficient troops. The Security Council is often slow to act, beset by internal wrangling, or approves resolutions that impede timely action. For instance, the joint AU/U.N. peacekeeping operation in Darfur is falling short of troops necessary to fulfill its mandate, not because of a lack of countries willing to provide troops, but because the Security Council agreed to Sudan's demand that only African peacekeepers be deployed.

CONCLUSION

This chapter has examined in some detail the relationship between U.N. involvement and conflict resolution in three cases. It could be argued that the seemingly permanent presence of U.N. peacekeepers in Lebanon, Cyprus, and Congo has, despite periodic relapses, contributed to the mitigation of armed conflict and kept apart communities that could not live together in Cyprus. However, a less charitable critique could also identify a

68. The operations in the Democratic Republic of the Congo, Côte d'Ivoire (Ivory Coast), Lebanon, and Darfur have recently experienced difficulties in increasing the numbers of troops authorized by the Security Council.

69. Robert C. Johansen, ed., *A United Nations Emergency Peace Service to Prevent Genocide and Crimes Against Humanity* (Global Action to Prevent War, Nuclear Age Peace Foundation, and World Federalist Movement, 2006), 22, at www.responsibilitytoprotect.org/index.php?module = uploads&func = download&fileId = 255 (accessed November 29, 2008).

70. U.N. Department of Peacekeeping Operations, "United Nations Standby Arrangements System (UNSAS)," April 30, 2005, at www.un.org/Depts/dpko/milad/fgs2/unsas_files/sba.htm (accessed November 29, 2008).

number of ways that the U.N. has exacerbated these three conflicts, cementing problems its intervention was designed to help resolve.

The complexity of the crises affecting all three countries requires bold and innovative thinking and strategies, based on the unique circumstances on the ground. Instead the U.N. response has too often been characterized by a "do what we can" rather than a "do what we must" mentality. Some will argue that this is inevitable. The U.N. is, to paraphrase Churchill, the best of the worst systems that we know—imperfect, but nevertheless the only global organization able to carry out the formidable tasks we ask of it.

They would be wrong. Peacebuilding and international interventions are likely to become much more complex and challenging, especially in Africa. The continent has been blighted by conflict since independence largely because the states inherited from the colonial powers were weak and often without ethnic or even religious foundation, and their "artificial" borders served to protect and bolster weak regimes. Consequently, although Africa has not balkanized, it has suffered continuous instability.

Yet Africa's fixation with borders may be eroding. Rather than forcibly living together or being kept apart, nations may choose to go it alone. Such processes are at work in the comparatively successful breakaway republic of Somaliland, southern Sudan, and elsewhere. The U.N. will need to decide whether to assist in the establishment of new states or to apply muscle to prevent it. Whatever it decides, the U.N. and its member states will need better analysis and new tools to meet the challenges.

4

Dysfunction in International Environmental Policy

How the U.N. Undermines Effective Solutions

Christopher C. Horner

"Global problems require global solutions." This seemingly reasonable call for concerted multilateral action to address shared problems conceals a host of concerns. Leading these concerns is that the "global solution" being proposed is often drafted, overseen, and implemented under the auspices of the United Nations through the U.N. General Assembly, affiliated technical and specialized U.N. agencies, or multilateral treaties. Mere domestic policies, adopted through democratic processes, are deemed inadequate without supranational coordination, even if they effectively address the problem at hand. Worse, the U.N. process is often designed to avoid the impediment of democratic decision making, and efforts to develop multilateral environmental initiatives outside the U.N., such as the original, U.S.-led Asia–Pacific Partnership on Clean Development and Climate (Clean Development Partnership, or CDP), elicit reflexive criticism from those who prefer a U.N.-orchestrated solution.

The U.N.-centric focus of these efforts is presented as an asset because the U.N. allows every nation to have input in responding to the issue. However, global input through the U.N. should not be confused with shared responsibility in addressing the problem. In part, this is because few countries have direct interests in a specific environmental problem or are in a position to contribute to resolving the problem. A few countries will bear

95

the burden, while the presence of the rest often serves more as a costly distraction than as a helpful addition. The situation is further complicated by the increasingly influential role played by nongovernmental special interest groups that advocate ideological agendas, allegedly on the behalf of civil society. In fact, they represent relatively narrow constituencies. Too often, these negotiations produce a tilted field on which a few, usually developed, nations are forced to adopt onerous policies or conform to new negotiated norms crafted by the many.

This approach sets the stage for dramatic expansions of international governance over activities and policies historically considered the province of local governance. Jessica Tuchman Matthews, then vice president of World Resources Institute and current president of the Carnegie Endowment for International Peace, observed years ago, "The United Nations charter may still forbid outside interference in the domestic affairs of member states, but unequivocally 'domestic' concerns are becoming an endangered species."[1]

In recent years, this has become increasingly obvious in discussions of "global warming." Despite the ineffectiveness of large-scale, U.N.-negotiated regimes such as the Kyoto Protocol, the drive to impose such policies on the United States—policies that the United States is clearly reluctant to impose on itself domestically—continues internationally. The U.N. hopes to have a successor treaty to Kyoto adopted in 2009.

Kyoto is not the only example. The Stockholm Convention on Persistent Organic Pollutants (POPs) seeks to ban certain chemicals. This treaty, which the United States signed in 2001, began with a list of banned chemicals, most of which the United States had already banned. However, it also provides a pathway for pressuring the United States to expand its list of banned substances without requiring Senate approval. One target is to ban industrial uses of chlorine, a building block of modern chemistry. This radical move was briefly floated in the United States early in the Clinton administration, only to be slapped down, but it has reemerged in the POPs process. Of course, codifying a bad policy in a treaty gives it a currency that it otherwise would not have and makes it resistant to reversal, even by a party to the agreement. For example, the POPs ban on DDT continues, even though assertions about its destructive environmental effects were subsequently disproved or otherwise defeated, and despite its effectiveness in combating malaria.[2]

---

1. Jessica Tuchman Matthews, "Chantilly Crossroads," *Washington Post*, February 10, 1991, C7.

2. See Roger Bate and Richard Tren, "Malaria and the DDT Story," Institute of Economic Affairs (London), 2001, at www.fightingmalaria.org/pdfs/malaria_and _DDT_story_IEA.pdf (accessed September 16, 2008).

Such is the paradox of international discourse on environmental issues. The insistence on addressing them through the U.N. ultimately undermines real efforts to resolve them because in the U.N. the votes and often the views of small island countries such as St. Kitts carry as much weight as those of the United States. Common sense and practical experience indicate that an alternative approach—possibly any other approach—would be preferable.

The United States and other nations are already exploring other multilateral approaches. In the case of global warming, they are beginning to recognize the need to limit the process to specific countries and practical measures. For example, the Major Economies Process on Energy Security and Climate Change, the CDP's coalition of the willing, and the annual G-8 meetings bring together those states that have the most direct interests in specific problems and that are called on to implement the potentially costly steps necessary to achieve the objectives.

Regrettably, internationalists ridicule and oppose such alternatives because they threaten the influence that the U.N. and radical environmental nongovernmental organizations (NGOs) exert over international environmental policy and limit the influence of small states over large economic powers.

The United States should reassess its willingness to address international environmental problems through the U.N., its funding of U.N. environmental organizations and conferences, and its minimum standards for ratifying and implementing environmental pacts. Working outside the U.N. framework, but within the Article II treaty process, may prove more effective in addressing international environmental problems, benefiting both the United States and the global environment.

THE EVOLUTION OF INTERNATIONAL ENVIRONMENTAL POLICY

Environmental policy is a relatively recent development in international affairs coinciding with the spread of wealth creation around the world because a society must attain a particular level of wealth before placing a high value on environmental protection in the prevailing sense of the term.[3] Using treaties to resolve environmental disputes among nations became increasingly common in the twentieth century as did the critical involvement of the United Nations in promoting and advancing this trend.

---

3. See Iain Murray, *The Really Inconvenient Truths: Seven Environmental Catastrophes Liberals Don't Want You to Know About—Because They Helped Cause Them* (Washington, DC: Regnery Publishing, 2008), esp. 216–24.

The U.N. sponsored the 1972 Conference on the Human Environment in Stockholm, the first major international conference on environmental issues. The Stockholm Conference touted the need for global action on most major environmental concerns of the time. It was followed by the U.N. Conferences on Environment and Development (UNCED) in Rio de Janeiro (1992) and Johannesburg (2002), several U.N. Conferences on Human Settlements/Habitat, the U.N. Conference on Population and Development in Cairo, various U.N. Food Summits, and other conferences. At the core of most of these conferences was the notion that population growth ensures that human activity is environmentally destructive and must therefore be governed, regulated, and often constrained or at least discouraged.

U.N. Environmental Bodies

The Stockholm Conference paved the way for the creation of several new U.N. agencies, including the U.N. Environment Program (UNEP) in 1972 and the Global Environment Facility (GEF) in 1991.[4] The key U.N. organizations involved in international environmental issues are the U.N. General Assembly, the Economic and Social Council (ECOSOC), UNEP, and GEF.

The U.N. General Assembly: The General Assembly approves the U.N.'s annual budget and is funded through it; this money is provided by member states according to their individual assessments, which are also determined by the General Assembly. The General Assembly frequently approves draft treaties, which are then open to signature and ratification by individual nations. It approves the treaties according to its rules on "important questions," which require a two-thirds vote on a one-country, one-vote basis.[5]

The Economic and Social Council: The United Nations conducts much of its business on environmental issues through the Economic andSocial Council. ECOSOC describes itself as "the principal organ tocoordinate economic, social, and related work of the 14 U.N. special-

---

4. Both the U.N. involvement in environmental issues and the modern environmental movement were guided by the Club of Rome. Indeed, the agendas of these U.N. organizations were driven by some of that group's stars, such as Maurice Strong. A longtime U.N. undersecretary-general, Strong was chief organizer and secretary-general of both the 1972 Stockholm Conference and the 1992 U.N. Conference on Environment and Development (the first "Earth Summit") in Rio de Janeiro. He also served as UNEP's founding executive director.

5. Charter of the United Nations, art. 18.

ized agencies, functional commissions and five regional commissions" and "the central forum for discussing international economic and social issues, and for formulating policy recommendations addressed to Member States and the United Nations system." ECOSOC's "green" subsidiary bodies include functional commissions on population, sustainable development, and forests; a standing committee on NGOs; the Ad Hoc Open-Ended Intergovernmental Group of Experts on Energy and Sustainable Development; and an expert Committee for Development Policy. "With its broad mandate the Council's purview extends to over 70 per cent of the human and financial resources of the entire UN system."[6] From this framework, many U.N. reports emerge, plans are made for priorities, and conferences are arranged. From within these bodies, green and related NGOs (e.g., food, population, and rights of women) work to advance the environmentalist agenda.

U.N. Environment Program: UNEP arose from the Stockholm Conference to coordinate international environmental protection, and it has assumed a leading role in developing international environmental agreements. Otherwise, it works mostly with developing countries to ensure sustainable development policies, largely through conditioning aid and project development funds on adoption of that agenda. Like other U.N. offices, it distributes millions of dollars each year through green activist groups.[7]

The Global Environmental Facility: GEF is actually a fund for Third World "environment projects" (biological diversity, climate change, international waters, and ozone depletion) supervised by the World Bank, U.N. Development Program (UNDP), and UNEP. It has openly cited activist groups such as the World Wildlife Fund (WWF), the International Union for the Conservation of Nature (IUCN), and Greenpeace as the executing agencies or collaborating organizations for millions of dollars in activities.[8]

These activities are funded through the U.N. regular budget and additional assessed and voluntary contributions from member states. It also

6. U.N. Economic and Social Council, "Background Information," at www.un.org/ecosoc/about (accessed September 16, 2008).

7. For more information on UNEP and its activities, see U.N. Environment Program website, at www.unep.org (accessed September 16, 2008).

8. For more information on GEF and its activities, see Global Environment Facility website, at www.gefweb.org (accessed September 16, 2008).

receives direct and in-kind funding from outside interests, including corporations, wealthy individuals, and foundations (notably Ted Turner's United Nations Foundation). Support goes well beyond UNEP and GEF. The U.N. Commission on Sustainable Development (UNCSD), UNDP, ECOSOC, Food and Agriculture Organization of the United Nations (FAO), U.N. Fund for Population Activities, and U.N. World Heritage Committee receive similar funding. This funding serves to wed them to the goal of advancing global governance of environmental issues, enhancing U.N. power and influence in this area, and, not coincidentally, increasing the influence of the nongovernmental financiers. Fueling this is an environmental alarmism that claims that failing to act on the U.N.'s proposals will bring dire consequences.

In the same year as the Stockholm Conference, the Club of Rome published *The Limits to Growth*.[9] Maurice Strong, a Club of Rome member, chaired the conference. Unsurprisingly, the mentality and agenda of *The Limits to Growth* were echoed in Stockholm. Projects flowing from Stockholm included UNEP efforts with WWF and IUCN to promote the World Conservation Strategy. The Stockholm conference document reads much like *The Limits to Growth*, touting resource scarcity as a rationale to curb population, advance global governance, and otherwise adopt the global environmentalist agenda. This sustainable development philosophy then bred further U.N. agencies to echo the call.

In recent years, the environmentalist agenda has permeated the U.N. system to the point that nearly every U.N. agency and program emphasizes claims that its actions benefit the environment. Among other examples, programs such as UNDP and the U.N. Educational, Scientific and Cultural Organization (UNESCO) have extended their missions into environmental issues and incorporated environmental objectives among their key purposes. This advances global governance over environmental issues and further elevates the environmental agenda in the U.N.'s broader set of activities. For instance, the U.N. Millennium Development Goals (MDGs) project lists sustainable development as one of its eight key goals. The Global Compact, run out of the U.N. secretary-general's office, asks companies to "embrace, support and enact" a set of principles, which includes three environmental principles: supporting a precautionary approach to environmental challenges, undertaking initiatives to promote greater environmental responsibility, and developing and diffusing environmentally friendly technologies.[10] The U.N.

---

9. Donella H. Meadows, Dennis L. Meadows, Jørgen Randers, and William W. Behrens III, *The Limits to Growth* (London: Earth Island Limited, 1972).

10. See U.N. Development Program, Millennium Development Goals, "Goal 7: Ensure Environmental Sustainability," at www.undp.org/mdg/goal7.shtml (accessed September 16, 2008), and U.N. Global Compact, "The Ten Principles," at www.unglobalcompact.org/AboutTheGC/TheTenPrinciples/index.html (accessed September 16, 2008).

General Assembly and most member states now subscribe to the MDGs and have pledged to implement and fund them.

Environmental Agreements and Treaties

U.N. environmental bodies may set policy and influence discussions and actions on international environmental issues, but international law remains the primary means for coordinating international action on environmental issues. This is done through drafting and adopting multilateral treaties and environmental norms.

Environmental treaties range from bilateral agreements between two nations to regional or multilateral pacts involving a handful of nations to "universal" or "global" conventions involving nearly all of the more than 190 U.N. member states. Until quite recently, multilateral environmental treaties were relatively issue specific, limited in scope, and evenly applicable to treaty parties. For instance, the 1973 Convention on International Trade in Endangered Species of Wild Fauna and Flora (CITES) focused on a discrete issue—prohibiting trade in endangered species or related goods—and applied treaty requirements equally to state parties. Similarly, the 1972 Convention on the Prevention of Marine Pollution by Dumping of Wastes and Other Matter governs deliberate dumping of waste at sea from vessels, manmade structures, and aircraft.

More recent environmental agreements differ significantly from earlier treaties. They are broader and increasingly intrude into the internal affairs of nations by seeking to establish norms for domestic behavior. If there was a discrete fulcrum for the move toward broader and more intrusive environmental agreements, it was the U.N. Conference on Environment and Development (Earth Summit) in Rio de Janeiro.

In the summer of 1992, nations of the world convened in Rio de Janeiro for the U.N. Conference on Environment and Development under UNEP auspices. Fitting nicely with the emerging U.S. political campaign narrative, Rio became the most prominent international meeting since the 1986 Reykjavík Summit between Ronald Reagan and Mikhail Gorbachev. It served as a platform for posturing and pressuring nations to act on an unprecedentedly ambitious environmentalist agenda, including outcome documents such as Agenda 21, the Rio Declaration on Environment and Development, the Statement of Forest Principles, the U.N. Framework Convention on Climate Change (UNFCCC), and the U.N. Convention on Biological Diversity (CBD).

The Convention on Biological Diversity is a good case in point. It cites three main goals: promoting conservation of biodiversity, sustainable use of its components, and fair and equitable sharing of benefits from using genetic resources "by appropriate access to genetic resources and by appropriate transfer of relevant technologies, taking into account all rights over those resources and to technologies, and by appropriate funding."[11] The peril lies in the interpretation of "appropriate," because the CBD also instructs parties to act according to the precautionary principle.

The precautionary principle requires that a good, substance, or activity be presumed harmful unless its proponents demonstrate that it will cause no harm. This perniciously shifts the burden of proof and imposes a nearly impossible standard of proving "safety." For example, the 2000 Cartagena Protocol on Biosafety to the CBD requires member nations to enact regulatory policies for biotech products based on the precautionary principle.[12] Consequently, countries establishing such regulatory policies generally approve no biotech products because "precautionary" policies give regulators many easy justifications to block approval based on objections from anti-growth, antipopulation, and antitechnology interest groups in the environmentalist movement. Even Calestous Juma, the first executive secretary of the CBD, objected to the Protocol on Biosafety and still considers it a bad idea.[13]

In addition, the protocol provides countries with an excuse to shirk their General Agreement on Tariffs and Trade (GATT) and World Trade Organization (WTO) obligations to base sanitary and phytosanitary regulations on demonstrated scientific concerns. Because the European Union is an important agricultural export market, strict EU adherence to the precautionary principle is especially damaging. Countries that are otherwise pro-biotech (e.g., China, Thailand, and Australia) and many very poor countries in Africa and Asia have imposed serious restrictions on domestic cultivation of biotech crops because they do not want to jeopardize the exportability of their products to the EU.[14]

When a number of less-developed countries balked at ratifying the Biosafety Protocol or adopting such regulatory policies, the GEF established a project in 2002 to create the regulatory infrastructure for testing and approval of biotech products in less-developed countries. Some observers describe this UNEP-GEF program as an organized system to bribe poor countries into ratifying the protocol.[15] However, since many of those coun-

---

11. Convention on Biological Diversity, December 29, 1993, at www.cbd.int/convention/convention.shtml (accessed September 16, 2008).

12. See Henry I. Miller and Greg Conko, "The Protocol's Illusionary Principle," *Nature Biotechnology* 18, no. 4 (April 2000): 360.

13. David Adam, "UN Attempts to Boost Biosafety in Developing World," *Nature* 415, no. 6870 (January 24, 2002): 353.

14. See Robert Paarlberg, "Are Genetically Modified (GM) Crops a Commercial Risk for Africa?" *International Journal of Technology and Globalisation* 2, no. 1/2 (2006): 81–92.

15. Kenyan Calestous Juma, former executive secretary of the Convention on Biodiversity and current director of Harvard's Science, Technology and Innovation Program, said the UNEP-GEF program was "like offering swimming lessons to people in the Sahara." Adam, "UN Attempts to Boost Biosafety in Developing World."

tries essentially have no functional environmental regulation, offering a couple of million dollars to establish a biotech regulatory apparatus not only effectively prohibits biotech products in these countries, but also diverts scarce domestic resources away from legitimate environmental and public health problems such as water pollution.

Not only have treaties expanded in scope and increasingly intruded into domestic affairs, but the number of treaties has proliferated. Notable environmental treaties drafted in the 1990s include the CBD, the International Convention to Combat Desertification in Those Countries Experiencing Serious Drought and/or Desertification, the Basel Convention on the Control of Transboundary Movements of Hazardous Wastes and their Disposal, the UNFCCC, and the Kyoto Protocol.[16] Even the Comprehensive Test Ban Treaty, the Rome Statute of the International Criminal Court, and the revived U.N. Convention on the Law of the Sea have been touted by environmental advocates as critical "environmental" agreements.

U.S. Involvement

The United States aided and abetted this evolution during the 1990s. While previous U.S. administrations had generally supported international efforts to resolve international environmental issues by participating in drafting international treaties and financially supporting organizations like UNEP, they had viewed these efforts in the context of broader foreign policy concerns. For instance, President Ronald Reagan declined to advance the Law of the Sea Treaty negotiated by President Jimmy Carter out of concern that it would impose significant economic costs and impede U.S. intelligence and military efforts.[17]

The practice of regarding international environmental issues as important, but subservient to other foreign and national security priorities, shifted dramatically under the Clinton administration. Secretary of State Warren Christopher openly argued for elevating environmental issues to the level of other foreign policy priorities, such as combating proliferation of weapons of mass destruction and fighting terrorism.[18] Numerous environmental initiatives were increasingly justified as key foreign policy objectives because they were critical to the international environment or had dire foreign policy or security implications. Environmental agenda items and

---

16. See Terry L. Anderson and Henry I. Miller, eds., *The Greening of U.S. Foreign Policy* (Stanford, CA: Hoover Institution Press, 2001).

17. See editorial, "George W. Haig," *New York Sun*, November 8, 2007, at www .nysun.com/editorials/george-w-haig/66109 (accessed September 16, 2008).

18. Warren Christopher, "Secretary's Message to State Department Employees," U.S. Department of State, February 8, 1993, at http://findarticles.com/p/articles/ mi_m1584/is_n6_v4/ai_13594491 (accessed September 16, 2008).

related buzzwords, such as "sustainable development," began appearing in all manner of foreign aid programs.

Before the Clinton administration, U.S. diplomats had acted as a moderating force in environmental treaty talks. Their counterparts could posture and preen on the environment for consumption back home, knowing that U.S. officials would eventually return the discussion to practicalities, metrics, and outcomes. Under the Clinton administration, the United States adopted a new posture in both formal and informal environmental treaty talks. Indeed, after negotiations for the International Joint Commission on the Great Lakes concluded, a Canadian diplomat lamented to a U.S. counterpart, "Now, you agree to anything!"[19]

Indeed, the United States signed all the 1990s environmental treaties listed above, but the Senate has not been as quick to ratify them. The potential consequences of these treaties are severe, which explains the Senate's deliberation. For example, the Kyoto Protocol would have cost trillions of dollars in reduced economic growth due to constraints on greenhouse gas (GHG) emissions.[20]

The U.N. Framework Convention on Climate Change

In addition to establishing obligations, environmental treaties often create entities to administer their terms and further advance the relevant agenda beyond the initial parameters. For instance, the Kyoto Protocol and its precursor, the 1990 U.N. Framework Convention on Climate Change, are administered by the UNFCCC Secretariat.[21]

---

19. This comment was related to the author by a former observer to, and offered in the context of, talks on the International Joint Commission on the Great Lakes, ca. 1995.

20. See U.S. Department of Energy, Energy Information Administration, *Impacts of the Kyoto Protocol upon U.S. Energy Markets and Economic Activity,* October 1998, at www.eia.doe.gov/oiaf/kyoto/kyotorpt.html (accessed September 16, 2008).

21. U.N. agreements routinely establish a new office within or affiliated with the U.N. to execute relevant functions delegated to it. Other, nonglobal multilateral treaties are typically managed by the parties' existing diplomatic and other bureaucratic infrastructure. The UNFCCC has a core budget of over $30 million per year and an annual income of $70 million or more. As with many other U.N. bodies, the UNFCCC has been subject to mismanagement. The UNFCCC's board of auditors has criticized the UNFCCC for its lack of transparency in its expenditures, failing to account for millions of dollars, resisting an internal audit, and failing to adopt fraud detection and protection plans. See U.N. Framework Convention on Climate Change, "Audited Financial Statements for the Biennium 2004–2005," FCCC/SBI/2006/14, November 1, 2006, at http://unfccc.int/resource/docs/2006/sbi/eng/14.pdf (accessed September 16, 2008). Additionally, the treaties provide that covered parties underwrite much of the participation by the rest of the world

The UNFCCC has been the leading advocate for global action and regulation to curtail projected global warming. To increase support for its own scheme to address climate change, it routinely conveys unrealistically optimistic cost assurances and worst-case climate scenarios while ignoring countervailing evidence.[22]

Among these false, questionable, or exaggerated claims is the 2007 insistence on "90–95 [percent] scientific certainty"[23] that humans are responsible for twentieth-century warming. Prior to that was the 2001 depiction of purportedly aberrant modern temperatures in the subsequently debunked "hockey stick" graph. The "hockey stick" graph purported to show a history of stable, slightly declining temperatures, which was suddenly and radically reversed by the onset of the Industrial Revolution. This claim was easily debunked once it was finally subjected to something resembling peer review.[24]

The UNFCCC promotes these claims through its science arm, the Intergovernmental Panel on Climate Change (IPCC). Although the IPCC conducts no scientific research, it represents itself as the final word on climate

---

in the name of "capacity building." Most of these free-riding parties fail to remit or are delinquent with their contributions.

22. The IPCC excludes research if produced during the two years preceding writing of the IPCC reports, but selectively ignored the exclusion to include alarmist material. Excluded papers that challenge the IPCC's premise include updated and enhanced understanding of how tropical weather and clouds act as planetary cooling thermostats, the effect of natural oscillations on climate over decades, how solar wind and magnetic effects may significantly influence climate, and how the impact of incoming energy from the Sun is amplified near Earth's surface. See Roy W. Spencer, William D. Braswell, John R. Christy, and Justin Hnilo, "Cloud and Radiation Budget Changes Associated with Tropical Intraseasonal Oscillations," *Geophysical Research Letters* 34, no. 15 (August 2007); American Geophysical Union, "Synchronized Chaos: Mechanisms for Major Climate Shifts," *ScienceDaily*, August 2, 2007, at www.sciencedaily.com/releases/2007/08/070801175711.htm (accessed September 16, 2008); and H. Svensmark and E. Friis-Christensen, "Reply to Lockwood and Fröhlich—The Persistent Role of the Sun in Climate Forcing," Danish National Space Center *Scientific Report*, no. 3 (2007), at www.spacecenter.dk/publications/scientific-report-series/Scient_No._3.pdf/view (accessed September 16, 2008).

23. For example, see Intergovernmental Panel on Climate Change, "Summary for Policymakers," in *Climate Change 2007: The Physical Science Basis—Contribution of Working Group I to the Fourth Assessment Report of the Intergovernmental Panel on Climate Change* (2007), at http://ipcc-wg1.ucar.edu/wg1/Report/AR4WG1_Print_SPM.pdf (accessed December 2, 2008).

24. See Stephen McIntyre and Ross McKitrick, "Corrections to the Mann et. al. (1998) Proxy Data Base and Northern Hemispheric Average Temperature Series," *Energy & Environment* 14, no 6 (November 2003): pp. 751–71, at www.uoguelph.ca/~rmckitri/research/MM03.pdf (accessed September 16, 2008).

science. However, the IPCC is led by political activists, not practicing research scientists. Indeed, IPCC guidelines "explicitly state that the scientific reports have to be 'change[d]' to 'ensure consistency with' the politically motivated Summary for Policymakers."[25] IPCC author Dr. John Christy has expressed astonishment over the IPCC's overt political agenda:

> At an IPCC Lead Authors' meeting in New Zealand . . .
>
> After introducing myself, I sat in silence as their discussion continued, which boiled down to this: "We must write this report so strongly that it will convince the US to sign the Kyoto Protocol." Politics, at least for a few of the Lead Authors, was very much part and parcel of the process.[26]

OMNIPRESENT NGOS: BLAME IT ON RIO

U.N. environmental policy advocacy coincided with and was greatly influenced by the emergence of the modern environmental movement.[27] The relationship was mutually beneficial. Rendered largely irrelevant to international peace and security by the Cold War, the U.N. saw international environmental issues as an arena in which it could exert influence. Meanwhile, the modern environmental movement saw the U.N. as a sympathetic venue for advancing environmental policies that were often resisted on the national level. As a result, although NGOs are active in every relevant sphere of the foreign policy universe, nowhere are they as well funded or more influential than in the environmental arena.[28]

---

25. James Inhofe, "Global Warming Alarmism Reaches a 'Tipping Point,'" speech in the U.S. Senate, October 26, 2007, at http://epw.senate.gov/public/index.cfm?FuseAction = Minority.Speeches&ContentRecord_id = dceb518c-802a-23ad-45bf-894a13435a08 (accessed September 16, 2008).

26. John Christy, "Viewpoint," BBC News, November 14, 2007, at http://news.bbc.co.uk/2/hi/science/nature/7081331.stm (accessed September 16, 2008).

27. The modern environmental movement differs from traditional conservationism in many ways, particularly in its abandonment of traditional property rights and common law remedies for environmental degradation in favor of state primacy in resource management and centralized regulation.

28. There are many types of NGOs: business-organized NGOs, such as the World Business Council for Sustainable Development, an erstwhile Enron vehicle for global warming rents, now headed by companies with similar business interests; government-organized NGOs (GONGOs); big international NGOs, such as Greenpeace and the World Wildlife Fund; and ordinary NGOs operating on the local, state, and national levels, such as church groups, unions, think tanks, and charities.

The Rio Earth Summit ushered in a boom era of mass NGO participation in U.N. environmental discussions and conferences.[29] In addition to delegations from all recognized national governments, including scores of heads of state, Rio hosted some ninety-five accredited NGOs and their subsidiaries representing regional, national, and international interests and agendas.[30] Only fifteen years later, the December 2007 U.N. Climate Change Conference in Bali, Indonesia, admitted more than 750 NGOs as observers among the more than ten thousand participants.[31]

In Rio and at subsequent U.N. conferences, NGOs have played a significant role in setting the agenda and pressuring government delegations. NGO activities at U.N. conferences and meetings range from the informal (e.g., availability to media and distributing pamphlets and newsletters) to the quasi-formal (presenting petitions in the plenary and subsidiary body

---

29. The author attended numerous Kyoto talks, beginning with the November 2000 session in The Hague (typically as a media representative, due in part to the difficulties in gaining widespread NGO accreditation), and observed that the U.S. State Department informally addressed two discrete constituencies in separate, restricted briefings: pro-Kyoto NGOs and a group of industry representatives inaccurately characterized as anti-Kyoto. Representation of groups that would be directly affected by potential commitments—industry and labor—was relatively limited in Rio (approximately 20 percent of the accredited NGOs) and split between those opposed to the treaty because it threatened their industries (e.g., the coal industry and mine workers) and those hoping to benefit from possible commitments and the ensuing governmental programs and subsidies. Contrary to common belief, industry groups were among the most aggressive "direct" protreaty lobbying forces at treaty negotiations and elsewhere. They were aggressive in their indirect advocacy by funding green groups and business and joint advocacy groups. The money at stake for potentially regulated entities and the rents to be gleaned from mandates and subsidies explain their zeal in pushing a pact so antithetical to U.S. interests. As Enron's senior staffer tasked with gaining U.S. participation in Kyoto wrote, the treaty was "precisely what we have been lobbying for" and "this agreement will be good for Enron stock!!" Most revealing was the urging for Enron to "monitize [sic] our relationship with the green groups." The disproportionate representation by pro-Kyoto industry attendees skewed input to the U.S. delegation. For NGO claims of influence, see Paul J. Georgia, "Greens' Success at Kyoto," *Cooler Heads Digest* 2, no. 6 (March 17, 1998), at www.cei.org/gencon/014,02873.cfm (accessed September 17, 2008).

30. These interest groups ranged from scientific and professional societies to industry and labor groups to gender and environmentalist pressure groups to spiritual leaders and indigenous peoples.

31. U.N. Framework Convention on Climate Change, "The United Nations Climate Change Conference in Bali: Parties & Observers," at http://unfccc.int/parties_and_observers/items/2704.php (accessed September 17, 2008).

sessions). While NGOs do not have voting privileges or formal status as negotiators, they provide significant input as lobbying organizations. NGOs representing every conceivable interest group are allowed, even encouraged, to participate in the process as long as they are approved by the U.N. This gives them a quasi-formal role and unique credentials that allow them privileged access to the talks and the negotiators.[32]

NGOs are also involved in decisions on text and outcomes.[33] For instance, in 2007 the Associated Press reported:

> A draft report of about 60 pages—distilling the previous three reports totaling more than 4,000 pages—has been circulating for months to governments, environmentalists and scientists for comment. . . . Each line must be adopted by consensus—and sometimes the use of a single word can be heatedly contested.[34]

In some instances, NGOs have effectively gained veto power in international environmental documents—a level of influence rivaling that of nations.

This increased NGO influence has a distinct downside for the United States. As the gatekeeper, the U.N. consciously favors NGOs that expressly support the enterprise at hand and thereby the U.N. agenda, which is often at odds with U.S. interests.[35] Specifically, to the extent that the U.N. favors

---

32. Disclaimers notwithstanding, members of accredited NGOs are generally accorded preferred access and privileges to facilitate interaction with U.N. operations. "The Department of Public Information and NGOs cooperate regularly. NGOs associated with DPI disseminate information about the UN to their membership, thereby building knowledge of and support for the Organization at the grassroots level." NGO Global Network, "Non-Governmental Organization," at www.ngo.org/index2.htm (unavailable September 17, 2008), reposted at http://everything2.com/node/694534 (accessed September 17, 2008). Indeed, the U.N. NGO Network asserts that the goal of NGOs is to "more effectively partner with the United Nations and each other to create a more peaceful, just, equitable and sustainable world for this and future generations." NGO Global Network, at www .ngo.org/index2.htm (accessed September 17, 2008).

33. As Senator Inhofe noted, "Left unreported by most of the media was the fact that Bill Hare, an advisor to Greenpeace, was a lead coauthor of a key economic report in the IPCC's 4th Assessment. Not surprisingly, the Greenpeace co-authored report predicted a gloomy future for our planet unless we follow the UN's policy prescriptions." Inhofe, "Global Warming Alarmism."

34. Associated Press, "'Synthesis' U.N. Warming Report to Be Issued," MSNBC, November 9, 2007, at www.msnbc.msn.com/id/21710833 (accessed September 17, 2008).

35. For example, see U.N. Department of Public Information, Non-Governmental Organizations, "DPI/NGO Partnership," at www.un.org/dpi/ngosection/ngo

NGOs that support its preferred policies, NGO participation can artificially strengthen certain views in the process and undermine opposing views.

For instance, the Bali organizers of the Thirteenth Session of the Conference of the Parties to the UNFCCC denied media credentials to outlets that might not support the agenda. It later denied access to others who had made their dissent known, and abruptly cancelled a media event at which the dissenters would have expressed their views.[36] Meanwhile, the IPCC provided nine hundred international journalists with lists of sympathetic NGOs, such as Greenpeace and the Union of Concerned Scientists, to contact for "independent" views. Such practices tend to disproportionately weigh against U.S. interests, particularly in pacts such as Kyoto that apply unevenly to the treaty parties.

Trumpeting their role at U.N. conferences is also a lucrative fund-raising tool for NGOs. Maintaining this funding is a key motivation behind their support of the U.N.-led global warming effort.[37] Bonner R. Cohen, a senior

---

_partnership.asp (accessed September 17, 2008). The U.N. has long recognized the importance of working with and through NGOs to advance U.N. interests. Establishing its Department of Public Information (DPI) in 1946, the General Assembly "instructed DPI and its branch offices to 'actively assist and encourage national information services, educational institutions and other governmental and NGOs of all kinds *interested in spreading information about the United Nations.*' . . . In 1968, the Economic and Social Council, by Resolution 1297 (XLIV) of 27 May, called on DPI to associate NGOs, bearing in mind the letter and spirit of its Resolution 1296 (XLIV) of 23 May 1968, which stated that an NGO '. . . *shall undertake to support the work of the UN* and to promote knowledge of its principles and activities, in accordance with its own aims and purposes and the nature and scope of its competence and activities.'" U.N. Department of Public Information, Non-Governmental Organizations, "NGOs and the United Nations Department of Public Information: Some Questions and Answers," updated November 2005, at www.un.org/dpi/ngosection/ brochure.htm (accessed September 17, 2008) (emphasis added).

36. Reporters from *Environment & Climate News* "were refused press credentials" for the Bali conference. The newspaper "has been in continual publication for 10 years; is sent to more than 75,000 elected officials, opinion leaders, and environmental professionals in the United States; and is one of five newspapers published by the 23-year-old Heartland Institute." Noel Sheppard, "Skeptics Denied Press Credentials at UN Climate Meeting in Bali," NewsBusters.org, December 4, 2007, at http://newsbusters.org/blogs/noel-sheppard/2007/12/04/skeptics-denied-press-cre dentials-un-climate-meeting-bali (accessed September 17, 2008). See also PR Newswire, "Skeptical Scientists Kicked off UN Press Schedule in Bali . . . Again," Breitbart .com, December 13, 2007, at www.breitbart.com/article.php?id=prnw.20071213 .DC09846 (accessed September 17, 2008).

37. Many agreements, whether they address environmental issues or human rights, offer the potential for such business opportunities. That is one way the NGOs elevate their negotiating presence. Matters are simply magnified in the Kyoto Proc-

fellow with the National Center for Public Policy Research who has extensively researched funding of environmentalist NGOs, describes the U.N. as
the NGOs' "indispensable global partner."[38] The NGOs have turned global
warming advocacy into a lucrative industry, having received $150 million
to $210 million per year over the past fifteen years.[39] NGOs have called for
tripling this amount.[40] Yet these figures do not include billions of dollars
spent annually by official bodies, national governments, and industries
engaging the issue.[41] For instance, according to the BBC:

> The European Commission is giving millions of pounds of taxpayers' money
> to environmental campaigners to run lobbying operations in Brussels. . . .
>   Among the organisations to benefit is Friends of the Earth Europe (FoE),
> which received almost half of its funding from the EU in 2007. . . .
>   In 2006 the EU gave more than 7.7m euros (£5.5m; $11.2m) to at least 40
> environmental organisations to help them lobby in Brussels.
>   They included big campaign groups such as WWF (World Wide Fund for
> Nature) and FoE Europe.
>   They are both in the Green 10, a powerful environmental lobbying network
> which works closely with the European Commission, the European Parliament
> and the Council of Ministers.[42]

Of course, money is fungible, and these groups also lobby at U.N. summits, subsidiary body meetings, and preparatory sessions in which they are
permitted to participate. These financial rewards are a powerful incentive

---

ess given the volume of interests seeking to ride the issue to increased revenues and
influence.
    38. Bonner Cohen, *The Green Wave: Environmentalism and Its Consequences* (Wash-
ington, DC: Capital Research Center, 2006), 145.
    39. This is according to an unpublished foundation study leaked to *Grist* maga-
zine. Ken Ward, "What to Do Now?: Conclusions and Recommendations," *Grist*,
May 7, 2007, at http://gristmill.grist.org/story/2007/5/7/114214/8796 (accessed
September 17, 2008). See also James M. Sheehan, "Cashing in on Global Warming,"
Competitive Enterprise Institute, June 1, 1998, at www.cei.org/gencon/005,01248
.cfm (accessed September 17, 2008).
    40. For example, see California Environmental Associates, "Design to Win: Phi-
lanthropy's Role in the Fight Against Global Warming," August 2007, at www.heart
land.org/custom/semod_policybot/pdf/22245.pdf (accessed September 17, 2008).
    41. NGOs have received millions of U.S. taxpayer dollars to advocate the Kyoto
agenda and are routinely brought in by companies desperate for an environmental
seal of approval or at least cessation of criticism by environmental groups. See Sheehan, "Cashing in on Global Warming." For a comprehensive assessment of NGO
participation, see Sheehan, *Global Greens* (Washington, DC: Capital Research Center, 1998).
    42. Simon Cox, "EU 'Wasting' Cash on Lobby Groups," BBC News, December 6,
2007, at http://news.bbc.co.uk/1/hi/world/europe/7127182.stm (accessed September 17, 2008).

for NGOs to emphasize, exaggerate, and even distort the severity and immediacy of international environmental issues. After all, without a crisis, there is little need to increase funding to environmental NGOs. Examples of such alarmism are rampant, as a visit to any environmentalist website will confirm.

Worse, this necessitates a race to the bottom because the threat of losing funding or credibility from being exposed as alarmist leads many environmental NGOs to ignore, dismiss, or more often attack evidence and research that question their extreme predictions of environmental consequences for failing to adopt the various environmental treaties and measures advanced by the U.N. For instance, the thirty-one thousand scientists and economists who signed the Global Warming Petition Project, a letter disputing global warming, and other organizations skeptical of global warming or the efficacy of constraints on greenhouse gas emissions are dismissed by the Union of Concerned Scientists as fronting for the energy industry or lacking credibility.[43]

THE TRIUMPH OF POLITICS OVER SCIENCE AND ECONOMICS

The process of drafting and adopting multilateral environmental agreements is fraught with flaws and perils. Allowing equal and active participation by states not exposed to cost, and only receiving financial benefit from, the terms of an agreement complicates efforts to achieve consent on specifics. Such parties can and often do hold negotiations hostage, demanding extraneous or counterproductive provisions. Of the major multilateral environmental agreements, none better exemplify the triumph of politics over science and economics than the agreements surrounding the Kyoto Protocol, generally referred to as the Kyoto Process.

The 1997 Kyoto Protocol requires a small group of nations to cap certain, mostly domestic emissions of greenhouse gases, which are produced by burning fossil fuels (hydrocarbon energy sources).[44] However, enormous

43. See Global Warming Petition Project, "Frequently Asked Questions," at www.petitionproject.com/gwdatabase/GWPP/Frequently_Asked_Questions.html (accessed September 17, 2008); and Union of Concerned Scientists, "Global Warming Skeptic Organizations," at www.ucsusa.org/global_warming/science/skeptic -organizations.html (accessed September 17, 2008).

44. Greenhouse gases (GHGs) are atmospheric gases widely assumed to absorb radiation, principally water vapor, carbon dioxide, nitrous oxides, and methane. GHGs are necessary for life on earth and are produced largely through natural processes in enormous, albeit varying, quantities from year to year. Combustion of fossil fuels, agriculture (livestock and soil tilling), and other activities produce relatively small quantities of GHGs.

loopholes prevent the treaty from achieving its ostensible goal of real emission reductions. The net result is that the Kyoto Protocol would not affect climate change, even accepting any premise or scenario used to advocate its terms.

Exemption of Major GHG Emitters

Kyoto is based on the premise of "common but differentiated responsibilities," a condition of disparate treatment of donor and donee states set forth in its parent treaty, Rio, and incorporated by reference in Kyoto.[45] The protocol explicitly states that more than 150 state parties have no reduction requirement, including China, which has since become the world's largest GHG emitter. It also exempted India, the world's fourth-largest emitter, and Mexico, South Korea, and Indonesia, which rank in the top fifteen. Excluding major GHG emitters from the agreement's restrictions renders the Kyoto Protocol inherently ineffective because net GHG emissions will continue to rise, albeit theoretically more slowly. Even the latter is dubious due to proven "carbon leakage," or relocation of industry from covered countries to exempt nations, an inescapable reality when agreements cover only a select few. Thus, if GHG emissions from human activity are the primary cause of global warming, then the Kyoto Protocol will at best delay, rather than prevent, global warming.

At one time, the U.N. acknowledged that efforts to address global warming would not succeed unless binding reductions also covered major developing-country emitters and that such emitters should be included in any agreement after 2008–2012. Yet the Kyoto Protocol, which declares all nations to be indispensable parties while simultaneously exempting many of them from any restrictions, no longer assumes foreseeable, meaningful participation by these countries. In fact, the U.N. now expressly dismisses the notion of including them.

The 1990 Gambit

In the negotiations of the Kyoto Protocol, the European Union insisted on calculating emissions reductions using 1990 as the base year—an

---

45. Generally, this meant that developed countries, because of their greater wealth and as the sources of most GHG emissions, should accept more stringent restrictions and donate resources to help developing countries comply with efforts to reduce their rate of emissions growth. However, this was not universally true, as illustrated by Australia's "reduction" from 1990 emissions, which was really a restricted increase not to exceed 8 percent above 1990 levels (averaged over 2008–2012). International Energy Agency data since 2000 reveal that CO_2 emissions in the EU are increasing faster than in the United States, despite generally faster growth in the U.S. population and economy.

unusual choice for a 1997 agreement that would go into effect beginning with 2008 emissions, or nearly two decades later. Under this provision, nearly all EU members were actually allowed to increase GHG emissions under the Kyoto emissions reductions scheme. By selecting 1990 as the base year, the EU could take advantage of the U.K.'s "dash to gas" and the shuttering of East Germany's dirty industrial capacity after reunification.[46] These two occurrences in the early 1990s were unrelated to Kyoto, but sharply reduced GHG emissions in two of the largest EU economies between 1990 and 1997.

The Kyoto Protocol also treated the EU-15 (the fifteen members of the EU in 1997) as one source, allowing them to collectivize their obligations to reduce GHG emissions. Thanks to these two provisions, the U.K. and Germany "achieved" nearly all of the EU's collective reduction quota under Kyoto, allowing most other EU countries to avoid the economic consequences of reducing GHG emissions. Indeed, this arrangement allowed five EU countries to *increase* emissions as much as 25 percent above 1990 levels. Finland and France promised no reductions under this scheme. Three other EU countries pledged emissions reductions less than they originally ratified under Kyoto.[47] Russia and Central and Eastern Europe also benefited from the 1990 date, which turned the supposed emission reduction requirement into permission to massively increase emissions or to sell the difference because they were unlikely to eclipse their emission ceilings.

Wealth Transfers in Lieu of Reducing Emissions

The thirty-five nations (including the EU-15) that are required to reduce emissions under the treaty can also use a loophole to meet their GHG emission cap through direct wealth transfers to and/or foreign direct investment in other nations, whether the recipient nations are covered or exempt.

For instance, Russia and some Eastern European countries experienced severe economic declines during the 1990s and have since replaced inefficient capital stock with less-polluting modern substitutes. It was unimaginable that they would eclipse the 1990 ceiling established by Kyoto. The small handful of countries with real emission reduction requirements

---

46. For a more technical discussion of these pollution reductions, see Mark Winskel, "When Systems Are Overthrown: The 'Dash for Gas' in the British Electricity Supply Industry," *Social Studies of Science* 32, no. 4 (August 2002): 563–98; and P. Klingenberger, "The Electricity Supply Industry in Germany After Unification," IEE Colloquium on Electricity Supply Utilities—Experience Under Privatisation, February 18, 1992.

47. For the respective promises assumed by EU-15, see Climate Action Network Europe, "Burden-Sharing Agreement of the EU," at www.climnet.org/resources/eu burden.htm (accessed September 17, 2008).

(Japan, Canada, and to a lesser extent the EU-15) could meet their emissions reductions requirements by paying these countries not to exceed their 1990 quota. For instance, Russia anticipated a financial windfall from selling credits up to the amount of the gap between its quota and its actual emissions. Russia also received investments under Kyoto's joint implementation mechanism, which provides an incentive for other covered countries to modernize and build out Russia's infrastructure in lieu of actually reducing their own emissions. This paper reduction allows most covered countries to escape the real reductions that Kyoto was supposed to effect, which would have reduced economic activity and incurred political risk.

Other concerns flow directly from this dynamic. It drives the process toward wealth transfers, which creates constituencies for continuing the process regardless of its effectiveness and feeds demands that subsequent agreements preserve this wealth transfer loophole.[48]

Even if the Kyoto Protocol were implemented perfectly for fifty years—meaning that the bound countries actually reduce emissions rather than use loopholes and paper reductions to "meet" their quotas—the agreement is projected to delay projected warming by an undetectable 0.07 degrees Celsius, and for just six years.[49]

While Kyoto had a political impetus, it lacks any real prospect for reducing greenhouse gas emissions. For those few countries actually vowing to reduce emissions, to the extent that they do not simply purchase "reductions," current and foreseeable technology ensures that Kyoto effectively rations and redistributes energy-intensive activities. Indeed, the Kyoto Protocol and other efforts to constrain GHG emissions would be prohibitively expensive. Even if perfectly implemented, complying with Kyoto could cost the United States more than $397 billion per year (1992 dollars).[50] Other initiatives to reduce GHG emissions outside of the Kyoto Protocol, such as the 2008 Climate Security Act[51] sponsored by senators Joe Lieberman (ID-CT) and John Warner (R-VA), would similarly limit GHG emissions from

---

48. For example, see Christopher C. Horner, "Kyoto's Future, Post-Nairobi and Going Forward in 2007: How a Post-2012 Kyoto Pact Is Impeded Not by U.S. Actions, but the Failure of Europe and Other Kyoto Parties to Reduce Emissions, and Continued Rejection of Rationing by the Vast Majority of the World," Center for Science Public Policy, January 2007, at http://ff.org/centers/csspp/pdf/200702_horner.pdf (accessed September 17, 2008).

49. This also assumes a CO_2 forcing effect, which has largely been disproved over the past decade, when global warming halted despite ongoing increases in GHG emissions. T. M. L. Wigley, "The Kyoto Protocol: CO_2, CH_4 and Climate Implications," *Geophysical Research Letters* 25, no. 13 (1998): 2285–88.

50. U.S. Department of Energy, *Impacts of the Kyoto Protocol.*

51. Climate Security Act of 2007, S. 2191, 110th Cong.

the combustion of hydrocarbons, which would cost the U.S. economy "at least $155 billion per year (by 2030) and realistically could exceed $500 billion (in inflation-adjusted 2006 dollars)."[52]

Thus, Kyoto is an economic instrument in practice. Assertions by leading diplomats, and the treaty's design, lead to the conclusion that Kyoto was specifically intended to mitigate U.S. competitive advantages under the guise of preserving the global commons. For example, former French president Jacques Chirac hailed it as "the first component of an authentic global governance,"[53] and EU Environment Commissioner Margot Wallström called it an effort to "level the playing field" economically.[54] Indeed, when in 2005 Saudi Arabia proposed making Kyoto's GHG reductions binding—a stated desire of Europe—Europe blocked the proposed amendment given that by then it had become clear that the U.S. Senate would not ratify Kyoto.[55]

Officially, Europe continues to insist that the extant formula and approach continue, although time is not on the side of perpetuating the Kyoto Protocol, which expires at the end of 2012. To avoid a gap between regimes, a successor agreement would need to be negotiated at the December 2009 talks in Copenhagen. A rare European overture at tweaking the disastrous Kyoto scheme to also bind developing countries has been rejected.[56]

Meanwhile, numerous leaders from exempt, less-developed countries have made it clear that they view the agreement as something of a restitution pact and a new source of foreign aid.[57] They, like the leaders of India

---

52. William W. Beach, David Kreutzer, Ben Lieberman, and Nicolas Loris, "The Economic Costs of the Lieberman-Warner Climate Change Legislation," Heritage Foundation *Center for Data Analysis Report*, no. 08–02 (May 12, 2008), at www.heritage.org/Research/EnergyandEnvironment/cda08-02.cfm.

53. Jacques Chirac, plenary address at the Sixth Conference of the Parties to the U.N. Framework Convention on Climate Change, The Hague, November 20, 2000.

54. Margot Wallström, quoted in the *Independent* (London), March 19, 2002, 14.

55. See Horner, "Kyoto's Future, Post-Nairobi and Going Forward in 2007," 6–7.

56. See Gerard Wynn, "EU Wants Developing Nations to Do More on Climate," Reuters, March 2008, at www.reuters.com/article/latestCrisis/idUSL11262051 (accessed September 17, 2008).

57. For example, one Chinese diplomat said, "Negotiations on a new treaty to fight global warming will fail if rich nations are not treated as 'culprits' and developing countries as 'victims.'" Associated Press, "China: Rich 'Culprits' on Climate Change," February 16, 2008. Brazilian president Luiz Inacio Lula da Silva weighed in, calling the Third World "victims of deforestation" and "victims of the global warming." "Although Lula admitted the importance of preserving the environment, he said it was necessary to take into consideration the social and economic needs of local populations." Xinhua News, "Brazilian President Says Rich Countries Do Not Follow Kyoto Protocol," *People's Daily* (Beijing), February 22, 2008, at http://

and China, intend to withhold their "indispensable" participation unless the free ride and wealth transfers continue. Russia has signaled a similar posture in recent Kyoto talks.

The Stalled Kyoto Process

Basing the Kyoto Process on incentives to reward political constituencies, avoid domestic economic pain, and transfer wealth doomed the stated goal of emission reductions. The wealth transfers inherent in the Kyoto system are too tempting for developing nations to give up voluntarily, or at least not until they milk the loss of these rents for other advantages. The exempt countries insist on remaining exempt. Much of the covered world, particularly Europe, has no interest in promising real emission cuts after having received a free ride to one degree or another, which still did not allow most European countries experiencing reasonable economic growth to comply.[58]

Yet the United Nations and environmental NGOs have generated enormous pressure to "do something" about global warming. Their objective is to maintain the failed design of the Kyoto Process. This is reflected by U.N. secretary-general Ban Ki-moon's call for completing a post-Kyoto agreement by the end of 2009. In his speech, he rededicated "the UN system to support countries in the implementation of existing agreements, and any future agreements under the UNFCCC, including in the areas of adaptation, technology and transfer, and capacity building."[59]

---

english.people.com.cn/90001/90777/90852/6358958.html (accessed September 17, 2008). Lula also complained that "rich countries consume 80 percent of the natural resources of the planet. They have to pay a trade-off to poor countries for them to conserve the environment." Reuters, "Brazil Urges Rich to Fund Environment Reform," February 22, 2008, at http://uk.reuters.com/article/oilRpt/idUKN 2145533820080222 (accessed September 17, 2008).

58. Even with the generous "reductions" arranged through the 1990 gimmick, most EU countries are vastly exceeding their Kyoto obligations. Europe's collective burden is also far out of reach, so they are trading wealth for credits to meet their obligations. Beyond 2012, the EU will need to reduce its collective emissions to 20 percent below 1990 levels. The EU now must confront, to some extent at least, the economic realities of its climate policies as it is deadlocked over which countries will bear the pain of meeting its promise to cut emissions in any post-Kyoto agreement. Internal EU talks have predictably fallen apart several times, with deadline after deadline passing. Carsten Volkery, "Europa will Weltmeister im Klimaschutz werden" [Europe wants to become the world champion of climate protection], *Der Spiegel*, March 9, 2007, at www.spiegel.de/politik/deutschland/0,1518,470889,00 .html (accessed September 17, 2008).

59. Secretary-General Ban Ki-moon, "Remarks at Town Hall Meeting on Climate Change," U.N. News Center, June 29, 2008, at www.un.org/apps/news/infocus/sg speeches/statments_full.asp?statID = 278 (accessed September 18, 2008).

The United States and other countries resisting arbitrary GHG emission restrictions successfully pushed back to make any successor agreement to Kyoto an improvement. For instance, the United States, Japan, and Canada have opposed further unrealistic commitments, called into question the hard-cap approach, and proposed abandoning Kyoto's 1990 baseline year. However, pressure to continue the failed Kyoto Process and structure is pervasive throughout the U.N. system and the NGO community and led to harsh criticism of past U.S. efforts to negotiate alternatives to that framework. Indications are that the Obama administration is sympathetic to this criticism and will retreat from past U.S. policy.

U.S. "Unilateralism"

Participating in the Kyoto Process has done little to advance U.S. policy interests. On the contrary, engaging in extended negotiations has already caused great harm by encouraging the process to continue. By initially dignifying the Kyoto Process by agreeing to its terms in 1997 and then signing the pact in 1998, the United States set in motion and lent legitimacy to a counterproductive approach for addressing international environmental issues. Indeed, going forward with Kyoto or a similar agreement would also have significant implications for U.S. law and the international trading system by opening the door to frivolous international lawsuits and justifying trade barriers on environmental grounds.

U.S. ratification of the Kyoto Protocol would arguably elevate the agreement's respective rights and responsibilities to a "law of nations" or otherwise expose the U.S. under customary international law. U.S. ratification would formalize U.S. acceptance of particular standards of behavior and responsibility regarding GHGs in accordance with Kyoto's "common but differentiated responsibilities." This is a significant milestone in international law,[60] surpassing the limited stature of a signed-but-not-ratified agreement.[61]

It would also set the stage for untold legal turmoil. For example, if the United States ratified Kyoto or a similar agreement, U.S. courts would be far more likely to allow plaintiffs to use the 1789 Alien Tort Claims Act as

---

60. The Constitution recognized "a law of nations" in granting Congress the power to remedy offenses against it. U.S. Constitution, art. 4, sec. 8.

61. The Vienna Convention on the Law of Treaties obligates a state to refrain from acts that would defeat the object and purpose of a treaty it has signed. Ironically, the United States has signed but not ratified the Vienna Convention, but this provision is generally considered customary international law, and the United States has observed it in practice.

a vehicle for filing claims of climate-related damages against U.S. citizens.[62] Plaintiffs from around the world could be granted primary jurisdiction in American federal courts for tort claims for damages allegedly caused by U.S. emissions, such as damage from severe weather, increases in sea levels, desertification, and other climatic and geophysical phenomena that the IPCC ties to GHG emissions.

A binding treaty or accepted customary international law on GHG emissions would also create tension in the international trading system. For example, the World Trade Organization claims its "overriding purpose is to help trade flow as freely as possible" by eliminating barriers to increased trade in goods and services. Further, the "WTO does not permit any member to impose its own policies extraterritorially under the threat of trade bans . . . and it does not permit members of the WTO to discriminate amongst each other in trade policies."[63] However, three multilateral environmental agreements (the Basel Convention, Montreal Protocol, and CITES) and the potential restrictions under Kyoto oblige their parties to use trade bans to enforce the treaties' environmental objectives. The sole relevant WTO ruling indicates that trade restrictions for the environmental protection might be deemed acceptable, depending on how the protections are designed.[64]

This opens an opportunity for nations intent on forcing the U.S. to adhere to GHG restrictions. Kyoto has already been invoked as an excuse for imposing trade barriers in the name of saving the environment. French, Italian, and EU officials have threatened to submit WTO complaints against the United States or to impose border adjustments on U.S.-manufactured imports.[65] These claims would be based on the argument that the United States unfairly subsidizes domestic manufacturing by not imposing higher taxes to incorporate the societal costs (e.g., climate change) allegedly caused by energy use. Viability of such claims will be uncertain until the WTO rules on the matter directly or a Kyoto successor agreement resolves the conflict, but pressure is increasing to allow "climate" protectionism under trade agreements or a Kyoto successor pact.

---

62. See Christopher C. Horner, *The Perils of 'Soft' and Unratified Treaty Commitments: The Emerging Campaign to 'Enforce' U.S. Acknowledgements Made in and under the Rio Treaty and Kyoto Protocol Using Customary International Law, WTO, Alien Tort Claims Act, and NEPA* (Competitive Enterprise Institute, July 2003), at http://cei.org/pdf/3297.pdf (accessed September 18, 2008), esp. 77–90.

63. Alan Oxley, "Environmental Protection and the WTO," in *Sustainable Development: Promoting Progress or Perpetuating Poverty*, ed. Julian Morris (London: Profile Books, 2002), 7.

64. Oxley, "Environmental Protection," 103–22.

65. See, generally, Alan Beattie, "Green Barricade," *Financial Times*, January 24, 2008, at www.ft.com/cms/s/0/429375de-ca1e-11dc-b5dc-000077b07658.html (accessed September 18, 2008).

Unacceptable Compromises

An additional peril of the United States ratifying the Kyoto Protocol or a similar framework that insists on universal participation is the tendency of international negotiations to use bait-and-switch tactics. The consensus language of the Kyoto Protocol exemplifies this phenomenon because it lacks, by necessity or design, sufficient detail to make it effective, clear, and transparent in its effect. Subsequent negotiations (and breakdowns) affirmed that even though Kyoto purported to be an enforceable agreement worthy of Senate consent and U.S. ratification, the details required to make it so were actually left to be filled in later. Essentially, the United States was expected to sign a blank check in terms of how it could fulfill the promise and the consequences in the event it failed to do so, with the particulars to be decided after the United States had signed away most of its negotiating leverage and was under the magnifying glass of the rest of the world. Many parties to Kyoto were determined to force the United States to accept the most onerous specifics possible once it had officially accepted the object, purpose, and necessity of the agreement.

Compromises are inherent in treaty negotiations, but the Kyoto construct encourages such bait-and-switch tactics. It also sets the stage for isolating and criticizing the United States as acting "unilaterally" when negotiations yield unacceptable terms and the United States refuses to accede to the desires of other nations. This is abetted by homegrown internationalists in the United States. For example, the then minority leader Tom Daschle (D-SD) criticized the Bush administration for its "unilateral" foreign policy in an October 2002 interview, citing its opposition to ratifying the Kyoto Protocol as an example, even though Daschle opposed the treaty in the Senate in 1997.[66]

The practical outcome of such criticism is not to clarify the threshold at which U.S. actions become unilateral. Instead, it constrains U.S. decision making and pressures the United States to engage in negotiations even to the detriment of U.S. interests. This pressure explains why the United States has remained entangled in the failed Kyoto Process despite President Bill Clinton, President George W. Bush, and a unanimous U.S. Senate all stating that the U.S. would not ratify any global warming treaty that did not include binding commitments on leading developing-country emitters.[67]

---

66. U.S. Senate, roll call vote on S. Res. 98, 105th Cong., 1st Sess., July 25, 1997, at www.senate.gov/legislative/LIS/roll_call_lists/roll_call_vote_cfm.cfm?congress=105&session=1&vote=00205 (accessed November 18, 2008).

67. See CNN.com, "Clinton Hails Global Warming Pact," December 11, 1997, at www.cnn.com/ALLPOLITICS/1997/12/11/kyoto (accessed September 18, 2008), and "Bush Firm over Kyoto Stance," March 29, 2001, at http://edition.cnn.com/2001/US/03/29/schroeder.bush/index.html (accessed September 18, 2008).

EMERGING ALTERNATIVE APPROACHES

To escape this politically charged environment, which undermines constructive efforts to address environmental issues with legitimate multinational dimensions, the United States and other countries must break with
the bad precedents of recent decades and avoid further concessions to the
intransigent constituencies created by the U.N.'s approach of universal participation and consensus. This will not be easy. The NGO community in
particular will strongly oppose any effort to restrict its growing influence
over international negotiations and its access to funding.

However, the United States is not alone. Canada, China, and India have
emerged as key partners, and anecdotal evidence indicates that other
nations, including some European nations, are increasingly cognizant of
the problems with the current process.

In the past few years, the ground seems to have shifted on global warming, the most high-profile and highly politicized environmental issue. As
host of the 2005 Gleneagles summit, even Kyotophile Prime Minister Tony
Blair of the U.K. placed climate change on the agenda and invited key
developing countries to participate in what is inarguably an alternate
forum:

> Blair was the author of the G8-plus-five process at Gleneagles in 2005, an
> attempt to get a small group of the major carbon emitters to come to an agree-
> ment on how to address climate change. . . .
>   Blair stressed he was not opposed to the UN process, but in those smaller
> forums "you are more likely to get people to do some hard negotiating instead
> of 100 countries to deal with, since you have the major emitters. In . . . the G20
> and the Major Emitters Group [Major Economies Process] there is no central
> secretariat, which is why I have convened these different experts, and had good
> input from experts in every country."[68]

This process has continued to advance as the Kyoto Process's weaknesses
have become more evident.

President George W. Bush engineered the Major Economies Process on
Energy Security and Climate Change, a separate, overlapping initiative to
bring together the largest emitters. Representatives of the United States and
sixteen other major emitting nations attended the first Major Economies
Meeting in September 2007.[69] The Bush administration also launched the

---

68. Patrick Wintour, "It Has to Be Politically Doable," *Guardian*, March 14, 2008,
at   www.guardian.co.uk/politics/2008/mar/14/greenpolitics.tonyblair   (accessed
September 18, 2008).

69. U.S. Department of State, Oceans and International Environmental and Scientific Affairs, "Attendee Participant List," Major Economies Meeting I, September
28, 2007, at www.state.gov/g/oes/climate/mem/92889.htm (accessed November
15, 2008).

Asia–Pacific Partnership on Clean Development and Climate (CDP), which attracted Australia and Japan (states covered by Kyoto) and China, India, and South Korea (exempt major emitters). From the beginning, these efforts achieved what Kyoto could not: bringing the major parties to the table without the condition precedent of Kyoto-style exemption. Instead, these parties were driven by a desire to find common ground on which to proceed toward a constructive enterprise that would actually reduce or, at minimum, avert avoidable growth in GHG emissions, without disruptive influences of the hanger-on industries, ancillary rent-seeking nations, self-interested NGOs, and U.N. bureaucracies.

Through the Asia–Pacific Partnership, the United States and other countries have agreed to facilitate country-to-country and company-to-country steps to remove barriers to using advanced technology to address environmental issues, instead of rationing emissions and creating broad schemes for rent seekers to profit from. For example, if a suspect record on respecting intellectual property is the major hurdle to deploying a low-emission technology, the CDP's aim is to alleviate the specific concerns and deploy the technology. Admittedly, this is still done with taxpayer-funded aid, but at least it is more of a technology transfer than a direct wealth transfer and therefore poses fewer moral hazards and can better address the purported problem.

While environmental groups deride the CDP as insufficient because it abandons the pretense of "binding" hard emission caps, it is superior to Kyoto if only because its agenda is realistic. In addition, by focusing on potentially covered major-emitter parties willing to buck the Kyoto Process, the CDP has expanded involvement well beyond the "global" Kyoto pact. (While Kyoto covers thirty-five countries, these include many minor emitters such as Iceland, Slovenia, Slovakia, Lithuania, Latvia, Estonia, and Romania.) By contrast, the CDP "involves countries that account for about half of the world's population and more than half of the world's economy, energy use, and GHG emissions [building] on existing multilateral climate initiatives."[70] After a false start under the leftist government of Paul Martin, Canada came on board as a full member, and discussions have centered on whether to expand the group further.[71]

---

70. U.S. Department of State, Office of the Press Secretary, "The Asia–Pacific Partnership on Clean Development and Climate: Implementation, Action, and Results," January 11, 2006, at http://georgewbush-whitehouse.archives.gov/news/re leases/2006/01/20060111-8.html (accessed May 25, 2009).

71. That conversation triggers several key strategic considerations. For example, Poland and the Czech Republic are possible partners, both rich in coal and dependent on it for energy. For historical reasons, both countries deeply mistrust Brussels's pleas for them to rely on Russian gas instead of domestic coal. Governmental representatives of both countries have privately expressed great interest in the proc-

The July 2008 G-8 meeting also represented a welcome move away from the U.N.-centric process. The United States has laid out a superior approach for addressing international environmental issues through the Major Economies Process instead of compounding the mistakes of Kyoto after 2012.[72] Strong backing of the U.S. position by Japan and Canada led the G-8 to offer a more realistic strategy to address GHG emissions in any post-2012 agreement. The summit limited itself to hortatory calls for reducing emissions by 50 percent by 2050—although the parties could not agree on a baseline year—with no new calls for deeper, binding promises. This represents a step back from the Kyoto rhetoric. Even European representatives at the July G-8 meeting agreed to demote climate below pressing issues such as spikes in food prices.[73]

It is instructive that European leaders had the courage to deviate from the Kyoto mantra in the G-8 forum, but their environment ministers are significantly less bold in the politically charged, rent-seeking atmosphere of U.N.-led talks. Regardless, the G-8 stance bled into the Kyoto Process in 2009, contributing to the likely stalemate, which would be a victory. The United States should build on this extra-U.N. model to address future international environmental issues.

THE PATH FORWARD

International discourse on environmental issues is often at cross-purposes with the practicalities of resolving them. The obsessive drive to address international environmental problems—real, imagined, or exaggerated—solely through the U.N. lessens the effectiveness of proposed responses. It enables indirectly involved parties to hold discussions and proposals hostage to tangential issues, such as wealth transfers to developing countries. It also allows some countries to game the system to avoid shouldering burdens matching their rhetoric.

By agreeing to address international environmental issues exclusively through the U.N., the United States places its negotiators in a position of weakness. Influential NGOs, nations with little direct stake in the outcome

---

ess. If either partners with the CDP, that would fracture the EU's negotiating stance and end the Kyoto stranglehold on international climate policy.

72. See "Bush Holds Joint Press Conference with E.U. Leaders," *Washington Post*, June 10, 2008, at www.washingtonpost.com/wp-dyn/content/story/2008/06/10/ST2008061001522.html (accessed September 18, 2008).

73. For a description of 2008 G-8 outcome on global warming, as agreed on in advance at the June ministerial meeting, see Government of Japan, Council for Science and Technology Policy, "The G8 Science and Technology Ministers' Meeting Chair's Summary," June 15, 2008, at www8.cao.go.jp/cstp/english/others/g8summary-e.pdf (accessed September 18, 2008).

of negotiations, and the U.N. manipulate the process to satisfy their vested financial and professional interests. The end result is often an ineffective, costly initiative that unnecessarily demands that the United States cede control over some element of its own economic and individual liberties. To break this cycle, the United States must advance a firm, new policy that defines which types of pacts the United States will pursue and which environmental entanglements it will avoid. Specifically, the United States should:

Preserve and defend the treaty process

Treaty commitments inherently cede some level of sovereignty by permitting other nations input into decisions that otherwise would exclusively be made by the U.S. government. Sometimes treaties transfer power, resources, and/or responsibility to a supranational authority or establish processes without the safeguards, checks, and balances of the U.S. system. Thus, pursuing treaties is a serious responsibility that should not be undertaken recklessly; this is why the Founding Fathers required that two-thirds of the Senate consent to a treaty prior to ratification.[74]

Environmental advocates have long been frustrated by the inability of various international environmental agreements, such as the Kyoto Protocol, to pass Senate muster, and they are seeking to avoid the supermajority requirement by employing executive agreements instead. "Unlike treaties, which require the advice and consent of two-thirds of the Senate, executive agreements are entered into either solely by the President based on previously delegated constitutional, treaty, or statutory authorities, or by the President and Congress together pursuant to a new statute."[75]

This approach has apparently found favor with President Barack Obama's administration. In the case of a global warming treaty, such a "fast track" amounts to simple majorities of both houses of Congress granting the administration, at its request, authority to enter into an international agreement that will later require implementing legislation. As proposed in theory, Congress would be signing a blank check of negotiating authority that would essentially force Congress to later implement a pact regardless of the content negotiated. This would not only greatly diminish Congress's political leverage, but by outsourcing that power to the executive branch, Congress would abdicate its responsibility to legislate in the interests of its constituents.

---

74. U.S. Constitution, art. 2, sec. 2.

75. Nigel Purvis, "Paving the Way for U.S. Climate Leadership: The Case for Executive Agreements and Climate Protection Authority," Resources for the Future (Discussion Paper 08–09, April 15, 2008), 1, at www.rff.org/News/Features/Publishing Images/DP-08-09.pdf (accessed October 24, 2008).

Although executive and congressional–executive agreements are well-established tools in certain contexts (e.g., trade agreements), the proposal to use them to make international environmental agreements—particularly one requiring energy taxation or other suppression—is advanced not because this is inherently a more sensible way of proceeding on the issue, but because it circumvents a decade of demonstrated inability to obtain sufficient support from elected representatives of the American people. It would undermine the system of checks and balances in the U.S. government and mock constitutional intent.

Along these same lines, the United States should end the practice of leaving signed but unratified treaties unresolved for decades on end. The Vienna Convention and customary international law state that the signatories should not undertake actions inconsistent with signed treaties, which gives such documents influence over U.S. foreign and domestic policy even though they have not been ratified. If the Senate has not given its advice and consent within a reasonable period, the United States should, as a standard practice, notify the treaty depository or other relevant authority that the United States has no intention of ratifying the treaty and no longer has legal obligations arising from its signature.[76]

Minimize involvement with U.N. environmental bodies

The various U.N. organizations expressly dedicated to environmental issues occasionally serve useful roles, albeit in limited circumstances. For example, UNESCO retains some legitimate functions, despite adding a modern environmentalist portfolio. Other bodies, such as the UNFCCC, should be supported on an ad hoc basis by nations that lack capacity on relevant projects. However, the positive aspects of these bodies seldom exceed their detrimental or counterproductive impacts. Any U.S. involvement should be undertaken with the limited expectations and commitment because of the long-standing and widespread lack of accountability and transparency in U.N. bodies.[77] The best course for the United States would be to cut most funding in favor of targeted support to specific projects that are deemed useful.

---

76. Kim R. Holmes, *Liberty's Best Hope: American Leadership for the 21st Century* (Washington, DC: Heritage Foundation, 2008), 118.

77. As with many other U.N. bodies, the UNFCCC has been subject to mismanagement. The UNFCCC's board of auditors has taken it to task for lack of transparency in disclosing its expenditures, failing to account for millions of dollars, resisting an internal audit, and failing to adopt fraud detection and protection plans. See U.N. Framework Convention on Climate Change, "Audited Financial Statements for the Biennium 2004–2005," FCCC/SBI/2006/14, November 2006, at http://unfccc.int/resource/docs/2006/sbi/eng/14.pdf (accessed September 18, 2008).

Other organizations do not merit support because of their ideological agendas, such as UNEP's actions on the Convention on Biodiversity. The CBD instructs its parties to "consider the need for and modalities of a protocol" regulating "the safe transfer, handling and use of any living modified organism resulting from biotechnology that may have an adverse effect" on biological diversity. In 1993, a scientific panel convened by UNEP recommended against establishing such a protocol, concluding that "a protocol would, for no clear purpose: (1) divert scientific and administrative resources from higher priority needs; and (2) delay the diffusion of techniques beneficial to biological diversity, and essential to the progress of human health and sustainable agriculture."[78] Yet UNEP ignored this expert advice and proceeded with negotiations that culminated in the 2000 Cartagena Protocol on Biosafety, which predictably failed to address these problems. The United States would be better served by completely severing ties with such organizations.

Explore alternative coalitions and efforts

The U.N. practice of guaranteeing every nation an equal voice in negotiations regardless of its exposure to the resulting policies and affording nongovernmental interests formal or semiformal roles impedes negotiation of focused, effective agreements to address international environmental issues. This practice is so deeply embedded in the U.N. that any U.N.-led discussions will likely suffer from it. This militates against using a U.N. global approach to resolve international environmental problems. Instead, the relevant parties need to confer and act outside of the U.N.

The U.S. effort to address global warming outside of the failed Kyoto Process offers a sound model. The U.S.-led Major Economies Process has proven to be a superior approach for bringing key parties together to agree to realistic, achievable steps and is a sound strategy to avoid compounding the Kyoto mistake after 2012.[79] The CDP is a complementary effort to expand the group and has likewise made progress without the problems inherent in a U.N.-led process.

The Obama administration should build on this model. For instance, it

---

78. U.N. Environment Program, "Report of Panel IV: Consideration of the Need for Modalities of Protocol Setting Out Appropriate Procedures Including, in Particular, Advance Informed Agreements in the Field of the Safe Transfer, Handling and Use of Any Living Modified Organism Resulting from Biotechnology Diversity, UNEP Arguments for a Protocol Pursuant to Article 19.3 of the Convention I 42(ii), at II," U.N. Doc. UNEP/Bio.Div/Panels/Int.4, 1993, quoted in Thomas P. Redick et al., "Private Legal Mechanisms for Regulating the Risks of Genetically Modified Organisms: An Alternative Path Within the Biosafety Protocol," *Environmental Lawyer* 4 (1997): 37.

79. See "Bush Holds Joint Press Conference with E.U. Leaders."

could include individual, interested European nations in the CDP. Superficial impediments, such as the fact that Europe is neither Asian nor Pacific, could be removed by dropping "Asia–Pacific" from its name, leaving a geographically unconstrained Partnership on Clean Development and Climate to effectively address climate change globally.

The Major Economies Process and the CDP offer useful, real-world examples of how nations can address international environmental problems outside of the U.N. system more quickly, effectively, and efficiently. The United States should use these successes as a model for addressing other environmental issues worthy of international cooperation and action.

Working through forums outside of the U.N. system also reduces the sway of NGOs that increasingly influence negotiations. The groups and their constituencies would retain their influence with individual governments, but be denied their current unwarranted quasi-official role at the negotiating table.

Limit negotiating parties to key nations

In negotiations to address an international environmental (or any other) issue, the incentives, constituencies, and alliances that could undermine an effective negotiation increase with the number of extraneous parties participating in the talks. This reality is a powerful argument in favor of limiting the number of negotiating parties in multilateral environmental agreements to those potentially subject to the agreement's terms and restrictions. In the context of a purportedly binding agreement, including only necessary parties to an agreement is the approach most likely to yield a focused, effective outcome.

Claims that including only a core group of countries unfairly excludes poor developing nations, which could be affected by any decisions, should be taken with a grain of salt. The Kyoto Process is dysfunctional in part because it includes countries that have insufficient direct interest in the matter to assume some of the core group's burdens in addressing it.

In such an arrangement, other countries would be free to form their own group, comment on actions taken by the core group, and even observe negotiations.[80] However, these countries would be granted a say over the obligations of other countries only if they accept restrictions on their own activities that are legitimately of like kind and quality.

---

80. This may prove wise or further folly, but the Bush administration worked behind the scenes with the UNFCCC to coordinate CDP efforts under the U.N. group's auspices. This arrangement is rhetorical and informal, may be revoked at any time, and looks increasingly tenuous as anxiety rises among Kyoto supporters over their project's being supplanted.

Accommodate economic growth

The Kyoto Process has also exposed the insidious nature of absolute caps on nontoxic and nonhazardous substances. These caps, particularly on carbon dioxide, are thinly veiled efforts to restrict energy use and/or constrain economic growth. When applied to a limited number of parties, they create a wealth-transfer regime, if only through the outsourcing of growth from covered parties.

The United States should insist that any standards be sectoral (e.g., steel) and/or use a metric of efficiency or energy/carbon intensity specific to particular industries. These are more viable options because they accommodate economic growth, but they will be unacceptable to most environmentalists for precisely that reason.

Oppose the precautionary principle

The United States should do nothing that would formally accept the precautionary principle. The precautionary principle perniciously shifts the burden of proof for restricting a substance or activity from demonstrating that it causes harm to proving that it will cause no harm. This leads countries to impede approval of products based on unsubstantiated objections from the antigrowth, antipopulation, and antitechnology wings of the environmental movement.

In addition, the precautionary principle and the treaties endorsing it provide the EU and other countries with an excuse to shirk their GATT and WTO obligations to base trade regulations (e.g., sanitary and phytosanitary) on demonstrated scientific concerns. Some countries now hope to extend the precautionary principle in one form or another to carbon emissions, in essence promoting "carbon protectionism" under which countries refusing to adopt restrictions (e.g., EU energy taxes or emission regimes) are prohibited from Europe's markets.

Trade and scientific innovation are the lifeblood of economic growth and future prosperity, and GHGs are simply the latest excuse for protectionism. The United States should challenge the application of the precautionary principle in international treaties and its use as a nontariff trade barrier.

Observing these principles would greatly minimize the downsides of multilateral efforts to address international environmental issues. Of course, such steps will have only limited effect unless the United States strictly adheres to these principles and is willing to walk away if negotiations go offtrack. Precisely when such a point is reached will differ by the occasion, but any reasonable standard would require that negotiations expressly begin with an objective that advances clearly articulated U.S. interests. This condition inherently rules out any process like Kyoto, in which the United States was called on to accept and even ratify an agreement that was still so broad and ambiguous that the political, policy, and economic ramifications of implementing it could not be predicted.

Similarly, the United States should pursue only agreements with parties that face equal or similar obligations. This principle was articulated in the unanimously adopted Byrd-Hagel resolution, which set the conditions for the Senate's support of the Kyoto Protocol.

Absent such conditions, further U.S. participation only encourages negotiations to continue along counterproductive paths. Indeed, the incentive of U.S. involvement may be the leverage necessary to correct missteps.

CONCLUSION

Obsessive insistence on maintaining a U.N. monopoly on efforts to address transnational environmental issues and to include all parties—great and small, public and private, industry and (particularly) NGO—has crippled the ability of international environmental negotiations to reach effective agreements that address international matters.

In recent years, the Kyoto Process has illustrated the folly of the "global" approach. Even if the Kyoto Protocol were implemented perfectly for fifty years, the agreement would reduce projected warming by an undetectable 0.07 degrees Celsius. Yet the U.N. and NGO industries require obeisance to the process, regardless of whether it will achieve its express objectives. This is a strong indication that other, unexpressed objectives may be driving the process.

The Kyoto experience demonstrates the significant downsides of the United States continuing along this path. When the United States agrees to cede control and oversight to the U.N. in these matters, as opposed to allowing a core group of nations with the most at stake to maintain control, it places its negotiators in a position of weakness and threatens its own interests.

The problems plaguing the current system do not necessitate condemning all international efforts to address environmental issues. In many cases, environmental matters with international implications merit multilateral engagement. It is the form of the multilateral engagement that has proven singularly problematic. Limited, focused processes like the CDP and the Major Economies Process are superior to the U.N. template for the simple reason that they are less vulnerable to manipulation by third parties and more likely to achieve their objectives. Any commitments, however, must not circumvent the Article II treaty process, as some now recommend.

If the United States is to pursue international environmental agreements that support rather than undermine its interests, it must fundamentally reevaluate its policies regarding international environmental issues, multilateral environmental treaties, and international environmental organizations. It must also reshape its relationship with the various governments, supranational bodies, and NGOs that have used these issues to promote ineffective, costly treaties that advance their unrelated agendas more than they address actual environmental problems.

5

Human Wrongs

Why the U.N. Is Ill Equipped to Champion Human Rights

Brett D. Schaefer and Steven Groves

Since the birth of the United Nations, protecting and advancing fundamental human rights has been one of its primary objectives and responsibilities. The drafters of the U.N. Charter included a pledge by member states "to reaffirm faith in fundamental human rights, in the dignity and worth of the human person, in the equal rights of men and women."[1] U.N. treaties and declarations, such as the Universal Declaration of Human Rights, which the U.N. General Assembly passed in 1948, form the core of international standards for human rights. Sadly, adoption of the Universal Declaration has been in many ways the high-water mark of U.N. efforts to promote human rights. As explained and illustrated in this chapter, the U.N.'s record in persuading member states to honor, enforce, and protect fundamental human rights has been gravely disappointing.

For nearly six decades, the U.N. Commission on Human Rights (CHR) epitomized this failure. Despite being the premier U.N. human rights body charged with reviewing the human rights performance of U.N. member states and promoting human rights around the world, the CHR devolved into a forum that human rights abusers used to block criticism of their own conduct.

The CHR's disrepute grew so great that former U.N. secretary-general Kofi

---

1. Charter of the United Nations, preamble.

131

Annan acknowledged in 2005, "We have reached a point at which the Commission's declining credibility has cast a shadow on the reputation of the United Nations system as a whole, and where piecemeal reforms will not be enough."[2] After lengthy deliberations and negotiations, the General Assembly voted in March 2006 to replace the CHR with a new Human Rights Council (HRC).[3] Regrettably, during the negotiations, many basic reforms and standards that had been proposed to ensure that the HRC would not repeat the CHR's mistakes failed to gain the necessary support in the General Assembly.[4] Moreover, nothing was done to address the problem of allocating seats based on regional groupings that had made the CHR vulnerable to manipulation through regional bloc voting and influential groups like the Organization of the Islamic Conference (OIC). On the contrary, it exacerbated the problem. As a result, in its first three years, the HRC has proven itself to be a weak and ineffectual instrument in promoting fundamental human rights—a record that is unlikely to be improved by having the U.S. on the HRC starting in 2009.

Other parts of the U.N. have been slightly more effective in promoting basic human rights. Each year, the Third Committee of the General Assembly—which deals with social, humanitarian, and cultural issues—musters enough support to pass a handful of resolutions condemning the human rights practices in some of the world's most despotic regimes, such as Burma and North Korea. The treaty bodies in charge of implementing various multilateral conventions have, if unevenly, chastised nations for failing to meet their treaty obligations. Individual human rights experts called "special rapporteurs" have also succeeded in highlighting human rights

---

2. Kofi Annan, "Secretary-General's Address to the Commission on Human Rights," Office of the Spokesman for the U.N. Secretary-General, April 7, 2005, at www.un.org/apps/sg/sgstats.asp?nid = 1388 (accessed November 21, 2008). See also Mark P. Lagon, "The U.N. Commission on Human Rights: Protector or Accomplice?" testimony before the Subcommittee on Africa, Global Human Rights, and International Operations, Committee on International Relations, U.S. House of Representatives, April 19, 2005, at www.state.gov/p/io/rls/rm/44983.htm (accessed November 21, 2008).

3. Press release, "General Assembly Establishes New Human Rights Council by Vote of 170 in Favour to 4 Against, with 3 Abstentions," U.N. General Assembly, March 15, 2006, at www.un.org/News/Press/docs/2006/ga10449.doc.htm (accessed November 21, 2008).

4. For more information, see Brett D. Schaefer, "The United Nations Human Rights Council: Repeating Past Mistakes," Heritage Foundation *Lecture*, no. 964 (September 19, 2006), at www.heritage.org/Research/WorldwideFreedom/hl964 .cfm, and "The United Nations Human Rights Council: A Disastrous First Year and Discouraging Signs for Reform," Heritage Foundation *Lecture*, no. 1042 (September 5, 2007), at www.heritage.org/Research/InternationalOrganizations/hl1042.cfm.

violations, however irregularly, even though rogue regimes often prevent them from even visiting the countries to do their assessments.

Regrettably, even these institutions have been undermined by the weaknesses that hobbled the CHR and continue to plague the HRC: the ability of nations that do not observe human rights to manipulate the system and vulnerability to political manipulation designed to undermine their focus. For instance, while the Third Committee can muster support for resolutions condemning a few notorious human rights violators, most violators escape even cursory criticism. The treaty bodies have abused their authority by reinterpreting the texts of their respective treaties in ways never envisioned when the treaties were ratified. Some treaty bodies repeatedly castigate nations for failing to enact domestic legislation to enforce norms as interpreted by the treaty body, whether or not these norms were explicitly expressed in the treaty. Similarly, some special rapporteurs have tended to engage in polemics and to push political agendas rather than focus on their mandates.

ˋ Another troubling issue is unprecedented influence that nongovernmental organizations (NGOs) have gained over the human rights debate in the U.N. system in recent years. Their efforts have both enhanced and debased the effectiveness and focus of the U.N. on human rights. NGOs serve a valuable role—often a brave and dangerous task—by providing local input and factual reports on the human rights situations in countries that discourage such scrutiny. NGOs clearly inform the human rights process in the U.N., which frequently is unable or unwilling to confront human rights problems. However, the NGOs often seek to use their influence to force states to observe or acknowledge controversial or disputed human rights norms to the detriment of advancing widely recognized, fundamental human rights. Worse, countries that place little value on civil and political rights have worked with sympathetic NGOs to successfully conflate civil and political rights with economic, social, and cultural "rights" in a manner that muddles the obligations of the state and disregards a necessary hierarchy of rights.

Quite simply, the U.N. system has proven to be a flawed, at times even counterproductive, vehicle for advancing fundamental human rights. The prospects for improved performance in the future are slim due to the carefully preserved principle of universal membership for all nations regardless of their human rights records. This undermines the effectiveness of the organization and distracts the focus of human rights bodies toward secondary or tertiary issues.

While working outside the U.N. system is potentially more effective, such efforts have generally been undermined by broad adherence to the idea that the U.N. is the most appropriate and legitimate vehicle to advance human rights. This view is more than incorrect; it has shielded states that violate human rights from scrutiny and concerted international action. Member states routinely use their influence in the organization and its human rights bodies to blunt efforts to hold them accountable for their human rights failures.

The best hope for advancing human rights is to reevaluate the U.N.-centric approach to promoting human rights, eliminate the redundant or ineffective parts of the U.N. human rights apparatus, and work with states committed to advancing civil and political human rights to create a new alternative multilateral body that will effectively and consistently undertake joint policies and actions to advance these principles.

THE FOUNDATIONS OF HUMAN RIGHTS

The history of human rights is the history of the relationship between the nation-state and the individuals subject to the authority of the nation-state. At the core of this relationship is an evolving understanding that individuals possess universal rights and freedoms of themselves. These rights are not awarded by government and cannot lawfully be abridged by government. The development of modern government is in many ways the story of the development of legal and customary constraints and restrictions on government authority to protect these universal rights and other rights deemed desirable by society. The progression of this relationship can be traced back to antiquity. For instance, the Code of Hammurabi listed crimes, guidelines for conduct, and means for settling common disputes. Greek and Roman philosophy and legal traditions explored the nature of societies and behavior and codified them into legal traditions that form the basis for modern Western legal traditions.

Philosophers, both in antiquity and during the Enlightenment, articulated the concept that certain rights—often referred to as "natural rights"—exist even when not enforced by a government. These include the rights to life and liberty and are distinct from legal privileges or responsibilities that governments can establish and enforce, such as access to education and health care. This concept was critical in establishing wide recognition of the modern concept of human rights and freedoms.

The need to translate philosophical theories and vague definitions of natural law or natural rights into practical guidelines for governance and laws led to such documents as the Magna Carta, the U.S. Constitution and Bill of Rights, and the French Declaration of the Rights of Man. These documents sought to clearly define the respective rights, authorities, and obligations of government and the governed. Of particular importance is the idea expressed in the U.S. Declaration of Independence that individuals have rights independent of government—"We hold these truths to be self-evident, that all men are created equal, that they are endowed by their Creator with certain unalienable Rights, that among these are Life, Liberty and the pursuit of Happiness"[5]—and that, if government violates these rights, it negates its legitimacy.

The idea of natural rights, including the right to liberty, also contributed to the broadening appeal of the antislavery movement of the early nineteenth century and the development of universally recognized customary international law condemning the slave trade. Agreements among nations articulating rules of warfare (known as "international humanitarian law"), such as those expressed in the Geneva Convention of 1864, extended from a national to an international obligation the idea of natural rights and the notion that states should constrain their freedom of action in certain areas out of respect for the rights of noncombatants. These efforts built on and codified long-standing traditions regarding appropriate rules and conduct during war dating back to the code of chivalry and customs regarding neutrality.

The concept of international obligations and rules of conduct in war were expanded at various points throughout the twentieth century. Acts of genocidal violence on populations, such as the slaughter of Armenians in World War I and the massacre of Assyrians in Iran in the 1930s, received increasing scrutiny and criticism in the years leading up to World War II. The Holocaust firmly ingrained the unacceptability of these crimes and led directly to the drafting and entry into force of the Genocide Convention and an unprecedented criminal prosecution in the Nuremburg trials.

Acceptance of the idea that certain crimes were so heinous that they constituted violations of international law bolstered the notion that governments had obligations to provide their citizens certain rights and privileges, and when nations met to draft the U.N. Charter, they included a mandate for the organization to promote and protect human rights internationally. Thus, the notion that the U.N. should promote and propagate observance of "international human rights law" became firmly entrenched in the organization and paved the way for a bureaucratic and legal expansion of internationally recognized human rights into the system.

THE POOR RECORD OF THE
U.N. HUMAN RIGHTS SYSTEM

The U.N.'s mandate to promote and protect human rights was the result of a political compromise to resolve two competing principles: promotion and protection of human rights and the sovereign right of nonintervention

---

5. Declaration of Independence, par. 2.

into a nation's internal affairs. While not inherently conflicting, these two principles come into frequent conflict. Indeed, both the United Kingdom and the Soviet Union resisted U.S. proposals to include promotion of basic human rights among the purposes of the U.N. and objected to proposals to empower the organization to intervene in the human rights practices of member states on the basis that such issues are domestic affairs and that intervention would violate national sovereignty.[6] As a result of this disagreement, the U.N. Charter provides for only a limited mandate to promote human rights, compared to the Charter's mandate to protect international peace and security:

- The preamble states, "We the peoples of the United Nations determined . . . to reaffirm faith in fundamental human rights, in the dignity and worth of the human person, in the equal rights of men and women and of nations large and small."
- Article 1 states that the purposes of the U.N. include developing "friendly relations among nations based on respect for the principle of equal rights and self-determination of peoples" and "promoting and encouraging respect for human rights and for fundamental freedoms for all without distinction as to race, sex, language, or religion."
- Article 13 charges the General Assembly with initiating studies and making recommendations for the purpose of "assisting in the realization of human rights and fundamental freedoms for all without distinction as to race, sex, language, or religion."
- Article 55 charges the U.N. with promoting "universal respect for, and observance of, human rights and fundamental freedoms for all without distinction as to race, sex, language, or religion," based on the premise that "the creation of conditions of stability and well-being which are necessary for peaceful and friendly relations among nations [is] based on respect for the principle of equal rights and self-determination of peoples." Article 56 pledges member states to take "joint and separate action in co-operation with the Organization for the achievement of the purposes set forth in Article 55."
- Article 62 authorizes the U.N. Economic and Social Council (ECOSOC) to "make or initiate studies and reports with respect to international economic, social, cultural, educational, health, and related matters and may make recommendations with respect to any such matters to the General Assembly to the Members of the United Nations, and to the specialized agencies concerned," to "make recommendations for the purpose of promoting respect for, and observance

---

6. For instance, see Evan Luard, *A History of the United Nations*, vol. 1, *The Years of Western Domination, 1945–1955* (New York: St. Martin's Press, 1982), 31–32.

of, human rights and fundamental freedoms for all," and to "call, in accordance with the rules prescribed by the United Nations, international conferences on matters falling within its competence."

Consistent with this limited role, at least compared to its charge to maintain international peace and security, the Charter does not specifically authorize the U.N. to take coercive action to enforce human rights, except in instances that "endanger the maintenance of international peace and security" or represent a "threat to the peace, breach of the peace, or act of aggression."[7] At the same time, the organization has not felt obligated to block admittance of countries that fail to observe human rights of its citizens or to censure members for failing to honor the pledge to uphold the human rights principles identified in the Charter. On the contrary, a majority of U.N. member states have less-than-ideal human rights records, according to assessments of independent NGOs, which are often corroborated by reports and investigations by governments and multilateral organizations. For instance, Burma, China, Cuba, North Korea, Sudan, and Zimbabwe are U.N. members in good standing despite extensive and well-documented instances of human rights violations. Moreover, the U.N. does not prohibit any nation, regardless of its record on human rights issues, from holding key positions of influence on the U.N. General Assembly's Third Committee, key human rights bodies such as the Human Rights Council, or related activities. For instance, in 2003 Libya was elected president of the now-defunct U.N. Commission on Human Rights, and China and Cuba are elected members currently sitting on the U.N. Human Rights Council.

Nonetheless, in an effort to fulfill the human rights objectives expressed in the Charter, the U.N. has developed an extensive and complex network of bodies, committees, and reporting mechanisms to look into a broad array of human rights issues. The primary U.N. bodies charged with promoting and protecting human rights are the Third Committee, the Human Rights Council (which replaced the CHR in 2006), the Office of the High Commissioner for Human Rights (OHCHR), and the human rights treaty bodies that monitor implementation of international human rights treaties. In addition, the Security Council, the General Assembly, Economic and Social Council, and International Court of Justice (ICJ) dedicate time to promoting and protecting human rights.[8]

---

7. Charter of the United Nations, arts. 34 and 39.

8. In addition, the Office of the High Commissioner for Human Rights indicates that a host of other U.N.-related bodies are "involved in the promotion and protection of human rights and interact with the main human rights bodies," including the U.N. High Commissioner for Refugees; Office for the Coordination of Humanitarian Affairs; Inter-Agency Internal Displacement Division; International Labor Organization; World Health Organization; U.N. Educational, Scientific and Cultural

The Third Committee's Limited Effectiveness

The U.N. Charter empowers the General Assembly to "discuss any questions or any matters within the scope of the present Charter" and "establish such subsidiary organs as it deems necessary for the performance of its functions."[9] The process of establishing the U.N. after the signing of the Charter resulted in a proposal for six main committees of the General Assembly, including the Third Committee, which focuses on social, humanitarian, and cultural issues. The Third Committee is a committee of the whole, meaning that all U.N. member states are members of the committee.

The Third Committee considers a range of social, humanitarian affairs along with human rights issues, including the advancement of women, protection of children, indigenous peoples, treatment of refugees, racism and racial discrimination, and self-determination. The committee also addresses social issues related to crime, criminal justice and drug control, aging and youth, disabled persons, and family issues. The committee receives reports of the Human Rights Council and the HRC's special procedures. In addition, the Third Committee has involved itself in expanding and codifying human rights by drafting instruments such as the Convention on the Elimination of Discrimination Against Women.

From the beginning, there was a regrettable confluence within the Third Committee of political and civil rights with economic, social, and cultural issues.[10] This was further muddled by the existence of the Economic and Social Council, which examines some of these issues and created the U.N. Commission on Human Rights as a subsidiary body. By having the CHR report to ECOSOC rather than the Third Committee, the U.N. was deliberately conflating fundamental civil and political rights with economic, social, and cultural issues within the organization.

The Third Committee has been marginally effective in confronting gross

---

Organization; Joint United Nations Program on HIV/AIDS; Inter-Agency Standing Committee; U.N. Department of Economic and Social Affairs; Commission on the Status of Women; Office of the Special Adviser on Gender Issues and the Advancement of Women; Division for the Advancement of Women; U.N. Population Fund; U.N. Children's Fund; U.N. Development Fund for Women; U.N. Development Program; Food and Agriculture Organization of the United Nations; U.N. Human Settlements Program; and U.N. Mine Action.

9. Charter of the United Nations, arts. 10 and 22.

10. For more information, see James Jay Carafano, Lee A. Casey, Helle C. Dale, Jennifer A. Marshall, David B. Rivkin, Grace V. Smith, and Janice A. Smith, "Reclaiming the Language of Freedom at the United Nations," Heritage Foundation *Special Report*, no. 08 (September 6, 2006), at www.heritage.org/Research/World wideFreedom/SR08.cfm.

and systematic violations of human rights. Specifically, the Third Committee regularly passes resolutions condemning the human rights practices of specific countries. In 2006, a Third Committee resolution condemned human rights practices in Belarus, Iran, and North Korea, and in 2007, it added Burma to the list.[11] In 2008, it condemned Burma, Iran, and North Korea. However, the limited number of condemnations—at least in relation to the number of governments committing human rights abuses—that pass the Third Committee shows that it also falls victim to the universal membership problem of the U.N., in which countries that regularly violate human rights can undermine the committee's activities and block its resolutions. Yet the limited success of the Third Committee only highlights the dire state of the Human Rights Council.

The CHR and HRC: A Record of Failure and Ineffectiveness

In 1946 the U.N. Economic and Social Council established the U.N. Commission of Human Rights, which was replaced by the Human Rights Council in 2006. As the premier human rights body in the U.N. system, the CHR was charged with holding "public meetings to review the human rights performance of States, adopt[ing] new standards and promot[ing] human rights around the world."[12] The CHR was responsible for drafting the Universal Declaration on Human Rights—a notable achievement. Regrettably, due primarily to the lack of any membership standards, the CHR became a tool for human rights abusers to block criticism of their own actions and stymie efforts to promote human rights.

In the years leading up to the General Assembly's decision to replace the CHR, a number of members with dubious human rights records were elected to the CHR, including Algeria, China, Cuba, Pakistan, Russia, Saudi Arabia, Sudan, Syria, Vietnam, and Zimbabwe. Libya served as chairman of

---

11. U.N. Department of Public Information, "General Assembly Adopts 46 Third Committee Texts on Human Rights Issues, Refugees, Self-Determination, Racism, Social Development," GA/10562, December 19, 2006, at www.un.org/News/Press/docs/2006/ga10562.doc.htm (accessed November 21, 2008); "Third Committee Approves Three Country-Specific Texts on Human Rights Despite Opposition Led by Developing Countries," GA/SHC/3909, November 20, 2007, at www.un.org/News/Press/docs/2007/gashc3909.doc.htm (accessed November 21, 2008); and "Third Committee Approves 11 More Drafts for Assembly Including One More Country-Specific Text That Again Draws Heavy Criticism," GA/SHC/3910, November 21, 2007, at www.un.org/News/Press/docs/2007/gashc3910.doc.htm (accessed November 21, 2008).

12. United Nations, "UN in Brief," at www.un.org/Overview/uninbrief/chapter 3_humanrights.html (accessed November 24, 2008).

the CHR in 2003, despite its ties to the 1988 Lockerbie airliner bombing and its own domestic human rights abuses. In 2004, Sudan was elected to the CHR, despite its role in the atrocities in Darfur, prompting the U.S. ambassador to walk out of the Economic and Social Council.[13]

In addition, the CHR routinely singled out Israel for discriminatory treatment. For instance, CHR's agenda devoted a special item to censuring Israel. Debates in the CHR focused disproportionately on condemning Israel. Indeed, over a forty-year period, almost 30 percent of the CHR's country-specific resolutions targeted Israel.[14] Its emergency special sessions and special sittings were frequently dedicated to condemning Israel. By contrast, human rights violations in Sudan, China, Cuba, and other nations were subject to minimal scrutiny.[15]

In addition, the CHR's historical inability to impartially discharge its responsibility to review human rights practices of U.N. member states led U.N. secretary-general Kofi Annan to observe:

> The Commission's capacity to perform its tasks has been increasingly undermined by its declining credibility and professionalism. In particular, States have sought membership of the Commission not to strengthen human rights but to protect themselves against criticism or to criticize others.[16]

Although the CHR regularly passed country-specific resolutions condemning a few states for human rights abuses, it very rarely or never condemned a host of countries that regularly violated the fundamental rights of their citizens. It was widely regarded as an ineffective champion of human rights susceptible to political pressure from human rights abusers. The CHR's disrepute eventually grew to the point that Secretary-General Annan acknowledged:

> The Commission's ability to perform its tasks has been overtaken by new needs, and undermined by the politicization of its sessions and the selectivity of its work. We have reached a point at which the Commission's declining

13. Associated Press, "Sudan Retains U.N. Human Rights Post," MSNBC, May 4, 2004, at www.msnbc.msn.com/id/4898975 (accessed November 21, 2008).

14. Anne Bayefsky, "Discrimination and Double Standards: Anti-Israeli Past Is Present at the U.N.'s Human Rights Council," _National Review_, July 5, 2006, at http://article.nationalreview.com/?q = ODIOMWMzYzQyMmE3MTBkZTUwYjk5Yj gzNGRiZDNkYWM (accessed December 8, 2008).

15. See Eye on the UN, Human Rights Actions, at www.eyeontheun.org/browse -un.asp?ya = 1&sa = 1&u = 50&un_s = 0&ul = 1&tp = 1&tpn = Resolution (accessed November 21, 2008).

16. Kofi Annan, "In Larger Freedom: Towards Development, Security and Human Rights for All," U.N. General Assembly, A/59/2005, March 21, 2005, p. 45, at www.un.org/largerfreedom/contents.htm (accessed November 21, 2008).

credibility has cast a shadow on the reputation of the United Nations system as a whole, and where piecemeal reforms will not be enough.[17]

The secretary-general went on to recommend replacing the CHR with a new, smaller Human Rights Council that would review the human rights practices of all U.N. member states.

The HRC: Deeply Flawed from the Beginning

Regrettably, negotiations in the General Assembly fell considerably short of proposals by the secretary-general, NGOs, the United States, and other countries interested in making the Human Rights Council more effective than the CHR. Specifically, the resolution lacked criteria for membership other than geographical representation. Even states under Security Council sanction for human rights violations are eligible for HRC membership. Council members are elected by an absolute majority of the General Assembly, not the two-thirds majority sought by the secretary-general and the United States, but the resolution set a higher bar (two-thirds vote of the General Assembly) to suspend a council member. While the council is charged with conducting a universal periodic review of all U.N. members, the conclusions of the review will not bar from council membership countries found complicit in human rights violations. Furthermore, special sessions may be called by agreement of only one-third of the council's membership, too low a threshold to prevent politically driven special sessions.

These failings led the United States to vote against the General Assembly resolution that created the Human Rights Council, while well-known human rights abusers Burma, China, Cuba, Ethiopia, Libya, Saudi Arabia, Sudan, Syria, and Zimbabwe voted in favor. In reaction, the Bush administration announced that the United States would not run for a seat on the council in 2006, and it renewed that decision in 2007 and 2008. Subsequent evidence of the council's ineffectiveness led Congress and the administration to withhold U.S. contributions to the council.[18] In June 2008, the United States announced that it would scale back its already low level of

---

17. Kofi Annan, "Secretary-General's Address to the Commission on Human Rights," Office of the Spokesman for the U.N. Secretary-General, April 7, 2005, at www.un.org/apps/sg/sgstats.asp?nid=1388 (accessed November 21, 2008).

18. See Brett D. Schaefer, "The U.S. Is Right to Shun the U.N. Human Rights Council," Heritage Foundation *WebMemo*, no. 1910 (May 2, 2008), at www.heritage.org/Research/InternationalOrganizations/wm1910.cfm (accessed November 21, 2008).

participation in the council based on the HRC's poor performance.[19] Although the Obama administration has re-engaged with and was elected to a seat on the HRC, the presence of the U.S. is unlikely to greatly improve its performance.[20]

With little justification, council supporters, including U.N. high commissioner for human rights Louise Arbour, were quick to declare that the new body represented the "dawn of a new era" in promoting human rights in the United Nations.[21] The council has clearly not lived up to these lofty expectations. Among its dubious accomplishments, the HRC discontinued consideration of the human rights situations in Iran and Uzbekistan under the 1503 procedure,[22] eliminated the special rapporteurs on the situations

19. The State Department spokesman stated that the U.N. Human Rights Council "has a rather pathetic record in that regard. Instead of focusing on some of the real and deep human rights issues around the world, it has really turned into a forum that seems to be almost solely focused on bashing Israel. . . . The Secretary has taken the decision that we will engage the Human Rights Council really only when we believe that there are matters of deep national interest before the Council and we feel compelled; otherwise, we are not going to." Sean McCormack, "Daily Press Briefing," U.S. Department of State, June 6, 2008, at www.state.gov/r/pa/prs/dpb/2008/jun/105716.htm (accessed November 21, 2008).

20. Brett D. Schaefer, "The Obama Administration Will Not Make the Human Rights Council Effective," Heritage Foundation *WebMemo*, no. 2432 (May 11, 2009), at www.heritage.org/Research/InternationalOrganizations/wm2432.cfm.

21. UN Watch, "Dawn of a New Era? Assessment of the United Nations Human Rights Council and Its Year of Reform," May 7, 2007, at www.unwatch.org/atf/cf/%7B6DEB65DA-BE5B-4CAE-8056-8BF0BEDF4D17%7D/DAWN_OF_A_NEW_ERA _HRC%20REPORT_FINAL.PDF (accessed November 21, 2008). U.N. General Assembly president Jan Eliasson, who oversaw the reform negotiations, called the council "a new beginning for the promotion and protection of human rights" and declared that the council would be "principled, effective and fair." See press release, "General Assembly Establishes New Human Rights Council."

22. The 1503 procedure is named after the ECOSOC resolution that established the procedure by which reliable reports or claims from NGOs of consistent patterns of gross human rights violations were considered. The HRC established the Working Group on Communications and the Working Group on Situations to examine NGO complaints and alert the HRC of "consistent patterns of gross and reliably attested violations of human rights and fundamental freedoms." The chairperson of the Working Group on Communications screened "manifestly ill-founded and anonymous communications." Complaints passing the initial screening were shared with the state concerned to include its views on the alleged violations. The Working Group on Communications was supposed to consist of five independent, highly qualified experts from the five regional groups. The working group assessed the admissibility and the merits of a communication, including whether it appeared to reveal a "consistent pattern of gross and reliably attested violations of human rights

in Belarus and Cuba, repeatedly singled out Israel for condemnation, and failed to address deplorable human rights situations in places such as Belarus, China, Cuba, North Korea, and Zimbabwe.

Weakened Special Procedures

When it adopted its institution-building measures in 2007, the HRC significantly weakened the special procedures inherited from the CHR. The term "special procedures" covers the various thematic independent experts, special rapporteurs, and working groups inherited from the CHR. With some notable exceptions, the special procedures are one of the more effective legacies of the CHR. The council's 2007 institution-building measures made it harder to adopt country-specific resolutions against human rights abusers, singled out Israel as the only country subject to a permanent council mandate, and created a restrictive code of conduct designed to impede the autonomy of the independent experts.

In addition, some experts who operate through the special procedures have demonstrated a troubling susceptibility to politicization and the selection of U.N. special rapporteurs has often left much to be desired. Former Swiss Socialist Party politician Jean Ziegler was appointed as an expert by the HRC in March 2008. He helped to found the Moammar Khadaffi Human Rights Prize in 1989 shortly after Libya bombed Pan Am flight 103, killing 270 people including 189 Americans, and was awarded that prize in 2002.[23] In March 2008, the council appointed Princeton professor Richard Falk as the special rapporteur on the situation of human rights in the Palestinian territories. Professor Falk is a skeptic of the official version of the

---

and fundamental freedoms." Admissible communications and recommendations were then transmitted to the Working Group on Situations. The Working Group on Situations was also made up of five members appointed by the regional groups from the states on the council. It presented a report to the council on "consistent patterns of gross and reliably attested violations of human rights and fundamental freedoms" along with recommendations on what actions the council should take. The council was then expected to adopt a decision on the situations reported to it. The 1503 procedure involved confidential communications between the relevant U.N. bodies and the state under examination. U.N. Human Rights Council, "Human Rights Council Complaint Procedure," at www2.ohchr.org/english/bod ies/chr/complaints.htm (accessed November 24, 2008). See also U.N. Economic and Social Council Resolution 1503, May 27, 1970.

23. Press release, "To Sounds of Cheers, UN Human Rights Council Elects Khaddafi Prize Founder to Expert Post," UN Watch, March 26, 2008, at www.unwatch .org/site/apps/nlnet/content2.aspx?c = bdKKISNqEmG&b = 1316871&ct = 5137875 (accessed November 21, 2008).

events of September 11, 2001, and has called for an investigation into whether neoconservatives were behind the attack.[24]

Moreover, HRC members and other U.N. member states have sought to abolish mandates for human rights experts who are studying particular nations of concern. Cuba, China, North Korea, and Algeria have repeatedly criticized country experts as unhelpful and demanded that their mandates be terminated. The council abolished the two mandates dealing with Cuba and Belarus during its inaugural year.

This is cause for concern because country-specific mandates are a crucial part of the U.N. human rights system. When independent experts on country situations submit reports to the council, the council must debate the reports. The reports have proven useful in highlighting human rights violations that the CHR and the HRC have been reluctant to discuss.

Council members have also sought to force the council to endorse constraints on free speech in the form of prohibitions on defamation of religion, particularly defamation of Islam. At the urging of the Organization of the Islamic Conference (OIC), the council passed a resolution in March 2007 that expressed "deep concern at attempts to identify Islam with terrorism, violence, and human rights violations" and urged states to "take all possible measures to promote tolerance and respect for all religions and their value systems and to complement legal systems with intellectual and moral strategies to combat religious hatred and intolerance." The resolution asserts that the right to freedom of expression may be limited out of "respect for religions and beliefs."[25] In essence, the OIC is seeking to encourage states to prohibit language that the OIC deems offensive, even if it tramples long-held protections of the freedom of expression. In March 2008 and March 2009, the OIC again persuaded the council to pass a resolution on "combating the defamation of religion."[26]

Universal Periodic Review

Despite the HRC's weaknesses and failure to confront critical human rights violations in places such as Tibet or Zimbabwe, human rights activ-

---

24. Eli Lake, "U.N. Official Calls for Study of Neocons' Role in 9/11," *New York Sun*, April 10, 2008, at www.nysun.com/news/foreign/un-official-calls-study-neo cons-role-911 (accessed November 21, 2008).

25. U.N. Human Rights Council, "Combating Defamation of Religions," A/HRC/RES/4/9, March 30, 2007, at http://ap.ohchr.org/documents/E/HRC/resolu tions/A-HRC-RES-4-9.doc (accessed November 24, 2008).

26. U.N. Human Rights Council, "Combating Defamation of Religions," A/HRC/RES/7/19, March 27, 2008, at http://ap.ohchr.org/documents/E/HRC/resolu tions/A_HRC_RES_7_19.pdf (accessed November 24, 2008); and U.N. Human Rights Council, "Resolutions, decisions, and President's statements adopted by the

ists held out hope that the Universal Periodic Review (UPR) called for in the resolution establishing the council would make the HRC more effective than the CHR. This hope was based on the requirement that each of the U.N.'s 192 member states, including the sitting members of the council, submit to a review of its human rights record. This new feature was intended to prevent a repeat of the CHR's selective scrutiny. Each year the council is required to convene three UPR sessions to examine a total of forty-eight countries, which means that over a four-year period it will review all 192 U.N. member states.

However, significant concerns about the UPR process hinder its utility in promoting human rights and exposing violations. The UPR modalities, established in June 2007, virtually ensure a nonconfrontational and meek process. Despite the requirement that the UPR incorporate information from NGOs, NGOs' contribution to the process has been strictly curtailed. NGOs and other stakeholders cannot speak during the three-hour working group examination of a country. Although they are allowed to submit reports based on "credible and reliable information" to the UPR Working Group for consideration, the OHCHR distills and summarizes their reports down to the strict limit of ten pages for NGO material—a fraction of what is usually presented to expert treaty bodies. In addition, the many recommendations of the expert treaty bodies are only selectively presented to the Human Rights Council, again with a ten-page limit. During the council's consideration of the UPR reports, many NGOs complained that key issues were ignored or not included in the document prepared by the OHCHR. In addition, a number of countries used points of order and other procedures to intimidate NGOs making statements or to strike their comments from the record if they did not strictly reference comments in the report.[27]

The UPR process is still driven primarily by the country under review and is limited by the country's willingness, or lack thereof, to volunteer infor-

---

Council at its tenth session," A/HRC/10/L.11, May 12, 2009, p. 78, at www2.ohchr .org/english/bodies/hrcouncil/docs/10session/edited_versionL.11Revised.pdf.

27. U.N. Human Rights Council, "Institution-Building of the United Nations Human Rights Council," A/HRC/RES/5/1, June 18, 2007, at http://ap.ohchr.org/ documents/E/HRC/resolutions/A_HRC_RES_5_1.doc (accessed November 24, 2008). For an example, see the HRC's consideration of the UPR reports for Bahrain and Morocco, particularly the webcast of the presentation of the Cairo Institute for Human Rights Studies. Egypt repeatedly interrupted the Cairo Institute presentation on the basis that it failed to focus specifically on the UPR report. This was followed by a lengthy debate over how much input NGOs should have in the process under the council's rules. Slovenia, representing the EU, referred to Egypt's interpretation of the rules, which was supported by the council's president, as a "farce." Human Rights Council, 8th sess., audio files, June 9, 2008, at www.un.org/webcast/unhrc/ archive.asp?go=080609 (accessed November 21, 2008).

mation on human rights violations. Moreover, the review process and oral interventions are conducted by the forty-seven council members, including some human rights abusers. Allies of countries seeking to avoid scrutiny queue up in an effort to dominate the allotted comment period. As described in a recent report from Human Rights Watch, an international human rights NGO, the result is "kid gloves" treatment of allies and sharp questioning of nonallies:

> Algeria's interventions on Tunisia, Bahrain, and the United Kingdom provide a good example of the double standards applied by some. The Algerian ambassador trod softly with regard to both Tunisia and Bahrain, noting the difficulties the Tunisian government faced protecting human rights while combating terrorism and asking only if Tunisia believed it would be "a good idea to have a seminar" on that subject, while congratulating Bahrain for the progress it has made with regard to protection of women's rights. In contrast, Algeria gave a strong, detailed statement when the United Kingdom was reviewed, raising concerns over its rate of incarceration of children, the violation of the U.K.'s commitments under the Convention Against Torture, excessive use of pre-trial detention, and the lack of protection for asylum seekers and migrants.[28]

Finally, countries wary of scrutiny are attempting to use the UPR process as an excuse to eliminate all country-specific mandates. These countries, which are invariably human rights abusers, contend that country-specific mandates are no longer necessary because all nations will be reviewed under the UPR process. This argument is baseless and disingenuous because country-specific mandates entail comprehensive study of a country, including visits by the human rights expert to witness the human rights situation firsthand. Nevertheless, the country-specific mandates for Belarus, Cuba, Liberia, and the Democratic Republic of the Congo had already been terminated as of mid-2009, and the opponents of human rights scrutiny will surely use the UPR process to argue against extending the seven remaining renewable country-specific mandates (Burundi, Cambodia, North Korea, Haiti, Burma, Somalia, and Sudan) and against creating new mandates. The exception will be the only permanent "country"-specific mandate, the special rapporteur on the situation of human rights in the Palestinian territories occupied since 1967, which is directed to investigate Israel's actions in the territory indefinitely.

Multilateral Human Rights Treaties

When the full breadth of the atrocities committed by Nazi Germany became apparent following World War II, a number of people sought to

---

28. Human Rights Watch, "UN: Mixed Results for New Review Process," April 18, 2008, at http://hrw.org/english/docs/2008/04/18/global18606.htm (accessed November 21, 2008).

expand the human rights provisions recognized under international law beyond those included in the U.N. Charter. This notion was first realized in the 1948 Universal Declaration of Human Rights.[29] Additional treaties have expanded on this broad expression of the basic rights guaranteed to all people.

The eight "core" human rights treaties, as recognized by the OHCHR, are:

- The International Covenant on Civil and Political Rights
- The U.N. Convention against Torture and Other Cruel, Inhuman or Degrading Treatment or Punishment
- The Convention on the Elimination of Racial Discrimination
- The International Covenant on Economic, Social and Cultural Rights
- The Convention on the Elimination of All Forms of Discrimination against Women
- The U.N. Convention on the Rights of the Child
- The International Convention on the Protection of the Rights of All Migrant Workers and Members of Their Families
- The Convention on the Rights of Persons with Disabilities

Each treaty is monitored and implemented by its respective treaty body. Most of these bodies receive secretariat support from the OHCHR, although the Human Rights Council has created a competition for resources. Parties to these treaties are generally required to submit regular reports (usually every four years) to the respective committees on their compliance with the various treaty obligations. The committees examine the reports and make observations and recommendations regarding treaty compliance.

Human Rights Committee

The Human Rights Committee, which operates separately from the Human Rights Council, is a body of eighteen independent experts that monitors compliance with the International Covenant on Civil and Political Rights (ICCPR). Parties to the ICCPR vow to protect and preserve key human rights such as prohibiting arbitrary execution, upholding the rule of law, protecting free speech and assembly, and ending discrimination based on race, religion, and gender. The committee holds three sessions each year in Geneva or New York and engages in a dialogue and review of

---

29. John Peters Humphrey of Canada was the principal drafter and was assisted by Eleanor Roosevelt of the United States, Jacques Maritain and René Cassin of France, Charles Malik of Lebanon, and P. C. Chang of the Republic of China, among others. The U.N. General Assembly passed the declaration in 1948 by a vote of 48 in favor and 0 against, with 8 abstentions from the Soviet bloc states, South Africa, and Saudi Arabia.

the human rights record with the delegations of four to six state parties in each session.

Committee against Torture and Subcommittee on the Prevention of Torture

Both bodies consist of ten members and monitor the U.N. Convention against Torture and Other Cruel, Inhuman or Degrading Treatment or Punishment (CAT) and its protocol. Parties to CAT are obligated to prevent acts of torture within their territories and prevent extradition of people from their countries to countries where they would face torture. The CAT Committee meets in Geneva twice yearly and reviews the records of approximately six to eight state parties. Parties to the optional protocol are obligated to allow the subcommittee to inspect places of detention.

Committee on the Elimination of Racial Discrimination

This eighteen-member committee monitors compliance with the International Convention on the Elimination of Racial Discrimination (ICERD). Parties to the ICERD are obligated to eliminate all forms of discrimination based on race, color, descent, and national or ethnic origin within their territories. The committee holds two three-week sessions in Geneva each year and reviews the records of approximately one dozen state parties each session.

Committee on Economic, Social and Cultural Rights

This eighteen-member committee meets twice yearly in Geneva and is responsible for implementing the International Covenant on Economic, Social and Cultural Rights (ICESCR), which obligates state parties to guarantee certain "rights," such as an adequate standard of living, health, a job, and other social and cultural aspirations. Approximately ten state parties are reviewed each year.

Committee on the Elimination of Discrimination against Women

This committee of twenty-three experts on women's rights monitors compliance with the Convention on the Elimination of All Forms of Discrimination against Women (CEDAW), which obligates state parties to prohibit discrimination that impairs the rights of women in any matter. It meets three times yearly in Geneva and reviews the records of eight to ten countries in each session.

Committee on the Rights of the Child

This committee of eighteen experts monitors compliance with the U.N. Convention on the Rights of the Child (CRC), which aims to protect the human rights of children from dilution or exploitation. Parties to the CRC must acknowledge that children have basic civil and political rights and certain child-specific rights, such as the rights to have a name and identity, to be raised by parents within a family or cultural grouping, and to have a relationship with both parents, even if they are divorced. The committee meets three times yearly in Geneva and reviews the record of approximately twelve state parties each year.

Committee on Migrant Workers

This ten-member committee monitors compliance with the International Convention on the Protection of the Rights of All Migrant Workers and Members of Their Families. Parties to this convention are obligated to respect the fundamental human rights of migrants and guarantee that migrants will receive equal treatment and the same working conditions as citizens. The committee meets yearly in Geneva and reviews one to two countries.

Committee on the Rights of Persons with Disabilities

The committee monitors compliance with the Convention on the Rights of Persons with Disabilities (CRPD), which is the most recent of the "core" human rights treaties. It was opened to signatures in March 2007 and entered into force in May 2008. Parties to the convention are obligated to "promote, protect and ensure the full and equal enjoyment of all human rights and fundamental freedoms by all persons with disabilities, and to promote respect for their inherent dignity."[30] As of this writing, the committee has not yet been formed, but plans to meet twice yearly in Geneva.

Some treaty bodies, including the Human Rights Committee and the Committee on the Elimination of Discrimination against Women, also have optional protocols that permit individuals to present particular complaints for review and remedy under the treaty norms, even between the periodic state reports. The state party is given an opportunity to respond on the facts and the law in these cases. Compliance with treaty recommendations is not as high as some might wish, but it gives an opportunity to signal to the state that its record is under scrutiny.

There is significant overlap among these various treaty obligations and the monitoring functions of the respective treaty bodies. For example, the separate conventions dealing with discrimination based on race and gender are essentially more specific iterations of the rights guaranteed to these classes of people by state parties to the ICCPR. Indeed, the experts on distinct treaty bodies have made a concerted effort not only to refer to and

---

30. Convention on the Rights of Persons with Disabilities, art. 1.

support decisions and recommendations by other bodies, but also to coordinate their criticisms of countries.

Problems and Concerns with Human Rights Treaties

For a number of reasons, the United States is party to only three of the eight core human rights treaties: the ICCPR, CAT, and ICERD. The U.S. Senate has thus far refused to ratify the Convention on the Elimination of All Forms of Discrimination against Women and the International Covenant on Economic, Social and Cultural Rights due to problems with their specific obligations. President Jimmy Carter signed both treaties. President Bill Clinton also signed the Convention on the Rights of the Child in 1995, but it has never been submitted to the Senate for its advice and consent, which is necessary for ratification.

A common concern about these treaties is that the obligations may violate provisions of the U.S. Constitution or the division of authority between the federal and state governments. For instance, the CEDAW Committee has interpreted CEDAW to require state parties to guarantee highly controversial rights. Recommendations of the CEDAW treaty body have included encouragement of abortion rights, legalization of prostitution, quotas to achieve gender parity in parliamentary bodies, same-sex marriages, and discouragement of references to motherhood as "stereotypical attitudes," even going so far as to call for eliminating Mother's Day.[31]

Moreover, the United States is not fully satisfied with the treaties to which it is a party, and has registered a number of reservations when ratifying the agreements. For instance, upon ratification of the ICERD, the United States declared that "the United States does not accept any obligation under this Convention . . . to restrict those rights, through the adoption of legislation or any other measures, to the extent that they are protected by the Constitution and laws of the United States." That reservation was made to ensure that the United States would not be required to enforce a blanket ban on all "hate speech" and "hate groups" in contravention of the First Amendment's protection of freedom of speech and assembly. Despite clear reservations, the United States and other parties are routinely chastised by the Committee on the Elimination of Racial Discrimination for failing to comply completely with the treaty's prohibition on all hateful language.

The treaty bodies and experts have also demonstrated a troubling tendency to reinterpret existing treaty text or "discover" new requirements not

---

31. Patrick F. Fagan, "How U.N. Conventions on Women's and Children's Rights Undermine Family, Religion, and Sovereignty," Heritage Foundation *Backgrounder*, no. 1407 (February 5, 2001), at www.heritage.org/Research/InternationalOrganiza tions/BG1407.cfm.

apparent in the text and to apply them as new treaty obligations. For example, when the ICCPR was being drafted, it was decided after much debate that the treaty obligations would apply to each party only for "individuals within its territory and subject to its jurisdiction."[32] However, in 2004, the Human Rights Committee decided to ignore the territorial restriction on the treaty so that the United States' obligations would extend to enemy combatants held at the U.S. naval base in Guantánamo Bay, Cuba, essentially rewriting the treaty to read "within its territory *or* subject to its jurisdiction." Obviously, the committee does not have the authority to reinterpret the plain language of the ICCPR in that manner. Such a change would require a treaty amendment and consent by all the treaty parties. Not only is this a gross, unjustified expansion of the committee's authority, but it specifically overturns a hotly debated provision sought and attained by Eleanor Roosevelt, the U.S. representative, during treaty negotiations to protect U.S. bases in other countries.[33]

Objectionable provisions in the treaty texts combined with concern about how the treaty bodies might interpret the agreements has led the United States not to sign the International Convention on the Protection of the Rights of All Migrant Workers and Members of Their Families and the Convention on the Rights of Persons with Disabilities. For instance, upon adoption of the CRPD by the General Assembly, U.S. ambassador Richard T. Miller stated:

> The United States believes that the most effective way for states to improve the real world situation of persons with disabilities from a legal perspective is to strengthen their domestic legal frameworks related to non-discrimination and equality. This approach is rooted in our own national experience with legislation such as the Americans with Disabilities Act. We hope that the Convention will assist states in this process at the national level. . . .
>
> The United States called for a separate vote on [preambular paragraph (u) of the Convention] and voted against it because we saw it as an attempt to politicize what had otherwise been a very productive and focused negotiation process.
>
> We were also concerned that the reference in this human rights convention to armed conflict and foreign occupation, which are governed by international humanitarian law and not human rights law, would create unnecessary legal confusion and thus potentially undermine the extensive protections already available under international humanitarian law to protected persons in those situations. The United States wishes to note for the official record its continued concerns related to this preambular paragraph in the Convention. We note that

---

32. International Covenant on Civil and Political Rights, art. 2, par. 1.

33. See Steven Groves, "The U.S. Deserves a Fair Report from the U.N. Human Rights Envoy," Heritage Foundation *WebMemo*, no. 1470 (May 24, 2007), at www.heritage.org/Research/InternationalOrganizations/wm1470.cfm.

these concerns also apply to Article 11, which deals with situations of armed conflict.[34]

THE OHCHR: A SELECTIVE
CHAMPION OF HUMAN RIGHTS

The Office of the High Commissioner for Human Rights was created in 1993 to coordinate the work of U.N. human rights bodies, provide them with expertise, and support them within the U.N. system. It is, in essence, the bureaucratic backbone of the U.N. human rights system and it supports the U.N.'s activities, good and bad. The OHCHR provides secretariat support for the Human Rights Council and provides legal research and secretariat support for the treaty bodies. The OHCHR also directly supports the work of special procedures of the Human Rights Council (the special rapporteurs, independent experts, and working groups) by assisting them as they conduct research trips or visit the field and receive and consider complaints from victims of human rights violations. The OHCHR also provides expertise and technical training in administration of justice, legislative reform, and the electoral process.

The OHCHR is headquartered in Geneva, but also has an office in New York City and eleven country and seven regional offices in other parts of the world. As of December 2007, the OHCHR employed over nine hundred staff, with roughly half based in Geneva and New York and half in other parts of the world. It is funded from the U.N. regular budget and voluntary contributions by member states, non-U.N. governmental organizations like the European Commission, foundations, and individuals.[35]

The high commissioner for human rights is the head of the OHCHR and the principal U.N. human rights official. The position was established by the General Assembly in 1993 to lead the OHCHR and oversee all U.N. human rights efforts. The high commissioner is part of the U.N. Secretariat, holds the rank of undersecretary-general, and coordinates the U.N.'s human rights efforts across the world, including working closely with the Human Rights Council. As noted by UN Watch, a Geneva-based NGO:

---

34. Press release, "Explanation of Position on the Convention on the Rights of Persons with Disabilities, Agenda Item 67(b), in the General Assembly," U.S. Mission to the United Nations, December 13, 2006, at www.usunnewyork.usmission .gov/press_releases/20061213_396.html (accessed November 21, 2008).

35. Office of the U.N. High Commissioner for Human Rights, "Funding and Budget," at www.ohchr.org/EN/AboutUs/Pages/FundingBudget.aspx (accessed November 21, 2008).

Functionally, it can be said that the High Commissioner wears two hats. First, she heads the OHCHR, the Geneva-based division of the UN Secretariat that serves the various UN human rights agencies, including the Human Rights Council, and implements human rights decisions taken by several UN bodies. In this sense, the High Commissioner and her staff are subject to the member states. Separately, however, the High Commissioner also has a significant role as an independent voice to promote human rights. . . .

The UN human rights chief has neither the power of sword nor of purse. With her moral voice alone does she go to battle against human rights violations around the world. This power, limited though it may be, is by no means insignificant. Nations large and small exert considerable effort to avoid being named and shamed in the international arena as a violator of human rights. The UN official with the greatest ability to do this is the High Commissioner for Human Rights.[36]

The utility of the high commissioner depends considerably on the officeholder. He or she is in a position to speak authoritatively and urge the U.N. or the Human Rights Council to consider or take action on human rights situations. Former high commissioner Louise Arbour had a decidedly mixed record.[37] During her tenure, she oversaw a number of positive actions, such as criticizing the Zimbabwe government for attacking and oppressing its political opposition. However, Arbour also demonstrated a troubling willingness to provide cover for authoritarian regimes, including congratulating the totalitarian regime in Cuba for taking "significant" actions in the field of human rights and praising the Arab Charter on Human Rights as "an important step forward" to help "strengthen the enjoyment of human rights,"[38] despite the Arab Charter's explicit calls for

36. UN Watch, "The Right to Name and Shame: An Analysis of the Tenure of Former UN High Commissioner Louise Arbour with Recommendations for New High Commissioner Navanethem Pillay," August 4, 2008, at www.unwatch.org/atf/cf/%7B6DEB65DA-BE5B-4CAE-8056-8BF0BEDF4D17%7D/THE_RIGHT_TO_NAME_AND_SHAME_FULL_REPORT.PDF (accessed November 21, 2008).

37. For a number of examples of the high commissioner's potential to use the office to advance or inhibit the effectiveness of U.N. human rights activities, see UN Watch, "The Right to Name and Shame."

38. U.N. Department of Public Affairs, "Arbour Sees 'Unprecedented' Commitment from Cuba on Human Rights," *Earth Times*, February 8, 2008, at www.earth times.org/articles/show/184623,arbour-sees-unprecedented-commitment-from-cu ba-on-human-rights.html (accessed November 26, 2008), and U.N. Office at Geneva, "High Commissioner for Human Rights Welcomes Ratification Bringing into Force Arab Charter on Human Rights," January 24, 2008, at www.unog.ch/80256EDD006B9C2E/(httpNewsByYear_en)/385A138D2DCAA53FC12573DA005 63DEB (accessed November 25, 2008).

the elimination of Zionism (i.e., Israel).[39] Only after she was challenged did Arbour clarify that she did not endorse that part of the Arab Charter.[40]

SYSTEMIC DEFECTS IN THE
U.N. HUMAN RIGHTS SYSTEM

The U.N. serves as a useful forum for multilateral meetings and discussion to address mutual concerns. U.N. interventions through peacekeeping operations, humanitarian missions, and political missions, such as election monitoring, are often more politically acceptable than unilateral or multi-lateral efforts outside of the United Nations. Crises or other problems that are not central to the interests of the United States or other major powers are often addressed through the U.N. or not at all. However, the record clearly demonstrates that the U.N. human rights system is an inadequate vehicle for advancing human rights, civil liberties, individual freedom, and the rule of law.

A System Dominated by Human Rights Abusers

The primary reason for failure of the U.N. human rights system is the organization's universal membership. In civil and political rights, only a minority of the 192 U.N. member states qualify as "free" in Freedom House's *Freedom in the World 2009*.[41] Similarly, the *2009 Index of Economic Freedom*, published annually by The Heritage Foundation and the *Wall Street Journal*, reports that a majority of U.N. member states remain "mostly unfree" or "repressed" in terms of economic freedom.[42] When countries do

---

39. League of Arab States, Arab Charter on Human Rights, May 22, 2004, at www1.umn.edu/humanrts/instree/loas2005.html?msource=UNWDEC19001& tr=y&auid;eq3337655 (accessed November 25, 2008). For more information, see Brett D. Schaefer, "The United Nations: Adieu Arbour, but Will Her Successor Be Worse?" Heritage Foundation *WebMemo*, no. 1833 (March 4, 2008), at www.heri tage.org/Research/InternationalOrganizations/wm1833.cfm.

40. Press release, "Statement by UN High Commissioner for Human Rights on the Entry into Force of the Arab Charter on Human Rights," United Nations, January 30, 2008, at www.unhchr.ch/huricane/huricane.nsf/view01/6C211162E43235 FAC12573 E00056E19D (November 21, 2008).

41. Freedom House, "Freedom in the World 2009: Tables and Graphs," in *Freedom in the World 2009*, at www.freedomhouse.org/Uploads/fiw09/FIW09_Tables& Graphs ForWeb.pdf (accessed May 19, 2009).

42. Terry Miller and Kim R. Holmes, *2009 Index of Economic Freedom* (Washington, DC: Heritage Foundation and Dow Jones & Company, Inc., 2009), at www.her itage.org/index (accessed May 19, 2009).

not value freedom at home, it is not surprising that they do not value it at the U.N. These unfree U.N. member states have used their majority status and influence in regional and other voting blocs (e.g., the OIC) to hijack the U.N. human rights system, undermining efforts to promote and protect fundamental human rights.

Membership in U.N. subsidiary bodies, including the Human Rights Council, is formally based on regional groups that dominate the U.N. system. For example, the HRC has forty-seven members with seats allotted among the regions in proportion to the number of member states from that region: Africa has thirteen seats, Asia has thirteen, Latin America and the Caribbean have eight, Eastern Europe has six, and the Western European and Others Group (WEOG) has seven seats. This guarantees that countries located in the African and Asian groups—regions with the weakest records of promoting and protecting human rights—will always outnumber the countries in the WEOG, which includes Europe, the United States, Canada, Australia, and New Zealand. Since the WEOG countries historically have been the most forceful proponents of fundamental human rights, the geographic composition of the HRC places countries supportive of a more assertive council in a weak position.

The regional arrangements are also problematic because countries that depend on regional support for their selection will tend to abide by the views of their regional caucus. These views are often set by regional powers, such as Egypt, Nigeria, and South Africa in the Africa region. The Organization of the Islamic Conference also has political influence over its African, Middle Eastern, and Southeast Asian members. Moreover, OIC members constitute a majority of both the Asian and African regional groups allowing the OIC to influence policy positions and votes by those regional groups. Openly dissenting from a stated caucus position is typically extremely risky for a state because it depends on the regional group for candidacies, political support, and a share of U.N. economic aid.

In addition, HRC membership does not require any proof of respect for human rights. Indeed, a majority (24 of 47) of the HRC members in 2008 were not considered "free" in Freedom House's annual assessment of civil and political rights. In 2008, the HRC included 16 OIC members, constituting more than one-third of the HRC's membership. Of those 16 nations, only Indonesia and Senegal were considered "free" by Freedom House in 2008.[43] The OIC has repeatedly demonstrated that its agenda rarely comports with traditional notions of human rights. OIC members have actively tried to prevent other HRC members from openly discussing certain issues by raising repeated and disruptive points of order. Because even liberal and democratic states have positions and posts that they may wish to secure,

43. Freedom House, "Table of Independent Countries, 2008."

the OIC's censorious activity has been extremely effective in barring the discussion of contested points regarding Israel and the human rights records of Islamic states.

The results in the HRC are sad and predictable:

- The "defamation of religions" agenda, pushed through the Human Rights Council by the OIC and its allies, has effectively replaced freedom of religion as a core action item. Religious liberty—once universally considered an individual right not to be abridged by government—has become a pretext for groups to avoid any discussion of their belief systems or the conduct of politicized groups.
- In the same vein, the council ordered the special rapporteur on the promotion and protection of the right to freedom of opinion and expression to report on incidences of religious discrimination, instead of concentrating on violations of the right to freedom of speech and expression.
- The HRC, led by the OIC, repeatedly singles out Israel for criticism, condemning it in twenty-six separate resolutions and decisions as of mid-2009, while ignoring human rights abuses committed by Hamas and Hezbollah.[44]
- Resolutions condemning the world's major human rights violators are rarely or never offered, as in the cases of North Korea and Cuba, or are substantially watered down, as in the cases of Burma and Sudan.
- In addition, the council discontinued consideration of the human rights situations in Iran and Uzbekistan under the 1503 procedure and eliminated the experts focused on Belarus, Cuba, and the Democratic Republic of the Congo, even though the human rights situations in those countries had not improved.

Regrettably, the composition of council membership is unlikely to substantially improve in the future. There is little possibility that the U.N. will apply criteria for membership beyond regional representation. For better or worse, the U.N. has decided as a body that membership on its human rights committees, treaty bodies, and subsidiary organs will be unrestricted and based on regional geographic representation, not on special expertise or national commitment to fundamental human rights.

While such an arrangement appears fair and equitable on the surface, its consequences have been uniformly negative for the promotion and protection of fundamental human rights. Until HRC membership is based on a

---

44. For an up-to-date account, see UN Watch, "Anti-Israel Resolutions at the HRC," at www.unwatch.org/site/?c = bdKKISNqEmG&b = 3820041 (accessed May 1, 2008), and Eye on the UN, "Human Rights Action."

proven commitment to human rights and the world's worst abusers are excluded from controlling the council's agenda, the council will continue to disappoint.

The U.N.'s Distorted Human Rights Priorities

The U.N.'s reluctance to recognize a hierarchy among individual human rights has resulted in distorted priorities. The 1993 Vienna Declaration and Program of Action of the World Conference on Human Rights established as official U.N. policy the moral equivalence of all "rights":

> All human rights are universal, indivisible and interdependent and interrelated. The international community must treat human rights globally in a fair and equal manner, on the same footing, and with the same emphasis.[45]

Thus, the Vienna Declaration stated that the U.N.'s development agenda to eliminate poverty should be treated "on the same footing" as the prevention of genocide, ethnic cleansing, and summary executions. In other words, the U.N. as an organization does not believe that some rights are more important than others. Instead of focusing its efforts on the most important and fundamental civil and political rights—such as the rights to choose one's government, enjoy equal status and protection under the law, or be free from arbitrary execution, torture, and arbitrary detention—the U.N. system spends an inordinate amount of resources on promoting certain "rights" listed in the International Covenant on Economic, Social and Cultural Rights, such as the "right to an adequate standard of living" and the "right to health."

While the ICESCR is part of the so-called International Bill of Human Rights—consisting of the ICESCR, the Universal Declaration of Human Rights, and the International Covenant on Civil and Political Rights and its optional protocols—it should be secondary to prevention of arbitrary death, detention, torture, and other grievous violations of human rights. Yet, the official policy of the U.N. system is that ICESCR principles such as the "right to work," "right to an adequate standard of living," and "right to health" have equal standing with the fundamental civil and political rights protected by the International Covenant on Civil and Political Rights. The U.N. system fails to recognize that without the institutional guarantees provided by civil and political rights—an independent judiciary, the rule of law, and representative government—all other rights are essentially unen-

---

45. World Conference on Human Rights, "Vienna Declaration and Programme of Action," June 25, 1993, at www.unhchr.ch/huridocda/huridoca.nsf/(Symbol)/ A.CONF.157.23.En (accessed November 21, 2008).

forceable. That is, a population may possess some ethereal "right to health," but that right is likely unattainable without an accountable government and accessible judiciary.

Although the Vienna Declaration does not have the standing of a treaty document, it carries the imprimatur of the 171 nations that signed it, including the United States. Moreover, the Human Rights Council has undeniably placed great significance on the principles of the Vienna Declaration, placing the Declaration and Program of Action as a permanent item on the council's agenda. Indeed, former high commissioner Arbour expressed support for placing emphasis on such "rights": "For various reasons, economic social and cultural rights have not always received the same amount of attention as civil and political ones. It is now time to change that."[46]

The resulting allocation of U.N. resources is predictably distorted. The developmental "rights" promoted by the ICESCR receive the same—perhaps more—attention as the civil and political rights protected under the ICCPR. For example, for every special rapporteur on key HRC thematic mandates such as torture, arbitrary detention, and freedom of religion, there is a special rapporteur or working group on issues such as adequate housing, transnational corporations, the right to food, the right to health, and the "effects of foreign debt and other related international financial obligations of States on the full enjoyment of human rights, particularly economic, social and cultural rights."[47] Moreover, the U.N. system tends to

---

46. Louise Arbour, statement to the Commission on Human Rights, Open-Ended Working Group, January 14, 2005, at www.unhchr.ch/huricane/huri cane.nsf/0/ECAE2629449C1EBCC1256F8C0035047D (accessed November 21, 2008).

47. The HRC's thirty thematic mandates are: (1) special rapporteur on adequate housing as a component of the right to an adequate standard of living; (2) Working Group on People of African Descent; (3) Working Group on Arbitrary Detention; (4) special rapporteur on the sale of children, child prostitution, and child pornography; (5) special rapporteur on the right to education; (6) Working Group on Enforced or Involuntary Disappearances; (7) special rapporteur on extrajudicial, summary, or arbitrary executions; (8) independent expert on the question of human rights and extreme poverty; (9) special rapporteur on the right to food; (10) independent expert on the effects of foreign debt and other related international financial obligations of states on the full enjoyment of human rights, particularly economic, social, and cultural rights; (11) special rapporteur on the promotion and protection of the right to freedom of opinion and expression; (12) special rapporteur on freedom of religion or belief; (13) special rapporteur on the right of everyone to the enjoyment of the highest attainable standard of physical and mental health; (14) special rapporteur on the situation of human rights defenders; (15) special rapporteur on the independence of judges and lawyers; (16) special rapporteur on the situation of human rights and fundamental freedoms of indigenous

promote aspirational rights over individual rights when this suits its ends, such as when it subordinates intellectual property rights to the U.N.'s broader development agenda.

While the health and welfare of the world's people are worthy causes deserving of U.N. attention, the human rights system is the wrong venue for promoting and protecting these causes. The U.N.'s development agenda is well represented throughout the U.N. system. Multiple U.N. agencies and programs are devoted to promoting the values enumerated in the ICESCR. For instance, the World Food Program, the U.N. Development Program, the International Labor Organization, and the World Health Organization are just a few of the U.N. organizations dedicated to the attainment of an "adequate standard of living" for all the peoples of the world.

ADVANCING HUMAN RIGHTS OUTSIDE THE U.N.

As outlined above, the United Nations has been charged with advancing and promoting human rights for more than six decades. The results have been disappointing. Representative government and recognition of fundamental human rights have expanded remarkably, particularly since the end of the Cold War, and the U.N. system deserves some credit for this progress

people; (17) representative of the secretary-general on the human rights of internally displaced persons; (18) working group on the use of mercenaries as a means of impeding the exercise of the right of peoples to self-determination; (19) special rapporteur on the human rights of migrants; (20) independent expert on minority issues; (21) special rapporteur on contemporary forms of racism, racial discrimination, xenophobia, and related intolerance; (22) special rapporteur on contemporary forms of slavery, including its causes and consequences; (23) independent expert on human rights and international solidarity; (24) independent expert on the effects of foreign debt and other related international financial obligations of states on the full enjoyment of human rights, particularly economic, social, and cultural rights; (25) special rapporteur on the promotion and protection of human rights while countering terrorism; (26) special rapporteur on torture and other cruel, inhuman, or degrading treatment or punishment; (27) special rapporteur on the adverse effects of the illicit movement and dumping of toxic and dangerous products and wastes on the enjoyment of human rights; (28) special rapporteur on trafficking in persons, especially in women and children; (29) special representative of the secretary-general on human rights and transnational corporations and other business enterprises; and (30) special rapporteur on violence against women, its causes, and consequences. Office of the U.N. High Commissioner for Human Rights, "Special Procedures Assumed by the Human Rights Council: Thematic Mandates," May 1, 2008, at www2.ohchr.org/english/bodies/chr/special/themes.htm (accessed November 21, 2008).

through its early efforts to establish standards for fundamental human rights and subsequent efforts to hold nations to those standards. However, it is also vital to acknowledge that the U.N. human rights system has often shielded violators, prevented scrutiny, and retarded progress.

The U.N. human rights system is extremely complex and seemingly designed to obfuscate and conflate human rights in order to make clear assessments of specific human rights situations practically impossible. A moral equivalence pervades the system to the point that exemplary states such as Sweden are dutifully considered on par with genocidal states such as Sudan, that is, neither state is perfect and needs to improve. This false moral equivalence is driven by political motivations, including an obsessive focus on the Israeli–Palestinian problem to the neglect of other grave human rights situations. The system is focused on claiming ever more tenuous norms and asserting new "rights," as detailed in Susan Yoshihara's chapter. This may serve the purposes of international diplomats and human rights professionals, but it falls far short for those around the world who have been deprived of their dignity and liberty.

The U.N. has no monopoly on the promotion of human rights in the world. A number of initiatives outside of the U.N. system are dedicated to examining and promoting human rights. For instance, the United States promotes international human rights in a number of ways through federal legislation, including the Foreign Assistance Act of 1961, the Millennium Challenge Act of 2003, the Trafficking Victims Protection Act, and the International Religious Freedom Act. The U.S. government also places unilateral economic, political, and military sanctions on governments with deplorable human rights records, including Burma, North Korea, Sudan, Syria, and Zimbabwe. Both the United States and the European Union produce annual reports regarding the current state of human rights practices. Human rights are also promoted by several regional, multilateral human rights organizations, including the Organization for Security and Co-operation in Europe, the Inter-American Commission on Human Rights, the African Commission on Human and Peoples' Rights, and the Council of Europe.

The United States and other countries interested in promoting fundamental human rights should not tolerate institutionalized mediocrity or ineffectiveness. Given the U.N.'s ineffectiveness, the United States should explore and take the first steps toward establishing alternative means to promote respect for fundamental human rights. A more transparent and global forum of freedom-loving countries is needed to promote and scrutinize human rights practices, such as Kim R. Holmes of The Heritage Foundation has suggested in *Liberty's Best Hope*:

> The United States could consider launching a Liberty Forum for Human Rights. It would provide a venue for countries to discuss and better understand

critical linkages of freedom, good governance, and the rule of law; human rights and security; and economic and political freedoms; and the role of the free democratic sovereign state in upholding liberty, justice, and equality before the law. Abusers of liberty would likely stay away, and even some of our friends (particularly in Europe) would at first be lukewarm, but scores of other countries would attend.[48]

Whatever the body is called, it must be structured to avoid the inherent flaws and key impediments of the U.N. system. Specifically, it must restrict membership to states that actually observe basic human rights, transcend the bloc voting tendencies of the regional groups, focus on fundamental civil and political rights, and welcome robust NGO input within that focus. Of critical importance, the new human rights body should be financed through a voluntary funding mechanism. A well-run, effective organization will garner financial support from its membership, while a poorly run or ineffective institution will not. A voluntary funding system as described by Ambassador John Bolton in the foreword to this book would serve as a critical check on the new body and create incentives for strong performance. Such a mechanism should also help to prevent excessive growth of the organization. It should remain a lean institution with minimal staff—perhaps seconded to the organization directly from member states as in-kind contributions—to undertake its responsibilities and no more.

Membership Criteria for the New Body

This alternative institution should be based on participation and membership of national governments. However, mere status as a national government should not be sufficient qualification for membership. As the failures of the CHR and HRC have definitively proven, the key to a successful multilateral human rights organization is ensuring that its membership observes the principles that the organization seeks to promote. Membership must be based on strict criteria, with scant leeway given. A nation's respect for human rights should not be assumed simply because it is a U.N. member, the rights appear in that nation's constitution, or the nation has ratified various human rights treaties.

While no list of qualifications is perfect, membership criteria should be based on each nation's human rights record and its commitment to preserve and protect fundamental human rights within its borders while promoting human rights around the world. At a bare minimum, a qualified member state will make no distinction among its citizens along racial, ethnic, gender, or religious lines in connection with their enjoyment of life,

---

48. Kim R. Holmes, *Liberty's Best Hope: American Leadership for the 21st Century* (Washington, DC: Heritage Foundation, 2008), 122.

expression of liberty, and possession of property. Suffrage must be universal, and citizens should be able to select their government through a free and fair electoral process. The citizens of a member state must also be able to protest infringements of their rights. Robust protection for free speech, free press, and peaceful assembly are also necessary prerequisites. The nations must possess an independent and impartial judicial system charged with protecting civil liberties and private property rights.

In addition to a proven respect for the human rights of its citizenry, each member nation of the new body must be adjudged to provide the means of enforcing and protecting those rights. Human rights cannot exist in a vacuum as a theoretical entitlement. Even natural rights must be affirmed by member states. Possession of a right without an avenue for relief for violations of that right is an empty entitlement. Member states must therefore have avenues for redressing violations of fundamental human rights in their governments' executive and/or judicial branches.

These membership criteria will likely exclude many nations. Yet the principle of universal or nondiscriminatory inclusion has been the downfall of U.N. human rights organizations. While the new body will not be immune from power politics, bloc voting, and the members' national interests, the members' universal and proven commitment to human rights should greatly reduce the negative consequences of such problems.

Nations that have not yet achieved the highest standards of human rights should not be wholly excluded from the body's activities. This would discourage nations that have the best of intentions, but have unresolved and intractable problems. Therefore, nations that can establish a commitment to human rights should be permitted to participate as observers until they meet the criteria for full membership. Unlike in the U.N. system, to join this body a nation must demonstrably meet these criteria for an extended period, perhaps encompassing the peaceful transition between elected civilian governments. A nation's written submission claiming that it meets the qualifications would be insufficient. Similarly, members that fail to observe the criteria should be subject to censure, demotion to observer status, or expulsion. Such action should be taken through member voting rather than consensus; voting would facilitate holding nations accountable and would force countries to defend their votes publicly. Transparency in the voting process would enhance countries' accountability for their positions because they would expect to be criticized and held to a high standard by NGOs and other countries.

NGOs should be encouraged to inform members of the new human rights body about human rights concerns and to contribute information and reports to the body, but they should not be treated as equal partners of nation-states. This is not to dismiss the NGOs' valuable contribution to human rights, but for all their strengths they do not broadly represent the peoples of a nation and are not held as accountable to their citizens as are elected representatives. They also often lack basic accountability and transparency in terms of motives, membership, and financing. Furthermore, NGOs serve as a valuable external check and critic of multilateral institutions, and that role would suffer if they became too entwined with the body.

Activities of the New Body

Like the U.N. human rights system, the new human rights body would engage in activities aimed solely at promoting the universal enjoyment of fundamental human rights. The new body should seek to coordinate joint sanctions for gross and systematic human rights violations and to coordinate efforts to promote protection of civil and political rights through technical and other assistance. It should also explore the possibility of issuing joint statements on the civil and political rights practices of its members and of other countries around the world. The joint statements should incorporate input from NGOs and could be modeled on the U.S. Department of State's *Country Reports on Human Rights Practices*. Given that elected representative government is in many ways the keystone of civil and political rights, the body should also offer electoral assistance, observers, and judgments on the freedom and fairness of elections of its members and other nations.

However, the new body should be specifically set up to promote human rights as those rights are traditionally understood and recognized. One key difference between the new body and the HRC is that the new body's activities should prioritize promoting fundamental civil and political rights over economic, social, and cultural rights and controversial new "discovered" rights.

Beyond promotion of fundamental human rights (e.g., universal suffrage, equal rights under the law, free speech, a free press, and the right to peacefully assemble), issues such as genocide, ethnic cleansing, arbitrary execution, war crimes, human trafficking, and torture should take precedence on the new body's agenda. Social, cultural, and economic issues may be examined within the context of how fundamental human rights contribute to the attainment of enhanced economic, cultural, and social gains, but not as discrete rights recognized by the body.

The new body should place special emphasis on governments that violate fundamental civil and political rights in a systematic manner. While the body should not ignore human rights abuses occurring on a less systematic level around the world, it would properly emphasize examining nations or situations that represent the world's worst human rights violations. For example, the human rights situations in nations like Burma, North Korea,

Sudan, and Zimbabwe should be given special attention and resources, in contrast to the U.N. system, which devotes the extensive time and resources to Israel and the relatively minor human rights blemishes in Europe or the United States.

In contrast to the HRC trend of abolishing country-specific mandates, country-specific studies should be a mainstay of the new human rights body's activities. Unlike the U.N. system, it must not shy away from "naming and shaming" the world's worst human rights abusers.

Ultimately, respect for and protection of human rights depends directly on a government's commitment to observe those rights and indirectly on other governments' commitment to hold nations to those standards. Neither the U.N. human rights system nor any other human rights body possesses the authority or means to actually protect the rights of individual human beings living in its member states. The governments of each respective nation are the only entities that can provide such protection. Regardless, nations that believe in the importance of fundamental human rights have a moral obligation to coalesce, speak out, and, where appropriate, act against the world's worst abuses.

Some would argue that only a U.N. body with universal membership would possess the legitimacy necessary to assess and pass judgment on the human rights situations around the world and that a nonuniversal body would lack the means for encouraging positive change. These conclusions are belied by the poor record of the CHR and the HRC, which as U.N. bodies were open to all member states and ineffective in their mission. A new human rights body can facilitate that process more effectively than the U.N. system because it would not be impeded by universal membership and the historical legacies that serve to mollify and blunt frank consideration and condemnation of violations and violators in the U.N. system. Shared commitment to human rights by the members would likely lead the new body to adopt stronger joint actions in response to human rights crises. Properly constructed, it would be more effective, transparent, and credible than the U.N. system, specifically, the Human Rights Council. Success would create the normal incentives for countries to become members or observers. This would be aided by the notion that the group would be exceptional and exclusive, that is, that membership itself would convey a stamp of approval of actual practice of good governance rather than simply the fact that the government controls the country.

The creation of a new multilateral human rights organization is fraught with pitfalls. The new body should not operate under any illusion that its activities will supplant the U.N. human rights system. Most nations, even traditional protectors of human rights such as the nations of the European Union, are committed to the U.N. system. The new body is not intended to immediately replace the Human Rights Council or other U.N. activities, but to serve as a much-needed rival by showing how a proper human rights organization should act. Success in this goal will promote the cause of oppressed peoples around the world and eventually relegate the flawed U.N. human rights system to a secondary role and a justly earned irrelevance.

CONCLUSION

Despite assuming the mantle as the world's human rights arbiter and enforcer, U.N. human rights bodies and mechanisms have been gravely disappointing and ineffective. While many nations and human rights advocates acknowledge the weaknesses of the U.N. system in promoting human rights, they often exhibit a deep and strong resistance to creating alternative institutions outside of the United Nations. Considering the U.N.'s poor record, such resistance makes little sense. Institutionalized mediocrity or ineffectiveness in the defense of fundamental human rights should not be tolerated. An alternative institution could hardly fail to meet the low bar set by the existing system and could easily surpass it if structured to avoid the major flaws of the U.N. system.

The United States should explore and take the first steps toward establishing a more effective alternative body to examine human rights practices and to promote respect for fundamental human rights. To avoid the missteps of the current system, the alternative body must be structured to avoid the key impediments of the U.N. system. Of paramount importance is restricting membership to states that actually observe basic human rights, focusing the institution on fundamental civil and political rights, and welcoming NGO participation and input within that focus.

However, the United States must be cognizant of this inertia and investment in the current system when proposing and soliciting the participation of other nations in the new human rights body. To that end, the United States should expressly state that the alternative institution is not intended to replace the existing U.N. system, but to supplement it by offering a more assertive and effective body to examine and promote human rights without the restrictions of the U.N. system. The United States should point out that other regional multilateral bodies outside the U.N. currently evaluate human rights issues, and the new body would emulate their efforts on a global scale. A first step in establishing the alternative would be for the United States, European nations, and other interested nations to release a joint annual report on human rights practices in countries based on country information contained in the U.S. State Department's *Country Reports on Human Rights Practices*, the EU's Annual Report on Human Rights, other national publications, and relevant submissions from NGOs. Joint releases and collaborative efforts in producing the joint report should spur interest in joint meetings, hearings, and actions on human rights.

The United States should continue to participate in those parts of the U.N. human rights system that it finds relevant or useful. For example, the United States should continue participating in the Human Rights Committee and other treaty bodies of treaties that the United States has ratified. This is necessary, if only to forcefully reject expansive or unjustified interpretations of treaty provisions or to refute unwarranted criticism. The United States should also continue assertively proposing and supporting human rights resolutions in the Third Committee, which has proven to be more responsible than the Human Rights Council in confronting states about their human rights violations. Such a venue also allows the United States to express its position within the U.N. system.

However, the United States should not support, attend, respond to, or participate in U.N. human rights bodies simply because they exist. Reports, experts, investigations, and inquiries from any treaty body of a treaty that the United States has not ratified should be largely dismissed and ignored unless the United States ratifies that treaty. However, to the extent deemed necessary, the United States should observe and report on proceedings. Treaties that have remained signed for extended periods without earning Senate advice and consent should be unsigned to remove any pretense of privileges, restrictions, or obligations relating to observance of the treaty. Similarly, if a human rights body has proven irrelevant or hopelessly flawed, such as the U.N. Human Rights Council, the United States should not reward it with U.S. financial support, prestige, or participation.

There remains a slim hope that the Human Rights Council could right itself. The resolution creating the council requires the U.N. General Assembly to "review the status of the Council within five years," or by April 2011. However, that review is unlikely to lead to strict membership requirements, a mandate placing an emphasis on fundamental political and civil rights, a change in anti-Israel biases, strengthened country-specific mandates, or a more robust mechanism for universal periodic review. Any reforms falling short of those basic requirements will further prove the necessity to create an alternative arbiter of international human rights.

An alternative human rights body will rise and fall based on its actions and seriousness. A body willing to confront nations about their violation or abuse of fundamental human rights will naturally draw the interest, participation, and respect of human rights NGOs and nations committed to preserving fundamental human rights for their citizens and promoting those rights elsewhere. The contrast with the U.N. system will be stark, and nations will likely gravitate toward it as its prestige rises. The flaws of the U.N. system will become increasingly evident based on the differences in membership between the two bodies, and the U.N. role in human rights will gradually and inevitably fall even further into disrepute. The ultimate goal is not to replace the U.N. human rights system, although this may result, but to establish a credible body to promote and take action to protect fundamental human rights. Success in this goal will promote the cause of oppressed peoples around the world and benefit those who value freedom regardless of nationality.

ACKNOWLEDGMENTS

We would like to thank Lee Casey, Leonard Leo, and Ruth Wedgwood for their comments and suggestions for this chapter.

6

The Quest for Happiness

How the U.N.'s Advocacy of Economic, Social, and Cultural Rights Undermines Liberty and Opportunity

Susan Yoshihara

Sixty years ago, still shaken by the atrocities of World War II, nations entered final negotiations on the Universal Declaration of Human Rights (UDHR). Seeing its final adoption jeopardized by a standoff on the nature of rights, Charles Malik, one of the negotiators, warned:

> Even after man is fully secure in his so-called "economic rights" he may still be not-man. But, unless man's proper nature, unless his mind and spirit are brought out, set apart, protected, and promoted, the struggle for human rights is a sham and a mockery.[1]

Diverging perspectives on the meaning of human rights led to deep divisions over the primacy of two kinds of rights. On one hand were state-provided economic, social, and cultural rights promoted by the Soviet states. On the other were inherent individual and personal rights emphasized by the United States and United Kingdom in the tradition of the Magna Carta and U.S. Constitution.[2]

---

1. Charles Malik, quoted in Habib Malik, ed., *The Challenge of Human Rights: Charles Malik and the Universal Declaration* (Oxford: Center for Lebanese Studies, 2000), 108–9.
2. Malik, *Challenge of Human Rights*.

This fundamental difference endures today. There remains a tension between championing civil and political rights that expand individual liberty and efforts to include economic, social, and cultural rights to such things as government-mandated health care and access to clean water. Dominated by the United States and other Western nations, the U.N. in its early years held fast to the original focus on civil and political rights. However, as developing countries and Soviet client states gained in number and influence at the U.N., the organization began to focus increasingly on promoting economic, social, and cultural benefits as "human rights."[3] In the past three decades, human rights activists inside and outside the U.N. system have also dramatically shifted their priorities from promoting civil and political rights to demanding that governments provide their favored economic, social, and cultural rights.

Six decades after the U.N. was created, few disagree that far too many people still suffer oppression at the hands of abusive governments and the scandal of poverty unalleviated by repeated international efforts. Many objective indexes document the progress or regression in political, economic, and civil rights year to year. Regrettably, many who work in this area seem to have given up on the hard cases and instead spend their days lobbying the U.N. to pressure governments to respect particular rights and expand handouts to certain minorities and groups.

This troubling development accelerated in the 1970s and 1980s as the West and Soviet Union ramped up competition in the developing world to persuade countries to adopt their economic and political models. At the U.N., the dynamic played out in efforts to induce governments to commit to policies that would promote ideals cemented in conventions as aspirations. Binding legal obligations were ascribed to governments to make them accountable for these outcomes, which required a fundamental change in the international economic order. U.N. bureaucrats sought to obligate governments to redistribute wealth in order to fulfill their humanitarian pledges. More recently, they began to claim that the common good requires the protection of every possible social desire, including one's bisexual, homosexual, or transsexual orientation.

This chapter will examine how the United Nations is central to promoting this elitist approach to economic, social, and cultural concerns. Groups with their own narrow interests now understand that if they cannot persuade their governments to give them what they want, they can pressure the

---

3. For example, when the International Covenant on Economic, Social and Cultural Rights was negotiated in the 1960s, World Bank officials refused to participate, saying such issues were outside its mandate. However, the latest World Bank health strategy indicates that it is deeply interested in such issues, including contraceptive use by women in Madagascar.

U.N. to declare what they want a "right" and pursue a global governance structure to enact and provide for it.

For one who has not followed these issues, this may sound extreme, but the evidence is ripe and growing. This rights-based approach poses significant challenges not only to countries that promote and protect individual liberties, but also to multilateral and international agencies. At the U.N., the rise of civil society and the campaign to change minds by mandating a broad and evolving range of economic, social, and cultural "rights" have pitted U.N. programmatic functions against a sharply increasing legalistic function. The merging of mandates attendant to the rights-based approach has diminished the autonomy, focus, and effectiveness of premier U.N. programs such as the United Nations Children's Fund (UNICEF) by linking them to more controversial programs and agendas, such as those of the United Nations Population Fund (UNFPA).

Consequently, the U.N. bureaucracy has gained extraordinary skill at promoting new norms and standards, even as it is failing to dispense goods and services to the people most in need. This rights-based approach undermines the rule of law when it circumvents the role of sovereign states in setting standards. Instead, committees of unelected and unaccountable "experts" set the standards and impose them through the human rights system. The credibility of the U.N. in protecting and promoting universally accepted human rights has been destroyed in the process, as Heritage Foundation experts Brett Schaefer and Steven Groves describe in their chapter. Worse, this process undermines the very social and cultural institutions, such as the family and religious networks, that historically have provided the overwhelming majority of effective services.

The evolution of the rights agenda at the U.N. plays out in three troubling ways.

First, it has inherited the ideological mantle left by the end of the Cold War. By exploiting pressing moral and human crises such as extreme hunger, established human rights norms are being redefined, reappearing as radical new "universally agreed" norms.

Second, the international power structure is being moved decidedly against the sovereign state, particularly the United States, and toward political, geographic, and cultural groupings. The very nature of international law is being redefined from a body of legal instruments to the opinions of U.N. officials, who view U.N. human rights and humanitarian proclamations as the only legitimate and universal "laws" and who believe that U.N. committee interpretations of treaties that go well beyond the treaties' texts are judiciable in national courts.

Third, the movement counters the U.S.-inspired, but internationally embraced democracy movement. It seeks to pit economic, cultural, and social privileges against civil and political rights in a competitive way to advance materialist goals, undermining the freedoms of speech and religion and circumventing democratic deliberation and debate.

In the end, the U.N. has done little to advance the economic, social, and cultural freedom in repressive states, such as Cuba, Sudan, Zimbabwe, China, and Iran. Americans would like to see the U.N. do a better job, but they understand that there is little hope without radical reform and that alternative organizations might provide a better solution. The best way forward is a strategy that utilizes selective participation, demands strict adherence to the agreed language of treaties, and insists that treaty bodies and special rapporteurs adhere to their mandates. It would de-emphasize the U.N.'s top-down, activist-driven projects and would instead promote targeted bilateral and ad hoc approaches.

THE EVOLUTION OF RIGHTS AT THE U.N.

Recovering from the shock of genocide and war, the founders of the U.N. were intent on creating an institution that at its core respected fundamental human rights and freedoms. While not enumerating specific rights save the "equal rights and self determination of peoples," the U.N. Charter made it clear that member states must honor all human rights and freedoms. Notably, the Charter does not hold all rights equal. Article 1 distinguishes between the two goals of "solving international problems of an economic, social, cultural or humanitarian nature" and "promoting and encouraging respect for human rights and fundamental freedoms without distinction as to race, sex, language, or religion." Article 55 adds a third goal, promoting "higher standards of living, full employment, and conditions of economic and social progress and development."

The Universal Declaration of Human Rights, passed by the U.N. General Assembly in 1948, enumerates a broader list of rights than those that were, until then, understood and acknowledged as customary international law. These rights range from the widely accepted rights to life, liberty, and due process under the law to less universally observed rights to work, leisure, and a standard of living adequate for health and well-being. Many of the rights asserted in the declaration remain subject to considerable dispute over their interpretation and the specific obligations that they impose on governments.

Less controversial, in part because of their historical and philosophical grounding, are the political and civil rights enumerated in the International Covenant on Civil and Political Rights (ICCPR),[4] which was adopted in

---

4. International Covenant on Civil and Political Rights, March 23, 1976, at www2.ohchr.org/english/law/ccpr.htm (accessed December 16, 2008).

1966 and entered into force in 1976. The ICCPR identifies rights including self-determination of peoples; equal rights of men and women; right to life, liberty, and security of person; freedom of movement; equality before the law; freedom of thought, conscience, and religion; freedom of expression; peaceful assembly; freedom of association; the right of men and women to marry and found a family; the right of children to protection, name, and nationality; the right to vote; and a right to express one's culture and religion. The United States and 161 other states are party to the ICCPR. Repressive countries such as China, Cuba, and Saudi Arabia have not signed the covenant. Most notably, signatories had problems with language in the treaty and filed twenty-eight pages of reservations, understandings, and declarations. The United States filed a full two pages of explanation to clarify that certain statements in the treaty did not supersede the U.S. Constitution, federalist system of government, or laws.[5]

The economic, social, and cultural rights asserted in the International Covenant on Economic, Social and Cultural Rights (ICESCR) have caused considerably more controversy.[6] The ICESCR was adopted at the same time as the ICCPR and entered into force two months earlier. The ICESCR imposes a broad array of responsibilities on governments, including providing an adequate standard of living, the highest attainable standard of physical and mental health, education, freedom from hunger, labor and union rights, social security, participation in cultural life, and enjoyment of the benefits of scientific progress and its applications. There are 159 states party to the ICESCR, including repressive countries such as China. Except for the Carter administration, every U.S. administration judged the treaty as having no merit and considered it a threat to the U.S. constitutional system and economy. President Jimmy Carter signed it in 1979, but he did not submit it for ratification for political reasons. Each successive administration has examined the treaty and chosen not to press for ratification due to major legal and constitutional concerns.[7]

Why would the United States ratify the ICCPR but not the ICESCR? The difference lies in the role that government is expected to play in assuring civil and political rights on one hand and economic, social, and cultural

---

5. Declarations and Reservations to the International Covenant on Civil and Political Rights, at www2.ohchr.org/english/bodies/ratification/docs/Declarations ReservationsICCPR. pdf (accessed December 16, 2008).

6. International Covenant on Economic, Social and Cultural Rights, January 3, 1976, at www2.ohchr.org/english/law/cescr.htm (accessed December 16, 2008).

7. For an earlier Heritage Foundation study outlining the problems that the convention poses to the United States, see Andrew J. Cowin, "Human Rights Treaty Poses Dangers for America," Heritage Foundation *Backgrounder*, no. 361 (July 29, 1993), at www.heritage.org/Research/PoliticalPhilosophy/EM361.cfm (accessed December 16, 2008).

"rights" on the other. Broadly conceptualized, civil and political rights identify where government cannot impede on the freedoms of the governed. By contrast, economic, social, and cultural rights are focused on the government's responsibility to provide for citizens attaining some goal, stature, or aspirational state. Some liken this to the difference between rights and entitlements.

Many U.S. government lawyers and officials have obviously concluded that the U.N. effort to impose binding economic, social, and cultural rights through an international system, originally championed by the Soviet Union and its client states, is antithetical not only to state sovereignty and self-governance, but also to long-term economic prosperity. Helle Dale, a foreign policy expert at The Heritage Foundation, has gone so far as to propose that whereas the ten civil and political rights found in U.N. documents are consistent with the U.S. Constitution, the fifteen economic rights directly contradict American political philosophy, springing instead from European political thought, specifically Rousseau and Marx.[8]

During the UDHR negotiations, Malik surmised that fundamental questions were at the heart of the contentious debates: Is the nature of man simply animal or also spiritual? Is he subordinate to or prior to society and the state? Does his ultimate loyalty lie with the state or with intermediate institutions such as family and church?[9] Those who emphasized the first perspective were more likely to promote material needs through social and economic rights. The latter perspective evoked support for civil and political liberties. Echoing Malik, Heritage Foundation scholars Jennifer Marshall and Grace Melton posit that the European approach puts the "general will" or "common good" at odds with and ahead of the needs of the individual, family, and small community, which are at the heart of the entrepreneurial economic fabric of American civil society.

In this vein, a rights-based approach to development, health, and other social and economic factors can be seen as fundamentally out of step with the American democratic tradition. Furthermore, as this chapter demonstrates, the rights-based approach to economic, social, and cultural policy has become a tool in the broader movement to hold governments accountable to elite, unelected bodies that create and enforce novel and particularistic norms without the consent of the individuals whom they purport to represent.

The inherent tension between assuring civil and political rights and eco-

---

8. James Jay Carafano, Lee A. Casey, Helle C. Dale, Jennifer A. Marshall, David B. Rivkin, Grace V. Smith, and Janice A. Smith, "Reclaiming the Language of Freedom," Heritage Foundation *Special Report*, no. 8 (September 6, 2006), at www.heritage.org/research/worldwidefreedom/sr08.cfm (accessed December 16, 2008).

9. Malik, *Challenge of Human Rights*, 110–11.

nomic, social, and cultural rights is not simply a U.S. or Western perception. During the Cold War, the Soviet Union argued that the two types of rights were in a zero-sum relationship. It argued that political rights must be sacrificed so that the state could fulfill social and economic rights. One could argue that the U.N. system supports this viewpoint by how it treats these rights, particularly the proportion of resources dedicated to economic, social, and cultural rights versus the proportion dedicated to civil and political rights. Indeed, while the U.N. officially holds all such rights equal and without distinction for merit or hierarchy, the preference for economic, social, and cultural rights is evident in U.N. statements and debates. For example, in 2003, the Commission on the Status of Women listed the right to development as the first and only right in the opening statement of the "Agreed Conclusions" on violence against women. This effort ultimately failed to secure agreement.[10]

The structure of the U.N. system itself elevates economic, social, and cultural rights above civil and political rights. For instance, aside from the Human Rights Committee, which monitors implementation of the International Covenant on Civil and Political Rights by state parties, no other institution in the U.N. system is dedicated solely to civil and political rights.

Other U.N. bodies are involved in both civil and political rights and economic, social, and cultural rights. The Commission on Human Rights, which was replaced by the Human Rights Council, was a subsidiary body of the Economic and Social Council (ECOSOC) and split its time between civil and political rights and economic, social, and cultural rights. The Human Rights Council reports to the General Assembly, but similarly divides its time between civil and political rights and economic, social, and cultural rights.[11] The General Assembly shares time between these rights in its main committee for human rights, the Third Committee (Social, Humanitarian and Cultural). The Office of the High Commissioner for Human Rights (OHCHR) and the U.N. human rights system under its purview, particularly the treaty bodies and special rapporteurs that monitor and comment on treaty compliance, also cover the range of human rights issues.

---

10. See Center for Women's Global Leadership, "No CSW Agreed Conclusions on Women's Human Rights and Elimination of All Forms of Violence against Women and Girls," 2003, at www.cwgl.rutgers.edu/globalcenter/policy/csw03/noagreed.html (accessed January 2, 2009).

11. "[T]he work of the Council shall be guided by the principles of universality, impartiality, objectivity and non-selectivity, constructive international dialogue and cooperation, with a view to enhancing the promotion and protection of all human rights, civil, political, economic, social and cultural rights. . . ." U.N. General Assembly, "Human Rights Council," A/RES/60/251, April 3, 2006, p. 2, at http://www2.ohchr.org/english/bodies/hrcouncil/docs/A.RES.60.251_En.pdf.

By contrast, key U.N. institutions focused on promoting economic, social, and cultural rights are legion, including one of the six principal organs of the U.N. in ECOSOC; many regional economic commissions; offices of the U.N. secretary-general, such as the Department of Economic and Social Affairs and its divisions such as the Division on the Advancement of Women; the newly created Executive Committee on Economic and Social Affairs, which is to coordinate U.N. funds, programs, and agencies involved in social and economic affairs; and deliberative bodies, including functional commissions on sustainable development, social development, population and development, and the Commission on the Status of Women, which issue nonbinding outcome documents for the General Assembly's consideration.

To the extent that specialized U.N. agencies focus on human rights, which they have increasingly done over the past three decades, they typically focus on addressing economic, social, and cultural rights related to their operations. These specialized U.N. agencies include the World Health Organization (WHO) and the Food and Agricultural Organization (FAO), and U.N. development agencies, such as the U.N. Development Program (UNDP), UNICEF, UNFPA, and the World Food Program (WFP). The United Nations Educational, Scientific and Cultural Organization (UNESCO) in particular is rapidly promoting "norming" in its highly touted Management of Social Transformation (MOST).[12]

MUTUALLY REINFORCING AGENDAS

Advancing human rights is not easy. Even with civil and political rights, which have deep legal and historical foundations, efforts to hold governments accountable for violations are difficult.

Member States

The most evident example is that the U.N. includes a number of member states that routinely deny their citizens fundamental civil and political rights, notwithstanding the standards set forth in the U.N. Charter and the provision to expel those who do not abide by those standards. These states routinely use their privileged position to blunt scrutiny and criticism of their failings. Indeed, one of their preferred tactics to counter criticism of their violations of civil and political rights is to change the subject by point-

---

12. James P. Kelly III, "In the Name of Human Security: UNESCO and the Pursuit of Global Governance," *Engage* 7, no. 2 (2006), at www.globalgovernance watch.org/docLib/20080211_Kelly_Human_Security.pdf (accessed December 18, 2008).

ing out that other nations—typically the United States and other Western nations that generally observe civil and political rights—fail to provide the full range of economic, social, and cultural rights to their citizens.

For instance, China often deflects criticism for its lack of civil and political rights by touting its progress on the economic front. China's one-child policy violates various civil and political rights that China has agreed to recognize—a fact that has caused the United States to withhold funding from the U.N. Population Fund three times due to its association with the Chinese authorities who enforce the policy. In December 2008, Hao Linna, director of the International Cooperation Department of China's National Population and Family Planning Commission, said, "Without the family planning policy, China would not be able to provide sufficient social welfare for every single child that was born."[13] This policy puts the right to life at odds with other civil and political rights and with economic and social needs.

However, social projects are not necessarily promoted as economic and social rights. For example, according to those promoting a new international "right" to abortion, six of the seven rights "violated" when a country does not provide abortions are civil and political: life, equality, dignity, liberty, freedom from inhumane and degrading treatment, and freedom of conscience. The seventh "violated" right is the right to health.[14] Hence, it is inexact to say that advocates seek only to circumscribe civil and political rights by advancing economic and social rights. Rather, advocates of new social norms also seek to revolutionize the meaning of civil and political rights as they are commonly understood and certainly as they were understood when the major human rights treaties were negotiated.

Western governments, particularly European governments, contribute to this trend through their forceful endorsement of the need for a rights-based approach to international governance and human rights. European scholars have argued that the increasingly globalized and interconnected world of the twenty-first century is fundamentally different from the world of the past. Military force and "hard power" are outdated, and future influence will revolve far more around economic might, diplomatic influence, and cooperation with international decisions. Many Europeans argue that Europe's strategic advantage is to become the world's "normative power" by broaching and shaping the international legal framework. These analysts

---

13. Hao Linna, quoted in Xinhua, "Official: China Family Planning Policy Doesn't Contradict Human Rights," *People's Daily* (Beijing), December 3, 2008, at http://english.peopledaily.com.cn/90001/90776/90882/6545056.html (accessed January 2, 2009).

14. Nancy Northrup, address at the Women Deliver Conference, London, October 2007.

believe that Europe will come to rival and overtake U.S. global influence by using ever more salient "soft power" and by championing human rights. As the need for military power to offset the threat from the Soviet Union waned, European Union politicians latched on to this theory as a means for increasing their influence at the U.N. and around the world.

To succeed, the European Union must necessarily bolster the means of asserting its normative role in the U.N. system. One example of its normative standard-setting power over sovereign European states is its controversial Charter of Fundamental Rights. Unlike the U.N. human rights treaties, it explicitly requires nondiscrimination for "sexual orientation."[15]

The EU has been increasingly successful in asserting that it speaks for all European member states at the U.N. This is particularly the case during social policy debates, in which voting congruence among EU members has increased to over 85 percent on human rights issues.[16] The EU works closely with human rights activists to negotiate new norms into nonbinding texts and other instruments of "soft law," such as in Third Committee documents, Human Rights Council resolutions, outcome documents for international conferences, and reports issued by human rights treaty bodies. The EU and some fifteen affiliated states are often joined for press statements by regional leaders such as Brazil and South Africa. In 2007, the EU demonstrated its dominance on social issues by persuading the U.N. General Assembly, against the opposition of the Organization of the Islamic Conference (OIC), to call for a global moratorium on the death penalty.[17]

The EU's success is attributable to its ability to master the two bedrock principles of U.N. negotiation: agreed language and consensus. The reliance of member states on agreed language means that by gradually adding new words and phrases to existing language taken from other state-negotiated documents, the patient negotiator can eventually create new norms. By invoking the specter of parting the curtains and calling for a vote on an issue, negotiators can intimidate dissenting member states into accepting these incremental changes in the name of maintaining consensus and avoiding isolation, as Ambassador John Bolton observes in the foreword of

---

15. The Charter of Fundamental Rights of the European Union, art. 21, par. 1, at www.europarl.europa.eu/charter/pdf/text_en.pdf (accessed January 2, 2009).

16. Katie Laatikainen and Karen Smith, eds., *The European Union at the United Nations: Intersecting Multilateralisms* (New York: Palgrave, 2006).

17. On December 18, 2007, the General Assembly passed a resolution calling for a "moratorium on the death penalty" by a vote of 104 to 54 with 29 abstentions. The resolution was an initiative of Italy and the EU, which successfully lobbied for it in the Third Committee. See press release, "General Assembly Adopts Landmark Text Calling for Moratorium on Death Penalty," U.N. Department of Public Information, December 18, 2007, at www.un.org/News/Press/docs/2007/ga10678 .doc.htm (accessed December 18, 2008).

this book. In the past several years, U.S. negotiators have been nearly alone in their willingness to call for a floor vote.

Nongovernmental Organizations

The self-serving support for economic, social, and cultural rights by the EU and developing countries—which use the international commitment to fulfill those rights to call for increased economic assistance from developed countries—goes hand in hand with the aims of leftist nongovernmental organizations (NGOs) and transnational networks that seek to shift the focus of human rights from civil and political rights to economic, cultural, and social rights. Activists look to promote these new norms in the U.N.'s more pliable environment for several reasons. Most importantly, many of their policies are often too radical to succeed in the arena of democratic debate in their home countries.

A telling example is the case of the Declaration on Human Cloning. French and German delegates frustrated with their countries' restrictions on human cloning called for a negotiated document at the U.N. The new document would ban only reproductive cloning, but allow "therapeutic" cloning, thus overcoming their countries' restrictions.[18] However, their plan backfired when the media alerted their governments, which then demanded that their U.N. representatives uphold national laws. The result was a document that banned all forms of human cloning.

Disenchanted with the laborious, time-consuming democratic and bureaucratic process of national policymaking, many activists come to the U.N. for practical reasons. Many are also idealistic, believing in the supremacy of "elite discourse" over appeals to public opinion, especially when the public is not as "enlightened" on the issues of global scope as these U.N. elites claim to be. Frustration with their governments' lack of concern or progress for the poor and marginalized, many small groups return to U.N. meetings year after year as a sort of appeal of last resort. Many of these small groups are unaware that a few privileged NGOs dominate the arena, gradually encroaching on their issues. In recent years, these powerful NGOs have turned away from their traditional activism for civil and political rights toward social and economic rights—even rights not mentioned in any of the international covenants. Amnesty International is perhaps the best-known case.[19]

---

18. See press release, "General Assembly Adopts United Nations Declaration on Human Cloning by Vote of 84–34–37," U.N. General Assembly, at www.un.org/News/Press/docs/2005/ga10333.doc.htm (accessed December 18, 2008).

19. See Joel E. Oestreich, *Power and Principle: Human Rights Programming in International Organizations* (Washington, DC: Georgetown University Press, 2007).

U.N. Treaty Bodies and Bureaucrats

Various U.N. bodies and bureaucrats, which are poised to reap increased influence and resources, are eager partners of the NGOs. Indeed, because advocates for these rights broadly seek the same goals, including the justiciability and extraterritoriality of international law, the push for radical social policy has infected every corner of the U.N. human rights system.

To support this legalistic approach, advocates seek state acceptance of the idea that treaty implementing bodies—usually composed of "experts" who act on their own authority and do not represent their state governments—have the status of high legal authorities whose opinions on any issue can shape current understanding of international law. Yet the treaties themselves vest no such authority in their treaty bodies.

Despite their increasingly intrusive role in asserting new rights and state obligations, the treaty bodies have no enforcement authority or mandate to assert and impose new rights or interpretations of treaty text on member states. Even so, member states often find themselves under extreme pressure to bow to their dictates because of the weight that NGOs invest in their comments and reviews. Treaty bodies receive administrative support from the OHCHR budget, yet they increasingly depend on the legwork and policy support of NGOs. NGOs submit detailed "shadow reports," which the experts often use as evidence against state parties. These NGOs often have their own representatives serving in the relevant treaty bodies. For instance, half the committee overseeing the implementation of the Convention on the Elimination of All Forms of Discrimination against Women (CEDAW) Committee are members of women's rights NGOs. At least on this committee, activists have realized their goal of holding sovereign states directly accountable to their desires.

In the General Assembly, NGOs rightly lobby member states to support or oppose resolutions that advance their agendas. However, they are far more effective in lobbying the treaty implementing bodies to interpret the treaties in ways more favorable to their agendas, criticize states for failing to observe these interpretations, and press states to change their domestic laws accordingly.

As with the treaty bodies, special rapporteurs have no official legal authority and are largely unaccountable. Yet their activism is increasingly felt in the U.N.'s agenda for economic, social, and cultural rights. Funded through OHCHR, special rapporteurs have mandates from the Human Rights Council or the U.N. General Assembly to investigate, monitor, and recommend solutions to human rights problems.[20] The independence of

---

20. For detailed descriptions of the mandates of rapporteurs, see Office of the U.N. High Commissioner for Human Rights, "Special Procedures of the Human Rights Council," at www2.ohchr.org/english/bodies/chr/special/index.htm (accessed December 18, 2008).

the special rapporteurs allows them great discretion to interpret their mandates broadly. Often this is advantageous, allowing them to confront and report on abuses freely. However, many have used their positions inappropriately to advocate for economic, social, and cultural rights:

- Paul Hunt, special rapporteur for the highest attainable standard of health, said he used his recently ended tenure to promote "the right to health" and "sexual health rights for girls."[21] Shortly after succeeding Hunt, Indian HIV/AIDS activist Anand Grover met with reproductive rights and homosexual rights NGOs in Mexico City during the United Nations Joint Program on HIV/AIDS (UNAIDS) meeting and pledged support for their agenda.
- Special Rapporteur Yakin Ertuk, whose mandate includes violence against women, announced in 2006 that she would place special emphasis on eliminating religious resistance to new rights and asserted that treaty reservations based on religion are "incompatible" with the CEDAW treaty.[22] This conflicts with established human rights, which in many places guard religious traditions.[23] In defiance of evidence that religion has historically played a central role in protecting women's rights and that faith-based organizations have been instrumental in fighting HIV/AIDS, Ertuk called religious belief a root cause of violence against women and said that abstinence-based programs for combating HIV/AIDS "reinforce ideologies of men's control over women's sexuality (however they may be culturally framed) and thereby contribute to the perpetuation of the root cause of many forms of violence against women."[24]
- U.N. Special Rapporteur on Extrajudicial, Summary or Arbitrary Executions Philip Alston, a human rights expert, has argued—in the context of using a "right to food" to force governments to alleviate world hunger—that only a rights-based, litigious approach will make governments take social and economic issues seriously.[25]

---

21. Paul Hunt, quoted in Samantha Singson, "UN Special Rapporteurs Attack Religion, Promote Radical Rights at Human Rights Council," Catholic Family and Human Rights Institute *Friday Fax*, April 12, 2007, at www.c-fam.org/publications/id.509/pub_detail.asp (accessed December 16, 2008).

22. Singson, "UN Special Rapporteurs."

23. For instance, the ICCPR protects the "liberty of parents and, when applicable, legal guardians to ensure the religious and moral education of their children in conformity with their own convictions." International Covenant on Civil and Political Rights, art. 18.

24. Yakin Ertuk, quoted in Singson, "UN Special Rapporteurs Attack Religion."

25. See Philip Alston and Katrina Tomasevski, eds., *The Right to Food* (Utrecht, NL: Martinus Nijhoff, 1984).

As a practical manner, finding a nation in violation of the progressive attainment of economic, social, and cultural rights is much more difficult than finding violations of civil and political rights. For this reason, the ICESCR constructed a series of steps, often requiring a state to change specific domestic laws and policies, to indicate a nation's move toward progressive realization of economic, social, and cultural rights. Unsatisfactory implementation of these steps—not just the articles of the treaties negotiated by states—determines whether the committee holds states in violation of their treaty obligations under international law.

One of the hallmarks of this rights-based approach is giving social definitions to existing and newly negotiated rights such that any barrier to the right—including attitudes, thoughts, and religious and social moral teachings—constitutes a violation of the state's treaty obligations. The latest human rights convention does exactly this, giving a social definition to "disability" such that any "barriers," including thoughts and attitudes, may be interpreted as a treaty violation.[26]

Another characteristic of the effort is to tie all these rights together so that asserting acceptance of one right necessitates acceptance of all the others. For instance, ICESCR's nonbinding General Comment 14 asserts that the convention's Article 12 on health should be interpreted to include a broadly defined right that is interdependent and therefore necessitates other broad new rights such as a right to food and a right to work.[27]

A problem arises with making this social definition justiciable. Under optional protocols to the human rights treaties, private citizens may "communicate" directly with the human rights committees about perceived violations of their government's obligations under the treaties. In this way, treaty bodies such as the ICESCR Committee are transforming all treaty bodies from committees that monitor state compliance to quasi-judicial organs with the authority to supersede national courts. Because the committee does not consult member states in the creation of its interpretations and may add or subtract steps, nations no longer know what their obligations will be under a treaty.

U.N. agencies, in turn, use these steps to create targets and benchmarks in a rights-based approach to programming. This has significantly influenced the work of the agencies. For example, when UNICEF decided to promote the Convention on the Rights of the Child (CRC), it entailed a "substantial expansion of its mandate and agenda. . . . Whereas before the

---

26. Convention on the Rights of Persons with Disabilities, at www.un.org/dis abilities/convention/conventionfull.shtml (accessed December 19, 2008).

27. U.N. Economic and Social Council, "The Right to the Highest Attainable Standard of Health," E/C.12/2000/4, August 11, 2000, at www.unhchr.ch/tbs/doc .nsf/(symbol)/E.C.12.2000.4.En (accessed December 19, 2008).

CRC certain survival issues were considered of paramount importance, now all issues relating to children . . . are rights and therefore nonnegotiable."[28] In other words, it is much harder to put programmatic emphasis on the needs most central to child survival. Additionally, the imperative to promote children's empowerment, a hallmark of the rights-based approach, reoriented UNICEF's processes from neutral service provision to a politicized role of lobbying governments to recognize certain rights:

> To help children achieve their right to immunization differs from simply providing immunization by placing it in the political context . . . where children and their mothers become empowered to . . . demand them from the primary obligation holder, the government.[29]

CIRCUMVENTING STATE SOVEREIGNTY TO ESTABLISH A NEW SOCIAL ORDER

Advancing controversial interests under the guise of the common good threatens the very sinews of free societies. This growing confluence of interests among socialist-leaning states, leftist NGOs and activists who believe in global governance, and U.N. bodies eager to expand their influence is a threatening force pressing states to observe a radical interpretation of human rights. The following examples of how these interests cooperate to advance "rights" to health, food, water, abortion, and sexual orientation demonstrate how much the U.N. has become a tool of the leftist agenda and how seriously the United States needs to work to ensure that these efforts do not undermine the freedoms, rights, and prosperity that Americans have come to treasure.

Economic Rights

Activists have worked to advance the economic "rights" of health, food, and water, even though they are not recognized by any binding international treaty.

Health

No widely recognized treaty asserts a binding "right to health." The closest reference is Article 25 of the Universal Declaration of Human Rights, which mentions health in reference to an "adequate" standard of living:

---

28. Ostreich, *Power and Principle*, 35.
29. Ostreich, *Power and Principle*, 37.

Everyone has the right to a standard of living adequate for the health and well-being of himself and of his family, including . . . medical care . . . and the right to security in the event of unemployment, sickness, disability, widowhood, old age or other lack of livelihood in circumstances beyond his control.[30]

Although the Universal Declaration is nonbinding, it is universally recognized. Some argue that this means that it has reached the status of customary international law and that U.N. member states are required to honor the rights it enumerates. Yet this assertion is belied by the many nations that have signed the declaration and that fail to honor it in their actions and practices.

Moreover, states rejected the opportunity to codify an explicit right to health in the ICESCR. When states negotiated the covenant in the 1950s and 1960s, they specifically declined to adopt a definition for the "right to health" based on the Constitution of the World Health Organization, which defines health as the "state of complete physical, mental and social well-being, and not merely the absence of disease or infirmity."[31] Instead, nations adopted a loose obligation to protect the "right of everyone to the enjoyment of the highest attainable standard of physical and mental health," which was to be realized incrementally.[32] Although the United States is not a party to ICESCR, it accepts ICESCR's definition of the existing right, as do the European governments, even left-leaning governments. The governments rejected a broader definition because a broad right to health taken seriously (as the United States would do if it ratified such a right) would impose obligations to provide for such things as universal free health care for their citizens.

Advocates of a right to health are undeterred by sovereign decisions about the implications of a treaty. The Committee on Economic, Social and Cultural Rights (CESCR), which monitors ICESCR compliance, and the U.N. special rapporteur on the right of everyone to the enjoyment of the highest attainable standard of physical and mental health regularly argue that a universal right to health exists. The CESCR acknowledges that the social definition that it is advancing was rejected by the states negotiating the convention, but the CESCR argues that the member states were wrong and that its understanding of the legislative history is more authoritative:

In drafting article 12 of the Covenant, the Third Committee of the United Nations General Assembly did not adopt the definition of health contained in

---

30. Universal Declaration of Human Rights, art. 25, at www.un.org/Overview/rights.html (accessed December 19, 2008).

31. U.N. Economic and Social Council, "Right to the Highest Attainable Standard of Health."

32. International Covenant on Economic, Social and Cultural Rights, art. 12.

the preamble to the Constitution of WHO, which conceptualizes health as "a state of complete physical, mental and social well-being and not merely the absence of disease or infirmity." However . . . the drafting history and the express wording of article 12.2 acknowledge that the right to health embraces a wide range of socio-economic factors that promote conditions in which people can lead a healthy life, and extends to the underlying determinants of health, such as food and nutrition, housing, access to safe and potable water and adequate sanitation, safe and healthy working conditions, and a healthy environment.[33]

The CESCR further argues that states are bound to uphold this broader definition and that governments can be held in violation of the treaty's normative content if they do not realize such a right.

Food

Frustrated with the lack of progress toward ending hunger, human rights expert Philip Alston and others published a strategy for NGOs to reframe the issue of world hunger as an international human right to food.[34] As with the right to health, the right to food is not contained in any binding, widely recognized treaty. Advocates for the right also point to Article 25 of the Universal Declaration of Human Rights, which states that "everyone has the right to a standard of living adequate for the health and well-being of himself and his family, including food,"[35] and to the 1974 Universal Declaration on the Eradication of Hunger and Malnutrition, in which governments pledged to end hunger within the decade.[36] However, neither document is binding. Even the ICESCR addresses food only in the context of a "right to an adequate standard of living."

In fact, states have specifically rejected a binding right to food. According to the activist NGO International Food Policy Research Institute (IFPRI), they reject it and cultural and social rights in general because providing it would be "prohibitively expensive" and "impossible to define in legally enforceable terms" and because enforcing the right would require redistribution of privately held resources and such enforcement could easily be

---

33. U.N. Economic and Social Council, "Right to the Highest Attainable Standard of Health."

34. Alston and Tomasevski, *Right to Food.*

35. International Covenant on Economic, Social and Cultural Rights, art. 11, par. 4.

36. Universal Declaration on the Eradication of Hunger and Malnutrition, December 17, 1974, at www.unhchr.ch/html/menu3/b/69.htm (accessed December 19, 2008).

abused by repressive governments.[37] The United States and other countries have argued that the right is an "aspiration" best "realized progressively that does not give rise to any international obligations nor diminish the responsibilities of national governments toward their citizens."[38] However, opposition by states has not prevented advocates from moving forward.

The ICESCR obligates its signatories to recognize "the right of everyone to an adequate standard of living for himself and his family, including adequate food, clothing, and housing."[39] However, in General Comment 12, the CESCR redefined state obligations: "The right to adequate food is realized when every man, woman and child, alone or in community with others, has physical and economic access at all times to adequate food or means for its procurement."[40] Comment 12 claims that the right to food is "inseparable from social justice" and is the basis for a host of other rights. Moreover, it claims that the right to food is extraterritorial and that nations must regulate private citizens and companies to ensure that they comply with treaty obligations. This would require the "adoption of appropriate economic, environmental and social policies, at both the national and international levels."[41] The committee acknowledged that it based General Comment 12 on input from activists, in particular "the draft international code of conduct on the human right to adequate food prepared by international non-governmental organizations" as well as on the nonbinding outcome document of the 1996 World Food Summit.[42]

NGOs such as FIAN International[43] are implementing Alston's litigious strategy by preparing lawsuits against governments for violating the right to food, using the optional protocol to the ICESCR, and by lobbying courts

37. Per Pinstrup-Andersen, David Nygaard, and Annu Ratta, "The Right to Food: Widely Acknowledged and Poorly Protected," International Food Policy Research Institute *2020 Vision Brief*, no. 22 (June 1995), at www.ifpri.org/2020/BRIEFS/NUMBER22.HTM (accessed December 19, 2008).

38. "U.S. Opening Statement for FAO Right to Food Forum," Rome, October 1–3, 2008, at www.fao.org/righttofood/rtf_forum/files/Right%20to%20food%20statement.pdf (accessed December 19, 2008); and U.S. Department of Agriculture, Foreign Agricultural Service, "World Food Summit," modified February 22, 2005, at www.fas.usda.gov/icd/summit/interpre.html (accessed December 19, 2008).

39. International Covenant on Economic, Social and Cultural Rights, art. 11.

40. U.N. Economic and Social Council, "The Right to Adequate Food (Art. 11)," E/C.12/1999/5, May 12, 1999, at www.unhchr.ch/tbs/doc.nsf/(Symbol)/3d027 58c707031d58025677f003b73b9 (accessed December 19, 2008).

41. U.N. Economic and Social Council, "Right to Adequate Food."

42. U.N. Economic and Social Council, "Right to Adequate Food."

43. FIAN is a Germany-based NGO funded largely by FAO and the governments of the Netherlands, Norway, and Sweden and by major Belgian, British, Canadian, and German foundations.

and bureaucracies in fifty countries. Their purpose is to establish a legal, widely accepted right to food. One example of this effort is the 2004 decisions of the FAO's Committee on World Food Security to adopt voluntary guidelines. FAO's legal counsel hailed this as a "major breakthrough" because the guidelines would provide a "human rights-based tool" for identifying states' obligations under a right to adequate food.[44]

Such a right, if taken seriously by states, would require sweeping changes to the international economic order. The highly controversial Swiss sociologist Jean Ziegler, who occupied the special rapporteur position for this right from 2000 to 2008, argued that capitalism, particularly the globalization of neoliberal trade, is the *primary* cause of world hunger, causing a "daily genocide" of the poor by rich countries.[45]

While Ziegler's view is extreme, his policy prescriptions line up with those of other advocates, including the CESCR, IFPRI, and FIAN. Belgian university professor Olivier de Schutter, Zeigler's successor as special rapporteur, has worked with European institutions to regulate successful transnational corporations and to prosecute them and their executive directors under EU human rights law. Along with Socialist Party members of the European Parliament and the EU-funded NGO European Coalition for Corporate Justice, de Schutter is a leader in the international campaign to prosecute transnational corporations using a broad interpretation of "foreign direct liability," which currently applies only in very limited cases such as maritime law.

Water

No widely recognized, binding treaty establishes a "right to water." The Universal Declaration of Human Rights and the ICESCR do not even mention water. However, in 2002, the CESCR set forth a general right to water in General Comment 15. This determination is also based on the same article in the ICESCR that underpins the right to food. However, in General Comment 15, the committee interprets the right to water as including a breathtaking array of additional obligations, such as to (1) regulate corporations to expand agreed definitions of nondiscrimination to include sexual orientation; (2) guarantee noncitizens the same rights as citizens; (3) limit the "use and testing of weapons" and proscribe certain military tactics in warfare; (4) mandate technology transfers from rich to poor nations; and

44. See U.N. Food and Agriculture Organization, "Committee on World Food Security Adopts Right to Food Guidelines," September 24, 2004, at www.fao.org/newsroom/en/news/2004/50821/index.html (accessed December 19, 2008).

45. "Globalized Capitalism Blamed for Increasing Famine," *Guardian*, April 6, 2005, at www.cpa.org.au/garchve05/1222famine.html (accessed December 19, 2008).

(5) regulate lending policies among international financial institutions. These steps and interpretations of obligations are outlined in the CESCR's guidelines for states to avoid "violating" the ICESCR.[46]

The committee sees these steps as necessary to progressively realize a right to water. States that have not "taken the feasible and necessary steps toward the realization of a right to water" as interpreted in General Comment 15 have "failed to act in good faith" and will be found in "violation of the right."[47]

General Comment 15 takes advantage of the transborder nature of water resources to push even further the claim of extraterritoriality of human rights law set out in General Comment 14 on the right to food. The committee maintains that state parties are obligated to help other countries meet their treaty obligations, essentially making states responsible for citizens of other countries:

> For the avoidance of any doubt, the Committee wishes to emphasize that it is particularly incumbent on States parties, and other actors in a position to assist, to provide international assistance and cooperation, especially economic and technical which enables developing countries to fulfill their core obligations.[48]

Social and Cultural Rights

In addition to a variety of economic rights being broadened and increasingly asserted through the U.N. system, a mutually reinforcing group of NGOs, internationalists, and U.N. human rights experts have sought to promote extreme social and cultural activities by creating and imposing select human "rights." Two of the most contentious deal with abortion and sexual orientation.

Abortion

Long frustrated by the resistance of nations to abortion, advocates have turned increasingly to the U.N. to pressure governments to legalize abortion. The strategy involves claiming that abortion rights are a prerequisite

---

46. U.N. Committee on Economic, Social and Cultural Rights, "General Comment No. 15 (2002): The Right to Water (Arts. 11 and 12 of the International Covenant on Economic, Social and Cultural Rights)," E/C.12/2002/11, November 26, 2002, at www.unhchr.ch/html/menu2/6/gc15.doc (accessed January 4, 2009).

47. U.N. Committee on Economic, Social and Cultural Rights, "General Comment No. 15 (2002)."

48. U.N. Committee on Economic, Social and Cultural Rights, "General Comment No. 15 (2002)," par. 38.

for or are inextricably linked to all other human rights and desirable outcomes, such as human development and maternal and child health.

To provide legal footing for international recognition of this right, U.N. bodies interpret treaties in new ways to assert that restrictions on abortion violate human rights. For instance, even though the Convention on the Elimination of All Forms of Discrimination against Women does not mention abortion, the committee that monitors CEDAW implementation by its signatories has asserted in its General Recommendation 24 that abortion restrictions violate Article 12 on health. CESCR, the committee monitoring the International Covenant on Economic, Social and Cultural Rights, similarly asserted in General Comment 14 that Article 12 requires state parties to provide "sexual and reproductive health services," which abortion advocates claim includes abortion. The CESCR has pressured more than a dozen countries on the matter since 1998, including Bolivia and Benin in 2008.[49] The Human Rights Committee, which monitors implementation of the International Covenant on Civil and Political Rights, similarly began pressuring countries in 2003, claiming that the ICCPR includes abortion and sodomy rights. The committee recently attacked Botswana and Ireland for their laws restricting, respectively, sodomy and abortion during their 2008 reviews.[50]

NGOs assist the effort by encouraging citizens to bring lawsuits against their governments alleging failure to observe their "right to abortion." The NGO Center for Reproductive Rights (CRR) chose to look for a plaintiff in Brazil because of the favorable disposition of its left-leaning judges, backing the first case against Brazil in 2008.[51]

To circumvent resistance to a right to abortion, advocates have tried to link it to a new "right to maternal health." This strategy, called the Interna-

---

49. See U.N. Economic and Social Council, "Benin," 2008, at www2.ohchr.org/tbru/cescr/Benin.pdf (accessed December 19, 2008); and "Bolivia," May 16, 2008, at www2.ohchr.org/tbru/cescr/Bolivia.pdf (accessed December 19, 2008).

50. In its 2008 country reviews, the Human Rights Committee told Panama and Ireland that they should liberalize their abortion laws based on Article 6 (the right to life). The committee told Botswana to decriminalize sodomy, asserting that the law violated Article 17 on privacy and Article 26 on nondiscrimination based on "race, color, sex, language, religion, political or other opinion, national or social origin, property, birth or other status." See U.N. High Commissioner for Human Rights, "Letter to Permanent Mission of Panama to the U.N.," August 15, 2008, at www2.ohchr.org/tbru/cerd/Letter_Panama.pdf (accessed December 19, 2008).

51. Luisa Cabal, remarks at the Women Deliver Conference, London, October 2008. For details on the case, see Center for Reproductive Rights, "Center Challenges Brazil's Record on Maternal Mortality," December 7, 2007, at www.reproductiverights.org/ww_lac_brazil.html (accessed December 19, 2008).

tional Initiative on Maternal Mortality and Human Rights,[52] specifically links "unsafe" abortions (ostensibly all illegal abortions) to maternal mortality. The initiative was launched at the U.N.-sponsored Women Deliver Conference in London in 2007. It is the latest step in a legal strategy conceived at an exclusive 1996 meeting hosted by OHCHR, UNFPA, and the U.N. Division for the Advancement of Women. The meeting produced a roundtable report that served as a guide for persuading treaty bodies to reinterpret the rights to life, privacy, health, and nondiscrimination and a host of other rights to include abortion.[53] The advocates have since claimed that abortion is a prerequisite for human development under the U.N. Millennium Development Goals, specifically fulfilling goal 4, "Reduce Child Mortality," and goal 5, "Improve Maternal Health."[54] Claiming a new Millennium Development Goal (MDG) target for reproductive health, no matter how dubious, is important for securing U.N. funding.

U.N. treaty bodies increasingly depend on NGOs such as International Planned Parenthood Federation, CRR, International Women's Health Coalition, and others to provide detailed shadow reports, which experts can use to criticize states. In fact, according to Human Rights Watch, U.N. treaty bodies have pressured at least 93 countries 122 times to liberalize their abortion laws based on NGO reports citing novel treaty interpretations.[55] These special interest NGOs also sponsor citizens' lawsuits against governments to induce national courts to decide that legal abortion is a prerequisite for upholding a state's legal obligations under U.N. human rights treaties and also its alleged development commitments under the

---

52. See Center for Reproductive Rights, "International Initiative on Maternal Mortality and Human Rights," at www.reproductiverights.org/pdf/MMHR%20bro chure%20revised.pdf (accessed December 19, 2008).

53. Activists staged the 2007 Women Deliver Conference in London. It was launched by UNFPA's Thoraya Obaid, former U.N. high commissioner for human rights Mary Robinson, the then U.N. special rapporteur for health and the initiative's author Paul Hunt, and Nancy Northrop, president of the public interest law firm Center for Reproductive Rights, which serves as secretariat for the initiative. The core planning group, which called itself the Partnership for Maternal and Child Health, consisted of UNFPA, UNICEF, WHO, and the World Bank. The event was organized and run by a handful of large abortion providers and advocacy groups with U.N. accreditation, including International Planned Parenthood, Ipas, and Family Care International. Major backing included only four U.N. member states: Britain, the Netherlands, Norway, and Sweden.

54. See U.N. Department of Public Information, "Millennium Development Goals," at www.un.org/millenniumgoals (accessed December 19, 2008).

55. Human Rights Watch, "International Human Rights Law and Abortion in Latin America," July 2005, p. 5, at www.hrw.org/legacy/backgrounder/wrd/ wrd0106/wrd0106.pdf (accessed December 19, 2008).

MDGs. The effort arguably hit its high point in 2006 when Colombia's con-stitutional court overturned abortion restrictions, citing comments by U.N. human rights treaty bodies.

The United States is not immune to this campaign. For instance, in 2008, the U.S. House of Representatives passed H.Res. 1022, "Reducing Maternal Mortality at Home and Abroad," introduced by Representative Lois Capps (D-CA). The Senate passed a similar resolution introduced by Senators Blanche Lincoln (D-AR) and Olympia Snowe (R-ME). Conservative sena-tors successfully removed language that would have declared "maternal health as a human right."[56]

Other U.N. bodies often provide academic and medical reports to rein-force the advocates' claims. A WHO-sponsored paper claimed that "com-prehensive reproductive health care," including abortion, was one of the top three necessary responses to the problem of maternal mortality, even though WHO and other U.N. offices often refute this claim in their reports.[57]

U.N. conferences similarly advance this agenda. Among the 1,700 parti-cipants at the 2007 U.N. Women Deliver Conference were midwives and midlevel health providers from South Asia and sub-Saharan Africa, flown in courtesy of corporate sponsors such as Brazil's Tibotec, Exxon Mobil, and GlaxoSmithKline. UNFPA's Thoraya Obaid announced at the conference that the role of her and other U.N. agencies is to break down religious and cultural barriers to abortion and other progressive sexual norms in a cam-paign of "destigmatization."[58] Breaking down religious barriers was the stated goal of the only official outcome document from the conference. The

---

56. A Resolution Reducing Maternal Mortality Both at Home and Abroad, H.Res 1022, 110th Cong., 2nd sess., and A Resolution Reducing Maternal Mortality Both at Home and Abroad, S.R. 616, 110th Cong., 2nd sess.

57. U.N. Population Division and WHO reports show that developing countries do not report the cause or sex of the deceased, making such a figure impossible to verify. The claim that "comprehensive reproductive health services" tops the list of necessary medical responses is not supported by the majority of the medical com-munity, which identified access to skilled birth attendants and emergency obstetric care as the two best ways to reduce maternal mortality. See U.N. Economic and Social Affairs, Statistics Division, *The World's Women 2005: Progress in Statistics*, 2006, at www.globalpolicy.org/socecon/inequal/gender/2005/11unwomanstats .pdf (accessed December 19, 2008). Another problem is that WHO often uses the terms "comprehensive reproductive health" and "family planning" interchangeably, even though some U.N. officials use "comprehensive reproductive health" to include abortion and member states defined "family planning" in the Cairo Pro-gram of Action as excluding abortion.

58. Thoraya Obaid, executive director, UNFPA, address at the Women Deliver Conference, London, October 2007.

U.N. tightly controlled the press at the event, providing NGO escorts for each reporter and limiting access to the pressroom through a guarded entryway.

Indeed, supported by a network of activists, U.N. experts and bodies have become highly effective in their attempts to change norms. For instance, at the Commission on the Status of Women in 2007, EU negotiators defeated a resolution sponsored by the United States and South Korea that condemned the rising global trend of killing baby girls because the resolution criticized sex-selective abortion.[59] The Commission on the Status of Women's dogged silence on this increasing assault on the girl-child through sex-selective abortions indicates how much the activists have achieved.

Sexual Orientation

Advocates have been increasingly effective in garnering U.N. support for broadening the definition of gender and asserting a "right to sexual orientation," despite substantial objections from the member states. Perhaps no document better shows the defiance of U.N. officials against the consensus of member states than the 2007 "Yogyakarta Principles: The Application of International Human Rights Law in Relation to Sexual Orientation and Gender Identity." Authored by eleven special rapporteurs and U.N. human rights treaty body members in 2007, the principles were endorsed by former U.N. high commissioner for human rights Louise Arbour.[60] They take twenty-nine human rights already in binding international law and reinterpret each one to include broad homosexual rights that require nations "to take all legislative, administrative and other measures" to grant homosexuals the right to marry and serve in militaries; remove conscience clauses for churches; control the media's portrayal of homosexuality; change "notions of public order, public morality, public health and public security" to favor homosexuals; and implement other sweeping economic, social, and cultural changes.

Fundamental to the principles is the assertion that they are *already binding on state parties*.[61] The document gives sexual orientation a social definition and mandates a vast social and cultural engineering project to enforce

---

59. The author was a member of a civil society group that participated in the negotiations during the 2008 Commission on the Status of Women.

60. International Gay and Lesbian Human Rights Commission, "The Role of the Yogyakarta Principles," August 4, 2008, at www.iglhrc.org/site/iglhrc/section .php?id = 5&detail = 868 (accessed December 19, 2008).

61. "The Yogyakarta Principles on the Application of International Human Rights Law in Relation to Sexual Orientation and Gender Identity," March 2007, at www.yogyakartaprinciples.org/principles_en.pdf (accessed December 21, 2008).

it.[62] U.N. human rights experts who support it flout the member states' repeated refusal to include sexual orientation on the list of recognized non-discrimination categories. In 2003, Brazil tried and failed to pass a resolution on it at the Human Rights Commission in Geneva. Yet, a recent UNESCO document actually cites this failed effort as proof of international consensus in favor of a right to sexual orientation.[63]

Activists are also seeking to secure acceptance of these new rights by linking homosexuality to "gender," which they then use to claim the same rights as women for people who are homosexual, transgender, or transsexual. The U.N. General Assembly defined "gender" when it adopted the 1995 Beijing Platform for Action, which stated that gender was "commonly used and understood in its ordinary, generally accepted usage."[64] Moreover, the treaty creating the International Criminal Court states that gender "refers to the two sexes, male and female, within the context of society."[65]

However, examples of U.N. officials ignoring these precedents abound. The U.N. secretary-general's special adviser on gender issues maintains publicly that gender is a "social construct" that is open to many interpretations.[66] The 2007 UNICEF annual report refers to more than two genders.[67] At the June 2008 high-level meeting on HIV/AIDS, numerous activists asserted—and the U.N. did not deny—that the U.N. interprets gender to include transgender, transsexual, and even men-having-sex-with-men activities. The secretary-general went so far as to call for repealing laws that crim-

---

62. "Yogyakarta Principles."

63. U.N. Educational, Scientific and Cultural Organization, "UNESCO Guidelines on Language and Content in HIV- and AIDS-Related Materials," October 2006, p. 34, at http://unesdoc.unesco.org/images/0014/001447/144725e.pdf (accessed December 21, 2008).

64. *Report of the Fourth World Conference on Women*, A/CONF.177/20/REV.1, September 4–15, 1995, p. 218, at http://daccessdds.un.org/doc/UNDOC/GEN/N96/273/01/PDF/N9627301.pdf (accessed December 21, 2008).

65. Rome Statute of the International Criminal Court, A/CONF.183/9, art. 7, par. 3 (July 17, 1998), http://daccessdds.un.org/doc/UNDOC/GEN/N98/281/44/IMG/N9828144.pdf (accessed December 21, 2008).

66. Catholic Family and Human Rights Institute, "UN Agency Promotes Change in Traditional Understanding of Gender," *Friday Fax*, March 30, 2001, at www.c-fam.org/publications/id.183/pub_detail.asp (accessed January 7, 2009); and U.N. Department of Economic and Social Affairs, Office of the Special Adviser on Gender Issues and Advancement of Women, "Gender Mainstreaming: Concepts and Definitions," at www.un.org/womenwatch/osagi/conceptsandefinitions.htm (accessed January 7, 2009).

67. U.N. Children's Fund, *State of the World's Children 2007*, 2006, at www.unicef.org/sowc07/docs/sowc07.pdf (accessed December 21, 2008).

inalize "vulnerable groups . . . for their lifestyles," such as prostitution and sodomy laws.[68]

This deliberate confusion has important implications for U.N. funding and reform because plans are advancing for a new "gender architecture."[69] Gender has gone to the head of the line for U.N. reform along with governance, finance, and country team coordination—themes that member states decided to consider in the first basket of concerns for the U.N.'s systemwide coherence effort borne out of the 2005 World Summit.[70] According to proponents, a new gender office will have unprecedented influence, a budget on par with UNICEF's budget, and an executive director who reports directly to the secretary-general.[71]

The effort to impose these social and cultural norms extends throughout the U.N. system, involving even seemingly unrelated discussions on treaties such as the Convention on Rights of Persons with Disabilities. In the pursuit of new social norms and rights, the EU has become a prime mover at the U.N., adducing support by powerful NGOs, U.N. agencies, and developing states that Europeans cultivate through their assistance. Interest groups and neoclient states, in turn, accept the EU's progressive social agenda, without the knowledge of and regardless of the best interests of their people, in order to advance various causes. Thus, the EU and its affiliated states are often joined by regional leaders, such as Brazil and South Africa. On the other side is a core group within the Organization of the Islamic Conference, Group of 77, and sometimes the Group of Latin American and Caribbean Countries that parries and thrusts to preserve traditional societies—often in sheer displays of bloc politics.

In the final negotiating round of the Disabilities Convention, the EU successfully played the internal competing interests of the OIC off one another

---

68. Ban Ki-moon, "Remarks on Handover of the Report of the Commission on Aids in Asia," March 26, 2008, p. 3, at http://data.unaids.org/pub/Speech/2008/20080325_sg_asia_comission_report_speech_en.pdf (December 21, 2008).

69. The Department of Economic and Social Affairs houses the Office of the Special Adviser for Gender Issues, which is in charge of implementing the plan for the gender architecture.

70. Global Policy Forum, "Member States Move towards a 'Basket' Approach to System-Wide Coherence," March 21, 2008, at www.globalpolicy.org/reform/initiatives/panels/coherence/2008/0321basket.htm (accessed December 21, 2008).

71. According to Nafis Sadik, the office would act as "a system-wide watchdog" with the authority to set standards, enforce accountability, and intervene at all levels of decision making from country to regional to international. It would focus on overcoming religious and cultural resistance to new sexual norms. Conceivably, the new office would focus not only on women's rights, but also on advancing homosexual rights, despite the opposition of some member states.

to secure, for the first time, the term "sexual and reproductive health" in a binding U.N. treaty document.[72] This was arguably a major EU goal, and the victory was no doubt sweeter because they achieved it over U.S. objections. Along with the United States, Holy See, and others, the OIC, led by Egypt, worked to keep the terms "sexual and reproductive health" and "gender" out of the document, but ultimately yielded in order to include language aimed against the United States and Israel referring to situations of "foreign occupation."[73]

In its explanation of position in the General Assembly the day that body adopted the treaty, the U.S. representative expressed concern on another level. Specifically, the Americans warned that the references to "armed conflict and foreign occupation, which are governed by international humanitarian law and not human rights law, would create unnecessary legal confusion."[74] The confusion proliferates as human rights law increasingly permeates the functional areas of humanitarianism and security at the U.N.

UNDERMINING THE U.N.'S FUNCTIONAL OPERATIONS

In each of these cases, "rights" are being asserted and advanced without explicit legal founding, promulgated by a group of left-leaning NGOs and U.N. treaty body "experts" with minimal consultation with member states and in some cases in defiance of them. This process has significant implications for the legitimacy of these rights and their impact on state sovereignty, the international economic order, and international law. The effort to establish economic, social, and cultural rights also arguably jeopardizes the work and reputation of the U.N.'s operational, development, and humanitarian agencies.

UNESCO

The United Nations Educational, Scientific and Cultural Organization was created to "contribute to peace and security by promoting collaboration among nations through education, science and culture in order to further universal respect for justice, for the rule of law and for the human rights and fundamental freedoms which are affirmed for the peoples of the

---

72. Convention on the Rights of Persons with Disabilities, art. 25, at www2.ohchr.org/english/law/disabilities-convention.htm (accessed December 21, 2008).

73. Convention on the Rights of Persons with Disabilities, preamble.

74. Richard T. Miller, "Explanation of Position on the Convention on the Rights of Persons with Disabilities, Agenda Item 67(b), in the General Assembly," U.S. Department of State, December 13, 2006, at www.state.gov/p/io/rls/rm/81455.htm (accessed December 21, 2008).

world, without distinction of race, sex, language or religion, by the Charter of the United Nations."[75] Yet UNESCO has downgraded its operational activities, which actually serve its member states, in favor of advocating various rights because:

> It is not enough to build classrooms in devastated countries or to publish scientific breakthroughs. . . . [They are] the means to a far more ambitious goal: to build peace in the minds of men.
>
> Today, UNESCO functions as a laboratory of ideas and a standard-setter to forge universal agreements on emerging ethical issues.[76]

One example is UNESCO's work in human security. James Kelly, director of international affairs for the Federalist Society for Law and Public Policy Studies, has analyzed the work of UNESCO's MOST Program and found that its purpose is to spread UNESCO's influence in social and economic decision making throughout the world.[77] According to Kelly, the program was established in 1994 to network social science researchers to advise UNESCO; advance understanding of social transformations; establish sustainable links between social science researchers and decision makers; strengthen scientific, professional, and institutional capacities, particularly in developing countries; and encourage the design of research-anchored policy. The program set up liaison committees in fifty-nine countries and comprises seventeen international research networks, which include global governance, multicultural and multiethnic society, urban development and governance, poverty eradication, sustainable development and governance, and international migration.

Its 2006 meeting in Buenos Aires exemplifies how UNESCO seeks to internationalize European-style social and economic order through means such as the MOST Program. According to Kelly, the conference overwhelmingly rejected the global consensus for neoliberal policy framework (the Washington Consensus) in favor of a "'reformist' redistributive global social democracy that promoted economic human security."[78] The plan is to secure support for the global social democracy agenda by funding more research to back it, while activating civil society to agitate for the enactment

---

75. Constitution of the United Nations Educational, Scientific and Cultural Organization, art 1, par. 1, at http://portal.unesco.org/en/ev.php-URL_ID = 15244 (accessed December 21, 2008).

76. U.N. Educational, Scientific and Cultural Organization, "What Is It? What Does It Do?" updated October 8, 2007, at http://portal.unesco.org/en/ev.php-URL _ID = 3328 (accessed December 21, 2008).

77. Kelly, "In the Name of Human Security," 127.

78. Kelly, "In the Name of Human Security."

of UNESCO's redistributionist policies and then enforcing the new order through U.N. channels.

UNICEF

UNICEF's hallmarks are its large footprint in many countries, and quick and effective emergency responses to provide basic needs. Despite all its good work in the past, UNICEF leadership has increasingly incorporated the rights-based approach into its mission and work. In 1986, UNICEF made the fateful decision to include negotiation and promotion of the Convention on the Rights of the Child and promotion of CEDAW in its mandate.[79]

A tragic outcome of this decision is that UNICEF is now encouraging countries to permit the killing of unborn children. In October 2006, the UNICEF country team representative to Nicaragua signed a letter urging the Nicaraguan National Assembly to keep therapeutic abortion legal. Initially, UNICEF's press office claimed that the country representative was obliged to sign the letter to support the broader One UN program.[80] Later, UNICEF's regional director made it clear that, as far as he was concerned, speaking out to keep abortion legal was in keeping with UNICEF's mission, which includes advancing the rights of women.[81] UNICEF felt that keeping abortion legal was necessary because doctors were not providing adequate emergency care during pregnancy. Essentially, this is saying that giving women recourse to abortion is easier than giving them decent care. It perfectly captures the shifting mind-set at UNICEF from humanitarian and development assistance to human rights activism.

This case also shows an inherent danger of the One UN initiative, specifically that the agendas of other organizations could undermine the unique priorities of individual U.N. programs. The entire U.N. team, including a CEDAW Committee member, falsely represented Nicaragua's international obligations to justify intervening. They even argued that Nicaragua's support for the Cairo Program of Action, Beijing Platform for Action, and other nonbinding documents required them to permit abortions. This deliberately ignores Nicaragua's reservation to Cairo:

---

79. Ostreich, *Power and Principle*, 26–58.

80. The One UN program is designed to place overall responsibility for coordinating U.N. activities in a country under one U.N. authority, the scandal-ridden UNDP. Although reconciling often-contradictory U.N. activities may be necessary in some cases, the proposal could backfire and undercut U.N. reform by making assets fungible within a country. This would further remove national oversight and jeopardize other initiatives.

81. Nils Kasberg, UNICEF Latin American regional coordinator, interview with the author, February 2008.

The Government of Nicaragua, pursuant to its Constitution and its laws, and as a signatory of the American Convention on Human Rights, confirms that every person has a right to life, this being a fundamental and inalienable right, and that this right begins from the very moment of conception.[82]

UNICEF's annual report, *State of the World's Children 2007*, raises another red flag. Instead of focusing on children, it focuses almost exclusively on women's rights. It makes little mention of the top six killers of 10.6 million children each year: pneumonia, diarrhea, malaria, neonatal sepsis, preterm delivery, and asphyxia at birth. However, it did recommend imposing gender quotas on political office, funneling more money to gender equality issues, and increasing the number and activity of women's groups.[83] UNICEF's adoption of a rights-based approach has demonstrably undercut its credibility.

WHO

The World Health Organization works with UNICEF on some core initiatives, such as recently vaccinating over one million children in southern Afghanistan. WHO also aggressively promotes abortion in its fieldwork, even in countries where it is illegal. In 2008 WHO promoted abortion using plastic suction devices called "menstrual regulation kits," or manual vacuum aspirators (MVAs), in Bangladesh.

A 2006 report titled *Sexual and Reproductive Health: Forming the Foundation of a More Just World* details WHO's rights-based approach to health and documents its experimentation with new abortion techniques on women in traditional societies and training of scarce medical professionals to perform risky techniques in the developed world. WHO says it has trained one-third of Mongolia's gynecologists, some 100 physicians, in the use of MVAs for second-trimester abortions and has aggressively experimented with chemical abortions throughout the developing world.[84]

---

82. Quoted in Samantha Singson, "UNICEF Attempts to Intervene in Nicaraguan Abortion Debate," Catholic Family and Human Rights Institute *Friday Fax*, October 31, 2006, at www.c-fam.org/publications/id.485/pub_detail.asp (accessed January 7, 2009).

83. U.N. Children's Fund, *State of the World's Children 2007*. Early in her tenure, the current executive director expressed a desire to return UNICEF to its core mission of child survival, but whether UNICEF will be able to recover from the rights-based policies set in motion by her predecessor remains to be seen.

84. World Health Organization, *Sexual and Reproductive Health: Laying the Foundation for a More Just World through Research and Action* (2006), 22–24.

UNFPA

The United Nations Population Fund was founded in 1969 to "sanitize" Western funding for aggressive population control in the developing world.[85] Today, with developed countries struggling to cope with the social and economic fallout of their fertility declines, aging populations, and dwindling labor bases to sustain economic growth and entitlements, many argue that UNFPA has outlived its mandate.[86] Yet like many resilient bureaucracies, it has rebranded itself and assumed roles already in the purview of other U.N. agencies. For instance, it now claims its mission is to promote "the right of every woman, man and child to enjoy a life of health and equal opportunity" and "to reduce poverty and to ensure that every pregnancy is wanted, every birth is safe, every young person is free of HIV/AIDS, and every girl and woman is treated with dignity and respect."[87] These missions are already covered by WHO, UNICEF, UNAIDS, and a host of development organizations.

UNFPA couches these objectives as realizing international human rights. As a chief promoter of the Maputo Plan of Action, UNFPA worked against some African heads of state in 2006 to ensure that the document promoted abortion and other special interests. The Maputo Plan of Action asserts that it is a framework that operationalizes reproductive health and rights on the continent by setting specific benchmarks that countries must reach in order to meet international obligations such as the Millennium Development Goals.[88] UNFPA has announced it will use this controversial plan of action as part of its rights-based approach with the tacit understanding that achieving the targets would help to determine which countries receive development funds. This would occur even though the Maputo Plan of Action is nonbinding, many African countries have not ratified the Maputo Protocol, and it promotes abortion as a means of family planning against the consensus reached at the U.N. population conference in Cairo.

Moreover, despite U.S. objections, UNFPA executive director Thoraya

---

85. Matthew Connelly, *Fatal Misconception: The Struggle to Control World Population* (Cambridge, MA: Harvard Belknap Press, 2008), 286.

86. Matthew Connelly argues that fertility rates declined independent of population programs. His exhaustive history of the population control movement concludes that fertility rates plummeted similarly in states with and states without population control programs. Connelly, *Fatal Misconception*, 374.

87. U.N. Population Fund, "Our Mission," at www.unfpa.org/about/mission.htm (accessed December 21, 2008).

88. See African Union Commission, *Plan of Action on Sexual and Reproductive Health and Rights (Maputo Plan of Action)* (September 2006), at www.unfpa.org/africa/newdocs/maputo_eng.pdf (accessed December 21, 2008).

Obaid continues to claim a new MDG target under goal 5 that includes achieving "universal access to reproductive health by 2015."[89] The member states have rejected this target twice in open debate, but UNFPA claims that the General Assembly approved the new target in a routine document adopted in December 2007.[90] However, inclusion of that particular wording was never mentioned or debated, undercutting any claim that member states endorsed a new target.

World Food Program

The World Food Program (WFP) has similarly let a rights-based approach impede its operational focus. The world faces a global food crisis that is expected to last for years. Yet when food riots broke out in 2007 and 2008 in Burkina Faso, Cameroon, Egypt, Haiti, Somalia, and other countries, the WFP admitted that it had failed to keep its granaries full and would not be able to meet the need.

This admission followed nearly twenty-five years of efforts to advance the right to food. World leaders had signed the Universal Declaration on the Eradication of Hunger and Malnutrition in 1974, pledging to end hunger within the decade. Ten years later, the pledge remained unfulfilled, and Philip Alston and other human rights experts published their strategy to reframe the issue of hunger as an international human right. In 2004, the U.N. Food and Agriculture Organization's Committee on World Food Security adopted voluntary guidelines on the right to food, which they hailed as a major breakthrough and a "human rights–based tool" for inducing states to fulfill their obligations to provide a right to adequate food. The normative effort distracted the WFP and other humanitarian agencies from their primary missions.

The case of Kosovo illustrates how much the rights-based approach has affected U.N. efforts on the ground. At least fourteen U.N. agencies, programs, and funds and some four thousand NGOs flooded into Kosovo after the 1999 NATO bombing campaign expelled the Serbian army and ended the ethnic cleansing of Kosovar Albanians. When the Serbian province declared independence on February 17, 2008, it issued a draft constitution that is striking in its social and cultural progressiveness, including broad

---

89. Thoraya Ahmed Obaid, statement to UNDP/UNFPA Executive Board, June 16, 2008, at www.unfpa.org/news/news.cfm?ID = 1147 (accessed December 21, 2008).

90. U.N. General Assembly, "Report of the Secretary-General on the Work of the Organization," A/62/1, 2007, p. 67, at www.un.org/millenniumgoals/sgreport200 7.pdf (accessed December 21, 2008).

homosexual and reproductive rights. The people of Kosovo were never allowed to see the draft during the year that they were to publicly debate it. The draft was authored by the U.S.-based and George Soros–backed Public International Law and Policy Group, and it was rushed through parliament without debate.[91]

Thus, after a decade of U.N. management, the mainly Muslim people of Kosovo have only three hours of electricity per day, a 60 percent unemployment rate, and a sudden rise in problems such as prostitution and human trafficking. However, their constitution does guarantee expansive sexual freedoms. In Kosovo, the effort to promote economic, cultural, and social rights has clearly undermined the U.N.'s more fundamental and traditional objectives.

IMPLICATIONS

The drive for "global governance" lies somewhere between the extremes of conspiracy and chaos. At the U.N., it has been a deliberate and coordinated effort to transform the economic, social, and cultural order, too often in defiance of the will and interests of member states. Advocates from all sides agree that solving problems such as world hunger and maternal mortality simply requires the political will, and this may be true. However, the claim that the international political will must be expressed as the acceptance of the U.N.'s positions and its rights-based solutions to economic, social, and cultural problems is disingenuous.

Many people believe that everyone should have access to adequate food, water, and health care. Such moral imperatives not only underpin humanitarian relief and development programs, but informed the decisions of the founders of the U.N.

By contrast, the movement to solve global humanitarian crises through litigation and international norms is founded on an erroneous belief that world politics are essentially normative and that elites need to compel states to act by finding moral imperatives in previously negotiated legal agreements.[92] From this elitist perspective, genuine political will—the will of the people—is not enough because "the people" do not understand the issues. Elites must therefore do what they can to force states to enact their policies. While this movement's initial aims, such as relieving hunger and poverty, may have been just, the trend is toward injustice: destroying the

---

91. Author interviews with the president of Kosovo, parliamentarians, and civil society during the adoption of Kosovo's constitution, Pristina, April 2007.

92. Phillip Alston announced in 1984 that a rights-based approach to humanitarianism was needed to compel states to act morally. See Alston and Tomasevski, *Right to Food.*

cultural and social fabric of society. This approach is shortsighted and could undermine the very nature of international agreements and commitments to human development and human rights.

The way in which nations have allowed expansive definitions of rights to proliferate is a real cause for concern. Most of the nations have no intention of enforcing these rights. This calls into question whether they could reverse the trend even if they decided to do so. The fallout from giving so much authority and credence to NGOs and unaccountable "expert" committees is a profound lack of consensus and ownership among U.N. member states on all kinds of matters.

In this fractured environment, determined American leadership is essential. It can strengthen the resolve of other nations that also want to push back at activist U.N. committees and bureaucracies to protect their own societies. To that end, the United States should:

Seek to focus the Human Rights Council on its core purpose

The Commission on Human Rights was instituted sixty years ago to be the guardian and champion of the UDHR. Instead, it became, to paraphrase Charles Malik, "a sham and a mockery." Regrettably, the Human Rights Council, which replaced the commission in 2006, has suffered a similar fate. Some argue that the United States would improve the body by joining, enabling it to promote reform from the inside. This is the view of the Obama administration, which successfully ran for a seat on the Council in 2009. An effective Council requires more than U.S. participation, however. The U.N. could begin to reform the council during its mandatory review, which must occur before 2011, by restricting participation by states that are known violators of human rights. The United States could also use the degree of reform to guide its funding decisions for the council. If substantive reforms are not made, the United States should distance itself from the Human Rights Council and tightly restrict U.S. funding.

Reclaim the language of human rights and restore a proper understanding of treaty documents

Activists seeking controversial new rights have been defeated in the democratic process in the United States and in other countries. To overcome this resistance, they turn to activist judges and the U.N.'s expert committees and agencies for top-down enforcement of their agenda from international bodies. Lacking transparency and accountability, this process has resulted in outrageous interpretations of the most basic principles of human rights, such as the right to life, in the pursuit of narrow special interests. The

United States should affirm and insist on adhering to the original understanding of the language of the treaties through clear and consistent statements during its treaty reviews and in the General Assembly and other U.N. bodies.

Continue to reject the proliferation of new rights

The recent "no" vote from Ireland on the Lisbon Treaty shows that some other nations still want to protect their sovereignty due to social concerns. The United States needs to bring together that group to push back the move toward global governance that poisons international relations. Too often, NGOs and U.N. activists have assumed that they know best. For example, a U.N. University study in 2007 called for reopening the contentious cloning debates even though member states carefully negotiated a declaration on the matter. In 2008, UNESCO followed this by convening the International Bioethics Committee to provide more evidence that the consensus of sovereign states reached in 2005 was flawed.

At a time when the Security Council is seeking to hold egregious human rights violators such as the Burmese junta accountable, the U.N. needs to bolster states' commitment to human rights, not undermine it. One reason that so many states resist the new concept of "responsibility to protect" is that once it is codified in international agreements, it will need to be enforced by U.N. elites demanding other countries to intervene where they have no overriding security interest.[93]

Ensure that treaty monitoring bodies stay within their mandates

Treaty bodies increasingly overstep their mandates and misinterpret the documents that they are entrusted with monitoring. To counter this trend, the United States and like-minded countries should demand that the human rights monitoring bodies no longer issue general recommendations or general comments that are out of step with the treaties. Instead, the treaty bodies should issue revised recommendations and comments to overturn inappropriate earlier positions. As a party to the ICCPR, the United States could call for a conference of state parties to review committee interpretations. Mechanisms should be put in place to ensure that committee member comments and positions are recorded for more transparency. The United States and allies should insist that only representatives who display

93. Susan Yoshihara, "How to Think about the Responsibility to Protect," *First Things*, June 2008, at www.firstthings.com/onthesquare/?p = 1093 (accessed January 12, 2009).

a proper understanding of international law be appointed to the committees to avoid situations such as the CEDAW Committee, which is composed largely of representatives from activist NGOs. Finally, states should continue to push back at committees during reviews and in written reports when the experts misinterpret the documents.[94]

Insist that expert committees not depend unduly on the interpretations put forth by narrow special interests

Nongovernmental organizations have a long and distinguished history of good humanitarian and human rights work dating back to the founding of the Red Cross and numerous philanthropic foundations in the early twentieth century. Yet by 1990, renowned international political theorist James N. Rosenau identified a trend toward "post-internationalism" in which nations are becoming less influential in world decisions.[95]

This is troublesome for a number of reasons. Human rights activists who seek a world in which governments are more accountable to "civil society" may seem to have much in common with the American democratic ideal, but these networks do not legitimately represent all of civil society. Most NGOs lack even minimal standards of transparency and accountability that are applied to public institutions.

The growing role and influence of leftist NGOs at the U.N. is promulgated by U.N. bureaucrats who want to control what states do. The secretary-general's 2004 Panel of Eminent Persons on United Nations–Civil Society Relations issued the Cardoso Report, which exemplifies this strategy.[96] However, this reform effort failed when member states disagreed with its recommendation to eliminate the NGO Committee, the consultative body of member states that decides which NGOs are accredited to the Economic and Social Council.[97] While NGO participation has been a part of the process since the U.N.'s founding, the current situation is out of step with the founders' intentions. The work of powerful NGOs, backed by a handful of wealthy foundations and member states—sometimes called GONGOs (government-operated NGOs) for their level of government

---

94. Douglas Sylva and Susan Yoshihara, "Rights by Stealth: The Role of U.N. Human Rights Treaty Bodies in the Campaign for an International Right to Abortion," *National Catholic Bioethics Quarterly* 7, no. 1 (Spring 2007): 128.

95. James N. Rosenau, *Turbulence in World Politics: A Theory of Change and Continuity* (Princeton, NJ: Princeton University Press, 1990), 6.

96. U.N. General Assembly, "Strengthening of the United Nations System," A/58/817, June 11, 2004, at http://daccessdds.un.org/doc/UNDOC/GEN/N04/376/41/PDF/N0437641.pdf (accessed December 21, 2008).

97. Peggy Kerry, U.S. Mission to the United Nations, interview with the author, May 30, 2008.

involvement—should be made more transparent. At the same time the playing field should be leveled to allow the voices of smaller civil society groups to be heard. Expert committees have become unduly dependent on the research work of special interest NGOs and need to be held accountable for seeking a balance of sources from states and the full range of civil society organizations.

Consider voluntary funding of the U.N. instead of just giving the U.N. a blank check

According to the secretary-general's High-Level Panel on UN System-Wide Coherence in the Areas of Development, Humanitarian Assistance and the Environment, voluntary funding is to be used for development expenditure, while assessed funding is intended to support activities "in which all Member States have an interest, principally the setting of global norms and standards and ensuring the provision of global public goods."[98] The assumption that all member states want the U.N. to set global norms and standards should be questioned. The United States helped to create the U.N. to restore and preserve international peace and security, not to set sweeping normative agendas.

Shifting more budgets from assessed dues to voluntary funding would help to build accountability and results into the U.N.'s work. The U.N. regular budget is financed through assessed contributions, of which the United States pays 22 percent. This funds the general operations of the U.N. Secretariat and supports the Office of the High Commissioner for Human Rights, the Human Rights Council, the special rapporteurs, and activities in the Third Committee. Some of these offices and activities have merit; others do not. Nations should be able to choose which activities to fund. Yet under the current funding structure, countries that object to specific U.N. activities funded through assessed budgets have little ability to express their discontent. They can only choose to withhold voluntary funding or a symbolic amount of assessed dues proportional to their percentage of a committee's budget. For example, the United States has done this with the U.N. Human Rights Council.

Minimize the damage done by activist U.N. officials and experts

The United States should work with allies to revise the mandates of special rapporteurs who inappropriately use their autonomy to expand their

---

98. Secretary-General's High-Level Panel on UN System-Wide Coherence in the Areas of Development, Humanitarian Assistance and the Environment, "Funding

work to include economic, social, and cultural rights not expressly included in their mandates. Rapporteurs who continue to abuse their mandates should be replaced.

The Bush administration took a principled stand by not joining the Human Rights Council, and the U.S. has not ratified certain treaties that violate American constitutional principles. But the U.S. can and should do more to remedy the lack of credibility in the U.N. human rights system. Because funding for the treaty bodies is channeled through the OHCHR, the United States could tie its support for that office to specific reforms. The United States should work with the secretary-general to promulgate a regulation or a General Assembly resolution mandating that U.N. staff cannot serve on the boards of NGOs with consultative status. The secretary-general should be directed to take appropriate action to resolve any conflicts of interest. Finally, the United States should insist that NGO conferences backed by only a few member states not be promoted as U.N. events without General Assembly support. For example, the 2007 Women Deliver Conference in London was backed by only four member states.

Refuse to participate in, appear before, or fund committees for treaties that the United States has not ratified

The United States should not lend legitimacy to U.N. human rights bodies that flout the will and consensus of U.N. member states. The United States should not sign (and therefore be somewhat constrained by[99]) treaties that it is unlikely to ratify. A consistent approach would lead the United States to "unsign" dead-end human rights treaties, at least those that the Senate has not ratified within ten years of the United States' signature. Likewise, the United States should redirect its funding away from treaty bodies that it does not support and toward those to which America is party and which uphold their mandates.

Withdraw from U.N. bodies that do not support U.S. interests and prove immune to reform

Voluntary funding may not always provoke reform. UNFPA's current functions could be carried out by other U.N. bodies, such as the U.N. Popu-

---

for Results: Funding the UN System on Development, Environment and Humanitarian Relief," at www.un.org/events/panel/resources/pdfs/IN_business_prac.pdf (accessed December 21, 2008).

99. The Vienna Convention on the Law of Treaties specifies that signatories incur an obligation not to defeat the object and purpose of the treaty before it enters into

lation Division or the Commission on Population and Development,[100] but it has successfully resisted reform efforts by several U.S. administrations.[101] Legislatively, Americans have thrice tried to use a withdrawal of its contribution to prevent UNFPA from supporting China's brutal one-child policy. Other big donors have rushed in to fill the void. The United States may have little choice but to withdraw from those U.N. bodies that prove immune to reform. Such was the case with UNESCO in 1984 when U.S. and U.K. withdrawal precipitated changes that eventually led the United States to rejoin in 2002.

Use targeted, bilateral approaches rather than top-down, expert-imposed dictums when they are likely to lead to better results

A growing body of work in the humanitarian and development fields criticizes the U.N.'s top-down, expert-driven system on practical grounds. Alex De Waal, a British researcher on African issues at Harvard University, criticizes the "humanitarian international" that focuses too much on courting donors and hitting benchmarks while ignoring the role of corrupt governments propped up by international aid. William Easterly, a former World Bank economist, has shown why the U.N.'s technological "utopian social engineering" approach to development championed by Jeffrey Sachs, special adviser to the secretary-general on the Millennium Development Goals, fails to work despite the $2.3 trillion spent thus far.[102]

Easterly and others call for a more humble "piecemeal democratic reform" approach, including local initiatives such as oral rehydration and

---

force. Vienna Convention on the Law of Treaties, May 23, 1969, art. 18, at http://untreaty.un.org/ilc/texts/instruments/english/conventions/1_1e1969.pdf (accessed December 21, 2008).

100. ECOSOC commissions are comprised of fifty-four members, who serve three-year terms. They meet annually to address pressing development issues with the benefit of having direct oversight and involvement by member states. Likewise, the U.N. Population Division has gained a reputation as the world's most authoritative source of data on international demographic trends.

101. UNFPA was unique in that it would be held accountable only to the secretary-general and a small executive board, thus circumventing member state scrutiny. Since then, some U.S. administrations have tried to distance themselves from the abuses of this overzealous agency, such as its massive botched forced sterilization campaigns, dumping of defective IUDs, and public humiliation of families with more than two children. Connelly, *Fatal Misconception*, 278.

102. William Easterly, "A Modest Proposal," *Washington Post*, March 13, 2005, BW03, at www.washingtonpost.com/wp-dyn/articles/A25562-2005Mar10.html (accessed December 21, 2008).

vaccinations. Edward Green, who works on HIV/AIDS issues in Africa at Harvard's Center for Population and Development Studies, concludes that faith-based organizations work far better than the "commodities" approach promoted by UNFPA.[103] Targeted efforts such as the President's Emergency Plan for AIDS Relief (PEPFAR) take advantage of local social and cultural circumstances in recipient nations and have far greater and measurable outcomes. American ingenuity should be brought to bear on issues for which the U.N. has become too large, too bureaucratic, and too politicized to address.

CONCLUSION

"Since wars begin in the minds of men, it is in the minds of men that the defenses of peace must be constructed."[104] Thus begins the constitution of the United Nations Educational, Scientific and Cultural Organization (UNESCO). After the great wars, idealism about what man can accomplish was understandable. Hopes were raised high that by changing minds, men could transform the world. The problem is that totalitarians believe the same thing. Today, the United Nations, which was created to protect human rights and fundamental freedoms, often serves to undermine those very goals. Even if one has a more sanguine view of things, the tension at the U.N. between doing good and changing minds has clearly shifted toward the latter and morphed into changing cultures rather than celebrating them.

Aided and abetted by activist NGOs, the U.N. retains sweeping plans to remake the world, but at steep cost to its traditional role of providing vaccinations, medicine, clean water, and a helping hand. Without strong American leadership, the U.N. will continue to excel in promoting new norms at the expense of aiding those most in need. Far better than transforming the world into a single culture is a strategy that promotes development without undermining the ability of sovereign states to protect and promote the best of every culture to meet the needs of humanity. It is time for courageous leadership to restore respect for genuine human rights, those that unshackle human life, mind, and spirit.

---

103. Edward Green, *Rethinking AIDS Prevention: Learning from Successes in Developing Countries* (New York: Praeger, 2004), 14–15.

104. Constitution of the United Nations Educational, Scientific and Cultural Organization, at http://portal.unesco.org/en/ev.php-URL_ID = 15244 (accessed December 21, 2008).

7

The United Nations and Development

Grand Aims, Modest Results

Ambassador Terry Miller

U.N. development agencies are fond of stories illustrating their work in helping to improve the lives of poor people. Their annual reports are filled with beautiful pictures of happy and prosperous people accompanied by captions touting the U.N. agency's positive role in their lives. For example, the U.N. Development Program's annual report for 2008 has about two dozen such vignettes scattered through its thirty-six pages.[1] It is impossible not to feel good about both the hardworking people of developing countries and their benefactors in the U.N. system, both of whom are pictured.

What is missing from the reports is rigorous analysis that links the development agency's program to the happy outcome. At the U.N., finding out how much money is being spent is very easy, but finding out how and on what it is spent is very hard. It is even harder to know whether an expenditure is achieving the desired developmental result.

In reality, little evidence indicates that U.N. development assistance has contributed to economic growth in the recipient countries. In general, countries that receive significant U.N. assistance show no better develop-

---

1. U.N. Development Program, "Capacity Development: Empowering People and Institutions," June 2008, at www.undp.org/publications/annualreport2008/pdf/IAR2008_ENG_low.pdf (accessed January 14, 2009).

ment results than those that receive little aid. Although the U.N. Charter proclaims that one of the U.N.'s main goals is to promote better standards of living and freedom, in practice the organization falls short on both counts. It eschews the proven development strategies of classic liberal economics for aid-focused plans that almost certainly do more harm than good because they emphasize and enhance the role of government and central planning.

BAD IDEAS, POORLY IMPLEMENTED

U.N. development work is afflicted by bad economic theory and philosophy, cumbersome bureaucracy, confused and duplicative institutional mandates, poor and corrupt administration, and a general lack of accountability. While one might expect that any activity beset with such problems would not survive long, the U.N. development system caters to some specific needs of various groups in a number of ways.

Providing development assistance satisfies a strong need of rich donor nations to demonstrate their compassion and caring for the poor around the world. It helps to prop up the governments—some honorable, some corrupt—of poorer U.N. members, even paying the salaries and travel expenses of their delegates to U.N. meetings. It also enables academic and bureaucratic specialists in labor, the environment, statistics, housing, agriculture, and other fields to have their day in the sun by attending international meetings in "hardship" locations such as New York, Geneva, and Bali.

Each of these factors creates strong constituencies for the current U.N. development system. Absent from the process is any real measurement of how U.N. development expenditures and activities affect the lives of the poor. The quest for such measurement is a perennial item on the agendas of U.N. development bodies. Its appearance, however, is always as a quest, never as the actual adoption or consideration of development metrics, which by and large do not exist. The little research that has been done on the subject shows disturbing results: foreign assistance has either no effect or a small negative effect on development.[2]

---

2. For example, see Raghuram G. Rajan and Arvind Subramanian, "Aid and Growth: What Does the Cross-Country Evidence Really Show?" (Working Paper WP/05/127, International Monetary Fund, June 2005), at www.imf.org/external/pubs/ft/wp/2005/wp05127.pdf (accessed January 14, 2009); and William Easterly, *Can Foreign Aid Buy Growth? Journal of Economic Perspectives* 17, no. 3 (Summer 2003): 23–48, at www.nyu.edu/fas/institute/dri/Easterly/File/EasterlyJEP03.pdf (accessed January 14, 2009).

With such institutional factors at work, change is not easy, despite the perennially felt need for reform. Indeed, reform is one of the most common items on the agendas of U.N. meetings. Reform is the holy grail of U.N. management, always sought, but never achieved.

Bad Theories Leading to Bad Outcomes

Understanding the failure of U.N. development assistance and development programs to deliver the promised results requires looking no further than the fundamental assumptions and economic theories on which the system rests. Regrettably, at the U.N., these assumptions not only belie historical experience, but also often contradict the very policies being implemented with good results by both developed and developing countries.

The contradictions and muddled thinking begin with a flawed view of development itself. Development is a complex phenomenon that can be viewed as a process or as a state of being. The common practice of dividing countries into categories of "developed" and "developing" countries unhelpfully mixes the two concepts.

Currently, standard usage is to call the group of countries that enjoy the highest standards of living "developed," a static term implying arrival at a plateau from which no further progress is needed. Another group, which has lower standards of living, is called "developing," implying a group undergoing change. Of course, the truth is almost exactly the opposite.

Starting from a situation of rough parity some two centuries ago, some countries have changed rapidly, gradually institutionalizing an economic system—capitalism—that promotes continuous economic evolution. Economist and political scientist Joseph Schumpeter famously called this evolutionary process "creative destruction."[3] These rapidly evolving countries, which are more accurately described as continuously developing, have come to enjoy levels of prosperity unprecedented in human history.

Another group of countries has failed to embark on this process of change. To call them "developing" is a cruel joke. Their chief economic characteristic is that they are not developing, not changing at all. In fact, they are mired in the status quo, usually because of government policies that have protected the special privileges and status of the ruling elites. Government structures and policies, economic markets and infrastructure, and even political thought and respect for human rights are all "underdeveloped" in these countries.

Interestingly, we know the policy characteristics most responsible for differentiating the two groups. The prosperous countries, which have devel-

---

3. Joseph A. Schumpeter, *Capitalism, Socialism, and Democracy*, 3rd ed. (New York: Harper & Row, 1962), 83.

oped rapidly and are still developing, have societies in which individuals are protected against arbitrary government. The concept of human rights is understood and vigorously respected and defended. The state provides a rule of law rather than a rule of men. Property rights are protected. Equal justice is available to all. Individuals are allowed to interact freely with others in the pursuit of prosperity, contracting for their own and others' goods and labor as they see fit. The state's role is to enforce private contracts, not to participate directly in economic activity other than in exceptional circumstances.

By contrast, in the countries that have not developed, citizens still live in political and economic systems similar to medieval feudalism in Europe. Freedom of employment is constrained, and in the worst cases, even freedom of movement is restricted. The state actively intervenes to preserve the economic privileges of elites and uses its coercive powers to monopolize economic activity. Arbitrary and complex regulatory structures invite corruption, and property rights are reserved to the state or the privileged few.

Of course, countries do not fall neatly into one group or the other; they occupy a continuum between the two. Countries that comprehensively and strongly protect and promote individual economic rights and freedoms grow consistently and sustainably. These countries tend toward one end of the continuum. Countries where individuals enjoy fewer rights and freedoms stagnate economically and tend toward the other end of the continuum.

The *Index of Economic Freedom*, produced annually by The Heritage Foundation and the *Wall Street Journal*, is one of several indexes that attempt to place countries on the development continuum.[4] All such indexes show strong links between economic freedom and prosperity and between economic freedom and continuing development. We do, in fact, know what promotes rapid development. Regrettably, the economic institutions of the United Nations, with few exceptions, do not seem to have gotten the message.

Even worse is the habit of thinking of countries themselves as monolithic entities in a single stage of development, that is, country X is rich, and country Y is poor. In reality, every country in the world has both rich people and poor people. Every country has sectors that are highly developed and others that are poorer. The continuum of development exists within countries as well as among them. Ironically, those individuals who represent the interests of the developing countries in the U.N. and purport to speak for the poor and dispossessed are almost always rich and almost

4. Terry Miller and Kim R. Holmes, *2009 Index of Economic Freedom* (Washington, DC: Heritage Foundation and Dow Jones & Company, Inc., 2009), at www.heritage .org/index/Default.aspx (accessed January 14, 2009).

always come from elite and powerful groups in their own countries. More often than not, these delegates are the dispossessors, not the dispossessed.

Too Much Government

The U.N. is an organization of states. It is expected and even appropriate that it should reflect the values and views of its members. Regrettably, most U.N. members believe that the state has a primary role in promoting or directing development. That they are wrong does not change their beliefs. Most U.N. members are not democracies, including many that are democratic in name only. This lack of democracy and respect for human rights is inconsistent with the U.N. Charter, but this inconsistency does not change the nature of the repressive governments represented at the U.N. The inevitable result is that those who believe in freedom or that economic activity is most fruitfully left to the private sector will find the U.N. an alien and hostile place.

We know today that freedom, especially economic freedom, is the key to prosperity, and one can envision a U.N. system in which promoting economic freedom takes center stage. But that is not the U.N. that exists today. In today's U.N., the socialist leanings (or socialist/Marxist fantasies) of many of its members run riot in a proliferation of overlapping bureaucracies united only by their proclivities for centralization, central planning, and transferring wealth from the rich to the poor, or at least from countries in which a majority is rich to countries in which a majority is poor. Actually, these transfers may even be from taxpayers of relatively modest means in wealthy countries to rich elites in poorer countries.[5]

Too Much Aid

Not surprisingly, U.N. agencies and U.N. debates have fallen into the trap of focusing on resource transfers. It is one of the few economic subjects on which all U.N. members can agree, however weakly.

However, maintaining a constructive dialogue between aid's strongest champions and those who are more skeptical is extremely difficult. Aid champions tend to use the language of emotions to touch donors' hearts, their hopes, and even their guilt. They focus far more on the act of giving and the desperate needs of the poor than on the effects of the aid. A good case in point is the long-standing call for rich countries to give 0.7 percent

---

5. P. T. Bauer frequently observed that foreign aid was the process of transferring money from poor people in rich countries to rich people in poor countries. *The Economist*, "A voice for the poor," May 2, 2002, at www.economist.com (subscription required).

of their gross domestic product (GDP) as aid to poorer countries. The amount requested is not linked to any particular need on the part of the poor. The call to give is comparable instead to a religious tithe, in which the duty to give stands on its own merits, while how the donation is used is almost inconsequential.[6]

Aid skeptics, by contrast, seek to compare costs and benefits of various approaches. They long for measurable outcomes to guide their decisions. Their rational, scientific approach is often frustrated by the lack of data and the sheer complexity of the development process. The two positions are almost irreconcilable. U.N. agencies, caught between the camps, often pander to the rationalists, but have found operating in the realm of the emotionalists more comfortable and satisfying.

At the U.N., donor governments are asked to accept as a matter of faith that putting more money into the system will produce more good outputs. It is a matter of faith because no one knows how to measure or adequately evaluate the outputs. By contrast, inputs (expenditures) are easy to measure. However, development effects, positive or negative, are difficult to isolate in complex systems in which many inputs and factors combine to produce a result. For the most part, aid agencies do not even try to measure results, which is probably for the best from their perspective because of the lack of evidence that aid has even a minimal positive impact on economic growth. This is not exactly an aid agency's best talking point.

Too Much Talk, Not Enough Capitalism

While actively promoting foreign aid, few U.N. development institutions actually run development projects or wealth-making enterprises. They do not produce goods and services, unless reports of international meetings or trips by U.N. officials, development consultants, and other employees are counted as products. For the most part, they do not even fund development projects. However, they do excel at talking, especially about development, and they try to influence thinking about development. Mostly they try to promote and justify the transfer of resources from rich countries to poor countries.

U.N. development debates take place in the General Assembly, the Economic and Social Council (ECOSOC), ECOSOC subordinate commissions and committees, the regional economic commissions, the governing bodies of the specialized agencies, and numerous periodic special sessions and

---

6. For a fuller discussion of the 0.7 percent target, see Michael A. Clemens and Todd J. Moss, "Ghost of 0.7%: Origins and Relevance of the International Aid Target," (Working Paper 68, Center for Global Development, September 6, 2005), at www.cgdev.org/content/publications/detail/3822 (accessed January 14, 2009).

conferences sponsored by the U.N. The fundamental U.N. development debate is ideological, not practical. The practical ways of encouraging and sustaining economic growth are already known, but few governments have been willing to give up historical patterns of economic control and truly liberate their citizens' entrepreneurial abilities.

Of course, the talking at the U.N. rarely constitutes actual debate. Usually, delegates recite set speeches written days earlier in their capitals. Members of the U.N.'s numerous special interest member groupings—the Group of 77 (G-77), the Non-Aligned Movement (NAM), and even the European Union (EU)—often parrot talking points prepared by the group's spokesperson. Indeed, in the "dialogue," participants rarely actually listen and respond to what others are saying.

The capitalist system, which is triumphant throughout the real world of commerce and industry and responsible for the unprecedented levels of growth and prosperity in almost every country, receives scant notice in U.N. debates. Delegates from developed countries, which have societies that are fundamentally based on capitalism, seem to find value at the U.N. in picking at the system's edges. They are far more likely to criticize its marginal flaws than praise its core virtues. Perhaps this is a symptom of the democratic virtue of constant self-examination and self-criticism that keeps our open societies actively engaged in renewal and improvement.

However, for the developing countries that have not completely integrated into the world capitalist system, particularly those societies emerging from the failed experiments in socialism that all too often follow political independence, the message is confusing at best. The message can be downright harmful when it leads to hesitation to embrace the fundamental individual freedoms that capitalism requires to function effectively. A forum that includes nations struggling to escape poverty is not the place to denigrate the only system proven to lead to prosperity and certainly not the place to espouse centralized planning and government control, which appeal intellectually but have failed miserably every time they have been tried.

The bedrock of capitalism is private ownership and control of property. There has been a growing recognition within developing countries of the importance of property rights and the domestic policies that protect private ownership and unlock the capital it represents. Hernando de Soto's seminal work pointed out the importance of property rights in allowing for capitalization of assets.[7] De Soto estimated that over $9 trillion was lying fallow in developing countries because of inadequate property rights and poor legal

---

7. Hernando de Soto, "The Mystery of Capital," *Finance and Development* 38, no. 1 (March 2001), at www.imf.org/external/pubs/ft/fandd/2001/03/desoto.htm (accessed January 14, 2009).

regimes. Voluminous research, including some at The Heritage Foundation, demonstrates the importance of rule of law, property rights, and the elimination of corruption in spurring development.

However, no one should imagine that a decentralized, private-sector, capitalist approach to development receives a fair hearing at the U.N. Indeed, the alternative view that development requires massive aid flows from the North to the South has maintained its primacy within the U.N. Secretariat. It now has an important champion in economist Jeffrey Sachs, who was hired by the U.N. to promote a Secretariat creation: the Millennium Development Goals (MDGs).

The MDGs are development goals that the U.N.'s Millennium Summit adopted as part of a far-reaching economic and political declaration in 2000.[8] They include such laudable goals as increasing education and access to clean water and reducing poverty, child mortality, and maternal mortality,[9] but they do not constitute a comprehensive development philosophy or strategy, or even a coherent development plan of action. Still, they have captured the public's imagination and have proven to be an irresistible public relations and fund-raising tool for the United Nations, aid agencies, and nongovernmental organizations (NGOs) around the globe. From the U.S. perspective, the MDGs are at best inadequate and at worst a destructive distraction from the policy reforms needed to unleash the private sector's unparalleled ability to foster development. Sadly, the incessant clamor for more aid that accompanies the MDGs has tended in the U.N. to drown out any other ideas for development.

A COMPLEX U.N. SYSTEM

The promotion of development lies at the heart of the United Nations, enshrined in the U.N. Charter's call for "better standards of life in larger freedom."[10] Nearly every U.N. agency and committee addresses developmental issues in some way. Even the Security Council has gotten into the act, holding special meetings in recent years on climate change and post-

---

8. U.N. General Assembly, "United Nations Millennium Declaration," A/RES/ 55/2, September 18, 2000, at www.un.org/millennium/declaration/ares552e.htm (accessed January 14, 2009).

9. The Millennium Development Goals include seventeen or eighteen (depending on how they are counted) development-related targets and pledges established by the U.N. Secretariat and grouped under eight headings based on the agreed statement from the 2000 Millennium Summit. For a more detailed explanation, see United Nations, "Millennium Development Goals," at www.un.org/millennium goals (accessed January 14, 2009).

10. Charter of the United Nations, preamble.

conflict peacebuilding.[11] The International Atomic Energy Agency, which is normally associated with sanctions on Iraq and the struggle to prevent Iran and North Korea from developing nuclear weapons, includes in its charge a development mandate "to accelerate and enlarge the contribution of atomic energy to peace, health and prosperity throughout the world."[12]

Development has become so pervasive on the agendas of U.N. bodies, and the U.N. system so complicated, that the U.N. Development Group (UNDG) has been created as a special mechanism to coordinate development work within the system. The UNDG has twenty-eight agency members and five observers, and includes the U.N. regional economic commissions.

The total spent by the member agencies of the U.N. Development Group can be calculated in different ways. According to the U.N., the U.N. system for development cooperation activities received $15.5 billion in contributions in 2005.[13] Depending on one's point of view, that is either a lot of money or a little. If one billion people are suffering from poverty or hunger worldwide, U.N. development aid could provide $15 per year to each of them. This is a modest amount, but would undoubtedly be significant to the recipients. In reality, the funds support thousands of permanent staff, consultants, government politicians, and bureaucrats in developing and developed countries. The poor and needy receive only a small portion. In addition, overall aid flows, about $100 billion per year as calculated by the Organisation for Economic Co-operation and Development, are dwarfed by flows from trade, foreign investment, and even private remittances.[14]

Core U.N. Development Agencies

An annual investment of $15 billion should produce some positive results, but such results are rare in the U.N. system. Four large, voluntarily funded agencies—the U.N. Development Program (UNDP), U.N. Chil-

---

11. U.N. Security Council, Meeting Record S/PV.5663, April 17, 2007, and Meeting Record S/PV.5627, January 31, 2007.

12. Conference on the Statute of the International Atomic Energy Agency, "Statute of the IAEA," art. 2, October 23, 1956, at www.iaea.org/About/statute_text.html (accessed January 22, 2009).

13. U.N. General Assembly and U.N. Economic and Social Council, "Triennial Comprehensive Policy Review of Operational Activities of the United Nations Development System," A/62/73-E/2007/52, May 11, 2007, at http://documents-dds-ny.un.org/doc/UNDOC/GEN/N07/328/60/pdf/N0732860.pdf (accessed January 22, 2009).

14. For detailed information, see Hudson Institute, Center for Global Prosperity, *The Index of Global Philanthropy 2008*, at www.hudson.org/files/documents/2008%20Index%20-%20Low%20Res.pdf (accessed January 22, 2009).

dren's Fund (UNICEF), U.N. Population Fund (UNFPA), and World Food Program (WFP)—form the core of the UNDG.[15]

The United Nations Development Program

The UNDP is a complex and multilayered organization. This makes it extremely difficult to unravel the actual amounts being spent on various categories of activities. These "program expenditures" can include expenses for travel, meetings, consultants, and personnel. Outputs are even harder to define and measure. According to the U.N. Advisory Committee on Administrative and Budgetary Questions (ACABQ), "There is room for further improvement [in the UNDP budget] in order to streamline the presentation, avoid repetition, and promote greater clarity and transparency."[16]

The UNDP has more than 3,200 employees and operates in 166 countries. More than 10 percent of its staff works in New York City. The UNDP operates on a biennial budget, with overall contributions totaling about $7.5 billion for 2006 and 2007. This includes about $2 billion in regular contributions from donors, another $3 billion in donor cofinancing, and about $2.6 billion in recipient government cost sharing. Of its regular contributions, the UNDP spent only about $870 million on development programs in countries, and another $200 million on global and regional programs. Management and administration accounted for $729 million. In 2008–2009, the UNDP will spend an astounding $50 million just to ensure the security of UNDP staff and premises.[17]

The UNDP's goals include reducing poverty and achieving the Millennium Development Goals, expanding democratic governance, preventing crises and assisting in postcrisis recovery, and promoting environmental protection and sustainable development. The agency also operates the system of resident coordinators by which the U.N. maintains almost universal representation in its member states.

While a recipient state can relatively easily track the amount of UNDP

---

15. The World Bank, the largest international development agency by far, is an observer in the U.N. Development Group. The bank has about $100 billion in outstanding loans to developing countries and provides nearly $15 billion annually in very long-term, low-interest loans to the poorest countries.

16. U.N. Development Program and U.N. Population Fund Executive Board, "Budget Estimates for the Biennium 2006–2007," DP/2005/32, August 10, 2005, at http://documents-dds-ny.un.org/doc/UNDOC/GEN/N05/456/39/pdf/N0545639 .pdf (accessed January 22, 2009).

17. U.N. Development Program and U.N. Population Fund, Executive Board, "UNDP Budget Estimates for the Biennium 2008–2009," DP/2008/3, November 20, 2007, at http://documents-dds-ny.un.org/doc/UNDOC/GEN/N07/611/28/pdf/ N0761128.pdf (accessed January 22, 2009).

resources coming into the country and determine how much is being spent on office costs, personnel, and program activities, such information is almost impossible to collect on a worldwide basis. No donor devotes sufficient staff or attention to actually knowing with confidence how the UNDP is spending its contributions. In the U.S. government—neither the worst nor the best of the donors in attempting oversight—only one full-time person in the State Department oversees how the UNDP uses the $100 million that the United States gives in a typical year. Historically, the United States has relied on trusted U.S. citizens within the UNDP itself, such as longtime administrator Brad Morse, to provide oversight from within. This process has broken down as the UNDP has grown and as leadership has passed to nationals of other countries, and the U.S. government has not addressed the oversight deficit.

It is possible, although not easy, to dig a little deeper into specific projects, looking beyond the stories and pictures of prospering people portrayed in annual reports. One picture highlighted in the UNDP's annual report shows Albanian high school students hard at work in a computer lab. The caption says, "UNDP is helping Albania to equip high schools with computer labs benefiting some 140,000 students."[18] More information about the project is available on the UNDP's website,[19] which explains that the UNDP plans to spend $25 million on this project over three years. That works out to a modest $12,000 per school. The project is cofinanced by the Albanian government, Samsung, Intel, and Western Union. The total cost is not given, nor is the UNDP's share of the total. There is no way of knowing how the UNDP fits into the project's overall scheme or whether the Albanian children would have received their computer labs without the UNDP's involvement. Nor can the relative merits of this project be compared to the merits of other projects in Albania and in other countries. In other words, member governments have no way of providing meaningful oversight. The program may be doing some good, but whether it was the best use of the UNDP's resources is unknown.

Economists speak of "opportunity cost," which is the value of the thing not done when an expenditure choice is made. It is a vital concept because it asks the question, "Could the money have been used more profitably or effectively elsewhere?" The UNDP has total resources of about $7.5 billion to spend each year, more than $1 for every person on the planet. The UNDP

---

18. U.N. Development Program, "Capacity Development: Empowering People and Institutions," June 2008, at www.undp.org/publications/annualreport 2008/pdf/IAR2008_ENG_low.pdf (accessed January 22, 2009).

19. U.N. Development Program, "E-School Programme for Albania," at www.undp.org.al/index.php?page = projects/project&id = 92 (accessed January 22, 2009).

has chosen, in its three-year Albanian computer program, to spend about $175 on each schoolchild in Albania. Was that the best use of its resources? Were there better programs or more needy children elsewhere? Those questions are neither asked nor answered in the UNDP governance process.

Undoubtedly, Albanian schoolchildren are worthy recipients of help, and this project will probably improve the economic well-being of Albanians. Donors and readers of the UNDP's annual report will feel better when they hear about this activity. What they will not read—and the UNDP will not ask them to consider—is what could have been done instead in Haiti, Sudan, or Bangladesh.

The UNDP does not ask its clients or its executive board to consider the opportunity cost of projects because it does not know how to measure it. Indeed, it is essentially impossible to link specific developmental outcomes to the presence or absence of U.N. development programs. This is not a failure unique to the U.N. It afflicts bilateral aid agencies, such as the U.S. Agency for International Development, and many other governmental bureaucracies that produce outputs intended to contribute, catalyze, or stimulate activities by others. No one has yet devised a satisfactory way to judge the relative merits of such activities.

Instead, UNDP funds are allocated on a political basis. Dollars donated to the UNDP are either earmarked by donors for specific uses in specific countries or allocated according to an entitlement process that ensures that every developing country receives a share of the available funds. In the latter case, projects are developed or chosen to fit the available funds. It is a top-down process in which opportunity cost is not considered except within each country's given allocation.

Worse, to the extent that politics force the UNDP to finance projects in despotic countries, they make the organization and its funds vulnerable to misuse and manipulation. For instance, pressure to conduct activities in North Korea led the UNDP to accede to that government's demands to staff the UNDP office with North Korean nationals chosen by the North Korean regime. This permitted the government to skim salary payments to those office workers and obtain convertible currencies such as the dollar and euro. U.N. and independent audits concluded that these activities directly violated U.N. and UNDP standard operating procedures and basic best practices.[20]

---

20. Brett D. Schaefer and Steven Groves, "Congress Should Withhold Funds from the U.N. Development Program," Heritage Foundation *WebMemo*, no. 1783 (January 26, 2008), at www.heritage.org/Research/InternationalOrganizations/wm 1783.cfm; and George Russell, "Report Shows U.N. Development Program Violated U.N. Law, Routinely Passed on Millions to North Korean Regime," Fox News, June

In Burma, local NGOs have accused the UNDP of allowing the regime to use its funds to further its political agenda and undermine the rights of its citizens.[21] More recently, the UNDP allowed the Burmese regime to reap millions in profits from aid intended to benefit victims of Cyclone Nargis by forcing the UNDP to pay an overvalued exchange rate.[22] In these cases and others, the UNDP has resisted U.S. efforts to investigate UNDP activities and practices. Even though the United States sits on the UNDP's executive board and provides millions of dollars to the organization annually, the organization refuses to permit the United States unfettered access to its internal documents and audits.

United Nations Children's Fund

According to its mission statement, UNICEF (formerly known as the U.N. International Children's Emergency Fund) is "mandated by the U.N. General Assembly to advocate for the protection of children's rights, to help meet their basic needs and to expand their opportunities to reach their full potential."[23] Regrettably, the organization is guided in this endeavor by the Convention on the Rights of the Child, a flawed document that the United States never ratified because of its exaggerated and imbalanced emphasis on the rights of children and governments over the rights of parents and because of its incompatibility with the U.S. federal system of government.[24]

Like the UNDP and the other U.N. development agencies, UNICEF is awash in cash, expecting to receive more than $10 billion for 2008–2009. Regular resource income (the money provided without strings or earmarks from member governments) totals $3 billion, a 50 percent increase over the previous two-year budget. The two-year budget for administration and management is more than $900 million. The ACABQ notes with concern

---

11, 2008, at www.foxnews.com/story/0,2933,365676,00.html (accessed January 22, 2009).

21. Brett D. Schaefer, "The U.N. Must Stop Enabling the Burmese Regime," Heritage Foundation *WebMemo*, no. 1710 (November 27, 2007), at www.heritage.org/ Research/AsiaandthePacific/wm1710.cfm.

22. George Russell, "U.S. Asked U.N. about Exchange Rate Issues in Burma Year before Latest Scandal," Fox News, August 1, 2008, at www.foxnews.com/story/ 0,2933,396143,00.html (accessed January 22, 2009).

23. U.N. Children's Fund, "UNICEF's Mission Statement," at www.unicef.org/ about/who/index_mission.html (accessed January 22, 2009).

24. For an overview of problems with the Convention on the Rights of the Child, see chapter 6, "The Quest for Happiness," by Susan Yoshihara, and Patrick F. Fagan, "How U.N. Conventions on Women's and Children's Rights Undermine Family, Religion, and Sovereignty," Heritage Foundation *Backgrounder*, no. 1407 (February 5, 2001), at www.heritage.org/Research/InternationalOrganizations/BG1407.cfm.

that while regular resources account for only 30 percent of UNICEF's resources, they pay for more than 73 percent of support costs.

UNICEF has almost three thousand employees, of whom more than 30 percent work in New York City. The ACABQ also notes an alarming tendency toward grade creep in UNICEF's workforce, with the number of senior level (P-5 rank and above) jobs increasing by about 12 percent in just two years.

As with the UNDP, determining what UNICEF actually does with its extravagant resources is extremely difficult based on documentation provided to member states and the public. The ACABQ notes that it wants UNICEF "to present the biennial support budget in a clear manner and with the necessary degree of detail that would allow thorough analysis and scrutiny."[25] Yet not even the United States may be in a position to provide such scrutiny, because only one State Department employee follows UNICEF full-time, despite the annual U.S. contribution of $120 million to the organization.

The United Nations Population Fund

UNFPA's mission statement epitomizes both the blurred focus and the mission creep that leads to so much duplication and overlap in the U.N. development system:

> UNFPA . . . is an international development agency that promotes the right of every woman, man and child to enjoy a life of health and equal opportunity. UNFPA supports countries in using population data for policies and programmes to reduce poverty and to ensure that every pregnancy is wanted, every birth is safe, every young person is free of HIV/AIDS, and every girl and woman is treated with dignity and respect.[26]

In just two sentences, UNFPA injects itself into the work of the Human Rights Council and the U.N. High Commissioner for Human Rights ("promotes the right" and "equal opportunity"), the World Health Organization ("enjoy a life of health"), the Statistical Commission ("using population data"), UNDP ("to reduce poverty"), UNICEF and WHO again ("every birth is safe" and "every young person is free of HIV/AIDS"), and the Commission on the Status of Women ("every girl and woman is treated with

---

25. U.N. Economic and Social Council, "United Nations Children's Fund Support Budget for the Biennium 2008–2009," E/ICEF/2008/AB/L.2, January 4, 2008, at http://documents-dds-ny.un.org/doc/UNDOC/LTD/N08/201/96/pdf/N0820196 .pdf (accessed January 22, 2009).

26. U.N. Population Fund, "Mission Statement," at www.unfpa.org/about/mis sion.htm (accessed January 22, 2009).

dignity and respect"). The only phrase in the entire mission statement that reflects a unique and specific mandate is "to ensure that every pregnancy is wanted." Of course, this unique mandate may have been submerged in so much extraneous and duplicative rhetoric because it is so heavily charged with religious and social controversy related to birth control and abortion.

With an income of more than $750 million in 2007, UNFPA closed the year "in robust financial health."[27] Despite this total and a 24.2 percent increase from 2006, the agency claims on the first page of its Statistical and Financial Review for 2007 that "increased and predictable core resources are necessary to enable UNFPA to deliver its programs."[28] This appeal seems even stranger in light of the same report's calculation that UNFPA spent only $396.3 million on programs in recipient countries and regions. Support costs in 2007 exceeded $100 million, consuming more than 26 percent of regular resource expenditures.

UNFPA employs more than 1,110 people, including 201 who work in New York City. As with UNICEF, grade creep is a serious problem. UNFPA proposes in its 2008–2009 budget to reclassify 135 of its posts, increasing 113 (84 percent) of them in rank and salary.[29]

Like those of other U.N. development funds and programs, UNFPA budget presentations lack transparency and detail. According to the ACABQ,

[UNFPA's budget] presentation, as it is currently formulated, continues to be too general and does not provide distinct information on links with specific programmes of work or activities. In addition, it does not allow assessment of cost effectiveness and the degree of achievement of expected results.[30]

The United States did not contribute to UNFPA for several years because of congressional restrictions on funding U.N. agencies that support the practice of coercive abortion. The Obama administration reinterpreted those restrictions and resumed funding in 2009.

---

27. U.N. Development Program and U.N. Population Fund, Executive Board, "United Nations Population Fund: Statistical and Financial Review, 2007," DP/FPA/2008/5 (part 1, add.1), May 1, 2008, at http://documents-dds-ny.un.org/doc/UNDOC/GEN/N08/326/13/pdf/N0832613.pdf (accessed January 22, 2009).

28. U.N. Development Program and U.N. Population Fund, Executive Board, "United Nations Population Fund: Statistical and Financial Review, 2007."

29. U.N. Development Program and U.N. Population Fund, Executive Board, "United Nations Population Fund, Estimates for the Biennial Support Budget for 2008–2009," DP/FPA/2008/2, December 26, 2007, at http://documents-dds-ny.un.org/doc/UNDOC/GEN/N07/659/86/pdf/N0765986.pdf (accessed January 22, 2009).

30. U.N. Development Program and U.N. Population Fund, Executive Board, "United Nations Population Fund, Estimates for the Biennial Support Budget for 2008–2009."

The World Food Program

While all the major U.N. development agencies also engage in emergency relief activities, the WFP could be considered a relief agency that also undertakes development programs. According to the WFP, its development aid "temporarily frees the poor of the need to provide food for their families, giving them time and resources to invest in lasting assets such as better houses, clinics and schools, new agricultural skills and technology and, ultimately, a better future."[31]

Much of the WFP's income comes in response to specific appeals related to particular emergency situations. As of September 30, 2007, 76 percent of the $1.9 billion that it had received that year was for emergency response, and only 12 percent was for development activities.[32] The total 2006–2007 biennial budget was almost $6 billion, of which about $500 million was budgeted for development programs and about $375 million for program support and administrative expenses.[33]

The majority of the WFP's staff of about 9,000 is involved directly in the delivery of food. About 1,300 are engaged in program support and administration, including about 600 who are based in Rome.

Other Major U.N. Development Agencies

In addition to the core UNDG members, several other major U.N. specialized agencies have significant functions that are developmental.

International Labor Organization

The creation of jobs, real opportunities for individuals to earn income to support themselves and their families, is rarely on the agenda of U.N. development agencies. When employment is discussed, the ILO tends to concentrate on regulating employment, not increasing it. The ILO has promulgated an amazingly long list of 187 conventions dealing with labor

---

31. World Food Program, "Food Aid: Deterrent Against Poverty," at www .wfp.org/operations/introduction/development_projects.asp?section = 5&sub_sec tion = 1 (accessed January 22, 2009).

32. World Food Program, "Annual Report for 2007 to ECOSOC and FAO Council," WFP/EB.1/2008/4, January 4, 2008, at one.wfp.org/eb/docs/2008/wfp147 092~1.pdf (accessed May 14, 2009).

33. World Food Program, "Report of the Advisory Committee on Administrative and Budgetary Questions (ACABQ)," WFP/EB.1/2007/6(A,B,C)/2, February 16, 2007, at www.wfp.org/eb/docs/2007/wfp116672~1.pdf (accessed January 22, 2009).

standards.[34] The negotiation of many of these involved hairsplitting battles among developed-country delegates, with each country trying to enshrine its own particular vision of sound labor policy in international law. Meanwhile, delegates from developing countries, who had neither the governmental institutional capability nor the political will to implement even the most basic worker's rights, watched in bemusement, intent only on ensuring that the conventions included sufficient escape clauses and did not create any follow-up or enforcement mechanisms.

The United States, which has a highly developed structure of labor laws that protect workers and regulate employment conditions, has chosen to ratify only 14 of the 187 conventions,[35] viewing most as too rigid, incompatible with the U.S. federal regulatory regime, simply unnecessary, or irrelevant. The United States became so dissatisfied with the ILO process, which can be highly politicized, that it withdrew from the ILO from 1977 to 1980. In announcing the U.S. intent to withdraw, U.S. secretary of state Henry Kissinger said that the ILO members had allowed workers' and employers' groups in the ILO's unique tripartite governing system to fall under the domination of governments, had shown an "appallingly selective" concern for human rights, had disregarded "due process" in condemning member states "which happen to be the political target of the moment," and had increasingly politicized the organization.

The ILO's shortcomings are particularly disappointing given that a key goal of development is to create jobs. When people have the opportunity to work or work more productively, they can buy the things they need and want. This is the essence of development. Romantics deride the quest for material things, and on one level they are right. A life without art, poetry, music, or religion can be barren indeed, but a life without food and shelter is no life at all. The pathway from destitution to wholesome life is through a job, and the money that a job earns is the means to obtain the goods and services that support life in a dignified and fully adult manner.

Of course, money is only a medium of exchange, valuable for buying goods and services. When people work for money, they are really working for food, clothing, and shelter.

Development agencies could, of course, simply give people these commodities. Although few aid advocates would explicitly champion this idea today, this is the logical extension of an aid-focused development process.

---

34. International Labor Organization, "Official Titles of the Conventions Adopted by the International Labour Conference," 2006, at www.ilo.org/ilolex/english/conventions.pdf (accessed January 22, 2009).

35. International Labor Organization, ILOLEX, Database of International Labour Standards, at www.ilo.org/ilolex/english/newratframeE.htm (accessed January 22, 2009).

As evident in U.N. documents and deliberations, much of the aid that is being advocated is really for the provision by governments of food, clothing, shelter, or health care. These things are not treated as products that individuals would purchase out of the fruits of their own labor, but as rights to be provided by the state. It is a socialist autocrat's vision of the world and plays right into the hands of the dictators and presidents-for-life of poor countries.

However, the poor people themselves are treated like children, kept in a childlike dependent state. People who depend on the state for food, clothing, shelter, and health care have little scope for independence. They have little choice and are therefore scarcely free. Capitalism is the form of economic organization that provides choice and is ultimately the backbone of a free society.

The United Nations Educational, Scientific and Cultural Organization

UNESCO is charged with the development of education, science, and culture. The United States has also withdrawn from this U.N. body and subsequently rejoined it. As might be expected in areas as politically sensitive as education and culture, UNESCO debates are highly charged and rarely productive. In science, the value that it once added in areas like oceanography by facilitating the interaction of scientists with their colleagues from other nations has been eroded by the dramatic advances in communications technology that allow real-time connectivity between scientists anywhere in the world.

The Convention on the Protection and Promotion of the Diversity of Cultural Expressions, one of UNESCO's recent big ideas, typifies how elites and special interest groups can pervert the very meaning of words and concepts in a U.N. agency in their quest to impose their views on others. The convention, adopted over opposition from the United States and a handful of other nations, is deeply flawed in its conception of culture as embodying only the dominant culture of a given country or region. Individual diversity—for example, a citizen of Quebec embracing the English language—is seen as a threat to cultural diversity rather than as an example of it. Indeed, the convention espouses an ideology of cultural rigidity and conformity that is the antithesis of the cultural mixing and evolution that characterizes the United States, the most diverse country in the world.

At its heart, the convention on cultural diversity is about preserving the status quo. Indeed, one of its major goals is to provide excuses for countries to "protect" their citizens from imports of foreign cultural products and ideas. This is a far cry from the "free exchange of ideas and knowledge" called for in the UNESCO constitution.[36]

The Food and Agriculture Organization

FAO, another mammoth U.N. agency, is charged with helping to develop agricultural systems and increasing agricultural production and productivity. Like UNESCO, its core functions of data sharing, provision of expertise, and policy coordination are largely nugatory in the modern interconnected world. On the other hand, one core FAO function, the setting of food safety and plant health standards by the Codex Alimentarius and the International Plant Protection Convention, has become increasingly relevant and important as international trade in food has expanded.

The World Health Organization

WHO is yet another large specialized U.N. agency with a mandate for development, in its case "the attainment by all peoples of the highest possible level of health."[37] With a budget of more than $4.2 billion for 2008–2009, WHO has had success in coordinating worldwide campaigns to eradicate smallpox and polio. It has tackled high-profile health issues such as tobacco control and HIV/AIDS with less success. Indeed, the United Nations Joint Program on HIV/AIDS (UNAIDS) was established as a separate agency to coordinate international aid flows in support of AIDS prevention and treatment programs.

As detailed in the chapter by Roger Bate and Karen Porter, WHO is an organization with a noble purpose, but it lacks focus. Presumably, so noble a cause as advancing health would promote professionalism and international comity, yet WHO has often been paralyzed by politics, with debates over Taiwan, Palestine, and abortion distracting it from the pursuit of better health.

The Perennial Problem of Palestine

The issue of Palestine provides a particularly vivid example of the inherent limitations of organizations such as the United Nations. No issue receives more attention in debates and programs, yet no issue has proven more intractable. That the two sides claim historical and religious rights to

---

36. Constitution of the United Nations Educational, Scientific and Cultural Organization, November 16, 1945, preamble, at http://portal.unesco.org/en/ev.php-URL_ID = 15244 (accessed January 22, 2009).

37. Constitution of the World Health Organization, art. 1, at www.who.int/governance/eb/who_constitution_en.pdf (accessed December 3, 2008).

the same land is a difficult problem, to be sure, yet other such issues have been resolved justly through dialogue, understanding, reconciliation, and goodwill. Not so with the issue of Palestine. More than any other international question, it is associated with the U.N., in part because modern-day Israel was created by a U.N. resolution that partitioned the land. The U.N. Security Council has passed some 250 resolutions or statements on Israel, Palestine, and related subjects, far more than on any other issue.

Every U.N. agency features the Palestinian issue prominently on its agenda. For governing bodies and deliberative councils that have little real practical work to do, it is an almost irresistible issue. It provides opportunities for political posturing at its worst, and it is easily understood by diplomats who may have little relevant substantive expertise. When presented in simplistic terms with the U.N.'s traditional anti-Israel bias, the Palestinian issue has good guys and bad guys as clearly defined groups. It does not affect the daily lives or national interests of most U.N. members, so it is a "safe" issue for the vast majority of delegates, who suffer no consequences if their debates or votes sow conflict rather than concord. It is also a perfect foil for expressing religious rivalries, conflicts between races and ethnicities, and even Cold War rivalries.

The issue of Palestine, more than any other at the U.N., serves as a litmus test of countries' identities. They can, merely by castigating Israel (and often the United States), confirm their identities as radical and revolutionary states and express their sympathies with the downtrodden. Of course, none of it is real, except for the Israelis and the Palestinians who suffer from the absence of peace. For the rest, it is a morality play. The parts are easily understood and played, and the U.N. provides the perfect stage. Regrettably, the show seems to go on without end, and people's lives are being lost in the process.

Is "One UN" the Answer?

Faced with the myriad U.N. development agencies and programs with intersecting and overlapping mandates, some donors and recipients have called for simplifying and rationalizing the U.N. presence in developing countries through the principle of "One UN," which would involve consolidating offices, management, and even programming and budgeting processes for development activities. Under the One UN concept, the UNDP resident coordinator would head a country team of officials from all U.N. agencies that would collectively decide program priorities and implementation strategies. Interaction with recipient governments would be through one point of contact, and donors could contribute to a pool of resources that would be shared by all agencies.

In theory, One UN could provide greater efficiency and simplicity. In practice, it raises significant issues of accountability, overcentralization, and the elimination of competition. For these reasons, the United States and a number of other governments, both donors and aid recipients, have not embraced the idea. A number of U.N. agencies have expressed concern at their loss of autonomy and the UNDP's increasing power and influence. The One UN idea is currently being studied in eight pilot countries: Albania, Cape Verde, Mozambique, Pakistan, Rwanda, Tanzania, Uruguay, and Vietnam. Regrettably, both donors and U.N. agencies have tended to pump extra resources into the countries being studied, and it is not clear that the pilot programs are truly testing the long-term viability of the concept.

THE WAY FORWARD

Despite the lofty rhetoric that accompanies U.N. debates and activities on development, the system really does not matter much to most U.N. members. The symbolic gestures and political posturing that dominate the debates may be far more important to them than the lack of developmental results. The revolutionary upheaval needed to make the system truly effective would require changes in economic philosophy, U.N. funding and voting patterns, and hiring and management practices. For most U.N. members, the pain of such changes far outweighs the benefits, particularly when development progress has been strong anyway in recent years as a result of trade liberalization and globalization.

If the U.N. membership is to focus on reforms that would improve the effectiveness of its development efforts, it needs to start by recognizing the following development facts of life:

- Development is more of an individual process than a societal process. A country's development is the sum and result of the individual development efforts of each of its citizens.
- Aid to individuals can support their personal development and, by extension, the development of societies.
- Governments that provide an honest and stable economic environment, economically useful public goods such as roads, and fair access to justice help their economies to develop and their citizens to prosper. Aid to such governments for such purposes can promote development.
- Corrupt and repressive governments stifle development. Aid to such governments hurts rather than helps development.

U.N. agencies that honor these principles when devising their programs have a chance to promote development. There is no real way of determining how useful such aid is in developing societies overall, but one could have a high degree of confidence that the aid was at least doing no harm and almost certainly helping some individuals.

The largest U.N. agencies have great difficulty in operating in accordance with these principles, which conflict with time-honored U.N. shibboleths. For example, the principle of universality dictates that aid should flow to all U.N. members, irrespective of the nature of their governments. Aid programs are as likely, perhaps more likely, to be driven by donor interests, specialists, experts, and consultants as by the needs of the developing country. The general assumption is that developing countries need everything and are thus likely to accept anything that comes along, even if they do not regard it as what they need most. U.N. programs add breadth to developing countries' development agendas, but may distract them from higher priorities or even encourage different priorities from those they favored.

Any aid program not focused explicitly on helping poor people in underdeveloped countries work more productively and compete more effectively within the globalized capitalist system is likely to be of symbolic value at best and counterproductive at worst. This reality suggests several specific recommendations:

U.N. discussions need to be refocused away from sterile exchanges about aid levels and toward a more honest discussion of policies that either promote or hinder development

Nothing has poisoned the U.N.'s work on development more than the debate over foreign aid. It is corrupting in profound ways. It makes beggars out of the developing countries and their U.N. delegates, and it reinforces the image of the citizens of developing countries as children, incapable of providing for themselves or promoting their own development. It encourages a paternalistic, "we know better" attitude on the part of donors and raises expectations of quick fixes. Interestingly, money is often the easiest thing to find in the U.N. development system, but fundamentally changing laws and traditional practices, eliminating corruption, and overthrowing established elite privileges can take decades and generations.

The focus on aid also destroys the concept of accountability of donors and recipients. One of the most perverse features of today's aid flows is the inverse relationship between aid and economic performance. Development assistance flows mostly toward failed states because they are in the greatest need. Yet the aid itself allows wretched governments to continue their failed policies and kleptocratic practices. Donors run a real risk that their charitable impulses will turn them into enablers for dictators and despots. Even humanitarian aid, the noblest assistance flows in the international system, invites corruption by both donors and recipients. U.S. commodity donations to the World Food Program at least indirectly support governments in failed states and may be the most important factor in keeping despotic regimes in power in Burma, North Korea, and Sudan.

The United States should continue to resist efforts to focus the development debate on the level of assistance, such as the call for developed nations to provide a mythical 0.7 percent of GDP for development assistance. Instead, the United States should focus the debate on how poor nations can adopt policies that increase their chances for development. This means limiting the size and scope of government, constraining corruption, creating an economic environment conducive to entrepreneurship, and strengthening the judicial system and legal framework to make it more reliable, transparent, and impartial.

The U.N. needs to abandon its sixty-year fascination with socialism

One U.S. failure at the U.N. has been its reluctance to robustly defend the U.S. economic system, namely, capitalism. In 2002, when the State Department sent me to New York to participate in a debate on financing for development, I spoke of the need for developing countries to embrace capitalism wholeheartedly. The room erupted in a clamor at my mere use of the word. Capitalism has somehow become discredited at the U.N., even though it is the basis of U.S. prosperity, not to mention the prosperity of most of the world. Even the U.S. ambassador at the time was taken aback, summoning me to his office to explain myself and my "confrontational" approach. His concerns and criticisms notwithstanding, I managed to keep my job and was rewarded with the opportunity to engage in months of hard-nosed wrangling, mostly late at night in the U.N. basement, to reach a consensus.

Surprisingly, the reaction from a number of developing-country delegates was more welcoming. A few, including the delegate from Egypt, recognized the potential benefits to the poor of a stronger embrace of the free-market system that was working so well for so many, and he welcomed even more so the chance for a debate in which the United States and others would talk about the world of commerce as it really works rather than the utopian visions that are all too often promoted in the halls of diplomacy. Out of these debates emerged the Monterrey Consensus, an agreement that for the first time in U.N. history put the official transfer of government resources (foreign aid) in its proper context as a supporting element in the development process and as a small part of much larger international flows of capital, most of which result from trade and investment decisions in the private sector.[38]

Real-world experience of the past six decades provides conclusive evidence that market-based economic policies, bolstered by a sound rule of law, offer the surest path toward development. The world economic system is and will remain a market-based capitalist system. All U.N. development agencies should, as a primary goal, assist member governments in crafting economic policies likely to best enable the entrepreneurial abilities of their individual citizens. Most poor U.N. member states need help in clearly defining a limited role for government, encouraging political and economic empowerment of their poorer citizens, and enforcing the rule of law, property rights, and private contracts in a fair and impartial manner.

The United States should resist the "One UN" effort and similar proposals to consolidate U.N. development efforts under one authority

A U.N. development system that truly promotes development is likely to have the characteristics of a market itself. Economic efficiency requires competition, and the U.N. would similarly benefit from competition. Centralization should be resisted because it creates too much power and bureaucracy. Large agencies such as the UNDP, which have developed monstrous bureaucratic structures and budgetary and programming systems that defy analysis, should be split up. A clear line needs to be drawn between humanitarian relief and development assistance. Agencies that have strong roles in both areas should focus on one or the other.

UNICEF and the World Food Program should drop their development activities and focus solely on relief. The UNDP and UNFPA should be active only in countries where the security environment is stable and where the governments are committed to market-based capitalist economic policies, respect for human rights, and fair and dependable enforcement of the rule of law. The currently popular One UN idea should be rigorously evaluated and pursued only in those countries where it has clear advantages over a more competitive process, perhaps in the poorest and least capable countries or in the context of a humanitarian intervention, where domestic governance is poor or nonexistent.

---

38. United Nations, *Monterrey Consensus on Financing for Development*, 2003, at www.un.org/esa/ffd/monterrey/MonterreyConsensus.pdf (accessed January 28, 2009).

The United States should promote smaller, more focused U.N. agencies that have more freedom of action and are more likely to avoid negative results

U.N. development agencies that are smaller in size often provide greater developmental impact or at least a more transparent purpose and mode of action that makes measuring their impact easier. They also deliver far more useful information and service for each development dollar than their larger counterparts.

For instance, the U.N. Capital Development Fund (UNCDF), a semi-independent part of the UNDP, had a budget of only $28 million in 2007. With an innovative program of microfinance focusing on the local and enterprise level rather than the national level, UNCDF supports about three thousand investments in twenty-eight low-income countries. Similarly, the International Trade Center (ITC), a Geneva-based organization loosely affiliated with the United Nations Conference on Trade and Development (UNCTAD) and the WTO, has a staff of 236 and a total budget of about $60 million. This budget funded more than 3,500 specific interventions, many at the level of individual companies. More than 30 percent of the interventions reported positive results. This is not quite a grade of A+, but in the development world where macroeconomic measures generally show no results or even negative effects from aid, a 30 percent success rate is almost miraculous. Based on its own report, the ITC understands that development is about creating productive and competitive enterprises.[39] Such a focus on helping businesses is almost unique in the U.N. system, where private enterprise is often treated as the enemy rather than as a favored and essential client.

The United Nations Development Fund for Women (UNIFEM) provides a contrasting case study of how increasing size can lead to a loss of focus and the diminution of developmental impact. According to the 2004 report of a U.N. advisory panel charged with making an overall assessment of UNIFEM, the organization evolved between 1984 and 1996:

> UNIFEM moved, during this period, from an emphasis on direct support to women, mainly in rural areas and with a focus on productive activities and

---

39. "Businesses trade, not countries. Making trade work for development and poverty reduction means creating an enabling business environment and helping companies access the resources they need to become internationally competitive. Small and medium enterprises (SMEs) are the engines of export growth for developing countries. Harnessing the untapped potential of these enterprises is a key policy objective for governments and the mission of the International Trade Centre (ITC)." International Trade Center, "Leveraging ITC Skills for SME Export Success," at www.intracen.org/docman/JAG_11230.pdf (accessed January 22, 2009).

revolving loan funds, into the human development and human rights arenas, with a growing emphasis on policy and advocacy. It experienced an accelerating pace of change, partly due to the rapid succession of global conferences, especially the Beijing Conference, as well as in response to broader interests and activities of women's governmental and non-governmental organizations.[40]

In practical terms, this means that UNIFEM has evolved away from supporting individual development projects that directly assist poor women toward emphasizing "upstream" activities directed at government policy change, coordination, and planning. Even within the same organizational structure, the diminishing impact as size increases is evident.

A comparison of two specific programs, a UNIFEM project approved in 2006 and a program of the newer, but smaller and less "evolved" U.N. Trust Fund to End Violence against Women that UNIFEM administers, is instructive. The UNIFEM project provided $3.3 million for "building capacity and improving accountability for gender equality in development, peace and security. Against the background of the Paris Declaration on Aid Effectiveness, this joint program with the European Commission and the International Labour Organization aims to support advocacy and action to step up investments in gender equality as key to the effectiveness of development assistance."[41] The U.N. Trust Fund to End Violence against Women project provided $200,000 to a Nepalese nongovernmental organization "using a flagship women's radio programme to empower women to end stigma, violence and discrimination."[42]

The larger project talks about building capacity, presumably government capacity, to do an activity rather than actually financing the activity itself. Its overarching goal is gender equality, an admirable goal but scarcely more than a slogan. It talks about improving accountability, but shares responsibility for the program with the European Commission and the ILO. The project aims to "support" (step 1) "advocacy" (step 2) "to step up investments" (step 3) "in gender equality as key" (step 4) "to the effectiveness of

---

40. Advisory Panel to the Consultative Committee, "Organizational Assessment: UNIFEM Past, Present and Future," U.N. Development Fund for Women, December 1, 2004, par. 24, in U.N. General Assembly and U.N. Economic and Social Council, "Letter Dated 23 November 2004 from the Permanent Representatives of Canada, Jordan, Mexico, the Niger and Slovenia to the United Nations Addressed to the Secretary-General," A/60/62, January 31, 2005, p. 10, at http://documents-dds-ny.un.org/doc/UNDOC/GEN/N05/224/73/pdf/N0522473.pdf (accessed January 22, 2009).

41. U.N. Development Fund for Women, *UNIFEM Annual Report 2006–2007*, 2007, at www.unifem.org/attachments/products/AnnualReport2006_2007_eng.pdf (accessed January 22, 2009).

42. U.N. Development Fund for Women, *Annual Report 2006–2007*.

development assistance" (the ultimate goal). How much "effectiveness of development assistance" this $3.3 million will buy is unclear, as is who will be responsible for each of the steps toward that end.

By contrast, the U.N. Trust Fund project is smaller and clear. A specifically identified NGO will do the project, which is producing a radio program. The program will happen or it will not. Of course, whether the program empowers women "to end stigma, violence and discrimination" is a judgment call, but at least U.N. members will know exactly who did what with the money that was provided.

U.N. programs should have discrete and identifiable funding streams

Funds contributed to U.N. development efforts should be squarely under the authority and oversight of the donor and recipient countries. Other countries should refrain from involving themselves in governance debates or decisions. A U.N. development system that functions like a giant bazaar, with both donors and recipients purchasing development services of one kind or another, is likely to add the most value to the process. Donors should consider providing money directly to poor country governments or even directly to the poor citizens of underdeveloped countries, so that those governments and citizens can become the consumers and purchasers of U.N. development services. Such a process in which the purchasers and the consumers are the same is the most likely to encourage accountability. The current system in which the rich pay, but the poor consume, provides almost no accountability. Only activities capable of being monitored and evaluated should be approved.

In addition to promoting these changes, the United States should be more selective in its participation in U.N. development bodies and ensure that it devotes appropriate staff resources to oversee the agencies in which it participates. The U.S. government, which has a large bilateral aid program and diplomatic representation in almost every country in the world, gains little from participating in U.N. aid agencies and should consider withdrawing from many of them. U.N. development activities may be appropriate for smaller donors who lack such infrastructure, but they add little value for the United States.

CONCLUSION

The current U.N. development system promises too much and demands too little of its member governments. Its autocracy, secrecy, bureaucracy, and self-aggrandizement reflect the worst of its members. U.N. rhetoric that promises, as does one of the Millennium Development Goals, to halve poverty in fifteen years is seductive nonsense. The goal may be realistic, but it will not be achieved because of U.N. development programs. While the U.N. development goals are noble, they ignore the fact that development is ultimately a process of individual change that governments can, at best, facilitate. If it is achieved, it will be through the efforts of the poor, the entrepreneurs, the businessmen, and other private actors.

The solution is more openness, more competition, and an insistence by those members that know better—especially the United States, the U.N.'s most powerful member—that the U.N. reflect and promote the values on which their own societies, economies, and governments are based. A U.N. system that aspires to revolutionary change for the poor would dedicate itself unambiguously to those revolutionary doctrines of democracy and capitalism that have altered the course of civilization and brought freedom and prosperity to billions. A U.N. system that demands that its member governments uphold the U.N. Charter's call for justice, human rights, and an end to war will take the most important steps toward fostering development. U.N. programs that explain and defend the capitalist market system and extend its reach into the poorest areas of the world will do even more.

8

Promoting Free Trade through the United Nations

Daniella Markheim

In the waning days of World War II, the Allied leaders met in Bretton Woods to begin developing the institutions and policies to rebuild Europe and set the world economy on a long-term path to prosperity. With the lessons of the Great Depression in mind, one part of this agenda centered on creating the International Trade Organization (ITO) to establish the rules governing global trade and to prevent a return to the ruinous protectionist trade policies that had helped to prolong and deepen the Great Depression.

The ITO was never established, but the United States and twenty-two other nations agreed to start reducing trade barriers through the General Agreement on Tariffs and Trade (GATT). The GATT was expanded over the course of eight negotiating rounds, culminating with the establishment of the World Trade Organization (WTO) in 1995. Today, the regulation of international trade falls under the WTO's jurisdiction and the numerous bilateral and regional trade agreements that shape the patterns of global trade.

While the WTO is an autonomous and independent body only loosely associated with the United Nations, numerous organizations and agencies have been created over the past six decades within the U.N. system to address the role of trade in issues ranging from economic development to protecting the environment. Although unable to directly determine the rules underpinning international trade, organizations such as the United Nations Conference on Trade and Development (UNCTAD) maintain observer status in various WTO bodies as part of an effort to promote

237

greater "coherence" in global economic policymaking.[1] In general, these organizations can provide valuable analysis and technical expertise that contribute to expanding international trade. Regrettably, they can also provide excuses for countries to delay trade liberalization, especially countries struggling to develop their economies. All too often, these organizations overlap in their jurisdictions and offer conflicting advice.

Reconciling and pruning these disparate elements within the U.N. system is long overdue. With the creation and expansion of the WTO, there is much less need for U.N. bodies that focus on international trade matters. As of July 2008, the WTO has 153 members, including nearly all the world's major trading nations. Developed and developing countries have a voice and vote in the body, and views on trade are varied and freely expressed. The U.N. system has little to offer that the WTO does not already provide.

Where the U.N. can effectively complement the WTO is by helping developing countries better embrace open markets more quickly. Although UNCTAD it is not as well funded as other U.N. institutions and suffers from mission creep like so many other multilateral organizations, it is the most influential U.N. body on trade matters and the only U.N. body with the explicit mandate to address issues of economic development and trade policy. To reduce waste and duplication of effort and to improve the quality and coherence of the international trade-related policy work carried out in U.N. agencies, such work should be streamlined and shifted to UNCTAD. With the proper resources and mission focus, UNCTAD is the best-positioned U.N. agency to assume responsibility for conducting and coordinating all U.N. endeavors in advising countries on matters of international trade policy.

However, simply reforming the U.N. to promote better analysis will not accelerate the pace of global trade liberalization. After all, the WTO leads international trade negotiations to dismantle the tariffs and nontariff barriers inhibiting trade. The WTO has its own flaws and weaknesses, including a growing calcification in efforts to further open markets due to fundamental divisions among its membership over the positive role of free trade in economic development. Realizing its goal of expanding trade and unfettering the world's markets will require new, more effective approaches to communicate the benefits of free trade and to resolve the policy deadlock that prevents countries from achieving those benefits.

A new forum for like-minded reformers—separate from the WTO, U.N., and other multilateral institutions—could provide the problem-solving environment and multilateral consensus needed to find solutions to indi-

---

1. World Trade Organization, "The WTO and Other Organizations," at www .wto.org/english/thewto_e/coher_e/coher_e.htm (accessed August 1, 2008).

vidual trade-related issues thwarting progress in the WTO. These solutions could then be introduced into the WTO discussion to speed a breakthrough in the trade talks—a breakthrough needed to advance sustainable development and world prosperity.

THE EVOLUTION OF THE INTERNATIONAL
TRADE SYSTEM AND UNCTAD

Trade restrictions can take the form of tariffs (taxes on imports), taxes on exports, quotas, outright bans on trade, or other regulatory and institutional barriers to trade. Tariffs and other trade barriers increase the prices that local consumers and businesses pay for foreign imports, helping to boost consumption of less-competitive domestic products. These price distortions change incentives, driving production away from specialization in more internationally competitive goods and toward goods protected by trade barriers. As a result, labor and capital are used less efficiently, and consumers are left with a smaller variety of more expensive products from which to consume. Thus, by interfering with comparative advantage, trade restrictions impede economic growth.

Free trade allows a country to compete in the global market according to its fundamental economic strengths and to reap the productivity and efficiency gains that promote long-run wealth and prosperity. Countries with open markets realize real gains from freer trade, including a more competitive economic environment and better, more efficient domestic resource allocation. These effects drive greater long-term economic potential, create economic opportunity, and improve living standards at home, which in turn contribute to other desirable outcomes such as a cleaner environment.

Exporters and domestic producers that use lower-cost imported inputs gain a competitive boost that promotes investment, productivity, and growth in these industries. Lower prices for imported goods also help households to stretch their incomes, enabling them to buy more of everything, including goods and services that are produced domestically. With freer trade, resources flow from less competitive uses to more competitive and efficient uses, creating opportunity and bolstering long-run economic growth and job creation.

The benefits of free trade are illustrated by the protectionist policy experiment that helped to make the Great Depression deeper, longer, and more costly than it would have been if tariffs had been left at their original levels or reduced. The Great Depression started with the crash of the stock market on Black Tuesday in the United States in 1929 and spread to devastate the economies of most countries around the world. The resulting economic panic inspired both good and bad policy prescriptions to bring relief to families and struggling businesses. One of the most destructive policies was the Smoot-Hawley Tariff Act of 1930, which dramatically increased U.S. tariff rates on foreign imports to boost domestic output by making imports too expensive to compete. Predictably, other countries retaliated against the United States with their own high and prohibitive tariffs. These "beggar thy neighbor" policies sparked a contraction of global trade that greatly contributed to the cost and duration of the Great Depression.

In the postwar era, most countries were determined to establish an international trade system that would promote freer trade and prevent a recurrence of the trade war that occurred during the 1930s. The basis for the modern international trading system was established in 1947 as countries launched a host of new multilateral institutions dedicated to international economic cooperation, including the World Bank and the International Monetary Fund (IMF). As part of that process, more than fifty nations drafted a Charter for the International Trade Organization, a formal autonomous international agency within the United Nations system alongside the World Bank and IMF. Under the draft ITO Charter, ITO members agreed:

1. To assure a large and steadily growing volume of real income and effective demand, to increase the production, consumption and exchange of goods, and thus to contribute to a balanced and expanding world economy.
2. To foster and assist industrial and general economic development, particularly of those countries which are still in the early stages of industrial development, and to encourage the international flow of capital for productive investment.
3. To further the enjoyment by all countries, on equal terms, of access to the markets, products and productive facilities which are needed for their economic prosperity and development.
4. To promote on a reciprocal and mutually advantageous basis the reduction of tariffs and other barriers to trade and the elimination of discriminatory treatment in international commerce.
5. To enable countries, by increasing the opportunities for their trade and economic development, to abstain from measures which would disrupt world commerce, reduce productive employment or retard economic progress.
6. To facilitate through the promotion of mutual understanding, consultation and co-operation the solution of problems relating to international trade in the fields of employment, economic development, commercial policy, business practices and commodity policy.[2]

---

2. Havana Charter for an International Trade Organization, in U.N. Conference on Trade and Employment, *Final Act and Related Documents* (November 21, 1947–

The ITO Charter was concluded at the U.N. Conference on Trade and Employment in Havana in March 1948. However, in 1950, after repeated attempts to gain congressional approval had failed, the United States announced that it would not ratify the Charter. This left the ITO without a critical member and effectively spelled the end for the ITO.

Countries turned to an alternative approach to international trade cooperation in the General Agreement on Tariffs and Trade. The GATT adopted a less formal structure than the ITO and offered an easier, more gradual route to reducing tariffs and opening markets among interested member nations. Rather than create an organization that regulated trade and trade-related aspects of the international economy, the GATT was a treaty that focused more explicitly on reducing and eliminating specific tariffs, quotas, and subsidies.

The first round of negotiations among the twenty-three founding GATT "contracting parties" resulted in significant trade liberalization based on provisional acceptance of some of the trade rules contained in the ITO Charter. These tariff concessions and Charter rules entered into force as the General Agreement on Tariffs and Trade in January 1948. Successive negotiating rounds under the GATT widened and deepened international markets by cutting tariffs and nontariff barriers on goods. A key concept enshrined under the GATT is the most favored nation (MFN) principle, which prevents countries from discriminating between different trading partners. The Uruguay Round, the eighth and final round under the GATT, was launched in 1986 in Uruguay. It not only extended GATT rules for the trading system into several new, more difficult negotiating areas including trade in services, intellectual property rights, and rules governing trade in agriculture and textiles, but also led to the creation of the World Trade Organization in 1995.[3]

The GATT provided the context for significant trade opening among member countries from 1948 to 1994 and served as the foundation for creating the WTO in 1995. During the Uruguay Round, GATT membership increased from 89 countries in 1985 to 128 countries in 1994. More countries quickly lined up to join the newly formed WTO, demonstrating that the multilateral trading system has been recognized as an anchor for development and an instrument of economic and trade reform. By 2008, every major trading nation and most developing countries were either one of the 153 member states in the WTO or one of the 29 countries in negotiations to accede to the organization.

March 24, 1948), 14, at www.wto.int/english/docs_e/legal_e/havana_e.pdf (accessed November 24, 2008).

3. World Trade Organization, "The GATT Years: From Havana to Marrakesh," at www.wto.org/english/thewto_e/whatis_e/tif_e/fact4_e.htm (accessed August 1, 2008).

The multilateral trading system changed dramatically under the GATT and has changed even more significantly under the WTO. Most developing countries were not members of the GATT, and their involvement in trade negotiations was negligible. Those that were members benefited from GATT rounds, but were not required to reciprocate with significant tariff concessions of their own. Thus, their products gained new access to foreign markets, but they continued to protect domestic industries and the resulting price distortions and misallocation of resources inhibited domestic economic growth. In a sense, they were passive members of the multilateral trading system and consequently failed to realize the full benefits of trade liberalization.

Circumstances are much different today. Approximately three out of four WTO member states are developing countries, and all members—rich and poor—are responsible for advancing freer trade. One consequence of the growing number of developing countries in the WTO was the decision to premise the current Doha Round of multilateral trade negotiations on promoting economic development. The round was launched in November 2001 in Doha, Qatar.

After more than half a century of trade liberalization, the Doha Round's agenda includes some of the most politically sensitive and difficult trade issues: reducing agricultural trade barriers, further reducing nonagriculture tariffs, expanding market access for trade in services, improving WTO institutional rules and procedures, and solving developing-country issues, including the need to boost the trade capacity of those countries.

Regrettably, the WTO's success in expanding its membership may be undermining its ability to advance trade liberalization at anything more than an incremental pace. So far, negotiations have failed to produce a comprehensive agreement that is satisfactory to all WTO members. The collapse of the negotiations in July 2008 reflects both divergent thinking on the role that trade liberalization plays in advancing economic development and some members' intransigence in upholding their commitments to eliminating trade barriers.

THE U.N. AND INTERNATIONAL
TRADE THROUGH 1995

In December 1964, the U.N. General Assembly established the United Nations Conference on Trade and Development to analyze international trade patterns and recommend policies and programs to advance sustainable economic development and tighter integration between developing and developed countries. UNCTAD arose, in part, from a belief among developing countries that the General Agreement on Tariffs and Trade was primarily a forum for developed nations. However, UNCTAD also drew interest from many developing countries that were influenced by the communist and socialist economic theories prevalent at that time and believed that the liberal economic policies underpinning the GATT were disadvantageous to less-developed countries. They sought to make UNCTAD a foil to the classical liberal trade theory espoused by the GATT and a forum that, in their eyes, emphasized development concerns along with broader reform of the existing trade and economic order.

As a means to keep the development and trade debate moving forward, UNCTAD was institutionalized with a permanent secretariat and scheduled to meet every four years, with intergovernmental meetings between conferences. The General Assembly specifically directed the UNCTAD:

(a) To promote international trade, especially with a view to accelerating economic development . . . ;
(b) To formulate principles and policies on international trade and related problems of economic development;
(c) To make proposals for putting the said principles and policies into effect . . . having regard to differences in economic systems and stages of development;
(d) Generally, to review and facilitate the coordination of the activities of other institutions within the United Nations system in the field of international trade and related problems of economic development . . . ;
(e) To initiate action . . . for the negotiation and adoption of multilateral legal instruments in the field of trade . . . ;
(f) [To work to harmonize] trade and related development policies of Governments and regional economic groupings. . . .[4]

Initially, UNCTAD was an unabashed champion of state control over trade and international transactions and promoted socialist economic policies based on the assumption that such policies would hasten development. Indeed, secretary-general Raul Prebisch declared in his 1964 report to the first UNCTAD conference, UNCTAD I, that the GATT had not been "efficacious" for developing countries precisely because it "is based upon the classic concept that the free play of international economic forces by itself also leads to the optimum expansion of trade and the most efficient utilization of the world's productive resources."[5]

---

4. U.N. General Assembly, "Establishment of the United Nations Conference on Trade and Development as an Organ of the General Assembly," Resolution 1995 (XIX), December 30, 1964, sec. 2(3), at www.un.org/documents/ga/res/19/ares19 .htm (accessed January 12, 2009).

5. Stanley J. Mickalak Jr., *The United Nations Conference on Trade and Development: An Organization Betraying Its Mission* (Washington, DC: Heritage Foundation, 1983), 2.

To be fair, the facts of the day seemingly lent credibility to this conclusion. During the late 1950s and early 1960s, exports from developing countries—largely primary products—were increasing. However, international prices for many of these commodities and goods were falling. At the same time, developing countries that had not started to reduce their tariff rates as part of GATT were paying increasingly high prices for imports of finished and other goods from around the world. As a result, many developing countries experienced a worsening of their terms of trade that, when coupled with developed countries' high tariffs and taxes on the developing world's exports of manufactured goods, left them little opportunity to diversify and develop their economies. This worsening of developing countries' competitiveness in global markets ultimately led Prebisch to determine that the freer trade facilitated through the GATT and other multinational economic organizations institutionalized the exploitation of developing countries, preventing them from diversifying their economies and improving economic growth.[6]

In reality, excessive regulation, state control of economic assets, weak rule of law, protectionism, and other policy failures underpinned many of the economic problems experienced by developing nations. However, the sense of unfairness pervading trade discussions led these countries to blame the GATT framework and free trade instead of questioning their own economic policies. Thus, Prebisch envisioned UNCTAD as an alternative to GATT, providing a framework for a new collectivist, interventionist international economic order through which developing countries could address their interests and concerns. As laid out in UNCTAD's general principles, a "new economic order" would replace the existing liberal international economic system based on free, nondiscriminatory trade with a system that would use planning, regulation, and discriminatory rules to ensure that resources flowed from wealthy countries to developing countries.[7]

UNCTAD was created when newly independent developing countries were beginning to outnumber developed countries in the U.N. and were increasingly asserting their agenda. UNCTAD was seen as an opportunity to mount a challenge to the existing world order and to eradicate the inequities and imbalances that open, nondiscriminatory markets were perceived to bring. To coordinate these efforts, the Group of 77 (G-77) developing countries was established at UNCTAD I to serve as a policy forum for developing countries on trade and economic issues in the U.N. It helped to coordinate policy positions and tried to coordinate voting in the U.N. to advance economic and political objectives deemed to be in the

---

6. Mickalak, *United Nations Conference*, 19.

7. United Nations, *Yearbook of the United Nations, 1964* (New York: Columbia University Press, 1964), 198–201.

interest of developing countries. These positions often were in conflict with those promoted by developed nations.

With developing countries rallying behind the guiding principles espoused in UNCTAD I, developed countries often found themselves caught in a heated debate between capitalist and socialist economic ideologies. Indeed, the legacy of these positions continues to be a headache today because Cuba and other countries continue to use the G-77 and its historical policy positions to frustrate efforts to advance economic liberalization and free trade in the U.N. This debate drove the United States and other nations to criticize and distance themselves from UNCTAD, and it helps to explain the cautious nature of their current engagement.

The Shift in UNCTAD's Approach to Trade

The ideological tug-of-war between developing countries and the developed world dominated the first five UNCTAD conferences and the organization's first decade. Yet UNCTAD led to a few concrete actions in advancing a binding, interventionist approach to managing international trade in the name of promoting economic development.[8] At UNCTAD II (New Delhi, 1968), conference participants adopted Resolution 21 (II), which called for tariff preferences in favor of developing countries. The GATT Council adopted this measure in 1971 as the Generalized System of Preferences (GSP).[9] The GSP was initially a ten-year exception to MFN treatment to permit tariff preferences for developing countries. The exception was later made permanent during the Tokyo Round of trade negotiations. GSP schemes grant reduced or zero tariff rates over MFN rates to a wide range of exports from least developed countries. Currently thirteen countries grant GSP preferences: Australia, Belarus, Bulgaria, Canada, Estonia, the European Union, Japan, New Zealand, Norway, the Russian Federation, Switzerland, Turkey, and the United States.[10]

The UNCTAD secretariat spent a large part of the 1970s gaining experience working with and learning about the GATT and providing analysis and data for developing countries engaged in the 1973–1979 Tokyo Round. The lessons learned from interacting with the GATT trade framework— especially in successfully winning preferential treatment for developing

---

8. Conferences include UNCTAD III (Santiago, 1972); UNCTAD IV (Nairobi, 1976); and UNCTAD V (Manila, 1979).

9. U.N. Conference on Trade and Development, *Beyond Conventional Wisdom in Development Policy: An Intellectual History of UNCTAD 1964–2004* (New York: United Nations, 2005), 4, at www.unctad.org/en/docs/edm20044_en.pdf (accessed January 15, 2009).

10. U.N. Conference on Trade and Development, "About GSP," 2002, at www.unctad.org/Templates/Page.asp?intItemID = 2309 (accessed August 1, 2008).

countries—combined with economic stagnation and rising unemployment in the 1970s and 1980s to make UNCTAD's approach to developing countries' trade issues more pragmatic.[11]

Consequently, the 1980s ushered in new thinking on the prodevelopment aspects of freer trade among developing countries and the decline in UNCTAD's role in international economic policymaking. During this time, UNCTAD began to transform from an institution pitted against the GATT and seeking to regulate trade into an institution that worked within the GATT system to better enable developing countries to benefit from trade—an increasingly important responsibility as the international economy became more complex.

With GATT's success in reducing tariff rates among its member countries, policymakers began to implement new policy tools to protect struggling industries from increased foreign competition. Governments in North America, across Europe, and around the world increasingly used antidumping and countervailing duties, quotas, subsidies, and bilateral market-sharing arrangements to restrict trade and erect barriers against export competition. These tactics, together with an increasingly complex global trade regime, which included a great increase in international trade in services and a growing number of countries engaging the world's markets, progressively undermined the GATT's effectiveness in regulating international transactions.

As a result, after the 1983 Belgrade conference, UNCTAD sought to improve the GSP and other commitments providing preferential treatment for developing-country exports, address the misuse of antidumping and countervailing duties, eliminate quantitative restrictions and similar measures, and set up "an improved and more efficient safeguard system."[12] UNCTAD called for proposals within the context of preserving the principles of MFN treatment and nondiscrimination that would grant preferential access to developing countries and allow them to protect domestic industry in times of emergency.

In this regard, UNCTAD provided technical assistance to the increasing number of developing countries participating in the Uruguay Round of trade negotiations and provided the comprehensive analysis of global trade in services and the role of services trade in promoting development that became the foundation for the General Agreement on Trade in Services negotiated in the Uruguay Round and adopted within the WTO.[13]

---

11. U.N. Conference on Trade and Development, *Beyond Conventional Wisdom*, 5.

12. U.N. Conference on Trade and Development, *Beyond Conventional Wisdom*, 6.

13. U.N. Conference on Trade and Development, "A Brief History of UNCTAD," 2002, at www.unctad.org/Templates/Page.asp?intItemID = 3358 (accessed August 2, 2008).

UNCTAD AFTER FORMATION OF THE WTO

With the conclusion of the Uruguay Round and the founding of the World Trade Organization in 1995, UNCTAD's role in the international economic policy arena came under scrutiny. By this point, UNCTAD lacked "the power to promote changes or to enhance international justice through the adoption of trade rules worldwide (as the WTO), or the power to finance development (as the World Bank), and to alleviate the debt burden, or to prevent or to manage financial crisis (as the IMF)."[14] However, in 1994, the U.N. General Assembly adopted a resolution that maintained UNCTAD's role as the coordinator for better integrating U.N. work in development, trade, and other development-related areas.[15] Additionally, while the new guidance recognized that the WTO would engage in policy analysis, collect data, provide technical assistance and advice to potential and actual members, and work to build international consensus in trade policy matters—some of the very tasks assigned to UNCTAD by its member states—UNCTAD should avoid being redundant. Instead, the U.N. tasked UNCTAD with promoting greater coherence in global economic policymaking by collaborating with the WTO and other international organizations.[16]

In 1996, in preparation for UNCTAD IX in Midrand, South Africa, UNCTAD and the WTO released a joint study of the post-Uruguay trade regime entitled *Strengthening the Participation of Developing Countries in World Trade and the Multilateral Trading System.*[17] Together with the Midrand Declaration,[18] this document defined UNCTAD's role in advancing economic development and trade. The WTO would be a forum for ongoing, complex negotiations, and UNCTAD would provide the technical expertise needed to facilitate developing-country participation in the WTO and would assist countries in navigating the WTO accession process. Moreover, since developing countries often lack the appropriate level of economic and physical infrastructure to adopt and adhere to WTO rules, UNCTAD would

---

14. U.N. Conference on Trade and Development, *Beyond Conventional Wisdom,* xvi.

15. U.N. General Assembly, "International Trade and Development," A/RES/49/99, February 21, 1995, at www.un.org/Depts/dhl/res/resa49.htm (accessed January 13, 2009).

16. World Trade Organization, "WTO and Other Organizations."

17. World Trade Organization, "Participation of Developing Countries in World Trade: Overview of Major Trends and Underlying Factors," WT/COMTD/W/15, August 16, 1996, at www.wto.org/english/tratop_e/devel_e/w15.htm (accessed January 13, 2009).

18. U.N. Conference on Trade and Development, "Midrand Declaration and a Partnership for Growth and Development," TD/377, May 24, 1996, at www.unctad.org/en/docs/u9d377.pdf (accessed January 13, 2009).

again provide technical expertise and analysis to design effective domestic policies that would support trade facilitation, development, and growth. As a consequence of UNCTAD's work on developing-country accessions to the WTO, the WTO General Council adopted a decision in 2002 that was geared to facilitating developing-country accessions by advising current WTO members to exercise restraint in what goods and services concessions they would demand from developing countries acceding to the WTO and by allowing these countries to benefit from special and differential treatment under the WTO agreements.[19]

With this strengthened mandate for supporting capacity building and providing assistance for member accessions to the WTO, UNCTAD launched the Positive Agenda, a program to help developing countries identify their development interests, formulate trade objectives, and then pursue those objectives in international trade negotiations. Work under the program directly contributed to the positions that developing countries adopted in subsequent trade negotiations.

UNCTAD X (Bangkok, 2000) resulted in continued adherence to the concept that trade liberalization and economic development are compatible, but emphasized that developing countries should receive special consideration and assistance in pursuing greater global integration. In the wake of the Asian financial crisis, the Bangkok Declaration warned:

> [Globalization] has expanded the prospect for technological advances and for effective integration into the international economy. It has increased prosperity and the potential for countries to benefit. However, globalization also raises the risk of marginalization of countries, in particular the poorest countries, and the most vulnerable groups everywhere.[20]

Increasing attention to poverty and growing income disparity and the call for the international community to strive toward "enhanced cooperation" in trade and other international economic flows were central to the Bangkok Declaration. Thus, the declaration advocated fully implementing special and differential treatment for developing countries within the WTO and called for the new round of trade negotiations to more explicitly consider the problems of advancing development and globalization.

---

19. World Trade Organization, "Accession of Least-Developed Countries," WT/L/508, January 20, 2003, at http://docsonline.wto.org/imrd/directdoc.asp?DDF Documents/t/WT/L/508.doc (accessed January 13, 2009).

20. U.N. Conference on Trade and Development, "Bangkok Declaration: Global Dialogue and Dynamic Engagement," February 18, 2000, at www.unctad.org/en/docs/ux_td387.en.pdf (accessed January 2, 2009).

UNCTAD worked with developing countries to reconcile their proposals and formulate their approach to a new round of multilateral trade talks under the auspices of the Third WTO Ministerial in Seattle in 1999. UNCTAD's role was pivotal because developing countries' economic interests had become more diverse. UNCTAD focused them on a few common concerns, helping them to maximize their influence on the direction future trade negotiations would take. As a result, developing countries, through UNCTAD, assumed an active role in submitting content and negotiation proposals to the WTO General Council for the Seattle Ministerial. These proposals centered on ensuring that negotiations on services and agriculture would focus on their particular interests and that developing countries would receive special and differential treatment on a wide range of topics and gain meaningful new access to developed world markets.[21]

Developed countries were unprepared for an assertive developing-country bloc taking the initiative in defining the shape of future multilateral trade negotiations, precipitating the collapse of the Seattle WTO Ministerial. By the conclusion of the Fourth WTO Ministerial Conference in Doha in 2001, the development objectives of trade negotiations espoused in the Positive Agenda and highlighted in the Bangkok Declaration became the focus of the Doha Development Round of multilateral trade talks. The Positive Agenda had formed an effective rallying point for developing countries and led them to successfully influence the shape of future WTO trade liberalization.

The 2004 São Paulo Consensus from UNCTAD XI went further by recognizing the importance of international trade among developing countries as a means to enhance regional infrastructure and to create regional economies of scale to promote competitiveness and growth—a concept borne out in research and practice. Additionally, the consensus recognized that developed and developing countries alike share an interest in making progress in the Doha Round, which has the complicated goal of reducing trade barriers and making the trading system more development friendly.[22]

The evolution of UNCTAD from an organization pitted against free trade and open markets continues today and is reflected in the latest UNCTAD conference results. UNCTAD XII's 2008 Accra Accord builds on the São Paulo Consensus, while providing updated guidelines to better reflect economic realities and equip UNCTAD to serve its development role, influence policy, and increase its institutional effectiveness. The accord appropriately

---

21. U.N. Conference on Trade and Development, *Beyond Conventional Wisdom.*

22. U.N. Conference on Trade and Development, "São Paulo Consensus," TD/410, June 25, 2004, at www.unctad.org/en/docs/td410_en.pdf (accessed January 13, 2009).

affirms that each country has primary responsibility for its own economic and social development and that sustainable development requires strengthened efforts to improve government effectiveness, regulatory quality, transparency, and accountability.[23]

UNCTAD TODAY

UNCTAD was established to advocate an interventionist, nonmarket alternative to the neoclassical economic paradigm advanced under the GATT. After a decade passed, UNCTAD slowly began to recognize that policies facilitating trade liberalization and sustainable economic development could go hand in hand. Today, UNCTAD espouses a relatively pragmatic approach toward the trade and development that better embraces competition and other open-market principles, but it persists in advocating that developing countries should generally follow a slower path to full trade liberalization.

UNCTAD's role in influencing international economic policy has evolved over time and as a consequence of changes in U.N. and UNCTAD leadership and shifts in global economic fundamentals. Although UNCTAD's influence on international trade regulation is indirect, it is not inconsequential. Today, UNCTAD serves as a forum to debate issues affecting international trade and development, provides technical assistance and training to developing countries seeking to better integrate into the global economy, and conducts research, policy analysis, and data collection, which is used by governments, researchers, and businesses.

UNCTAD continues to evolve with changing economic and member requirements. One of UNCTAD XII's primary thrusts centered on evaluating progress in enhancing UNCTAD's development role, improving its institutional effectiveness, and heightening its impact on development policy. Effective reform of UNCTAD could go far in maintaining its relevance in today's international economic policy debate and, more importantly, it would promote effective economic development. However, this would depend on UNCTAD's accepting a more focused mandate that promotes sound economic policy—a role many hoping to expand UNCTAD's influence in all spheres of international economic policymaking would find unpalatable.

---

23. U.N. Conference on Trade and Development, "Accra Accord," advance copy, April 25, 2008, at www.unctad.org/en/docs//tdxii_accra_accord_en.pdf (accessed January 13, 2009).

UNCTAD MISSION CREEP

While UNCTAD has become more cooperative with the WTO and other organizations in reducing trade barriers, this has perversely undermined the distinctions that led to its establishment in the first place. Not surprisingly, UNCTAD and its developing-country supporters have sought to broaden its mandate in disparate areas deemed critical to trade and development policy. Regrettably, as UNCTAD's activities multiply and expand, it increasingly duplicates efforts in other institutions that are better equipped and staffed to fulfill those mandates. Moreover, as UNCTAD's mandate continues to grow, it is distracted from its core purpose of better understanding and promoting the role of international trade in effective development policy.

The Accra Accord provides the latest glimpse into UNCTAD's mission creep. It directs UNCTAD to continue conducting policy analysis and identifying policy options to advance globalization and development strategies by:

(a) Identifying specific needs and measures arising from the interdependence between trade, finance, investment, technology and macro-economic policies from the point of view of its effect on development;

(b) Contributing to a better understanding of coherence between international economic rules, practices and processes, on the one hand, and national policies and development strategies, on the other;

(c) Supporting developing countries in their efforts to formulate development strategies adapted to their specific circumstances and to the opportunities and challenges of globalization;

(d) Addressing the complex and wide-ranging special needs and problems faced by landlocked developing countries, small island developing States and other structurally weak, vulnerable and small economies; and

(e) Contributing to the global development policy debate by highlighting the inter-linkages between globalization, trade and development indicators based on reliable and timely statistics.[24]

UNCTAD is further directed to assist developing countries to create and implement domestic policies that promote growth, improve conditions for private sector investment and development, advance sound competition policies, and strengthen economic institutions.[25] While much of this assis-

---

24. U.N. Conference on Trade and Development, "Accra Accord," par. 36.

25. U.N. Conference on Trade and Development, "Overview of the Main Activities," 2002, at www.unctad.org/templates/page.asp?intitemid = 3359 (accessed August 2, 2008).

tance is focused on least developed countries, UNCTAD XII also dictated the secretariat to support the development efforts of middle-income countries, which also face difficulties promoting sustainable economic development and poverty reduction. In this regard, UNCTAD is to assist developing countries with integrating trade and development concerns into their national development plans.

Moreover, in coordination with the Organisation for Economic Cooperation and Development, World Bank, United Nations Industrial Development Organization, United Nations Global Compact, and International Organization for Standardization's Working Group on Social Responsibility, UNCTAD is to evaluate and promote voluntary enterprise policies on corporate social responsibility and other codes of conduct as a complement to national competition policy to facilitate the development role of corporate activities.

The growing importance of regional trade, especially among developing countries, serves as the impetus for UNCTAD to improve research and analysis of South–South trade, investment, and finance and regional developing-country trade to advance greater developing-country integration. Therefore, the accord instructed UNCTAD to promote coherence and consistency of regional trade agreements within the multilateral trading system.

Continuing with the drive to keep development issues on the radar in multilateral trade negotiations, UNCTAD has been advised to continue monitoring and assessing the broader evolution of the international trading system and of trends in international trade from a development perspective. It is to train countries in the negotiations process; build their capacity to negotiate and implement bilateral, regional, and multilateral trade agreements; and provide technical expertise to developing countries engaged in the WTO accession process.

Research into the global trade in services remains on UNCTAD's task list, with particular emphasis on increasing developing-country participation in services trade, helping to develop the regulatory regimes and other economic infrastructure to support efficient and competitive national and international services trade, directly supporting services negotiations within the WTO, and collecting and disseminating data and statistics on trade in services. In addition, UNCTAD is to continue to research and evaluate how improving market access affects temporary services workers.

As a more focused element of UNCTAD's trade agenda, the organization is directed to monitor developments and challenges in commodity markets and to assist commodity-dependent developing countries in harnessing development gains from high commodity prices and to develop national commodity strategies to bolster competitiveness and promote economic diversification. UNCTAD is also charged with promoting intergovernmental cooperation and consensus on ways of integrating commodity policies into development and poverty-reduction strategies and with developing policies and instruments to smooth commodity trade.

The Biotrade Initiative is also on UNCTAD's agenda. The program supports sustainable, private-sector trade in biodiversity products and awards strengthened intellectual property rights protection over the use of traditional knowledge and natural resources in products. UNCTAD continues to advocate the transfer of environmentally sound technology to developing countries and improved trade in environmental goods and services as part of an environmentally conscious development strategy. Further supporting this approach to development is UNCTAD's work in evaluating stronger provisions regulating the ecolabeling and certification costs.

Finally, UNCTAD has mandates to collaborate with the WTO and other multilateral institutions in helping developing countries build their capacities to efficiently engage international markets under the Aid for Trade initiative. UNCTAD is to facilitate improved production and infrastructure capacity in the developing world, help developing countries improve their customs management and their transportation links to the global market and competitiveness, assist them in developing and implementing institutional and legal frameworks to support enhanced market connectivity, and offer technical assistance to developing countries in negotiations designed to advance trade and sustainable development.

As a consequence of tighter cooperation between UNCTAD and the WTO, developing countries increasingly adopting open-market policies and liberalizing trade, and shifts in UNCTAD leadership,[26] the organization has adopted a more moderate and pragmatic approach to trade and development than in earlier years. However, with each new conference directive adding ever more mandates to UNCTAD's mission, both its members and outside parties are looking for ways to improve how UNCTAD operates.

THE U.N., WTO, AND TRADE

While UNCTAD maintains the mandate within the U.N. system to focus on international trade and development issues, numerous institutions strive to influence the workings of the WTO and to shape trade policy around the world. The list of these institutions includes more than thirty U.N. agencies, more than a dozen regional development banks, the World Bank, the IMF,

---

26. UNCTAD secretary-general Supachai Panitchpakdi was WTO director general before joining the U.N.

other multilateral organizations, countless nongovernmental groups, and various treaty bodies that conduct research and analysis of the international economy and educate and advise governments on trade policy.[27]

In the U.N., these groups span the range of trade concerns from the most technical legal aspects in the U.N. Commission on International Trade Law to general economic discussions in the regional economic commissions under ECOSOC. As is often the case with organizations seeking to maintain their relevance in policy debates, any mainstream concern even remotely associated with a group's mission is added to its agenda. As an agency's efforts become more complex, overlapping other agencies' efforts and spreading across myriad policy questions, any value that it may add to the pursuit of good economic policy is diluted. Moreover, as lines of accountability and responsibility become increasingly complex, governments find it more difficult to determine where to turn for information or assistance.

This single chapter could not possibly discuss all the U.N. bodies claiming a role in international trade and their contributions (or lack thereof) to shaping countries' trade policies. However, a few examples illustrate the redundancy of many U.N. efforts. The United Nations Industrial Development Organization has a range of programs to help transitional countries increase their competitiveness, better facilitate trade, and build trade capacity. The U.N. Research Institute for Social Development engages in significant research and analysis of the roles of markets, privatization, and businesses in economic development that influence the policies defining open markets. Various regional commissions, such as the U.N. Economic Commission for Africa, strive to assess effective regional trade policies sup-

---

27. Within the U.N. system, the organizations involved in trade-related policy concerns include the U.N. Commission on International Trade Law, the Economic and Social Council, various groups within the Commission on Sustainable Development, the Committee of Experts on International Cooperation in Tax Matters, the Committee (and subcommittee) of Experts on the Transport of Dangerous Goods and on the Globally Harmonized System of Classification and Labeling of Chemicals, the U.N. Development Group, UNDP, the U.N. Capital Development Fund, U.N. Environment Program, the U.N. Institute for Training and Research, the U.N. Research Institute for Social Development, the Secretariat of the Convention on Biological Diversity, the Secretariat of the Convention on International Trade in Endangered Species of Wild Fauna and Flora, the Secretariat of the U.N. Framework Convention on Climate Change, the Global Environment Facility, the International Labor Organization, the Food and Agriculture Organization (FAO), the FAO/WHO Codex Alimentarius Commission, the U.N. Educational, Scientific and Cultural Organization, the Universal Postal Union, the International Telecommunications Union, the World Intellectual Property Organization, the International Fund for Agriculture Development, the U.N. Industrial Development Organization, and the World Tourism Organization.

porting sustainable development. While each of these organizations may bring a different perspective to UNCTAD's efforts, they also undermine the U.N.'s efforts to advocate transparent and consistent policies to member countries.

In addition, these organizations waste resources trying to tackle too many issues with limited budgets and staffs. While UNCTAD is ostensibly an independent organization, it is funded through the U.N.'s regular assessed budget. UNCTAD's annual budget is approximately $50 million plus roughly $25 million in extrabudgetary technical assistance funds for a staff of about four hundred. This is a relatively tiny slice of the U.N.'s estimated $5.2 billion budget for the 2008–2009 biennium.[28]

By comparison, the WTO had a 2008 budget of just over $154 million for a regular staff of 629, who handle far more demanding responsibilities. With this comparatively small budget, the WTO administers trade agreements, monitors member nations' trade policy regimes, facilitates the resolution of trade disputes, organizes and provides a forum for conducting global trade negotiations, and provides technical assistance and training for developing countries. The WTO has done a better job than most organizations in keeping to a range of activities directly required to fulfill its mission. However, maintaining that focus is difficult with both countries and organizations trying to use trade policy to advance various tangential policy objectives, such as global labor and environmental standards and limits on commerce in the name of climate change.

Reconciling the existent system to improve lines of accountability and authority over trade-related policy concerns is an enormous challenge. Yet such reform is needed for the world to continue to benefit from trade liberalization.

CREATING A BETTER INTERNATIONAL TRADE SYSTEM

Ultimately, any reform of the institutions, rules, or regulations that influence international trade should focus on reducing the complexity and cost of the system. With so many institutions advising countries on trade policy and implementing programs to facilitate trade and educate governments, the economic landscape is littered with an uncoordinated mass of projects that work at cross-purposes and waste resources. The following recommen-

---

28. U.N. Conference on Trade and Development, "The UNCTAD Secretariat," 2002, at www.unctad.org/Templates/Page.asp?intItemID = 1931 (accessed November 24, 2008).

dations mark a path that would increase the transparency of the environment in which research, analysis, and communication of trade policy are conducted. They also identify a role for the U.N. and UNCTAD that adds value to member nations and promotes the benefits of trade liberalization for all countries. The recommendations also propose a new mechanism for countering some of the weaknesses within the WTO that impede the expansion of free trade.

Reforming the U.N. and UNCTAD

Since the establishment of the World Trade Organization, UNCTAD has struggled to match the pace of economic change with a mission that promotes UNCTAD's success and relevance in international economic policymaking. Regardless of one's opinion regarding UNCTAD's success or failure over its more than four decades of existence, UNCTAD has clearly gradually lost influence over trade and development issues. Not only did the WTO supplant UNCTAD's role in negotiating trade regulations, but the World Bank, IMF, UNDP, and other organizations have encroached on many of its policy areas.

Not all of UNCTAD's marginalization can be attributed to new multilateral institutions or mission creep of existing organizations. UNCTAD conferences in the early 1990s intentionally reduced UNCTAD's mandate in response to economic and institutional pressures. While UNCTAD's direct role in regulating trade has been eliminated, it has played a significant role in defining the developing world's relationship with the WTO. Successful reform would need to address the extent of UNCTAD's indirect influence on trade regulation.

Recent discussions at UNCTAD XII advanced the need, initially discussed at UNCTAD XI, to evaluate how UNCTAD ensures that the secretariat's efforts offer developing countries policy support that is consistent with changing international economic fundamentals and shifting requirements for effective, sustainable development. By providing timely and useful research, analysis, and technical support, UNCTAD hopes to augment its impact and institutional effectiveness in shaping international trade and development policy.

Specifically, UNCTAD should focus on helping developing countries to participate more effectively in the global economy, and it should discontinue its consensus-building activities in international trade negotiations.

Strengthening What Works

Today's UNCTAD is very different and much improved from the UNCTAD that waged an ideological war against open markets and freer trade forty years ago. In many ways, the organization does a good job of satisfying its fundamental rationale for existence: It engages in sound research, provides useful data, and offers a number of worthy training and technical assistance projects that help developing countries better engage with and function in the international economy.

As valuable as these activities are, they can be improved. Given the extent of U.N. activities in trade and trade-related policy, UNCTAD should coordinate and lead all U.N. research, analysis, and training efforts in the interrelated development issues of trade, investment, technology, and finance. Such coordination would help to ensure that U.N. products convey coherent and consistent policy prescriptions. Redundant or unneeded UNCTAD or U.N. programs or programs that infringe on UNCTAD's core mandate, such as the trade-related activities of the regional economic commissions and UNIDO, should be consolidated or eliminated. A basic metric for identifying unneeded programs is to prioritize and focus on those activities that separate UNCTAD from other institutions in the policymaking world. This would reveal which areas the organization can provide the most value added. Unfettered by duplicative projects and efforts that other institutions do better, UNCTAD and the U.N. would free resources for better use within a more streamlined and focused UNCTAD.

Given the increasingly divisive debate over the role of free trade in development policy, UNCTAD needs to ensure that its analytic work remains solidly grounded on evidence of improved economic growth and living standards that freer trade has wrought in developing and developed countries alike. The need for objective research and education is critical for addressing the various misperceptions that thwart sound economic policy.

Eliminating UNCTAD's Consensus-Building Activities

UNCTAD should eliminate its consensus-building activities, especially efforts to formulate multilateral trade negotiating strategies for developing countries as a bloc. The clash of members' interests within the WTO highlights the institution's fundamental weakness: as trade negotiations become larger, they become more cumbersome, impeding efforts to reach timely agreements. The tendency to pull many countries with varied trade agendas together into trade talks explains why many smaller, regional initiatives such as the Free Trade Agreement of the Americas fail to make progress. The scale of the problem is even bigger in the Doha Round, in which many external organizations are also vying for influence on the final trade deal.

Alternatively, the scope of an agreement could be limited to addressing a smaller number of trade barriers, or each member country could participate in only those aspects of a larger, comprehensive agreement that it likes, but these alternatives defeat the purpose of the round—to reduce trade barriers and promote sustainable development for the benefit of all member countries. One seeming solution to the deadlock is UNCTAD's tactic of advocating that all developing countries form into a single negotiating bloc against developed countries to ensure that they have some muscle in trade negotiations. Regrettably, while this certainly reduces the number of countries sitting around the table, it also muffles the influence of developing countries that have embraced free trade, especially when the countries representing the developing world are less ambitious about opening markets.

UNCTAD has evolved over the past four decades in part because many of its members in the developing world have also changed. Developing economies in Asia and the Americas have, to some degree, abandoned nonmarket development strategies. These countries and others in the developing world have embraced economic reform, with each moving at a pace that makes such reform politically feasible and sustainable over the longer term. As a result, developing countries should no longer be considered a truly unified bloc with identical development needs that can be addressed by the same development strategies.

UNCTAD has recognized this fact in many aspects of its work, but in multilateral trade negotiations, it still continues to aggregate developing countries through its consensus-building function. In the early days of UNCTAD, this tactic succeeded in introducing trade preferences into the international trade dialogue and in focusing the current WTO round on development issues, but it is questionable whether this approach is still necessary or effective in helping countries liberalize trade to further their economic development.

The past seven years of negotiations in the Doha Round have been contentious and halting largely because two big developing countries—India and China—continue to try to extract concessions and flexibilities that far exceed what is realistic for a comprehensive trade deal that would be acceptable to all WTO members. Interestingly, their demands reflect the very objectives that UNCTAD has long advocated: special and differential treatment for developing countries across a host of trade topics.

Whether cutting tariffs on agriculture, manufacturing, and services products or eliminating subsidies and quotas, UNCTAD has firmly maintained that developing countries should not be expected to dismantle trade barriers to the same degree or at the same speed as developed countries. Regrettably for the bloc of developing countries represented in negotiations by India, China, and other large members, the scope and pace of reform that India may desire is unlikely to match needs elsewhere in the developing world. Nor are developed countries likely to accept an agreement that treats small, poor, developing nations the same as rapidly developing countries such as India and China, which can engage the global economy on par with many developed countries.

By pulling the developing world together around the idea that development depends on keeping to a slow pace of trade liberalization, UNCTAD helped to ensure that the principle of special and differential treatment for developing countries would be at the core of Doha Round negotiations from the outset. Unfortunately, this has allowed some developing countries an excuse to avoid agreeing to any degree of meaningful trade liberalization, while still demanding that developed countries offer ambitious concessions. Yet the purpose of these trade negotiations is to advance freer trade around the world, not simply expand market access in developed economies, especially when exports from developing countries already face relatively low trade barriers in developed markets. The Generalized System of Preferences championed by UNCTAD in the 1970s and other preference programs have already lowered the barriers to most developing-country exports. The programs are not perfect, but they are substantial.

The biggest boost to freer trade and sustainable development would come from developing countries' making binding commitments to reduce their tariffs and other trade barriers—which are some of the highest and most restrictive in the world—both against the developed world and, even more critically, against one another. Indeed, "seventy percent of tariffs paid by developing countries go to other developing countries."[29] As research by UNCTAD and others has shown, greater competition and economic integration among developing countries would have a real, positive impact on development.

Opening developing-country markets to agriculture, manufacturing, and services products from the developed world would also provide real value because it would give developing countries access to new technologies and a wider array of less-expensive products, thereby helping farmers, businesses, and families. Moreover, freer trade would promote investment, a critical component of any long-term development strategy.

India and China were able to help derail a tentative deal that incorporated many of UNCTAD's multilateral trade objectives by demanding even greater flexibilities on protecting their agriculture sectors. These flexibilities would have further limited out not only exports from the developed world, but also exports from other developing countries. Clearly, India and China were not championing the best interests of the bloc that UNCTAD helped to create, but were advancing their own perceived interests. This alone was not a problem. The problem is that the bloc's existence deters other developing countries from identifying and advancing their own best negotiating positions.

---

29. U.S. Department of State, "The U.S. Approach to International Development: Building on the Monterrey Consensus," September 12, 2005, p. 3, at http://tira na.usembassy.gov/uploads/images/HnHV1GrzqOp3qWH5gbZsAA/monterrey.pdf (accessed January 2, 2009).

Without pressure to adhere to UNCTAD's negotiating objectives for the bloc of developing countries, many in the developing world, especially those aggressively pursuing reformist agendas, would likely seek and agree to terms better tailored to their own economic interests or align with like-minded countries to lobby for trade rules that genuinely reflect their interests. With developing countries continuing to diverge economically, UNCTAD should abandon its consensus-building efforts and instead augment its training and capacity-building efforts to help countries engage the WTO on their own terms so that they no longer need to rely on others to protect their economic agenda. This would not only benefit the developing countries themselves, but also reduce conflict within the Doha Round, giving all countries the chance to reap the benefits of a comprehensive trade pact more quickly.

Keeping Multilateral Consensus Building within the WTO

Multilateral consensus building on international trade rules and regulations would best be kept within the WTO. However, the formation of a new, independent organization populated by any country—developed or developing—committed to advancing freer trade could help to resolve specific issues that are thwarting progress in global negotiations or affecting the international economic system. Trade negotiations within the WTO Doha Round are complex and comprehensive, aimed at achieving an agreement that more than 150 members can accept and implement. Trade agreements made in the WTO are not binding until each member ratifies them and implements the laws needed to ensure compliance with the new trade regulations. Tariffs may need to be reduced, quotas cut, and subsidy programs eliminated. These trade barriers generally protect domestic firms and workers from foreign competition—protections few desire to lose and most are willing to fight to keep. As a consequence, governments find passing trade agreements politically difficult unless they can demonstrate that the country stands to gain more than it "loses" from further opening its domestic economy.

Of course, countries do not lose by opening their markets to trade. Freer trade enables more goods and services to reach consumers at lower prices, giving families more income to save or spend on other goods and services. Freer trade promotes a level of competition in an open economy that engenders innovation, job creation, diversification into new markets, and an improved investment climate. Regrettably, the reality of these benefits does not usually resonate with voters who see uncompetitive domestic firms close down and neighbors lose jobs, feeding their fears that they could suffer the same fate.

Thus, the final Doha Round trade pact will attempt to delicately balance the level of trade liberalization in each member country with reciprocal market access and trade opening by other member countries. Yet, a balanced deal can be ruined by countries insisting on further concessions, as has been recently seen. Negotiators are ever mindful of the comprehensive nature of the process; this can make it difficult to isolate and remove specific trade barriers.

Establishing a Global Economic Freedom Forum

Unfortunately, the longer the Doha Round takes to reach an agreement, the more likely countries will look to bilateral and regional free trade arrangements to more quickly reap the benefits of lower trade barriers, or they could succumb to protectionist pressures in response to the current economic downturn. Free trade agreements (FTAs) can help to reduce trade restrictions globally by demonstrating solutions to difficult trade problems, but they can also discriminate against countries that are not party to the agreements, and the differing rules can add to the cost of trade. FTAs are not a perfect substitute for multilateral trade liberalization and cannot resolve the deadlock within the WTO alone.

Because of these dynamics, international forums created to foster trade and open markets struggle to advance free-market principles. Too often officials at the World Bank, IMF, United Nations, and other multilateral organizations are sympathetic to policies that undermine open markets and the free flow of international trade and investment. Regrettably, attempts by high-performing free-market democracies to resist such policies often result in international policy gridlock.

Heritage Foundation vice president for foreign policy Kim Holmes and others at The Heritage Foundation have proposed creating new, post–Bretton Woods structures to advance the interests of the United States and other free economies throughout the world.[30] Holmes has specifically called for the United States to take the lead in establishing a Global Economic Freedom Forum in which the heads of state from twenty to twenty-five nations sharing America's commitment to open markets and democracy could seek "common solutions to such problems as international debt, weak financial institutions, and poverty in developing nations."[31] Such a forum could provide the problem-solving environment needed to find solutions to individual trade-related issues that are thwarting progress in the WTO or affecting the international economic system.

The forum would focus on one issue at a time, and country membership and participation would be voluntary, shifting to include those countries of concern that are most willing to find free-market solutions. Solving the

---

30. Kim R. Holmes, "Economic Freedom on a Global Scale," Heritage Foundation *Commentary* (September 26, 2008), at www.heritage.org/Press/Commentary/ed0926508a.cfm (accessed November 23, 2008).

31. Holmes, "Economic Freedom on a Global Scale."

world's trade problems one small issue at a time may provide just the perspective needed to build a real multilateral consensus on the best approach to freeing international trade.

CONCLUSION

Although numerous U.N. bodies have mandates involving trade and trade-related issues, the U.N. system has historically played a relatively marginal role in trade. The United Nations Conference on Trade and Development, the major U.N. organization focused on trade, is one of the few with an ongoing justification for continuing to involve itself in trade-related issues. However, UNCTAD needs to find a more effective mandate for advancing sustainable development. It should focus its resources to emphasize those programs that advance sound economic policymaking and demonstrate tangible success. In this vein, UNCTAD should eliminate projects that duplicate efforts carried out more effectively by other institutions. This would free more resources for advancing UNCTAD's primary mission of promoting sustainable economic development through trade.

Real reform relies on more than just simplifying and focusing UNCTAD's agenda. UNCTAD's reform should occur in the context of comprehensive U.N. reform that further rationalizes the roles of U.N. agencies and better coordinates U.N. efforts. In this regard, UNCTAD could serve as a center for U.N. work in trade and economic development and act as an important moderating voice within the U.N. to promote open-market principles as the best means for economic development.

While UNCTAD contributes sound research in the policy realm and helps countries learn how to better embrace world markets, the organization's role in building consensus among member countries to advance specific trade policy objectives has outlived its usefulness. A one-size-fits-all strategy of trade and development policy no longer serves developing countries. Instead, UNCTAD would more effectively advance sound, sustainable development and contribute to the success of multilateral trade negotiations by helping each developing country identify, pursue, and implement its own best strategy to promote economic growth and greater integration with the global marketplace.

With each developed and developing country having a voice in the complex debate over the future of trade liberalization, a new mechanism is needed to help the WTO open markets. A forum of like-minded reformers could more easily resolve specific, problematic issues within the comprehensive trade negotiations structure with solutions that can then be introduced into the WTO discussion. This could speed a breakthrough in the trade talks, which is needed to advance sustainable development and world prosperity.

9

Restoring the Role of the Nation-State System in Arms Control and Disarmament

Baker Spring

Arms control and disarmament sit at the intersection of foreign and defense policy. With the possible exception of policies governing decisions to use force or to form or break defense alliances, arms control and disarmament policy has the greatest potential to further or damage a state's national interest. As a result, sovereign states will not willingly cede control over arms control policy to outside forces unless the specific topic on the agenda is one in which they do not have a direct stake.

Given the compelling national interests at stake, it would be expected that the United Nations and its affiliated international organizations would be expected to play at most tangential roles in arms control and disarmament. This was certainly the case during the Cold War, when the United States and the Soviet Union addressed the most important arms control issues on a bilateral basis. The problem is that the United Nations and other international institutions have ambitions that far outstrip this appropriate and modest role. On this basis, they organize their institutions to address matters of arms control by raising the pursuit of irresponsibility to an art form.

In this context, the U.N. and its affiliated international organizations seek to expand both their bureaucratic structures and their claims to authority. Yet the U.N. as an international organization has no direct stake in the substantive outcome of any arms control or disarmament issue, only the purely procedural accomplishment of concluding agreements. The people who serve in the U.N. and its affiliated international organizations are not held accountable for protecting the lives and well-being of the people who may be made vulnerable by poorly conceived or biased arms control agreements and implementing measures. U.N. officials are not elected and claim no constituencies other than their colleagues and the nongovernmental organizations (NGOs) with which they work closely. These NGOs frequently see arms control and disarmament measures as ends in themselves and regard the national security interests of particular nations as only tangential concerns. Unsurprisingly, the U.N. disarmament and arms control structures tend toward far-flung and overlapping institutions that diffuse responsibility and accountability rather than a tight structure focused on outcomes and effectiveness.

In some cases, U.N. elites also seek governing authority without accountability to those whom they would govern. In arms control and disarmament policy, these elites disparage the concept of the national interest and see their neutrality as proof of their moral superiority. In reality, this neutrality is the height of irresponsibility because these elites maintain no direct obligation to provide security to the people over whom they claim authority to set policies that directly affect their safety. In short, these elites seek to destroy the nation-state system without offering a viable substitute that can assume responsibility for and ensure the security of peoples in nations around the world. If this international elite realizes these purposes, there will be catastrophic results.

To put the United Nations and its affiliated international organizations in their appropriately modest roles of creating and implementing arms control and disarmament agreements, it is necessary to examine the various component institutions of the U.N.:

1. The Security Council
2. The First Committee on Disarmament and International Security of the General Assembly
3. The Department for Disarmament Affairs (DDA) under the Secretariat
4. The Conference on Disarmament
5. The International Atomic Energy Agency (IAEA), the most important U.N.-affiliated international organization with arms control responsibilities
6. The myriad NGOs involved in arms control at the U.N

This chapter examines each of these component institutions, recommends appropriate reforms, and suggests alternative venues that could prove more effective. The recommendations are designed to narrow the scope of U.N. involvement in arms control and disarmament, in accordance with the more direct interests and responsibilities of sovereign member states to provide security to their people. The recommendations are also designed to increase the level of responsibility that U.N. institutions and alternative institutions must bear in the narrow areas where they have appropriate roles to play.

THE U.N. SECURITY COUNCIL

The U.N. Security Council is the United Nations' foremost institution for keeping the peace and responding to threats to peace and security at the international level.[1] As a result, the Security Council generally addresses arms control and disarmament matters in the context of both immediate and projected threats to international peace and security. This was the case, for example, when the Security Council adopted a series of resolutions after the first Gulf War that, among other things, imposed restrictions on Iraq's nuclear, biological, and chemical weapons programs and its ballistic missile program.[2]

The Security Council consists of fifteen members, including five permanent members (China, France, Russia, the United Kingdom, and the United States).[3] The permanent members have the power to exercise a veto on substantive matters. The ten nonpermanent Security Council members are elected for two-year terms by the U.N. General Assembly.

This organizational structure represents both the central strength and weakness of the Security Council. On one hand, veto power allows the United States and other permanent members to prevent the Security Council from taking action that is deemed unwise or unjust. On the other hand, the veto power undermines timely and aggressive action by the Security Council when it is called for and frequently results in a lowest-common-denominator approach to drafting resolutions that address important and pressing security issues.

For example, the United States has frequently exercised its veto when other Security Council members have offered resolutions that unjustly criti-

---

1. For a summary description of the Security Council's functions and powers, see U.N. Security Council, "Functions and Powers," at www.un.org/Docs/sc/unsc_functions.html (accessed May 8, 2008).

2. Brett D. Schaefer and Baker Spring, "Bush Is Right on Iraq: The Issue Is Compliance, Not Inspections," Heritage Foundation *Backgrounder*, no. 1592 (September 19, 2002), at www.heritage.org/Research/Iraq/bg1592.cfm.

3. For a list of the current Security Council members, see U.N. Security Council, "Membership in 2009," at www.un.org/sc/members.asp (accessed June 8, 2009).

cize Israel or that would undermine Israel's security.[4] It is easy to underestimate how much the adoption of such resolutions would undermine stability in the Middle East by isolating Israel and effectively encourage attacks on it. If not for the United States' vetoes, the Security Council—supposedly the United Nations' foremost institution for preserving peace and security—would have been encouraging aggression.

Conversely, the Security Council's tendency to adopt a lowest-common-denominator approach to important arms control problems has produced quite weak resolutions on Iranian and North Korean nuclear weapons programs. Former U.S. permanent representative to the United Nations John Bolton has described the Security Council's process of drafting these resolutions as one in which even France and the United Kingdom—allies of the United States—work to water down sanctions resolutions that respond to Iran's and North Korea's provocative behavior and enormously destabilizing weapons activities. The behavior of China and Russia, in threatening and casting vetoes, is even worse. In this process, adoption of any resolution, no matter how weak, is perceived as a success.[5] In the meantime, Iran has ignored Security Council demands to cease uranium enrichment activities and North Korea continues to pursue nuclear weapons, conducting explosive tests in October 2006 and May 2009.

The Insidious Assumption of Moral Equivalency

The source of the problem in the Security Council's process for drafting resolutions on arms control and disarmament is the assumption of moral equivalency between regimes. For example, the process too easily treats the structures and purposes of the regimes in Iran, Israel, and North Korea as morally equivalent. From this point of view, a particular kind of weapon in Israeli hands is the same as one in Iranian or North Korean hands. The result is a process that fails to differentiate between weapons programs that truly threaten international peace and security and those that would bolster peace and security.

Regrettably, no approach to institutional reform under the U.N. Charter is guaranteed to overcome this assumption of moral equivalency in U.N. bodies, including in the Security Council. The best the United States can do is to pursue an agenda that distinguishes among regimes, even in the Secur-

---

4. For example, see U.N. News Service, "US Vetoes Security Council Resolution on Israeli Operations in Gaza," November 11, 2006, at www.un.org/apps/news/story.asp?NewsID=20576 (accessed May 8, 2008).

5. John R. Bolton, *Surrender Is Not an Option: Defending America at the United Nations and Abroad* (New York: Threshold Editions, 2007), 291–340.

ity Council. The United States should undertake a long-term and determined effort in the General Assembly to identify regimes that pose such immediate threats to liberty and convince other U.N. member states that they should be ineligible to serve on Security Council.

For example, Iran launched a bid for a nonpermanent Security Council seat starting in 2009.[6] Iran is actively seeking nuclear weapons in defiance of international treaties and Security Council resolutions. Iran's president has threatened to attack and destroy Israel, a U.N. member state. Because nonpermanent seats are allocated geographically, the United States needs to work with Asian countries to defeat Iran's bid by promoting a more desirable Asian candidate, such as Japan. If the United States can successfully reduce support for unacceptable candidates, this effort will not only improve the quality of members on the Security Council, but also counterbalance the assumption of moral equivalency in Security Council deliberations.

If U.S. efforts to exclude those regimes most opposed to liberty from the Security Council do not progress in the General Assembly, the United States should pursue a different approach. It should seek to create a competitor to the United Nations that consists of a coalition of nations committed to global freedom and security. This Global Freedom Coalition should undertake similar responsibilities as the Security Council in maintaining world peace and security, including arms control and disarmament matters. Unlike the Security Council, it would not involve an international bureaucracy. Rather, the coalition would be based on the nation-state system, and its member states would contribute their own resources to coalition activities. Generally, the Global Freedom Coalition would serve as a balancer in international affairs. Its arms control initiatives would support this balancing role and be pursued on a selective basis. Accordingly, its arms control initiatives would support the balance and not become ends in themselves.[7]

As long as the Security Council remains a viable institution such that the United States determines to have value or influence over matters critical to its national interests, the United States should remain an active participant, if only to veto actions inimical to its interests, the interests of its allies, or the cause of liberty.

Undermining the Right of National Self-Defense

The Security Council and other U.N. institutions and affiliated organizations compound problems when they seek to operate outside the nation-

6. Betsy Pisik, "Iran Seeks Seat on Security Council," *Washington Times*, July 9, 2008, at www.washingtontimes.com/news/2008/jul/09/iran-seeks-asia-seat-on-security-council (accessed August 1, 2008).

7. Kim R. Holmes, "Time for 'Global Freedom Coalition,'" *Washington Times*, September 11, 2008, A4.

state system. This is most dangerous when the Security Council seeks to ignore both the letter and the spirit of Article 51 of the U.N. Charter by undermining the inherent right of states to individual and collective self-defense. Article 51 states:

> Nothing in the present Charter shall impair the inherent right of individual or collective self-defence if an armed attack occurs against a Member of the United Nations, until the Security Council has taken measures necessary to maintain international peace and security. Measures taken by Members in the exercise of this right of self-defence shall be immediately reported to the Security Council and shall not in any way affect the authority and responsibility of the Security Council under the present Charter to take at any time such action as it deems necessary in order to maintain or restore international peace and security.

The most alarming attacks on state sovereignty by Security Council members occurred in 2002 and 2003 during deliberations in advance of allied military actions against Iraq. In large measure, these deliberations were over how to respond to Iraq's unwillingness to comply with earlier Security Council resolutions requiring its disarmament in certain categories of weapons. For example, France and Germany asserted that the United States and its coalition partners could not take military action against Iraq unless specifically authorized by the Security Council.

Insofar as the United States and its coalition partners deemed Iraq a threat and considered the use of military force an exercise of their right to self-defense, the French and German position represented a de facto attempt to amend Article 51. The French and German argument claims that Article 51 does not recognize the inherent right of all states to defend themselves, but refers to a privilege that may be extended to states only by the Security Council—despite the clear language of Article 51 to the contrary. France and Germany, therefore, were effectively trying to use Security Council deliberations to amend the U.N. Charter by means other than those established by the Charter itself. Further, France attempted to use its veto to force this outcome. Its action was the international equivalent of Congress's attempting to repeal the First Amendment to the U.S. Constitution by simply enacting a statute. It utterly lacked legitimacy.

Bolstering the proposition that self-defense is a right and not a privilege should foreclose opportunities to repeat this abuse. The United States should make every effort to persuade the Security Council to adopt a resolution that affirms Article 51. Such a resolution should explicitly state that the Security Council recognizes the inherent right of all states to defend themselves and shall take no action that would subordinate that right to other specific Security Council actions. The language should clearly recognize that no state requires prior approval from the Security Council to engage in defensive actions, including the use of force. For its part, the United States should issue a unilateral statement of policy that it will not accept any U.N. Security Council action or withholding of action that in any way would impede both its right and ability to provide for its own defense and/or the defense of its allies.

Sadly, although its record in addressing arms control and disarmament matters is decidedly mixed, the Security Council represents the high-water mark of effectiveness of the U.N.'s component institutions. Its limited effectiveness stems from its semblance of a hierarchical structure (represented by the permanent members and their individual veto power) that has a small number of members, including at least some that have a sense of responsibility for the dangers and opportunities that arms control and disarmament efforts pose to international security.

Nevertheless, whether the Security Council in its current form furthers or undermines U.S. interests in arms control and disarmament is at best an open question. The question can be restated simply as: Can the United States use its veto in the Security Council to further its interests more effectively than the other permanent members can use their vetoes to thwart U.S. interests? If the United States can openly and honestly conclude that it can, then it should seek to preserve the Security Council in its current form. If the United States concludes the opposite, it should seek to create an alternative institution and use it in lieu of the Security Council to achieved desired multilateral outcomes in arms control.

THE GENERAL ASSEMBLY
AND ITS FIRST COMMITTEE

The U.N. General Assembly consists of all member states and operates under one-country, one-vote rules.[8] Article 11 of the U.N. Charter states:

> The General Assembly may consider the general principles of co-operation in the maintenance of international peace and security, including the principles governing disarmament and the regulation of armaments, and may make recommendations with regard to such principles to the Members or to the Security Council or to both.

Clearly, the Charter envisions that the General Assembly should serve a supportive rather than a leading role in disarmament and arms control matters.

---

8. For a summary description of the General Assembly's powers and functions, see U.N. General Assembly, "Functions and Powers of the General Assembly," at www.un.org/ga/about/background.shtml (accessed May 1, 2008).

This makes eminent sense considering the General Assembly's nonhierarchical structure. Yet as with other matters, the members' direct responsibility for the results of arms control and disarmament is inversely proportional to the power that they seek to exert. Under these circumstances, the General Assembly is prone to adopting resolutions that essentially criticize the few members that have a direct stake in arms control and disarmament matters and a sense of responsibility for the consequences of their actions. For these benighted few among the member states, the adage "no good deed goes unpunished" has become a way of life in the U.N.

Under these circumstances, the assumption of moral equivalency is even more strongly entrenched in the General Assembly. At times, the General Assembly even turns the concept of moral judgment on its head by focusing its criticism on member states that take responsibility for their actions within the body. Its propensity to approve resolutions criticizing Israel[9] and its silence on Syria's clandestine nuclear reactor program are cases in point.

The First Committee of the General Assembly suffers from the same defects. The only difference is that the First Committee focuses narrowly on arms control, disarmament, and international security. Its primary work is to assist in drafting resolutions for consideration by the General Assembly. It also issues reports and records.[10]

Counterproductive Procedures

The General Assembly's procedures encourage countries with limited interests in specific arms control and disarmament initiatives to involve themselves in these matters. Too many resolutions on arms control and disarmament issues brought before the General Assembly are sponsored by nations with only a distant or tangential interest in the subjects. Many are introduced on behalf of the Non-Aligned Movement (NAM).[11] The result is resolutions that tend to point out and complain about problems, but offer only abstract and/or impractical solutions.

For example, Indonesia sponsored a draft resolution in 2007 on the relationship between disarmament and development on behalf of the Non-

---

9. U.N. General Assembly, "Israeli Nuclear Armament," A/RES/39/147, December 17, 1984, at www.un.org/documents/ga/res/39/a39r147.htm (accessed June 25, 2008).

10. For a description of the work performed by the First Committee, see U.N. General Assembly, First Committee, "Documents of the 62nd Session," at www.un.org/ga/first/62/documentation.shtml (accessed May 1, 2008).

11. For a listing of the resolutions introduced in the General Assembly and referred to the First Committee during the 62nd Session of the United Nations, see U.N. Dag Hammarskjöld Library, at www.un.org/Depts/dhl (accessed August 1, 2008).

Aligned Movement.[12] This resolution would take a portion of the resources made available by the implementation of arms control agreements and divert them to economic and social development, thereby reducing resources for arms control (in which Indonesia has little stake) in favor of development (in which Indonesia is strongly interested). Because countries with little direct stake in arms control dominate the General Assembly, its resolutions make virtually no direct contributions to solving problems related to the threats posed by dubious countries that possess or are seeking to acquire certain kinds of weapons.

This unduly broad involvement in arms control and disarmament could be corrected by implementing the voluntary funding mechanism that Ambassador Bolton recommends in the foreword to this book. Participation in the execution of General Assembly resolutions on arms control and disarmament and other matters should be limited to those countries that are willing to play a direct role by contributing resources to the effort. The text of the resolutions themselves should be limited to instructions to the U.N. Secretariat's Department of Disarmament Affairs to provide clerical and organizational support to the countries (sponsors) directly involved in resolving the relevant matter.

For example, if outside monitors were needed to confirm that a country is divesting itself of certain classes of weapons, this approach would permit only member states that are willing to contribute resources to the monitoring system and monitoring activities to sponsor the resolution. Further, this kind of resolution should have a sunset clause that would terminate U.N. involvement in the activity if the specific pledges of resources by sponsoring countries did not materialize or if the prescribed monitoring activity had been concluded. This way the resolutions would clearly identify the problem to be solved, avoid an unfunded mandate that would likely be financed by all member states through the U.N. regular budget, and provide a more direct path to the practical resolution of the problem. It would also ensure that those countries most directly involved would guide the process.

The First Committee's Excessively Broad Roles and Functions

It is appropriate for the First Committee to assist in drafting General Assembly resolutions in a manner consistent with the process described above. However, it is not appropriate for the First Committee to issue reports on the general subjects of arms control and disarmament. Such reports have too often consisted of simple hectoring statements and are

---

12. U.N. General Assembly, First Committee, "Relationship between Disarmament and Development," Agenda Item 98(j), October 23, 2007.

largely criticisms of the United States, such as the committee's November 2007 report *General and Complete Disarmament.*[13]

Instead, the First Committee should be a small group. This means the First Committee and by extension all the main committees should no longer be committees of the whole. Limiting membership of the First Committee will require the General Assembly to adopt an implementing resolution under Article 22 of the Charter, which instructs the General Assembly to "establish such subsidiary organs as it deems necessary for the performance of its functions."

The smaller First Committee should focus on working with the sponsoring states to draft resolutions. As described earlier, these resolutions should generally consist of establishing mandates to the Secretariat's Department of Disarmament Affairs to provide clerical and logistical support to the sponsoring countries involved in the activities established by the resolutions. They should also catalog the specific contributions that the involved (sponsoring) countries have pledged to the activity. Effectively, the First Committee should become a drafting board for resolutions to be presented to the General Assembly. The other existing roles and functions of the First Committee, including the drafting of reports, should be eliminated.

THE SECRETARIAT AND THE
DEPARTMENT FOR DISARMAMENT AFFAIRS

The U.N. Secretariat performs the executive functions of the organization. Its management duties cover the full range of U.N. activities, including those related to arms control and disarmament.[14] At the heart of the Secretariat is its staff: 36,579 (excluding more than 200 on special leave without pay or seconded to other organizations) were under contract as of June 30, 2007. Of this total, 30,745 were employed on contracts of one year or more. Slightly less than one-third (11,253 people) were employed at U.N. headquarters in Geneva, Nairobi, New York, and Vienna.[15] A U.N. budget

---

13. U.N. General Assembly, First Committee, *General and Complete Disarmament,* A/62/391, November 15, 2007, at www.undemocracy.com/A-62-391.pdf (accessed August 4, 2008).

14. For a summary description of the U.N. Secretariat and its staff, see U.N. Department of Public Information, "Secretariat," 2004, at www.un.org/documents/st.htm (accessed May 1, 2008).

15. See U.N. secretary-general, "Composition of the Secretariat," A/62/315, August 31, 2007, 9, 11–12, table 1. According to the U.N. document, the global U.N. Secretariat staff "includes all staff with valid contracts as of 30 June 2007, irrespective of source of funding, type of engagement, duration of contract, level or duty

document indicates that 9,993 "established and temporary posts" in New York were proposed for the 2008–2009 biennium.[16]

Secretariat operations, led by the secretary-general, and its staff are funded out of the U.N. regular budget and through extrabudgetary resources. The personnel are identified as international civil servants and are answerable only to the United Nations for their activities. In fact, they take an oath that precludes them from seeking or receiving instructions from member governments.

The secretary-general's direct line of authority on arms control and disarmament proceeds through the Department for Disarmament Affairs.[17] Its breadth of activities cuts across the full range of arms control and disarmament matters, including such detached subjects as gender and disarmament.[18] By outward appearances, DDA staff spends the majority of its time advocating disarmament.

In 2007, secretary-general Ban Ki-moon understandably proposed rolling the DDA into the Department of Political Affairs, its companion institution inside Secretariat. The proposal drew criticism from both the Non-

---

station. It also includes for the first time data on the International Criminal Tribunal for the former Yugoslavia and the International Criminal Tribunal for Rwanda. Staff included in the analysis are those serving at headquarters duty stations (New York, Geneva, Vienna and Nairobi), at regional commissions (Economic Commission for Africa, Economic Commission for Europe, Economic Commission for Latin America and the Caribbean, Economic and Social Commission for Asia and the Pacific and Economic and Social Commission for Western Asia), in field locations where they are administered by the Department of Economic and Social Affairs, the Department of Political Affairs, the Department of Public Information, the Department of Peacekeeping Operations, the Office for the Coordination of Humanitarian Affairs, the Office of the United Nations High Commissioner for Human Rights, the Office of Internal Oversight Services, the United Nations Conference on Trade and Development, the United Nations Environment Program, the United Nations Human Settlements Program and the United Nations Office on Drugs and Crime, field missions administered by the Department of Peacekeeping Operations and in the international tribunals for the former Yugoslavia and Rwanda." U.N. secretary-general, "Composition of the Secretariat," p. 9.

16. U.N. General Assembly "Proposed Programme Budget for the Biennium 2008–2009: Foreword and Introduction," A/62/6, June 8, 2007, pp. 33–41, table 5, at www.un.org/ga/fifth/ppb89sg.shtml (accessed September 6, 2008).

17. For a summary description of the DDA, see U.N. Department of Public Information, "Disarmament," updated January 19, 2006, at www.un.org/issues/m-dis arm.html (accessed May 1, 2008).

18. U.N. Department for Disarmament Affairs, Office for Disarmament Affairs, "Peace and Security through Disarmament," at http://disarmament.un.org (accessed May 1, 2008).

Aligned Movement and NGOs that advocate arms control.[19] Shortly thereafter, the secretary-general dropped his proposal.[20] As in many other
instances, the permanent U.N. bureaucracy demonstrated considerable skill
in the art of institutional survival. Whether or not DDA should be a separate department under the secretary-general, however, is less important
than operating a responsible and effective institution for addressing arms
control and disarmament matters.

Lack of Accountability to Member Governments

The offices and personnel of the U.N. Secretariat are not accountable to
the member governments. The fact that Secretariat personnel, including
those in the DDA, are accountable only to the U.N. is tantamount to saying
that they are accountable to nobody. This is the chief problem with Secretariat, both generally and specifically in the DDA. The current system is
wrong to separate the Secretariat from member states. In fact, the entire
U.N. structure should serve the members.

Once again, a system of voluntary contributions from member governments to support U.N. activities would effectively correct the lack of
accountability. It would build on the process of adopting resolutions in the
General Assembly described earlier in this chapter. The resolutions, which
would be sponsored by the members committed to participating in the
activity established by the resolution, would establish the task for the Secretariat. A task-oriented Secretariat would be manned by officials from the
participating governments, who would maintain their positions as officials
of their sponsoring governments. Inherent in this approach is elimination
of the oath currently administered to Secretariat personnel and their desig-
nation as international civil servants. Under this arrangement, seconded
staff from participating governments would enjoy the privileges and
immunities as U.N. staff, but strictly in the context of the missions assigned
to them by the cooperating member states. Furnishing manpower for these
purposes would constitute a voluntary in-kind contribution to the U.N.
and its value would be counted toward the member governments' overall
contributions to the activity established by resolution, whether that resolution is a Security Council resolution or a General Assembly resolution.
Other contributions, of course, could be purely financial.

---

19. Thalif Deen, "U.N. Move to Downgrade Disarmament Triggers Protests,"
CommonDreams.org News Center, January 17, 2007, at www.commondreams.org/
headlines07/0117-05.htm (accessed May 1, 2008).

20. Associated Press, "U.N. Drops Key Restructuring Proposal after Protests from
Non-Aligned Nations," Fox News, January 19, 2007, at www.foxnews.com/story/
0,2933,244819,00.html (accessed May 1, 2008).

For example, in a monitoring activity, the participating countries would provide the resources to establish the appropriate task force within the DDA. In the greater scheme of things, the DDA would henceforth consist of a variety of ad hoc task forces. All personnel participating in the task force would remain employees of their sponsoring governments, cooperating with one another under the terms of the relevant resolution. Financial and material resources would be contributed by the participating countries and would be managed and consumed by the task force. Given the task-oriented structure of the system and the required sunset clause in the authorizing resolution, the task force would be dissolved upon completion of the assigned task or its failure to complete the task by the established deadline. The sponsoring governments would then assign their personnel to new positions on other U.N. activities or national activities. The task forces would continue only if reauthorized under a new resolution. This system would make the Secretariat and its activities accountable to the member states and restore the concept of state sovereignty to its proper place in the Secretariat.

THE U.N. CONFERENCE ON DISARMAMENT

The United Nations touts the U.N. Conference on Disarmament as "the single multilateral disarmament negotiating forum of the international community."[21] It has sixty-five member states and is located in Geneva, Switzerland. The Conference on Disarmament provides an annual report to the General Assembly. Its 2007 annual report listed the following items on its agenda in 2007:

1. Cessation of the nuclear arms race and nuclear disarmament.
2. Prevention of nuclear war, including all related matters.
3. Prevention of an arms race in outer space.
4. Effective international arrangements to assure non-nuclear-weapon States against the use or threat of use of nuclear weapons.
5. New types of weapons of mass destruction and new systems of such weapons; radiological weapons.
6. Comprehensive programme of disarmament.
7. Transparency in armaments.
8. Consideration and adoption of the annual report and any other report, as appropriate, to the General Assembly of the United Nations.[22]

---

21. For a summary description of the U.N. Conference on Disarmament, see U.N. Office at Geneva, "Disarmament," at www.unog.ch/disarmament (accessed September 6, 2008).

22. U.N. Conference on Disarmament, annual report for 2007, CD/1831, September 13, 2007, pp. 5–6, at http://daccessdds.un.org/doc/UNDOC/GEN/G07/636/40/PDF/G0763640.pdf (accessed May 5, 2008).

The Conference on Disarmament operates by consensus. While it has not produced a major arms control treaty in recent years, earlier efforts by it and its institutional predecessors have produced:

- The Convention on the Prohibition of the Development, Production and Stockpiling of Bacteriological (Biological) and Toxin Weapons and on Their Destruction of 1972 (Biological Weapons Convention)
- The Convention on the Prohibition of the Development, Production, Stockpiling and Use of Chemical Weapons and on Their Destruction of 1993
- The Comprehensive Nuclear Test Ban Treaty (CTBT) of 1996

All three treaties are fatally flawed to the point that they cannot accomplish their purposes because some countries refused to join the regimes or because compelling evidence exists that countries that joined are prepared to or are currently violating their obligations under these treaties. For these reasons, the U.S. Senate soundly rejected the Comprehensive Nuclear Test Ban Treaty on October 13, 1999.[23] In this instance, the Conference on Disarmament was the primary contributor to this outcome because it unwisely overreached by negotiating a "zero-yield" test ban, ignoring the fact that a zero-yield ban is not verifiable.

An ongoing example of overreaching is the Chinese and Russian proposal for a treaty on the "prevention of an arms race in outer space" (PAROS). In May 2008, the Chinese and Russians issued a joint statement in Beijing reiterating their support for such a treaty.[24] In this case, the treaty will attempt to ban something (i.e., space weapons) that experience demonstrates cannot be defined. For example, the Soviet Union sought to define the U.S. space shuttle as a weapon during the Cold War.

It is far from clear why the broader U.N. system would want to have a single multilateral negotiating forum on arms control and disarmament. The varying agendas of the sixty-five participants have undermined any sense of coherence and purpose. Its unwieldy structure has also exposed it to pressure from outside NGOs that advocate an unrealistic disarmament agenda. For example, numerous NGOs pressed for adoption of the unverifiable and unenforceable CTBT.[25]

---

23. *CQ Almanac, 106th Congress, 1st Session* (Washington, DC: Congressional Quarterly, 2000), 9-40–9-46.

24. Peter Brookes, "Marking the Boundaries of Weapon Use in Space," *Jane's Defence Weekly*, July 22, 2008, reprinted at www.heritage.org/Press/Commentary/ed072508c.cfm.

25. International Physicians for the Prevention of Nuclear War et al., "Joint Statement Endorsed by 97 Non-Governmental Organizations (NGOs), Including IPPNW," September 5, 2003, at www.ippnw.at/presse/030905-ctbt-statement.shtm (accessed June 25, 2008).

Given the flawed products that the conference has produced, its suscepti-bility to pressure from NGOs, and its lack of productivity in recent years, the U.N. should abolish the Conference on Disarmament, as proposed by the United States Institute of Peace's Task Force on the United Nations.[26] The task force also recommended that the Security Council establish ad hoc negotiating bodies of manageable sizes to take on narrowly defined tasks.

The ad hoc approach recommended by the task force is the correct approach, except that the Security Council is not needed to establish these groups. Instead, the nations that are interested and willing to undertake such a narrowly defined arms control and disarmament negotiating task should form the groups themselves. If at an appropriate point the ad hoc group feels that it would benefit from Security Council support, it should appeal to the Security Council.

The Proliferation Security Initiative (PSI) is an example of a successful ad hoc arrangement. President George W. Bush proposed the establishment of the PSI at the G-8 summit in Poland on May 31, 2003. The PSI's governing principles were adopted at a meeting in Paris on September 4, 2003. The PSI established a means for participating states to cooperate in interdicting transshipments of weapons of mass destruction. Its strength is that, unlike U.N. bodies, it remains an activity and not an international organization. This permits it to harness the power of sovereign states and their institu-tions to achieve specific security, arms control, and nonproliferation goals.[27] While PSI is not a U.N. initiative—nor should it be—it is an existing and ongoing example of how a more flexible arrangement can be very suc-cessful where more traditional efforts have failed. Indeed, it is an excellent reason not to rely solely on the U.N. in pursuing arms control and disarma-ment efforts.

If the treaty under negotiation is designed to involve only the participat-ing states in the negotiations, then the treaty should specifically identify these states as parties to the treaty. If the treaty under negotiation is designed to appeal to a broader group of nations, then the treaty should establish accession arrangements that provide due regard for state sover-eignty. Under no circumstances should any arms control or disarmament treaty drafted by a group include provisions that could be binding on any state that has not signed and ratified it.

---

26. United States Institute of Peace, Task Force on the United Nations, "American Interests and UN Reform," 2005, p. 23, at www.usip.org/un/report/usip_un _report.pdf (accessed May 5, 2008).

27. Baker Spring, "Harnessing the Power of Nations for Arms Control: The Pro-liferation Security Initiative and Coalitions of the Willing," Heritage Foundation *Backgrounder*, no. 1737 (March 18, 2004), at www.heritage.org/Research/National-Security/bg1737.cfm.

THE IAEA AND OTHER
U.N.-AFFILIATED INSTITUTIONS

The U.N. includes not only the institutions within its structure, but also affiliated institutions that perform specific tasks, including a number of institutions that deal with arms control and disarmament issues. Among the most prominent is the International Atomic Energy Agency (IAEA). While each of the affiliated institutions has unique characteristics, their institutional structures are similar enough that the IAEA's structure can serve as a model for needed institutional reforms in this broader group of affiliated institutions.

The IAEA[28] consists of three bodies: the General Conference, the Board of Governors, and the staff. The General Conference consists of all the participating states. Typically, the General Conference meets annually and approves the budget and other matters brought before it by the Board of Governors. The Board of Governors is the IAEA's policymaking body and consists of thirty-five member states, which are elected by the General Conference. The outgoing board designates the new members for election based on each state's advancement in atomic energy technology and geographic distribution. The Board of Governors typically meets five times a year. It also selects the IAEA's director general. The director general leads the IAEA staff, which currently consists of 2,200 individuals from ninety countries. The staff is organized to perform work in three general areas: improving the safety and security at nuclear facilities, advancing nuclear science and technology for peaceful purposes, and applying safeguards and verification measures to ensure that peaceful nuclear programs are not diverted to weapons purposes. The safeguards and verification measures bring the IAEA into the field of arms control and disarmament.

Many other international institutions associated with the United Nations, including those with arms control and disarmament responsibilities, have similar structures. Generally, they consist of a general assembly of all the member states, a board with a smaller number of member states, and a staff that is led by an executive official. As such, these organizations possess both the strengths and weakness of the IAEA.

The IAEA's Unduly Broad Mandate

The IAEA is charged with simultaneously expanding access to advanced nuclear technology and preventing the spread of nuclear weapons; this dual

---

28. For a summary description of the IAEA, see International Atomic Energy Agency, "The 'Atoms for Peace' Agency," at www.iaea.org/About/index.html (accessed May 6, 2008).

function creates a tension between these responsibilities because expanding nuclear technology can easily increase the risk of nuclear weapons proliferation. When U.N.-affiliated organizations have broad areas of responsibility, these kinds of tensions are all but certain to arise.

In the IAEA, this tension can jeopardize international security. The 1968 Treaty on the Non-Proliferation of Nuclear Weapons (NPT) assigns the IAEA the responsibility to detect diversions of nuclear facilities and materials to weapons purposes. Effectively, this function is designed as a verification measure to ensure that nonnuclear-weapon states fulfill their treaty obligation of not pursuing nuclear weapons. Even though the risks to peace and security posed by diversion far outweigh the benefits of expanding nuclear technology, the IAEA's responsibility to safeguard against nuclear diversion is forced to compete against its responsibility to expand access to nuclear science and technology. Because these competing priorities are treated as equals, they can cause the organization to undermine its various efforts in either direction. In short, its unwieldy mandate has produced an unwieldy organization.

The answer to the IAEA's unduly broad mandate is to prioritize its competing responsibilities. Because its safeguard responsibilities are far more important than its responsibilities to expand access to nuclear technology and facilities, the IAEA Board of Governors should focus funding and staff on the safeguard mission and limit the scope of the assistance programs. It should make this prioritization explicit in its funding decisions, and its instructions to the staff to remove all doubt inside the organization about how it functions and where it should focus its attention. Preventing the diversion of nuclear material and facilities must come first.

Other U.N.-affiliated organizations with unduly broad mandates should also be forced to prioritize among their competing responsibilities.

The Director General's Involvement in Diplomatic and Political Matters

The director general's position is intended to be nonpolitical. He is to supervise the staff in fulfilling its bureaucratic functions. Dr. Mohamed ElBaradei, the current IAEA director general, has certainly exceeded his mandate by involving himself in diplomatic and political matters related to Iran's nuclear program. Reports indicate that he has specifically demanded that the United States offer economic and security concessions to Iran.[29] In outward appearances, he behaves like a mediator, not an executive agent.

---

29. George Jahn, "Diplomats Say IAEA Chief Urging More U.S. Flexibility on Iran," Associated Press, May 6, 2008.

The IAEA Board of Governors needs to rein in the director general, specifically warning him against involving himself in diplomatic and political affairs. It should reaffirm that his mandate is to put in place safeguards to detect attempts by nonnuclear-weapon states (e.g., Iran) to divert nuclear materials and facilities to weapons purposes. It should prohibit him from undertaking any negotiations on the substance of any suspect nuclear program. Rather, his interactions with any nonnuclear-weapon state, including suspect states, should focus on putting the necessary safeguards in place and reporting to the board if a state is limiting a safeguard system in any way.

Other U.N.-affiliated institutions with executive branches that inappropriately engage in diplomatic and political functions should take similar steps to rein in such behavior.

The IAEA's Monopolistic Behavior

The IAEA staff essentially considers itself the sole authority for designing and managing the safeguard system referred to in the NPT. Like all monopolies, it has become complacent and self-indulgent regarding its responsibilities. The discoveries of Iraq's clandestine nuclear facilities after the first Gulf War revealed that the IAEA staff was reluctant to challenge Iraq on the accuracy of its list of declared facilities prior to the conflict.[30] Prior to the second Gulf War, the IAEA staff's assessment regarding the lack of an Iraqi nuclear weapons program proved more accurate. However, it is entirely possible that its accuracy in this case was more the result of its traditional complacency than of a careful assessment of Iraq's program.

The argument demonstrating IAEA complacency is bolstered by its staff's failure to discover an illicit shipment of nuclear-related equipment to Libya. This discovery was a contributing factor in Libya's decision to declare and dismantle its nuclear weapons program in December 2003. In the aftermath of the Libyan declaration, the IAEA director general acknowledged that the IAEA would need to "kick start the process of verification."[31]

The answer to the IAEA staff's monopolistic behavior is for prominent states to break the monopoly. The United States should lead an effort by interested states to create a competing international institution to perform the safeguard mission. They can do this in two ways. First, the participating

---

30. Baker Spring, "Controlling the Bomb: International Constraints on Nuclear Weapons Are Not Enough," Heritage *Backgrounder*, no. 941 (May 19, 1993): 5, at www.heritage.org/Research/NationalSecurity/bg941.cfm.

31. Anjali Bhattacharjee and Sammy Salama, "Libya and Nonproliferation," James Martin Center for Nonproliferation Studies, December 24, 2003, at http://cns.miis.edu/pubs/week/031223.htm (accessed May 7, 2008).

states can agree to undertake safeguard measures among themselves. These measures should be stricter than the IAEA's safeguards and should be conducted in addition to IAEA measures. They should be performed by national inspection teams on a reciprocal basis. Second, those states involved in negotiations to ensure nonproliferation goals regarding suspect states (e.g., the six-party talks on North Korea) should not simply allow the IAEA to manage the safeguard and verification systems resulting from any agreement. Instead, they should insist on conducting safeguard and verification activities that augment IAEA measures. These inspections should also be performed by national teams.

These two steps would fill the gaps in the safeguard system created by the IAEA's complacency and self-indulgence and they would force the IAEA to compete in performing safeguard functions or risk becoming irrelevant.

As needed, other U.N.-affiliated organizations that are involved in arms control and disarmament matters should likewise be forced to compete with other safeguard, verification, and inspection regimes.

NONGOVERNMENTAL ORGANIZATIONS

A wide variety of nongovernmental organizations participate in U.N. arms control and disarmament efforts. Many are nothing more than arms control and disarmament advocacy groups. Such NGOs have little interest in protecting member states' inherent right of individual and collective self-defense as stated in Article 51. They are interested in elevating the cause of arms control and disarmament as an end unto itself, rather than as a means to enhance national security or international peace and stability. This even includes pressuring the U.N. on internal organizational decisions that could be perceived as downgrading the value of arms control and disarmament in purely abstract terms. As noted, some NGOs challenged the U.N. secretary-general's proposal to fold the Department for Disarmament Affairs into the Department for Political Affairs in the U.N. Secretariat.[32] The secretary-general abandoned his proposal shortly thereafter.

NGOs are too closely involved in the internal procedures of the U.N. This incident suggests that the NGOs are directly participating in the decision-making process in the U.N. structure, as opposed to performing an educational or advocacy function from outside the organization. To the extent that such participation leads the U.N. Secretariat to take one action instead

---

32. Global Action to Prevent War and Armed Conflict, "Secretary-General Ban Ki-moon: Don't Downgrade the Department for Disarmament Affairs!" February 7, 2007, at www.globalactionpw.org/UN/Downgrade_DDA.htm (accessed May 7, 2008).

of another, it undermines the U.N.'s primary purpose, which is to serve and be responsible to the member states. Indeed, some elements of the U.N. structure appear to answer more to the NGOs than to the member states.

In arms control, this shift started with the Ottawa Process, which produced a treaty banning antipersonnel land mines. In the Ottawa Process, the NGOs assumed roles functionally equivalent to the diplomatic representatives of states, although in collaboration with approving state delegations. Further, these NGOs did not even bother to claim that they represented a broad cross section of public opinion on the issue of banning antipersonnel land mines. They were explicitly advocates of a complete ban.[33]

The latest cause of the arms control and disarmament advocacy groups is to establish a treaty banning cluster munitions. Regardless of this proposal's merit or lack of merit, the conference convened in Dublin on May 19, 2008, reveals how NGOs are beginning to dominate the arms control process at the United Nations. First, the Dublin conference permitted a sponsorship arrangement in which the U.N. Development Program covered the participation costs of some states.[34] Many U.N. member states are pressed for funding and find it difficult to attend the multitude of U.N. meetings, conferences, and summits held every year. They frequently do not send representatives to events that they consider irrelevant or of limited interest. This is and should be their prerogative and serves as an important filter to limit attendance to those countries that highly value the particular conference. By funding attendance at these conferences, the U.N. discourages countries from appropriately weighing their priorities when deciding which conferences are most important to their governments and citizens and therefore justify the expense of attending. Instead, the U.N. is substituting nonnational priorities.

Second, the conference listed 259 individuals on the official list of delegates as NGO representatives.[35] These NGO representatives were provided direct access to the conference proceedings. This is the equivalent of the

---

33. For a description of the Ottawa Process, see David Davenport, "The Ban on Landmines, the International Criminal Court and Beyond," *Policy Review*, no. 116 (December 2002 and January 2003), at www.hoover.org/publications/policyreview/3458466.html (accessed July 15, 2008).

34. Government of Ireland, Department of Foreign Affairs, "Dublin Diplomatic Conference on Cluster Munitions: Information for Delegates," at www.clustermunitionsdublin.ie/delegation.asp (accessed June 26, 2008).

35. Government of Ireland, Department of Foreign Affairs, "Diplomatic Conference for the Adoption of a Convention on Cluster Munitions: List of Delegates," May 30, 2008, pp. 34–45, at www.clustermunitionsdublin.ie/pdf/CCM_INF_1_ListofDelegates_Final.pdf (accessed July 15, 2008).

U.S. House of Representatives granting floor privileges to lobbyists. It mocks the role and stature of government representation in U.N. activities. Worse, the NGO representatives were not broadly based. Judging from the names of their organizations, nearly all 259 were arms control advocates and almost certainly committed to adopting a ban on cluster munitions. None appeared to represent organizations concerned about the ability of national militaries to fulfill their assigned missions.

The first step to restoring an appropriate relationship between internal U.N. bodies and NGOs is to restore the sovereign state to its preeminent position in the U.N. If the U.N. insists that member states take direct responsibility for their actions in the various U.N. processes, the NGOs will be forced to advocate their positions at the domestic level. This will limit their efforts to circumvent the member states to push their own agendas supranationally within the U.N. structure.

The second step is to implement a voluntary contribution mechanism. If U.N. positions are filled only by employees of the member states at their own expense, the NGOs will be effectively barred from assuming roles that should belong to the participating governments.

The third step is to limit arms control negotiating groups to those states with a direct interest in the outcome. The NGOs have worked their way into inappropriate positions within U.N. arms control and disarmament institutions through states that have no interest in the outcome. If these disinterested states are excluded from a particular negotiating structure, the NGOs will not have the political space to involve themselves directly in the process.

The final step is for the U.N. to bar member states from granting proxies to NGOs to assume their responsibilities in U.N. activities. This step will eliminate the mechanism that the NGOs have used to assume inappropriate responsibilities, such as happened at the cluster munitions conference in Dublin.

THE U.N. CHARTER

Given the myriad structural shortcomings of the greater U.N. system in relation to arms control and disarmament issues, it is reasonable to ask whether adopting a new U.N. Charter would be the best way of reforming the entire system. If the changes to the U.N. system proposed in this chapter are not adopted, then the alternative of a new U.N. Charter should be examined. Too much has gone wrong with the U.N. in the field of arms control and disarmament since its creation in 1945 to let the problems continue to fester. Further, there is growing pressure to increase the size of the

Security Council. The United States, in principle, supports expanding the Security Council to include Japan.[36]

The wisdom of expanding the Security Council is questionable. Even a modest expansion would make the council more unwieldy, contribute to gridlock, and dilute U.S. influence in the council. Expansion would inevitably make the council less able to respond to crises and less supportive of the United States on many key issues.[37] Ambassador Bolton said,

> I felt strongly that any increase in the Council's overall size should be minimal, since it was hard enough to get any real work done with fifteen members, and each new addition increased that difficulty not just arithmetically but probably geometrically. The United States was certainly the most concerned about maintaining the Council's (limited) effectiveness as a decision-making body. Many aspirants for permanent membership never considered the consequences of expanding the body to twenty-four or twenty-five members, so eager were they to get a chair around that horseshoe table, regardless of what would follow. I must confess, from time to time I had an "Atlas Shrugged" moment, concluding that we should just let the Council expansion happen, and, as we predicted, watch the whole thing slide into a ditch. But then, my sense of responsibility would assert itself, and I would revert to diligent defender of the Council's effectiveness.[38]

Regardless of the consequences, there is considerable interest in expanding the council. Expanding the Security Council would require revising the Charter, thus the United States must be prepared to undertake a revision in the Charter in any event.

However, amending or revising the U.N. Charter is not easy. The Charter amendment process is appropriately challenging. It is not the sort of document that should be tampered with frequently or for insignificant reasons, nor should a few countries have the power to change a treaty affecting all nations. Yet this also means that amending the Charter to address the organization's weaknesses will be difficult. In particular, it would be extraordinarily difficult for the United States to gain support from two-thirds of the General Assembly for any proposal limiting the U.N.'s role, revising U.N. staffing and funding procedures, or limiting participation in activities long

---

36. John R. Bolton, "Statement on Security Council Reform," U.S. State Department, November 10, 2005, at www.state.gov/p/io/rls/rm/57420.htm (accessed May 8, 2008).

37. For a lengthier discussion, see Nile Gardiner and Brett D. Schaefer, "U.N. Security Council Expansion Is Not in the U.S. Interest," Heritage Foundation *Backgrounder*, no. 1876 (August 18, 2005), at www.heritage.org/Research/International Organizations/bg1876.cfm.

38. Bolton, *Surrender Is Not an Option*, 251.

considered the province of all U.N. member states to only those states with a direct interest. Nevertheless, considering the options for revising the Charter is necessary because the organization is seeking to override state sovereignty in a way that threatens liberty worldwide.

Given the difficult process of revising the U.N. Charter and the likelihood that other nations would use the opportunity to propose amendments inimitable to U.S. interests, the United States should be very wary of supporting a process to revise the Charter and should regard any such effort as a long-term enterprise. It would require a consistent vision, patience, and determination—qualities not usually associated with the U.S. State Department, which would likely oversee the negotiations.

The United States will come under enormous pressure to adopt the product of a Charter amendment process, even if it is clearly inconsistent with U.S. interests. Therefore, the United States must be certain and clear about what it wants to obtain through a revision in the U.N. Charter and publicly state that goal. Clarity of purpose and a public statement of intent will provide a basis for U.S. leaders in Congress and the executive branch and for the public to judge whether the revision process is running in the wrong direction and would make the U.N. even less effective, or if it would expand U.N. authority in a manner that threatens state sovereignty and the cause of liberty. Knowing that the result will be held to a public metric of what constitutes a desirable outcome will stiffen U.S. resolve when other governments and NGOs pressure the United States to accept a deleterious outcome.

The two options for amending or revising the U.N. Charter are set forth in chapter 8. Under the first option, the General Assembly can adopt an amendment by a two-thirds vote of its members. The amendment would enter into force when two-thirds of the members, including all five permanent members of the Security Council, have ratified it.[39]

Under the second option, two-thirds of the members of the General Assembly and any nine members of the Security Council can vote to convene a charter review conference.[40] The conference may recommend alter-

---

39. "Amendments to the present Charter shall come into force for all Members of the United Nations when they have been adopted by a vote of two-thirds of the members of the General Assembly and ratified in accordance with their respective constitutional processes by two-thirds of the Members of the United Nations, including all the permanent members of the Security Council." Charter of the United Nations, art. 108.

40. "A General Conference of the Members of the United Nations for the purpose of reviewing the present Charter may be held at a date and place to be fixed by a two-thirds vote of the members of the General Assembly and by a vote of any nine members of the Security Council. Each Member of the United Nations shall have one vote in the conference. Any alteration of the present Charter recommended by a two-thirds vote of the conference shall take effect when ratified in accordance with

ations in the Charter by a two-thirds vote. The alterations would enter into force when two-thirds of all members, including all the permanent members of the Security Council, have ratified them.

The United States should view an effort to revise the U.N. Charter as a long-term enterprise and should prepare to opt for the latter option if the revision process is being initiated. With this approach, the United States would signal to other members of the General Assembly its willingness to support a resolution calling for the convening of a review conference. This approach would allow initiation of the Charter revision process, which otherwise could be blocked at the outset by a recalcitrant permanent member of the Security Council.

However, entering into a Charter amendment process is far more likely to yield an unsatisfactory result. Indeed, a two-thirds majority of the member states is far more likely to expand U.N. authority in ways that would replicate or exacerbate the organization's current flaws than to restrict the U.N.'s role and make it more focused on and accountable to member states.

Moreover, if an effort to revise the Charter, whether initiated to expand the membership of the Security Council or for some other reason, were moving in the wrong direction, the United States would have little choice but to abandon the U.N. altogether. Once such misdirected amendments were submitted for ratification, many member states would eagerly press forward to ratify them, either because they would support increasing the U.N.'s authority and power or because they would face little consequence from such an expansion of power. Pressure on the permanent members of the Security Council to ratify such amendments would mount and ultimately prevail. At that point, the reform process would clearly have arrived at a dead end, and U.S. interests would be far better served by ending U.S. participation in the U.N. than by continuing to participate, with the notable exception of maintaining its presence on the Security Council to veto objectionable resolutions.

While reaching such a dead end in the U.N. reform process is not inevitable, the United States cannot just hope for the best. The United States will need to take steps in the interim to reserve its options. Simply leaving the U.N. would not be wise. While a number of national interests are not served by working through multilateral institutions, some indisputably are

---

their respective constitutional processes by two-thirds of the Members of the United Nations including all the permanent members of the Security Council. If such a conference has not been held before the tenth annual session of the General Assembly following the coming into force of the present Charter, the proposal to call such a conference shall be placed on the agenda of that session of the General Assembly, and the conference shall be held if so decided by a majority vote of the members of the General Assembly and by a vote of any seven members of the Security Council." Charter of the United Nations, art. 109.

best served by working through that framework. The United States will need to move to an alternative institution. It can do this by taking concrete steps to build such an institution. Kim Holmes, vice president of The Heritage Foundation, has proposed creating a Global Freedom Coalition.[41] While it need not be created as an explicit alternative to the U.N., a Global Freedom Coalition could evolve into that if circumstances warrant.

THE WAY FORWARD

The United Nations system has assumed a large and influential role in international efforts on arms control and disarmament. While the U.N. and some of its affiliated bodies certainly have roles to play in this arena, the United States should undertake an effort to revise and reform the U.N.'s arms control and disarmament infrastructure to make it smaller and more focused and to eliminate the processes and traditions that have proven counterproductive.

Preserving and Protecting the Primacy of National Sovereignty

The slow, incremental expansion of U.N. authority, power, and influence in a host of international areas is infringing on the authority and sovereignty of nation-states. This is unjustified and inappropriate because the nation-state is the sole means through which the rights and privileges of individuals can be protected and preserved. While numerous governments abuse their power by failing to promote the best interests of their citizens or even by oppressing them, no viable or superior alternative exists to a representative government with ample checks to prevent abuse. Certainly, subordinating national governments to a largely unaccountable international bureaucracy is not a recipe for success. The United States should:

- Press the Security Council to adopt a resolution that unequivocally affirms every state's right to self-defense
- Seek to make the offices of the U.N. Secretariat accountable to the member states through the system of voluntary contributions and by requiring all personnel participating in U.N. activities to remain the employees of their sponsoring states
- Block NGOs from directly participating in U.N. activities by forcing them to work through the governments of member states to further their positions

41. Kim R. Holmes, *Liberty's Best Hope: American Leadership for the 21st Century* (Washington, DC: Heritage Foundation, 2008), 118–30.

Promoting the Values of Liberty in the U.N.
and Elsewhere

The presence of despotic nations on key U.N. bodies, including the U.N. Security Council, can dramatically undermine the bodies' effectiveness. The United States should use its influence to impede those member states most opposed to liberty from election to the Security Council, or at the very least, seek to bar member states currently under Security Council sanctions from sitting on the Security Council.

The United States should also use its influence to convince regional groups to support good candidates for the Security Council, rather than spoilers such as Iran and Venezuela. If these efforts fail to improve the composition of the Security Council, the United States should seek to create a competitor institution to the United Nations composed solely of members committed to liberty. This alternative institution should include a body that has responsibilities similar to the Security Council's mandate to maintain world peace and security, including arms control and disarmament matters.

Overhauling the International Arms Control and
Disarmament System

The current system for dealing with disarmament and arms control issues has fallen increasingly under the U.N.'s purview. This shift away from a state-based system is undesirable and counterproductive because it gives undue influence to those who are not responsible for and are not accountable to the people who may be made vulnerable by poorly conceived or biased arms control agreements and implementing measures. The United States should seek to implement a series of changes to return the focus of international arms control and disarmament efforts to states that have a direct, vested interest in negotiating realistic, effective, and verifiable agreements. Specifically, the United States should seek to:

- Narrow participation in the General Assembly's First Committee on Disarmament and International Security to a smaller number of key countries central to the discussion, and narrow the committee's jurisdiction to assisting in drafting resolutions that recommend arms control measures for member states to consider, individually or in the General Assembly
- Reform the funding mechanism by shifting from assessed budgetary support to a voluntary contribution funding mechanism focused on executing specific General Assembly resolutions on arms control
- Review and reform the international organizations focused on arms

control and disarmament. Specifically, the United States should seek to abolish the U.N. Conference on Disarmament, clarify the mandate of the IAEA to emphasize its safeguard responsibilities over its mandate to access to nuclear technology, prohibit the IAEA director general from engaging in political and diplomatic activities, and establish alternative forums to compete with the IAEA and break its monopoly on nuclear safeguards

- Promote alternative institutions and options in arms control and disarmament. The Proliferation Security Initiative is a sound, successful example of how a non-U.N. effort can enhance arms control and disarmament efforts. The PSI option should be explored and replicated where appropriate.

Refusing to Sign or Ratify Arms Control Treaties That Would Undermine U.S. Interests

Recent arms control and disarmament treaties emanating from the U.N. system have proven greatly flawed. The Biological Weapons Convention and the Comprehensive Nuclear Test Ban Treaty are flawed to the extent that they are unable to accomplish their purpose. Yet the United States participated in formulating these agreements and even signed them. To avoid this in the future, U.S. negotiators should be instructed to demand that:

- Arms control treaties include provisions that further a relevant military or security goal outlined by U.S. strategy. For example, an arms control treaty could ease the burden on the U.S. military by eliminating targets that are difficult to hold at risk.
- The United States will not be bound in any way by a treaty that it does not sign and ratify or that fails to enter into force for other reasons

The United States should clearly state that failure to accommodate these principles in the treaty will lead the United States to refuse to sign future agreements, precipitate a decision to "unsign" existing agreements, and even lead the United States to consider withdrawing from current agreements to which it is a party.

CONCLUSION

To successfully reform U.N. institutions to better address arms control and disarmament, the United States must clearly understand its vital national interests and demonstrate a willingness to defend those interests. For example, the U.N. system was not entirely at fault for producing the fatally

flawed Comprehensive Nuclear Test Ban Treaty in 1996. In the negotiations, the Clinton administration completely lost sight of U.S. security
requirements. It actually pressed the U.N. system to produce a treaty that
so jeopardized the vital interests of the United States that the U.S. Senate
had no choice but to soundly reject its ratification in 1999.

Preserving a nation-state, including the United States, ultimately depends
on its people and institutions demonstrating a willingness to defend it and
its sovereignty. The disintegration of the Soviet Union demonstrates the
potential fragility of a state. Even the Soviet superpower ceased to exist
when its people and institutions stopped believing in its purpose, albeit
this loss of purpose came for good cause. The cause of the United States is
the preservation of liberty, starting with its own. It is the most noble of
callings, and U.S. leaders should never lose sight of this.

The shortcomings of the U.N. system, particularly in arms control and
disarmament, are coming dangerously close to being tantamount to an
attack on liberty. The arms control and disarmament processes at the U.N.
are increasingly becoming transparent attempts to disarm the defenders of
liberty around the world, starting with the United States. At the same time,
these processes seek to avoid confronting the arms buildups of forces for
repression, such as Iran.

Under these circumstances, the United States cannot afford to allow the
U.N. arms control and disarmament institutions to remain unreformed.
Nothing less than the future survival of the United States and the worldwide cause of liberty are at stake. There is no room for moral self-doubt, a
lack of understanding of the nation's vital interests, or a lack of willingness
to defend these interests by the leaders of the United States.

10

Curing the International Health System

Roger Bate and Karen Porter

The U.N.'s World Health Organization (WHO) has a unique role to play in global health. As the only membership U.N. entity concerned exclusively with health, it can theoretically provide a forum for health ministers to share information on rapidly transmitted and dangerous infectious diseases, such as avian flu and severe acute respiratory syndrome (SARS). Through its World Health Assembly, WHO can call attention to global health problems and help establish global health standards.

WHO can facilitate data sharing, although this process has been hobbled by distrust from developing countries, many of which view the organization as too close to Western business interests.[1] It can also provide approved

---

1. For example, in January 2007, Siti Fadilah Supari, Indonesia's health minister, began withholding virus samples and data on the country's avian flu pandemic from WHO, saying that its virus sharing system was exclusive and unfair to poor nations. In May 2008, Indonesia announced that it would begin sharing its data with the Global Initiative on Sharing Avian Influenza Data, an independent international consortium of avian scientists that promised to deposit data in the three publicly available databases (EMBL, DDBJ, and GenBank) participating in the International Sequence Database Collaboration. Robin McDowell, "Indonesia Hands Over Bird Flu Data to New Database," *USA Today*, May 15, 2008, at www.usa today.com/news/world/2008-05-15-4236239537_x.htm (accessed December 3, 2008); and Peter Bogner et al., "Global Initiative on Sharing Avian Influenza Data," *Nature* 442, no. 7106 (August 31, 2006): 981, at www.nature.com/nature/journal/v442/n7106/full/442981a.html (accessed December 3, 2008).

product lists for medicines, bed nets, condoms, and other health products purchased with public funds, especially for poor countries that lack capacity. Yet historically, it has failed to control quality of drugs and has acted as a bottleneck for other products. While other public and private actors might perform some of these roles more efficiently, WHO, as a multilateral organization, can garner more trust from all states, especially those wary of "Western-guided" development.

Based on its lack of accountability and poor performance, however, WHO desperately needs to reform. WHO has often failed to fulfill its assigned mandates and has been unable to implement the initiatives it has begun. It has sometimes allowed political concerns to undermine its technical expertise. It is no longer equipped to directly implement measures to combat disease because it lacks sufficient staff, the skill set, the correct incentive structure, and adequate financing. Other implementing organs— bilateral initiatives, such as the U.S. President's Malaria Initiative, and private actors, such as the Bill and Melinda Gates Foundation—have grown in number and influence over the past twenty years and are better suited to combating disease than WHO is. The organization should focus on roles in which it enjoys a comparative advantage (e.g., technical coordinator, health advocate or "cheerleader," and secretariat for various private and public agencies) and divest responsibilities not directly related to these roles.

As WHO's single largest financier,[2] the U.S. government has a powerful role to play in WHO reform. It can publicly pressure the organization to stop letting "politics get in the way of fundamental health needs," as it is doing with WHO's continued refusal to grant membership to Taiwan.[3] It can partner with like-minded states to withhold assessed contributions and push for more voluntary ones, making payment contingent on strong performance in WHO's areas of comparative advantage. When WHO fails to measure up, the U.S. government can and should invest its money elsewhere, with the plethora of other actors that now populate the international health arena.

THE INTERNATIONAL HEALTH ARENA

Today's international health arena is complex and sprawling, with myriad interconnected actors. At the pinnacle is the World Health Organization. Its

---

2. World Health Assembly, "Scale of Assessments 2008–2009," WHA60.5, May 21, 2007, at www.who.int/gb/ebwha/pdf_files/WHA60/A60_R5-en.pdf (accessed December 3, 2008).

3. Barney Frank, "Keep Politics Out of the WHO; Let Taiwan In," *Congressional Record* (July 24, 2008): E1555.

policy organ, the World Health Assembly, includes representatives from the 193 WHO member states and meets every year, usually in May. Policies are coordinated by headquarters in Geneva and carried out by six regional offices, 147 country offices, and more than 8,000 staff.[4]

WHO's regional offices operate as the implementing organs for the global body, but often have a high degree of autonomy and their own policy-organ assemblies. For example, WHO's regional office for the Americas goes by the independent-sounding moniker Pan American Health Organization and receives some funding directly from the U.S. government ($56.6 million in assessed contributions in 2007 plus voluntary funding) and other governments over which WHO has virtually no control.

WHO members are expected to donate a specified percentage of the overall budget, known as "assessed contributions," based on a formula designed to determine a country's ability to pay. Although members are technically obligated to provide assessed funds, they have often made such contributions contingent on policy reforms.

WHO's $4.2 billion budget for 2008–2009, approved at the May 2007 World Health Assembly, included $959 million for the regular assessed budget (an approximately 5 percent increase over 2006–2007) and $3.3 billion in projected voluntary contributions. Overall, this is a 15 percent increase over 2006–2007.[5] In 2006, the United States' assessed contribution was $101.4 million (set at 22 percent of WHO's total regular budget), and the president's total request for fiscal year 2009 was $106.6 million.[6] The United States also provides substantial voluntary contributions annually, including more than $130 million in 2006.[7] By comparison, in 2006, the U.S. government contributed $108.9 million to the United Nations Development Program (UNDP) and $125.7 million to the United Nations Children's Fund (UNICEF), which are more "implementation-driven."[8]

WHO is the most prominent and important international health organi-

---

4. World Health Organization, "WHO—Its People and Its Offices," at www .who.int/about/structure/en/index.html (accessed December 3, 2008).

5. World Health Organization, "Programme Budget 2008–2009," p. 10, at www .who.int/gb/ebwha/pdf_files/AMTSP-PPB/a-mtsp_4en.pdf (accessed December 3, 2008).

6. U.S. Department of State, *The Budget in Brief, Fiscal Year 2009*, p. 101, at www .state.gov/documents/organization/100033.pdf (accessed December 3, 2008).

7. World Health Organization, "Unaudited Interim Financial Report for the Year 2006," A60/30, p. 5, at www.who.int/gb/ebwha/pdf_files/WHA60/A60_30-en.pdf (accessed December 3, 2008).

8. Marjorie Ann Browne and Kennon H. Nakamura, "United Nations Systems Funding: Congressional Issues," Congressional Research Service *Report for Congress,* updated September 17, 2007.

zation, but it was not the first. When it was launched in 1945, it entered an arena already populated by several multilateral and bilateral institutions, including the Office International d'Hygiène Publique (founded in 1907), the mostly defunct League of Nations Health Organization (1923), the U.N. Relief and Rehabilitation Administration (1943), the Pan American Sanitary Bureau (1902), and the U.S. Malaria Control in War Areas (1942), which later became the Centers for Disease Control and Prevention (CDC) (1946), as well as quasi-governmental health organizations such as the International Red Cross (1863) and private charities including the Rockefeller Foundation (1913).

Within the U.N., WHO was later joined by several agencies that included health issues within their mandates. UNICEF was made a permanent agency in 1953, and UNDP was created in 1965, followed by the United Nations Population Fund (UNFPA) in 1969.[9] The U.N. has also created special programs and offices, such as the United Nations Joint Program on HIV/AIDS (UNAIDS) in 1994 and the Global Fund to Fight AIDS, Tuberculosis and Malaria in 2002. The structures of these special programs tend to reflect the programs' focus on implementation. Most include governing boards, but lack representative assemblies. Contributions are generally voluntary, rather than assessed.

Other international agencies also consider "health" within their purview. For example, the World Bank provides loans to developing countries for health-related projects. While the International Monetary Fund does not involve itself in specifics or priorities of health spending, it supports national poverty-reduction strategies that allocate additional spending to HIV/AIDS and other health programs.[10]

The size and scope of bilateral health initiatives have increased significantly over the past decade, primarily with targeted disease-specific programs such as the President's Malaria Initiative and the President's Emergency Plan for AIDS Relief. U.S. programs are funded through one or more of the following: the U.S. Department of Health and Human Services, U.S. Agency for International Development (USAID), Department of State,

---

9. For example, UNDP's strategic framework for 2004–2007 lists "responding to HIV/AIDS" as one of its five goals. UNICEF operates programs related to children's health (especially vaccine distribution), sanitation, and nutrition, as well as programs in basic education and child protection. The UNFPA funds programs for population and reproductive health care in more than 140 countries.

10. International Monetary Fund, "IMF Helping Countries on Health, Social Spending Policies," *IMF Survey*, July 25, 2008, at www.imf.org/external/pubs/ft/sur vey/so/2008/POL072508A.htm (accessed December 3, 2008); and "The IMF's Role in the Fight Against HIV/AIDS," August 2008, at www.imf.org/external/np/exr/facts/ hivaids.htm (accessed December 3, 2008).

National Institutes of Health, and CDC. A number of U.S. programs are increasingly funded through the Department of Defense because of cross-connections between health and security. For example, the President's Malaria Initiative is led by the U.S. Agency for International Development, but is overseen by a coordinator appointed by the president and an inter-agency steering group with representatives from USAID, CDC, U.S. Department of Health and Human Services, Department of State, Department of Defense, National Security Council, and Office of Management and Budget.

Outside of the strictly bilateral and multilateral governmental sphere, the picture becomes even more complex. Quasi-governmental organizations (e.g., the International Red Cross), large nonprofit private foundations (e.g., the Bill and Melinda Gates Foundation), and nongovernmental organizations (e.g., Oxfam and Médecins Sans Frontières) finance and implement health programs. Businesses provide pharmaceutical drugs, medical devices, and health-care services at cost or as charitable donations. These nongovernmental actors are becoming more influential and powerful. According to the Hudson Institute's Center for Global Prosperity, private resources (investment, remittances, and philanthropy) account for "over 75 percent of donor countries' entire economic dealings with developing nations." While health aid has been historically dominated by governments, private-sector participation is increasing. In 2007, corporations spent more than $5 billion on in-kind medical donations.[11] Since 1994, the Bill and Melinda Gates Foundation has pledged some $9.3 billion for global health out of $17.3 billion in total development aid.[12]

Within the international health arena, actors might be classified as financiers, implementers, vendors, or recipients. Sometimes an organization falls neatly into one category. For example, the Global Fund is a U.N.-coordinated partnership of "governments, civil society, the private sector and affected communities"[13] concerned exclusively with financing efforts against three diseases—AIDS, tuberculosis, and malaria. However, organizations more frequently fall into several categories and play numerous roles. Although each theoretically has its own comparative advantage, mandates and tasks often overlap. Because the World Health Organization is the

---

11. Hudson Institute, Center for Global Prosperity, *The Index of Global Philanthropy 2008*, pp. 3 and 68, at www.hudson.org/files/documents/2008%20Index%20-%20Low%20Res.pdf (accessed December 3, 2008).

12. Bill and Melinda Gates Foundation, "Funding from 1994 to Present," at www.gatesfoundation.org/grants/Pages/overview.aspx (accessed December 19, 2008).

13. Global Fund, "A New Partnership," at www.theglobalfund.org/en/partnership (accessed December 11, 2008).

principal international agency concerned exclusively with health, we anchor our analysis on it, explaining how it has interacted with myriad agencies and venturing to propose how it could do its job better.

THE NEW INTERNATIONAL
HEALTH ORGANIZATION

In April 1945, delegates from around the world gathered in San Francisco to hammer out a postwar order and launch the United Nations. Because few countries had the capacity to finance and organize broad-based international health operations and programs, an international body was appealing and seemed necessary. A proposal by the Brazilian and Chinese delegations for a new world health organization quickly gained support. In June 1948, delegates from fifty-three of the U.N.'s fifty-five member states convened the first World Health Assembly and proclaimed as its mission "the attainment by all peoples of the highest possible level of health."[14] Slogans proclaiming that "germs know no frontiers" and "carry no passports" echoed throughout the first assembly.[15]

WHO's Original Mission

Negotiations over the structure and authority of the new health organization borrowed from the mandate of the Health Organization of the League of Nations. Because participants deemed the Health Organization to have been too weak to meet many of the world's health needs, they designed WHO with a far more comprehensive role and greater authority to fulfill its mission. Among the twenty-one functions in its constitution, WHO would:

- Direct and coordinate international health work
- Establish and maintain collaboration with all international health actors, public and private, deemed "appropriate"
- Provide assistance for emergencies and for "strengthening health services"
- Work to eradicate, not only "epidemic" diseases, but also "endemic and other diseases"

14. The WHO constitution had come into force two months earlier on April 7, 1948, when the requisite twenty-sixth member state ratified it. Brock Chrisholm, "Landmark in World Health," *Chronicle of the World Health Organization* 2, no. 4 (April 1948), at http://whqlibdoc.who.int/hist/chronicles/chronicle_1948.pdf (accessed December 3, 2008).

15. Walter R. Sharp, "The New World Health Organization," *American Journal of International Law* 41, no. 3 (July 1947): 514.

- Establish international nomenclature and standards for health
- Provide administrative and technical services, including gathering epidemiological data
- Even "promote and conduct research"[16]

These functions were supposed to be performed only "upon the request or acceptance of governments" of member states, the organization's financiers and clients. As with any large organization, principal–agent problems quickly arose.

In its early years, the organization strayed little from what most member states considered to be its primary function: eradicating epidemic diseases.[17] This approach of focusing on mass disease prevention and control campaigns is generally categorized as "vertical," rather than "horizontal," which focuses on improving general health. WHO launched a series of disease-specific programs, which achieved varying degrees of success: the 1952–1964 program against Yaws (a bacterial infection), a 1974 effort against onchocerciasis, the celebrated eradication of smallpox by 1979 (in just over a decade), and a campaign against polio in 1988. The organization's early campaigns against malaria were launched in the mid-1950s in the Americas, Europe, Asia, and Oceania with pilot programs in Africa and were highly effective. By 1970, an estimated one billion people no longer lived in malaria-endemic areas, and malaria had been eradicated from fourteen wealthier tropical and subtropical countries.[18]

These programs succeeded for several reasons. For smallpox and malaria, the nature of the disease had been clearly identified, and methods for prevention and treatment were obvious. Funding was forthcoming from donor

---

16. Constitution of the World Health Organization, July 22, 1946, at www.who.int/governance/eb/who_constitution_en.pdf (accessed December 3, 2008).

17. At proceedings of the first World Health Assembly, member states agreed that the organization's first priority would be "malaria, maternal and child health, tuberculosis, venereal diseases, nutrition and environmental sanitation." World Health Organization, "Working for Health: An Introduction to the World Health Organization," 2007, at www.who.int/about/brochure_en.pdf (accessed December 3, 2008). Still, campaigns tended to focus on epidemic diseases rather than general health.

18. World Health Organization, "Informal Consultation on Malaria Elimination: Setting Up the WHO Agenda," 2006, at www.who.int/malaria/docs/malariaelimi nationagenda.pdf (accessed December 3, 2008). In India, malaria incidence decreased from 75 million cases per year to about 100,000 cases per year. See World Health Organization, "Implementation of Indoor Residual Spraying of Insecticides for Malaria Control in the WHO African Region," November 2007, p. 1, at www.afro.who.int/vbc/reports/report_on_the_implementation_of_irs_in_the_african_region_2007.pdf (accessed December 3, 2008).

countries, at least initially.[19] National governments in recipient countries were eager to participate.

Because paternalistic attitudes pervaded much international aid policy in the years following World War II (and WHO was no exception), it was politically acceptable for rich countries to fund and carry out health campaigns in poorer countries without consulting much with the countries' health leaders. With strong political support from donor and often from recipient nations, WHO did not hesitate to pursue aggressive, vertical strategies with firm timelines and tight management. Expert personnel were recruited from private and public organizations, and protocols were borrowed from and built on the strategies implemented by other organizations.

For example, Brazilian Marcolino Candau, WHO's second director general, who launched WHO's first major malaria eradication campaigns in 1955, had previously worked under Fred L. Soper, who directed many of the vertical disease control programs at the Rockefeller Foundation[20] and later the Pan American Sanitary Bureau.[21] In the smallpox eradication campaigns of 1966–1979, WHO borrowed scientists from the CDC, the Institute of Sera and Vaccines in Prague, and the Pasteur Institute in Paris, among others.

The strategy yielded positive results, at least initially. Between the early 1960s and the early 1980s, infant mortality and under-five mortality rates fell in sub-Saharan Africa, partly due to successful vertical campaigns. The decline in the infant mortality rate (2.9 deaths per thousand per year) was less than in East Asia/China (3.8 deaths) and the Arab countries (3.4 deaths), but greater than in South Asia (2.2 deaths).[22] Even in South Asia,

---

19. For malaria, initial eradication campaigns enjoyed enormous success, but poor management and the growing politicization of intervention initiatives, coupled with donor fatigue, hobbled later efforts. By the 1970s, the number of malaria infections was increasing, driven by a resurgence of the disease in Africa and in countries previously declared free of the disease. Roger Bate, "Rolling Back Malaria: Rhetoric and Reality in the Fight against a Deadly Killer," American Enterprise Institute *Health Policy Outlook*, no. 4 (April 2008), at www.aei.org/publications/pub ID.27859/pub_detail.asp (accessed December 3, 2008).

20. For more information on the Rockefeller Foundation's initiatives, see Darwin H. Stapleton, "Lessons of History? Anti-Malaria Strategies of the International Health Board and the Rockefeller Foundation from the 1920s to the Era of DDT," *Public Health Reports*, March 1, 2004.

21. Theodore M. Brown, Marcos Cueto, and Elizabeth Fee, "The World Health Organization and the Transition from 'International' to 'Global' Public Health," *American Journal of Public Health* 96, no 1 (January 2006): 64.

22. Giovanni Andrea Cornia and Germano Mwabu, "Health Status and Health Policy in Sub-Saharan Africa: A Long-Term Perspective," United Nations University,

the limited success owed largely to "global initiatives and vertical national programs" against diarrhea and acute respiratory infections.[23] Still, sustaining success critically hinged on the recipient country's economic growth and specifically on governmental and private support for health interventions.

Failure to achieve these goals is a key reason why improvements ultimately languished in sub-Saharan Africa.[24] Economic development in Africa stagnated,[25] with direct implications for future health.[26] By 1999,

---

World Institute for Development Economics Research, July 1997, p. 3, at www-1 .unipv.it/cds/userfiles/file/Papers/paper_cornia_3.pdf (accessed December 3, 2008).

23. Zulfiqar A. Bhutta, "Why Has So Little Changed in Maternal and Child Health in South Asia?" *BMJ* 321, no. 7264 (September 30, 2000): 809, at www .pubmedcentral.nih.gov/articlerender.fcgi?artid = 1118621 (accessed December 3, 2008).

24. Economic crises, wars, subsequent displacement of peoples, and widespread adoption of socialist policies that slowed economic growth and directly stifled innovation in the health sector meant that improvements in infant mortality and life expectancy slowed in the region after 1980. By 1995 with the emergence of HIV/ AIDS in sub-Saharan Africa, infant mortality and life expectancy had deteriorated in many countries. Germano Mwabu, Issidor Noumba, Rachel Gesami, and Dominique Njinkeu, "Health Service Provision and Health Status in Africa," paper presented at the Global Development Network Conference, Prague, April 2002, revised February 2003, p. 8, at http://gdnet.org/pdf2/gdn_library/global_research_ projects/MERCK_health/Kenya_Cameroon_study.pdf (accessed December 3, 2008).

25. According to the World Bank, the annual growth rate in per capita income in Africa barely rose above 1 percent, compared to growth rates of 2–3 percent in similar economies elsewhere. Mwabu, Noumba, Gesami, and Njinkeu, "Health Service Provision." See also Gary Gereffi and Stephanie Fonda, "Regional Paths of Development," *Annual Review of Sociology* 18 (August 1992): 428, at www.jstor.org/sici? sici = 0360-0572(1992)18%3C419%3ARPOD%3E2.0.CO%3B2-7 (accessed December 3, 2008).

26. Infant mortality in sub-Saharan Africa declined 1.7 per thousand annually during 1980–1990, but slowed to 1.2 per thousand during 1990–1995. This may have been partly due to Africa's starting point of very high mortality rates and low life expectancies. This meant that, while early policy changes or vaccination programs had immediate and noticeable impacts, achieving each subsequent incremental improvement became increasingly difficult. The robust connection between improvements in GDP and health is well recognized in the literature. See Ann L. Owen and Stephen Wu, "Is Trade Good for Your Health?" *Review of International Economics* 15, no. 4 (September 2007): 660–82; Michael D. Stroup, "Economic Freedom, Democracy, and the Quality of Life," *World Development* 35, no. 1 (January 2007): 52–66; James Gwartney and Robert Lawson, *Economic Freedom of the World: 2007 Annual Report* (Vancouver, BC: Fraser Institute, 2007), at www.freetheworld .com/2007/EFW2007BOOK2.pdf (accessed December 3, 2008); and World Health

thirty-two countries in sub-Saharan Africa were poorer than they had been in 1980,[27] even while countries in other regions were enjoying rapid economic growth.[28]

New Goals and Mission Creep

Despite a reasonable number of successes, questions and criticisms of WHO's approach to international health gathered momentum in the 1970s. Donor countries began to question the wisdom and sustainability of large foreign aid transfers. Newly independent states in Africa were demanding a role in crafting policy. WHO's top-down, "paternalistic" campaigns of the past were growing increasingly unpalatable. These trends crystallized into policy at the September 1978 International Conference on Primary Care held in Alma-Ata (now Almaty), Kazakhstan, where "health for all" and "primary health care" were proclaimed as WHO's new goals.[29] Both goals were subsequently endorsed by the U.N. General Assembly in December 1979.

These two goals revolved around the principles of "equity, community involvement, appropriate technology, and a multisectoral approach."[30] Their practical effect was to broaden WHO's mandate significantly. WHO would no longer focus primarily on disease-specific programs, but would now promote health "development" more broadly by improving health systems, building infrastructure, and fighting chronic diseases.

The Health for All and Primary Health Care initiatives made several important contributions to development discourse and practice. They identified the need to strengthen underlying health systems and thereby improve health capacity, which is essential for any sustainable, long-term development beyond epidemic disease control. They also emphasized the

Organization, Commission on Intellectual Property Rights, Innovation and Public Health, *Public Health: Innovation and Intellectual Property Rights*, April 2006, at www .who.int/intellectualproperty/documents/thereport/CIPIH2303200 6.pdf (accessed December 3, 2008).

27. Paul Collier and Jan Willem Gunning, "Why Has Africa Grown Slowly?" *Journal of Economic Perspectives* 13, no. 3 (Summer 1999): 3–22.

28. A comparison between Indonesia and Nigeria is illustrative. Until around 1970, Nigeria's economic performance was broadly superior to Indonesia's performance, but over the next quarter century Nigeria's performance declined markedly, even though both countries experienced oil booms in their predominantly agricultural economies. Collier and Gunning, "Why Has Africa Grown Slowly?"

29. International Conference on Primary Health Care, "Declaration of Alma-Ata," Alma-Ata, Kazakhstan, September 6–12, 1978, at www.who.int/hpr/NPH/docs/declaration_almaata.pdf (accessed December 3, 2008).

30. World Health Organization, "The Fourth Decade: New Visions," in *50 Years of WHO in South-East Asia, Highlights: 1978–1987*, at www.searo.who.int/EN/Section898/Section1444_5859.htm (accessed December 3, 2008).

interconnection between health and other development issues, including economic growth and education, and identified the importance of country-level, local ownership. WHO leadership had long recognized the need for such policies, but most WHO member countries had done little to fill policy gaps. In 1948, for example, WHO's regional director for South-East Asia, Dr. C. Mani, noted that reducing morbidity from communicable diseases would not be possible "until basic health services [were] strengthened and adequately supervised so as to play their part."[31]

However, given the paucity of competent health-care practitioners and the lack of good governance in many nations, the new Health for All ethos enabled, even encouraged, mission creep. WHO expanded into many highly politicized areas where it had less technical ability, managerial competence, or experience, duplicating the efforts of other organizations including the well-funded and managerially more competent World Bank. WHO was often unable to secure adequate funding for success. WHO also failed to recognize or at least acknowledge that the radical changes to existing health-care delivery systems required to achieve "health for all" were ultimately the responsibility of health ministries of national governments, not a global body. Indeed, research by Alex Preker of the World Bank would later show that efforts to provide resources for horizontal health initiatives were far less effective than predicted, partly because they crowded out domestic (national government) health expenditures.[32]

In the wake of the global financial woes of the 1970s and amid growing distrust of the WHO's ability to allocate funding effectively, the World Health Organization began to lose funding.[33] In 1982, the World Health

---

31. World Health Organization, "The First Decade: Laying the Foundations," in *50 Years of WHO in South-East Asia*. In his seminal 1965 paper "Mass Campaigns and General Health Services," C. L. Gonzales criticized the false dichotomy between the horizontal (general health services / Health for All) approach and vertical (mass disease prevention and control campaigns) approach. Quoting from the *Annual Report of the Director-General for 1951*, Gonzales acknowledged that "campaigns for the eradication of diseases will have only temporary effects if they are not followed by the establishment of permanent health services in those areas." Anne Mills, "Mass Campaigns versus General Health Services: What Have We Learnt in 40 Years about Vertical versus Horizontal Approaches?" *Bulletin of the World Health Organization* 883, no. 4 (April 2005), at www.who.int/bulletin/volumes/83/4/315.pdf (accessed December 3, 2008).

32. Roger Bate, "G8 on Health: Spend Faster, Not Smarter," *American*, June 15, 2007, at www.american.com/archive/2007/june-0607/g8-on-health-spender-faster-not-smarter (accessed December 3, 2008).

33. The *Washington Post* bemoaned the fact that WHO was one of those "good" U.N. agencies that was hit "inadvertently but painfully by blows aimed at arms of the U.N. system that had gone politically sour or succumbed to mismanagement." "Who's at WHO," *Washington Post*, December 19, 1987, A22.

Assembly voted to freeze the organization's budget. In 1984, the Guttmacher Institute noted that WHO's Special Program of Research Development and Research Training in Human Reproduction had downsized its goals in response, including eight budget reductions since 1980.[34] In 1985, the United States withheld its entire pledged contribution to WHO's regular budget, partly to protest WHO's recent launch of an essential drugs program partly designed, to a certain extent, to encourage countries to develop their own pharmaceutical production.[35] The United States actively encouraged the director general to make cuts to the organization's budget.

Meanwhile, supporters of the organization were bemoaning what appeared to be growing politicization of the "sort that [had] plagued other United Nations agencies." For example, following the retirement of director-general Dr. Halfdan Mahler in 1988, a political squabble ensued. Health agency officials alleged that Japan had pressed "third-world governments" to support the candidacy of Dr. Hiroshi Nakajima as Mahler's replacement, "in some cases offering foreign aid projects as inducements."[36]

By the end of 1995, unpaid contributions from all member states had reached $243 million. The organization had been forced to borrow its entire internal reserve of over $175 million, forgoing its ability to respond quickly to health crises and the interest on its reserve.[37] Meanwhile, WHO's extrabudgetary funding, which allowed donors to track the use of their funds more closely, increased from 25 percent of WHO's total budget in the 1970s to 40 percent in 1980 and over 50 percent in 1990.[38]

---

34. Guttmacher Institute, "WHO Human Reproduction Program Funded 600 Projects in 160 Research Centers in 1983," *International Family Planning Perspectives* 10, no. 3 (September 1984), at www.jstor.org/stable/pdfplus/2947615.pdf (accessed December 3, 2008).

35. The program was fiercely opposed by the largest pharmaceutical companies, of which eleven of eighteen were based in the United States at the time. Fiona Godlee, "WHO in Retreat: Is It Losing Its Influence?" *BMJ* 309, no. 6967 (December 3, 1993), www.bmj.com/cgi/content/full/309/6967/1491 (accessed December 3, 2008).

36. Paul Lewis, "Divided World Health Organization Braces for Leadership Change," *New York Times*, May 1, 1988, at www.nytimes.com/1988/05/01/world/divided-world-health-organization-braces-for-leadership-change.html (accessed June 1, 2009).

37. Fiona Godlee, "New Hope for WHO?" *BMJ* 312, no. 7043 (June 1, 1996): 1376, at www.bmj.com/cgi/content/full/312/7043/1376 (accessed December 3, 2008).

38. J. Patrick Vaughan, Sigrun Mogedal, Gill Walt, Stein-Erik Kruse, Kelley Lee, and Koen de Wilde, "WHO and the Effects of Extrabudgetary Funds: Is the Organization Donor Driven?" *Health Policy and Planning* 11, no. 3 (September 1996): 254, at http://heapol.oxfordjournals.org/cgi/reprint/11/3/253 (accessed December 3, 2008). Such funding was a mixed blessing. It added to the organization's budget

Even as financial constraints made it increasingly impractical, WHO did little to focus its activities and remained committed to a "full-menu" programming approach. Critics routinely lambasted the organization for spending too much on its own bureaucracy. In 2002, only 40 percent of WHO resources went to countries and regions.[39] Money that did make it to the regions was not being spent efficiently. In many countries, national governments demonstrated little willingness to invest in necessary health resources and infrastructure, and endemic corruption meant that even well-intentioned WHO-directed aid had little impact.[40]

WHO's strong, semiautonomous regional offices often could more clearly identify and respond to each region's unique problems and were generally perceived to be more representative of local peoples. Yet they also duplicated efforts of the WHO secretariat and offered little accountability. Because regional directors were elected by member states, they were not directly accountable to the director general of WHO, were not necessarily subject to the same technical scrutiny as secretariat staff, and tended to be less insulated from local politics.

Recent Reform Efforts

When Dr. Gro Harlem Brundtland, a former prime minister of Norway, became director general in 1998, the organization was in desperate need of reform. She raised performance standards at WHO's Geneva headquarters, placed more than half of the staff on short-term contracts, and tightened the chain of command between the executive board and what had been

and, according to a 1996 analysis, generally included "more elaborate systems for planning and evaluation than for other, usually smaller, regular [budget] programmes." At the same time, however, programs financed by extrabudgetary funding paid "little attention to functional coordination and collaboration between programmes," leading to wasteful replication. Extrabudgetary funding was also contingent on the demands and priorities of donors, which were predominantly Western. Some critics voiced concerns that this voluntary, extrabudgetary support had the potential to be unpredictable and thereby constrain WHO's ability to respond to countries' long-term needs. In practice, core donors for the larger programs had been "remarkably loyal over many years." Vaughan et al., "WHO and the Effects of Extrabudgetary Funds," 254, 258. See also Fiona Godlee, "WHO's Special Programmes: Undermining from Above," *BMJ* 310, no. 6973 (January 21, 1995): 182, at www.bmj.com/cgi/content/full/310/6973/178/a (accessed December 8, 2008).

39. Lee Jong-wook, "End-of-Year Message to All WHO Staff from Director-General," World Health Organization, December 20, 2005, at www.who.int/dg/lee/speeches/2005/endofyear2005/en/index.html (accessed December 3, 2008).

40. Maureen Lewis, "Governance and Corruption in Public Health Care Systems" (Working Paper 78, Center for Global Development, January 2006), at www.cgdev.org/files/5967_file_WP_78.pdf (accessed December 6, 2008).

"powerful and largely independent units" within the Geneva office.[41] Although WHO did not acknowledge the outright failure of its Health for All campaign, its 1998 evaluation report recognized the initiative's numerous shortcomings.[42] By the end of the report, the phrasing "health for all" had been abandoned for the more qualified language of "health development," with emphasis on ownership by countries themselves. This change in phrasing signaled a subtle, but important, clarification of WHO's goals.[43]

Brundtland also renewed WHO's focus on public–private partnerships. Emboldened by resources brought to the table by private NGOs and foundations, as well as donor confidence in these partnerships' responsiveness and flexibility,[44] WHO helped launch several new public–private partnerships within the U.N. system, including Roll Back Malaria, the Global Alliance for Vaccines and Immunization (GAVI), and Stop TB Partnership.[45] Brundtland also boosted the organization's long isolated and underfunded

---

41. "A Triumph of Experience over Hope," *Economist*, May 24, 2001.

42. Under-five mortality and infant mortality had fallen when aggregated across all countries, but these indicators had been declining for decades prior to the launch of Health for All. In Africa, while there were "successes in the control of a number of endemic diseases," maternal mortality remained high in most countries, and HIV and tuberculosis were inadequately controlled. In the Americas, "the improvements in general morbidity, mortality, and in life expectancy were not attributable exclusively to the implementation of [Health for All and Primary Health Care initiatives] but chiefly to the political will of many governments to move forward in this area." World Health Organization, *Evaluation of the Implementation of the Global Strategy for Health for All by the Year 2000, 1979–1996*, WA 540.1 98EV, 1998, pp. 207–8.

43. World Health Organization, *Evaluation of the Implementation of the Global Strategy*, esp. 214–22.

44. Prior to Brundtland's tenure, WHO had encompassed other partnerships, such as the Global Polio Eradication Initiative, launched in 1988 by WHO, Rotary International, CDC, and UNICEF. Global Polio Eradication Initiative, "The History," at www.polioeradication.org/history.asp (accessed December 8, 2008).

45. See Roll Back Malaria Partnership, at www.rbm.who.int (December 8, 2008); GAVI Alliance, "Innovative Partnership," at www.gavialliance.org/about/in_part nership/index.php (accessed December 8, 2008); and Stop TB Partnership, "About the Stop TB Partnership: WHO Housing Arrangement," at www.stoptb.org/stop_ tb_initiative (accessed December 8, 2008). For a comprehensive discussion of public-private partnerships in the international health arena, see Sania Nishtar, "Public-Private 'Partnerships' in Health: A Global Call to Action," *Health Research Policy and Systems* 2, no. 5 (July 2004), at www.pubmedcentral.nih.gov/articlerender.fcgi? artid=514532 (accessed December 8, 2008). Other initiatives include Safe Injections Global Network (SIGN), Action TB (led by the private sector), the Global Alliance for TB Drug Development, the Concept Foundation, Malaria Vaccine Initiative (NGO hosted), the Mectizan Donation Program (NGO hosted), and the HIV Vaccine Initiative (NGO hosted).

Special Program for Research and Training in Tropical Diseases (TDR) to a more prominent position. WHO helped create—and joined the boards of—several independent initiatives, including the International AIDS Vaccine Initiative and Medicines for Malaria Venture.[46]

While not without problems,[47] such partnerships allowed WHO to focus on its comparative advantages. In its public-private partnerships, WHO hosted at most a secretariat[48] and in many cases played merely a technical or advisory role. In the Multilateral Initiative on Malaria, a global alliance launched in 1997 to maximize the impact of scientific research against malaria in Africa, TDR's role (and by extension WHO's role) was limited to helping to evaluate research applications from African malaria scientists and, in general, strengthening research capacities. In the Medicines for Malaria Venture, WHO's role was to offer "technical and public health guidance."[49] Management and implementation were left to private and other nongovernmental actors better suited to the tasks.[50]

Dr. Lee Jong-wook, Brundtland's successor, also corrected some of WHO's many problems when he assumed office in 2003. His recruitment of strong, technically qualified personnel dramatically improved WHO's focus and effectiveness in several key programs.[51] He also continued internal management and finance reforms, with the aim of "putting most of the budget where it was needed—in countries—and building strong accountability mechanisms." By 2005, 60 percent of WHO resources was going

---

46. World Health Organization, "Public-Private Partnerships for Health: Medicines for Malaria Venture," EB105/8 Add.1, January 6, 2000, at http://ftp.who.int/gb/archive/pdf_files/EB105/ee8a1.pdf (accessed December 8, 2008).

47. For instance, collective "ownership" meant that partners could glory in successes and at the same time skirt responsibility for failures. Critics also suggested that close engagement with the private sector might jeopardize the organization's role as an "advocate for all." Judith Richter, "Public–Private Partnerships for Health: A Trend with No Alternatives?" *Development* 47, no. 2 (June 2004): 43–48, at www.haiweb.org/pdf/JRichterSIDArticle2004.pdf (accessed December 8, 2008).

48. This is true of SIGN. WHO hosts the secretariat through its Department of Essential Health Technologies. World Health Organization, "Injection Safety: The Objectives," at www.who.int/injection_safety/about/strategy/en/index.html (accessed December 8, 2008).

49. World Health Organization, "Public-Private Partnerships for Health."

50. As a 2000 WHO report acknowledged, industry engagement in the Medicines for Malaria Venture lent professionalism to the venture while the public sector shouldered "the direct costs of research and development and of the risk of failure." World Health Organization, "Public-Private Partnerships for Health."

51. Dr. Arata Kochi, who had worked in WHO's tuberculosis program, proved to be an effective leader of the revamped Global Malaria Program. Kevin DeCock was an effective performer in the field of HIV/AIDS.

directly to countries and regions.[52] Better internal management (WHO reduced administrative costs by 15 percent in 1999)[53] and greater transparency in spending improved donor trust. In 2005, member states increased WHO's regular budget by 4 percent, reversing earlier declines.[54] Extrabudgetary funding continued to increase, accounting for 71 percent of the budget in 2004–2005.[55]

Following Lee's untimely death in May 2006, Dr. Margaret Chan, a former assistant director for the organization's Communicable Diseases cluster, was elected director general.[56] It is still perhaps too early in Chan's tenure to assess her record. While she publicly acknowledges the need for reform, she at times seems reluctant to unambiguously endorse tailoring WHO's activities to its strengths.

For instance, Chan pledged to assess the performance of WHO's assistant director generals, introduced travel restrictions for senior staff, and affirmed the need to streamline the number of publications produced by the agency.[57] She also reaffirmed the need for WHO to focus its efforts and work with other actors in international health. Shortly after her election, she signaled strong willingness to coordinate WHO efforts with other agencies and NGOs by spending several weeks meeting with Bill and Melinda

---

52. Lee, "End-of-Year Message."

53. Barry Bloom, David Bloom, Joel Cohen, and Jeffrey Sachs, "Investing in the World Health Organization," *Science* 284, no. 5416 (May 7, 1999): 911, at www .sciencemag.org/cgi/content/summary/284/5416/911 (accessed December 8, 2008).

54. World Health Organization, Regional Office for South-East Asia, "Review of Detailed Workplans for Programme Budget 2006–2007," July 29, 2005, at www .searo.who.int/en/Section1430/Section1439/Section1638/Section1889/Section2036 _10335.htm (accessed December 8, 2008).

55. This does not include donations to non-WHO program activities including trust funds of various programs and entities (e.g., Trust Fund for the Joint United Nations Program on HIV/AIDS, International Agency for Research on Cancer, and Global Fund). World Health Organization, "Financial Report 2004–2005," at www .who.int/gb/ebwha/pdf_files/WHA59/A59_28-en.pdf (accessed January 5, 2009).

56. Chan had almost thirty years of public health experience, including a long tenure as Hong Kong's director of health, during which she led the country's response to two global health crises: avian influenza (1997) and SARS (2003). Bryan Walsh, "Who's Next at WHO?" *Time* Global Health Blog, July 25, 2006, at http://time.blogs.com/global_health/2006/07/whos_next_at_wh.html (accessed December 8, 2008); and Miriam Shuchman, "Improving Global Health—Margaret Chan at the WHO," *New England Journal of Medicine* 365, no. 7 (February 15, 2007), at http://content.nejm.org/cgi/content/full/356/7/653 (accessed December 8, 2008).

57. Editorial, "Margaret Chan Puts Primary Health Care Centre Stage at WHO," *Lancet* 371, no. 9627 (May 31, 2008): 1811.

Gates and "high-ranking officials at all the major international health agencies" to "identify priorities and decide who is doing what."[58]

In her 2008 address to the World Health Assembly, Chan said that she rejects the full-menu approach for WHO programming and has "a duty to steer the work of this Organization into areas where [its] leadership offers a unique advantage."[59] Yet she has also expressed a desire to resurrect the vision of primary health care articulated in the 1978 Alma-Ata Health for All declaration.[60] Health for All is a bold cheerleading vision, but only individual states can address its delivery. Two of the three "global crises"—food security, climate change, and a global influenza epidemic—that she identified in her address[61] lie outside of WHO's expertise or mandate. While lack of food has serious health consequences, it may be better addressed by other U.N. entities, such as the U.N.'s Food and Agriculture Organization, World Food Program, UNDP, and World Bank. While climate change may lead to deleterious impacts on health, policy solutions lie outside of WHO's expertise and authority.[62]

RECURRENT CHALLENGES
AND NEEDED REFORMS

The World Health Organization has begun a reform process that will hopefully direct it toward roles in which it complements—rather than competes with—the activities of other international health institutions, national health institutions, and private-sector health efforts. Still, the organization

---

58. Shuchman, "Improving Global Health."

59. Margaret Chan, address to the 61st World Health Assembly, Geneva, May 19, 2008, at www.who.int/dg/speeches/2008/20080519/en/index.html (accessed December 8, 2008).

60. "If we want to reach the health-related goals," she admonished delegates at the 2008 World Health Assembly, "we must return to the values, principles, and approaches of primary health care," including investment in human and institutional capacity, health information, and systems for delivery. Chan, address to the 61st World Health Assembly.

61. Ibid.

62. "In the developing world, the main defects [in health delivery] are in the social matrix—a scarcity of basic needs: shelter; food; clothing; electricity; clean water; a safe living environment; education and access to healthcare. . . . In nearly all cases, climate is at most a minor, often irrelevant parameter." Paul Reiter and Roger Bate, "Climate Change: A Challenge for Public Health," testimony before Committee on Health, Education, Labor, and Pensions, U.S. Senate, April 10, 2008, at www.aei.org/docLib/20080410_Bate_testimony.pdf (accessed December 8, 2008).

faces a long road ahead. Specifically, WHO and its member states need to correct the organization's:

- Ambiguous mandate and overambitious rhetoric
- Duplication of other agencies' efforts
- Susceptibility to political influence
- Failure to focus on results
- Tendency to exceed its mandate and capabilities
- Statist bias

Ambiguous Mandate and Overambitious Role

WHO's ambiguous mandate and inflated rhetoric have translated into a poorly defined, overambitious role. "The almost limitless scope of the international medical field," Melville Mackenzie warned in an address at Chatham House in 1950, meant that there were "certain problems that [lent] themselves to international collaboration and others which [did] not." Malaria and cholera—for which the causes, treatments, and preventions were known—were "ripe for international collaboration." However, research on cancer and leprosy might best be done nationally. It would be difficult, Mackenzie acknowledged, "to keep the work of the organization on the right lines . . . to prevent the development of projects in which we cannot hope to produce adequate results."[63]

A pertinent example is WHO's continued focus on chronic diseases and other "lifestyle" issues, such as substance abuse, high blood pressure, cholesterol, tobacco use, and obesity. These programs divert attention, time, and money from other, more immediate priorities such as epidemic diseases.[64] In 1998, the organization launched the Global Initiative on Primary Prevention of Substance Abuse. In 2002, the World Health Assembly issued a resolution urging member states to collaborate with WHO and calling on the director general to "develop a global strategy on diet, physical activity and health . . . for the prevention and control of noncommunicable

63. Melville Mackenzie, "International Collaboration in Health," *International Affairs* 26, no. 4 (October 1950): 515–21.

64. See World Health Assembly, "Diet, Physical Activity and Health," WHA55.23, May 18, 2002, at http://ftp.who.int/gb/archive/pdf_files/WHA55/ewha5523.pdf (accessed December 8, 2008); World Health Organization, "Process for a Global Strategy on Diet, Physical Activity and Health," February 2003, at http://whqlibdoc.who.int/hq/2003/WHO_NMH_EXR.02.2_Rev.1.pdf (accessed December 8, 2008); and Shanthi Mendis, Derek Yach, and Ala Alwan, "Air Travel and Venous Thromboembolism," *Bulletin of the World Health Organization* 80, no. 5 (2002): 403–6, at http://whqlibdoc.who.int/bulletin/2002/Vol80-No5/bulletin_2002_80(5)_403-4 06.pdf (accessed December 8, 2008).

diseases,"[65] which the director general later fleshed out to include high blood pressure, cholesterol, tobacco use, alcohol abuse, and obesity.

In 2002, WHO also convened an international meeting of medical experts, airline companies, and consumer groups to probe the potential causal link between air travel and venous thromboembolism. The group concluded that the "the risk was not quantifiable because of a lack of data" and "was likely to be small and mainly affect passengers with additional risk factors for venous thromboembolism." Yet the group agreed that WHO and the International Civil Aviation Organization would conduct a series of large clinical studies to consider its impact.[66]

Problems such as diabetes and heart disease predominantly afflict older people in more developed countries: the United States, European countries, and increasingly, countries such as India and China. In less-developed countries, many people simply do not live long enough to experience such health problems. Therefore, these problems can be addressed more effectively by (generally wealthier) developed-country governments or nongovernmental agencies. Instead of worrying about "economy-class syndrome (when passengers on long flights develop blood clots in their legs)" and international tobacco control, WHO should "concentrate on the biggest killers in the countries least able to cope without assistance": AIDS, tuberculosis, and malaria, especially in Africa.[67]

Even when formal mandates are complementary, overlapping authorities lead to "an unclear delineation of activities."[68] A relevant example is WHO's decision to reestablish its own HIV department at the beginning of 2001[69]—only a year after it helped to found the Accelerated Access Initiative, a public–private partnership of five pharmaceutical companies, WHO, UNAIDS, World Bank, and other U.N. agencies to accelerate and improve access to HIV/AIDS-related care and treatment in the developing world.

This problem is not exclusive to WHO. A third of U.N. initiatives involve more than ten U.N. agencies, inevitably duplicating administrative efforts and creating overlapping mandates.[70] The World Bank has also been faulted

---

65. World Health Assembly, "Diet, Physical Activity and Health."

66. Mendis et al., "Air Travel and Venous Thromboembolism," 405.

67. "A Shower of Lifesaving Dollars," *Economist*, January 30, 2003.

68. Kelley Lee, Sue Collinson, Gill Walt, and Lucy Gilson, "Who Should Be Doing What in International Health: A Confusion of Mandates in the United Nations," *BMJ* 312, no. 7026 (February 3, 1996): 302–7, at http://bmj.bmjjournals .com/cgi/content/short/312/7026/302 (accessed December 8, 2008).

69. Roger Bate and Lorraine Mooney, "WHO's Comprehensive HIV Treatment Failure: Will We Learn the Real Lessons from 3 by 5?" (Working Paper 133, American Enterprise Institute, November 2006), at www.aei.org/docLib/20061130_ AEIWP133.pdf (accessed December 8, 2008).

70. High-Level Panel on UN System-Wide Coherence in the Areas of Development, Humanitarian Assistance, and the Environment, "Delivering as One,"

for expanding into areas outside its traditional ambit. By 2001, it had acquired tasks as disparate as Balkan reconstruction, education for girls in Muslim countries, and the fight against AIDS, making its mission so complex as to be unwieldy.[71]

WHO's early efforts at malaria eradication ultimately fell short because donors grew tired of supporting what turned out to be decades-long initiatives. In September 1971, WHO admitted that it had "not been possible to pursue a vigorous campaign to eradicate malaria because of deficiencies in planning, management, administrative problems and *particularly lack of government funds.*"[72] Eradication in all countries, many of which lacked the necessary infrastructure to mount ongoing malaria control measures, proved to be an overambitious, unsustainable goal—much like many of the targets set in later decades.

In some cases, WHO has even launched unfunded programs with the hope that the subsequent media blitz would generate the necessary support. Its drug prequalification program was launched hurriedly, even though it was underresourced and underdeveloped. Yet funding was not forthcoming because the program lacked credibility, and the program languished, poorly funded and poorly implemented.

Duplication of Efforts

At the outset, WHO experienced difficulty in defining its relationship with nonmembers, both states and nonstates, including earlier regional initiatives and other U.N. funds, programs, and efforts. Considering their disparate origins and different political imperatives,[73] the difficulty of

---

November 9, 2006, at www.un.org/events/panel/resources/pdfs/HLP-SWC-FinalReport.pdf (accessed December 8, 2008).

71. Jessica Einhorn, "The World Bank's Mission Creep," *Foreign Affairs* (September/October 2001); and Alex Shakow, *Global Fund–World Bank HIV/AIDS Programs: A Comparative Advantage Study*, Global Fund to Fight AIDS, Tuberculosis and Malaria and the World Bank Global HIV/AIDS Program, January 19, 2006, at http://siteresources.worldbank.org/ INTHIVAIDS/ Resources / 375798-1103037153392/GFWB ReportFinalVersion.pdf (accessed December 8, 2008).

72. World Health Organization, Regional Committee for the Western Pacific, "Malaria," WPR/RC22.R5, September 23, 1971, at www.wpro.who.int/rcm/en/archives/rc22/wpr_rc22_r05.htm (accessed December 8, 2008) (emphasis added).

73. For instance, the Pan American Sanitary Bureau, which serves as the secretariat of the Pan American Health Organization, was created in 1902 as a regional organization to exchange and disseminate epidemiological information and other health data. In May 1949, the bureau became a WHO regional office. Walter R. Sharp, "The New World Health Organization," *American Journal of International Law*

coordinating efforts between Geneva headquarters and regional offices is not surprising. At its founding, WHO absorbed a host of long-standing regional health programs. Today, regional offices remain largely autonomous, with regional directors appointed by member states rather than the collective assembly, making it difficult for the director general to correct regional failings, remove duplication, or prioritize expenditures. For instance, a 2004 editorial in the *Lancet*, a British medical journal, accused the Africa office of "having an ineffective and self-serving management" that acted as a political rather than a technical agency. Although the entire organization was criticized for its staffing decisions, the Africa regional office was singled out in particular for recruiting staff "rarely based on competence or qualification."[74]

Outside the U.N. system, poor communication with nonmembers can exacerbate administrative waste and program duplication. In 2005, WHO attempted to rectify this for its HIV/AIDS initiatives by creating the Global Task Team on Improving AIDS Coordination among Multilateral Institutions and International Donors.[75]

Yet questions remain unresolved, including which agency will have the final say when initiatives with other U.N. bodies overlap, how to coordinate activities between WHO and its regional offices, and how WHO's chain of command can be enforced. WHO has little ability to demand— and whether it should is questionable—the participation of key bilateral initiatives involved with HIV/AIDS work, such as the President's Emergency Plan for AIDS Relief, even though reducing conflicts, reducing duplication, and bolstering cooperation are in the interests of such initiatives.

41, no. 3 (July 1947): 509–30. When determining the relationship between the pre-existing regional Pan American Sanitary Bureau and the new World Health Organization, "a controversy developed." Lleras-Restrepo of Colombia "raised the objection . . . that the Pan-American Sanitary Bureau should not be abolished, but rather 'coordinated' with the international health organization." "World Health Organization," *International Organization* 1, no. 1 (February 1947): 134–36.

74. Editorial, "WHO's African Regional Office," *Lancet* 364, no. 9433 (August 7, 2004).

75. Joint United Nations Program on HIV/AIDS, "Global Task Team," www.u-naids.org/en/CountryResponses/MakingTheMoneyWork/GTT (accessed December 8, 2008). Other efforts are also working independently of WHO to achieve effective coordination, such as the Comprehensive Development Framework, a concept developed by the World Bank, but officially embraced by U.N. agencies. Analysts hope that it will "lead to increased co-operation and a more constructive division of labour." Leiv Lunde, "Coherence or Dissonance in the International Institutional Framework: Overlapping Responsibilities," Center for Economic Analysis, December 2000, at www.g24.org/lunde.pdf (accessed December 8, 2008).

Susceptibility to Political Influence

In theory, one benefit of WHO is its "ability to bring scientific evidence to bear in political disputes that often lose sight of facts on the ground."[76] In practice, however, as a membership organization that relies on the funding and cooperation of its members, WHO is often constrained by political disputes that are unrelated to health.

This is especially evident in health crises that involve countries that include de facto authorities that WHO does not recognize. For example, in early March 2003, Taiwan became one of the first authorities in the region to report suspected SARS cases to WHO by offering to share information and cooperate with international organizations and governments fighting the disease. However, because the U.N. regards Taiwan as part of the People's Republic of China, Taiwan's participation is dependent on Beijing, which has consistently refused to let Taiwan become a member state of WHO. During the SARS crisis, WHO officials could only encourage the Taiwanese to contact authorities in Beijing, who had several months earlier refused to allow WHO to investigate a suspected SARS outbreak in China's Guangdong Province. Taiwanese authorities were denied access to WHO meetings and WHO's Global Outbreak Alert and Response Network, the organization's rapid global alert and reporting mechanism. According to Taiwanese health professionals, WHO was "hindering all the circulation of disease information" by adhering to its member-state-only policy.[77] Encouragingly, there were signs in early 2009 that WHO was beginning to relax its policy: Taiwan was admitted as an observer at the World Health Assembly and was also included in negotiations surrounding an International Health Regulations framework.

In some cases, WHO has foisted programs on member states without much consultation. For example, WHO did not spend sufficient time or resources developing country-specific plans for its 3 by 5 Initiative, which it launched in 2003 with the aim of treating three million people suffering from HIV by the end of 2005. This led it to push some poor country governments, including Sierra Leone and Lesotho, to attempt to treat more HIV/AIDS patients than could be sustained. In South Africa, the government opted to run and fund its own national program independently of

---

76. Steven Menashi, "The Politics of the WHO," *New Atlantis*, no. 3 (Fall 2003): 88, at www.thenewatlantis.com/publications/the-politics-of-the-who (accessed December 8, 2008).

77. Shao-Yen Chou, "2008 Taiwan's Proposal to the WHO Executive Board," Peace Forum, May 8, 2008, at www.peaceforum.org.tw/onweb.jsp?webno = 3333 333712&webitem_no = 1411 (accessed December 8, 2008). This agreement was articulated in the memorandum of understanding between China and the WHO Secretariat in 2005.

WHO because, as it argued among other less credible reasons, WHO set ambitious goals without providing the funding to support those goals.[78]

In other cases, WHO is viewed as too close to national governments and unable to provide impartial, scientific advice. In the 3 by 5 Initiative, participating countries were often "ambivalent" about WHO's role, sometimes seeing WHO as a barrier rather than a facilitator. Development partners in the U.N. system, civil society, and the private sector criticized WHO for "hiding behind government policy, not addressing controversial issues or neglecting other players."[79]

Failure to Focus on Results

All multilateral and even the best bilateral agencies do not measure performance well enough; they generally measure inputs such as *how much* money is spent rather than *how* it is spent and whether it achieves the desired goal of lower disease rates. WHO's failure to focus on results is both a cause and a consequence of unavailable (or else poorly interpreted) international health data, exacerbated by a self-perpetuating bureaucracy. At the end of September 2007, the *Lancet* published papers exposing the United Nations' misuse of scientific information on child mortality, especially in relation to malaria. "UN agencies are willing to play fast and loose with scientific findings in order to further their own institutional interests," the editorial soberly concluded.[80]

In another instance, Roll Back Malaria, the organization's antimalaria campaign launched in 1998, pledged to halve the incidence of malaria between 1998 and 2010, but lacked a baseline for malaria incidence and did not try to establish one.[81] UNICEF's latest assessment report of the Roll Back Malaria Partnership highlights the program's success in dispersing antimalarial resources: "Global funding has increased more than tenfold over the past decade. . . . There has been real progress in scaling up the use of insecticide-treated nets across sub-Saharan Africa." However, the report gives scant attention to the impact of such dispersion on actual health indi-

---

78. Shao-Yen Chou, "2008 Taiwan's Proposal"; and Maria Ines Battistella Nemes, Jean Beaudoin, Shaun Conway, George Washington Kivumbi, Anne Skjelmerud, and Ulrich Vogel, "Evaluation of WHO's Contribution to '3 by 5,'" World Health Organization, 2006, at www.who.int/hiv/pub/me/3by5evaluation/en/index.html (accessed December 8, 2008).

79. Bate and Mooney, "WHO's Comprehensive HIV Treatment Failure."

80. Editorial, "Science at WHO and UNICEF: The Corrosion of Trust," *Lancet* 370, no. 9592 (September 22, 2007): 1007.

81. Bate, "Rolling Back Malaria."

cators, such as infant mortality and life expectancy, although in practice, these indicators are hard to measure.[82]

In 2007, WHO announced that it was downgrading its 2006 estimate for the total number of people living with HIV by nearly 7 million, largely because of revised epidemiological methods in India and sub-Saharan Africa. WHO's acknowledgment and correction of the error is commendable, but calls into question the veracity and reliability of other WHO data.

Poor-quality, misreported data from member states—which WHO does not adequately monitor—is undoubtedly part of the problem. In 2008, the *Lancet* published a study revealing disparities between official reports (based on countries' own administrative data) and independent, multi-country surveys of the number of children vaccinated under programs such as the Universal Childhood Immunisation campaign and GAVI. According to multicountry surveys, only half as many children (7.4 million) had been vaccinated with the three-dose childhood diphtheria, tetanus, and pertussis vaccine (DPT3) as had been suggested by official reports to WHO and UNICEF (13.9 million). Because GAVI disperses payments in proportion to the number of additional children targeted or reported to have received DPT3, some experts feared that countries may have been artificially inflating their numbers. "That's how you get money," Ken Hill, a public health professor at Harvard University who was not linked to the study, told the Associated Press. "You exaggerate the number of people who die or who you save. . . . Somehow, numbers always end up bigger than they would be otherwise."[83] In an era of global target-oriented, performance-based initiatives, there is "urgent need," authors concluded, "for independent and contestable monitoring of health indicators."[84]

In addition to lapses in technical competency, WHO has sometimes strayed from its commitment to technical objectivity. The organization's oft-cited *World Health Report 2000* features a health performance index that reflects, as economist Glen Whitman has written, "implicit value judgments and assumptions." According to Whitman, only two of the index's five components are objective measures of actual health attainment.[85]

---

82. U.N. Children's Fund, "Malaria and Children: Progress in Intervention and Coverage," September 22, 2007, at www.unicef.org/health/index_malaria.html (accessed December 8, 2008).

83. Maria Cheng, "Dozens of Nations Inflated Vaccine Numbers," Associated Press, December 12, 2008.

84. Stephen S. Lim, David B. Stein, Alexandra Charrow, and Christopher J. L. Murray, "Tracking Progress towards Universal Childhood Immunisation and the Impact of Global Initiatives: A Systematic Analysis of Three-Dose Diphtheria, Tetanus, and Pertussis Immunisation Coverage," *Lancet* 372, no. 9655 (December 13, 2008).

85. Glen Whitman, "WHO's Fooling Who? The World Health Organization's Problematic Ranking of Health Care Systems" (Cato Institute Briefing Paper 101,

Until September 2006, WHO refused to actively endorse indoor spraying of DDT to combat malaria, despite evidence that such spraying posed minimal health risks and no environmental risks and was saving thousands of lives annually in southern Africa and other malarial areas. While it listed DDT as an approved insecticide, it had done nothing to promote its use, instead favoring alternative methods of malaria prevention. Furthermore, the World Health Assembly has still not repealed a 1997 directive that pushes against the use of all insecticides.[86]

Too often, WHO has concealed its shortcomings instead of acknowledging them, hoping to avoid international embarrassment and the funding cuts that would likely result. When it became clear in late 2005 that the vaunted 3 by 5 Initiative would not even approach its goal of treating 3 million people in poor and middle-income countries with antiretroviral drugs, the organization became strangely quiet about the program.[87] UNAIDS and WHO's 2005 "AIDS Epidemic Update," mentioned it only once, as a parenthetical reference for successful programs in Kenya and Brazil.[88] While treatment gaps were expected to narrow in these countries, they would not do so at a "pace required to effectively contain the epidemic," it admitted.[89] The report failed to ask why, which would have most certainly included a discussion of shortcomings of the 3 by 5 program.

While much of the blame must rest with national governments that failed to deliver treatment, WHO was fully aware of these limitations when it set its unrealistic, politically motivated targets for each country. In November 2005, South Africa's health minister, Dr. Manto Tshabalala-Msimang, bristled at suggestions that the government was deliberately

---

February 28, 2008), at www.cato.org/pubs/bp/bp101.pdf (accessed December 8, 2008). See World Health Organization, *The World Health Report 2000: Health Systems: Improving Performance*, 2000, at www.who.int/whr/2000/en/whr00_en.pdf (accessed December 12, 2008).

86. World Health Assembly, "Promotion of Chemical Safety, with Special Attention to Persistent Organic Pollutants," Resolution 50.13, May 1997, at www.who.int/ipcs/publications/wha/whares_53_13/en/index.html (accessed December 8, 2008). While this directive does not oppose insecticide use as strongly as many other U.N. pronouncements, such as the UNEP Stockholm Convention on Persistent Organic Pollutants, it is important because WHO is the most important body where health is allegedly the highest priority.

87. "Spin Doctors," *Economist*, November 24, 2005.

88. Joint United Nations Program on HIV/AIDS and World Health Organization, "AIDS Epidemic Update," UNAIDS/05.19E, December 2005, 8, at www.unaids.org/epi/2005/doc/EPIupdate2005_pdf_en/epi-update2005_en.pdf (accessed December 8, 2008).

89. Joint United Nations Program on HIV/AIDS and World Health Organization, "AIDS Epidemic Update," 5.

denying drugs to people by failing to meet the target set unilaterally by WHO. "[Our] Government is not withholding treatment for opportunistic infections, including [antiretroviral drugs]," said Tshabalala-Msimang. "Our objective is to promote quality healthcare. We are not just chasing numbers."[90]

Exceeding Its Mandate and Capabilities

WHO publishes lists of approved "essential medicines," which the World Bank, the Global Fund, and many private-sector donors use when determining which drugs to purchase for developing countries. However, WHO does not have the technical capacity to act as a drug authority, at least compared with the U.S. Food and Drug Administration (FDA) or the European Medicines Agency.[91] While WHO has the capacity in principle to analyze drug-quality data provided by independent laboratories commissioned by drug companies, it has not always received such data prior to granting approval.

In 2004, WHO withdrew five drugs manufactured by Indian companies from its prequalification list, and the companies voluntarily withdrew seven more. The companies had failed to provide adequate evidence of bioequivalence, which demonstrates that the generic drug works in the same way as the original product. Prior to this withdrawal, developing-country governments and aid organizations had used WHO's list as a guide when buying unproven drugs for the poor, with unknown consequences. Agencies still rely heavily on the WHO list, under the assumption that drug quality is acceptable.

The WHO Pesticides Evaluation Scheme (WHOPES) was another well-intentioned WHO "credentialing" program that lacked the capacity for broad effectiveness. Founded in 1961, WHOPES provides a four-phase evaluation and testing program for approval of insecticides applied to bed nets and used in insecticide residual spraying or larviciding. The program's approval of long-lasting insecticide nets has been criticized for delays in approving nets (an average of two years) and the lack of postmarket surveillance, or ongoing quality checks after initial approval.[92]

---

90. Manto Tshabalala-Msimang, quoted in Roger Bate, "WHO's AIDS Target: An Inevitable Failure," American Enterprise Institute *Health Policy Outlook*, no. 3 (January 19, 2006), at www.aei.org/publications/pubID.23712/pub_detail.asp (accessed December 8, 2008).

91. Jeremiah Norris and Catherine Fisher, "A Summary of Key Issues on National Drug Regulatory Authorities in the Developing World," Hudson Institute, March 2008, at www.hudson.org/files/documents/CSPP%20March%20White%20Paper%203%2007%2008.pdf (accessed December 8, 2008).

92. One critic suggests that this practice may have unfairly favored one company over another. Philip Coticelli, "WHOPES and Its Impact on Long-Lasting Insectici-

WHO openly acknowledges that it "is not a regulatory authority" and that "the regulatory approval of pesticide products is the sole prerogative of national authorities."[93] Its recommendations are designed to facilitate pesticide registration and use in countries that lack the technical capacity to assess such pesticides on their own or for products that more stringent regulatory authorities have little incentive to assess. For instance, having eradicated its own malaria scourge more than fifty years ago, the U.S. government may be hard pressed to rationalize significant funding for testing different brands of long-lasting insecticide-treated bed nets. Thus, the WHOPES program serves an important function, at least in principle. Still, it is not clear that the program has to be WHO specific.

Worse, WHO can greatly undermine future health through shortsighted intervention in areas in which it has broad, but insufficient, expertise, such as intellectual property rights. It is expected that WHO will champion immediate assistance for the poor, but immediate public health need is not the only criterion for assessing patent enforcement and drug pricing. WHO director general Chan demonstrated her uncertainty when she vacillated on the issue of access and innovation in pharmaceuticals when pressured by the pharmaceutical industry and Western governments on one side and the Thai government and antipatent NGOs on the other. When Thailand broke patents for several HIV/AIDS drugs and one heart disease medicine in early 2007, she initially seemed to rebuke Thailand, then appeared to support its right to break patents, and then went silent, leaving the situation in limbo. WHO could play a constructive role by driving patent-holding manufacturers to differentiate their prices (lowering prices further in the poorest nations, but raising them in mid-income nations), while appealing to member governments and NGOs to uphold intellectual property rights in mid-income countries.

Statist Bias

As an international governmental body composed of representatives of national governments—many of which are hostile to private markets—WHO sees public goods (and market failures) in more areas than most economists would. For example, it supports claims that pharmaceutical research for diseases that predominantly affect the developing world is a

dal Net Availability," Africa Fighting Malaria occasional paper, April 2007, at www.-fightingmalaria.org/pdfs/AFM_WHOPES_LLN.pdf (accessed December 8, 2008).

93. World Health Organization, response to Africa Fighting Malaria occasional paper, at http://rbm.who.int/docs/WHOPES_Coticelli.pdf (accessed December 8, 2008).

market failure and demands more research funded by taxpayers to provide the "public good" of treatments, immunizations, or cures for these diseases. It has already done this for malaria, leishmaniasis, and Chagas disease.

While more drugs for more developing-world diseases would be welcome, the major problem of combating most diseases is not the paucity of drugs, but lack of funds to buy and deliver them. These are failures of poverty and governmental inadequacy, not the market. WHO's support of positions anathema to private-sector research and development (e.g., its vacillation on intellectual property rights) has probably encouraged at least some large pharmaceutical companies to move away from such research. For example, pharmaceutical company Eli Lilly quietly left HIV/AIDS research many years ago. Companies that develop drugs for neglected diseases are generally unable to garner any profit from these enterprises and often incur losses, which are a considerable disincentive to future research and development.

In much of the world, the private sector provides nearly all health services. In Africa, over half of drugs are bought privately. WHO has been guilty of proposing to reform the private sector, or more often to replace it by state action, without input from the private sector itself. The latest manifestation of this problem is the Global Fund and WHO's Affordable Medicines Facility for Malaria (AMFm). The initiative would provide a $2 billion subsidy to lower the price of malaria drugs in the supply and distribution chains in Africa. Yet neither the Global Fund nor WHO has actively consulted with the main drugmakers or the wholesalers that they will use. Some fear that the AMFm may increase drug resistance by subsidizing substandard drugs. At its November 2008 meeting, the Global Fund board approved the pilot for the project.[94] Hopefully, WHO members and Global Fund financiers will demand evidence of success before rolling out the project elsewhere.

WHAT CAN BE DONE?

Although the World Health Organization has historically been an important international health organization, it is not alone. The World Bank has a prominent role in promoting health in developing countries. UNAIDS, the Global Fund, and other international organizations have been created to combat specific diseases. National organizations, such as the CDC and

---

94. Global Fund to Fight AIDS, Tuberculosis and Malaria, "Affordable Medicines Facility—Malaria," Decision Point GF/B18/DP7, 18th Board Meeting, November 7–8, 2008, at www.theglobalfund.org/documents/board/18/GF-BM18-Decision Points_een.pdf (accessed December 13, 2008).

U.S. Food and Drug Administration, are often better equipped than WHO to perform certain tasks. Nongovernmental organizations, such as Médecins Sans Frontières (Doctors Without Borders) and the Gates Foundation, have assumed an increasingly prominent role in influencing international health policy, financing health initiatives, and providing treatment and expertise. However, WHO officials can provide much-needed reflection on the role of these independent groups, as has already happened in at least one case.[95] If WHO is to find a place in the increasingly crowded arena of international health, it must reform. Specifically, WHO should divest itself of inappropriate roles, missions, and activities; focus the organization's mission around its comparative advantages; and enhance the authority and power of the director general.

Divesting Itself of Inappropriate Roles, Missions, and Activities

Compared to the performance of bilateral and private-sector initiatives, the U.N.'s track record is spotty in many instances. WHO is no exception. A 2007 Center for Global Development report found that the President's Emergency Plan for AIDS Relief bested the World Bank and the U.N.-backed Global Fund to Fight AIDS, Tuberculosis and Malaria in channeling aid money into on-the-ground initiatives in Zambia, Uganda, and Mozambique.[96]

When WHO engages in activities for which it is ill suited, it can do more harm than good. It may set goals for and direct money to policies that are antithetical to the realities on the ground. It may unduly focus on public-sector development initiatives when the private sector is already playing a greater role, squandering valuable time and resources in counterproductive or duplicative initiatives.

To correct these problems, WHO should:

- *End its implementation programs.* With the Global Fund well positioned to fulfill the niche of funding distribution and the myriad bilateral and nongovernmental initiatives pursuing disease and issue-specific programs, WHO should shed its implementation programs and instead

95. Roger Bate, "Stifling Dissent on Malaria," *American*, December 8, 2008, at www.american.com/archive/2008/december-12-08/stifling-dissent-on-malaria (accessed January 5, 2009).

96. Nandini Oomman, Michael Bernstein, and Steven Rosenzweig, "Following the Funding for HIV/AIDS: A Comparative Analysis of the Funding Practices of PEPFAR, the Global Fund and World Bank MAP in Mozambique, Uganda and Zambia," Center for Global Development, October 10, 2007, www.cgdev.org/content/publications/detail/14569 (accessed December 8, 2008).

focus on what it does best: providing technical, clinical, and public health advice to poor countries applying for aid money and to implementing agencies looking for the most cost-effective ways to use aid money.

- *Leave primary health care to other organizations and governments.* Primary health care with its emphasis on local ownership and strengthening the underlying heath systems is a laudable goal. However, it is not a goal best pursued by WHO. The organization needs to acknowledge that responsibility for development initiatives lies first with member states and will depend on their capacity and political will, which do not always match the international "consensus." WHO initiatives have repeatedly languished because countries simply do not have the means (e.g., staff, facilities, expertise, and systems) to implement them, much less in the time frame proposed by WHO. WHO can provide some technical advice, but the World Bank is better positioned to advise national governments on health systems.[97] The World Bank is also better equipped to provide technical assistance on health financing.

- *Cease or greatly constrain its regulatory efforts.* WHO is not a drug regulatory authority. It should either stop attempting to assess drug quality or undertake the initiative properly. If it chooses to retain this role, WHO should list only those drugs approved by stringent national agencies, including those of the United States, Canada, the European Union, Japan, and Switzerland, as long as those agencies are prepared and funded to undertake free assessments of drugs made in developing countries. In the past, the FDA has provided free assessments for HIV drugs.

  Unlike approval of drugs and other ingestibles for which strict governmental safety approval is desirable, approval of bed nets and other noningested products could potentially be undertaken by an NGO. A precedent has been set by numerous environmental approval mechanisms, including the Forestry Stewardship Council, which approves sustainable forest products. Although bed nets and sustainable-forest products are different, it is important to recognize the trade-off between the costs of safety regulation and the consumer safety benefits accrued therein. If the international community determines that regulating bed net safety is an essential public good that is best served by WHO, the organization should be careful that its endorsement of pesticides and nets is recognized for what it is: a limited guide, not stringent regulatory approval.

In short, WHO should yield to others when they are better positioned or equipped to lead. For health-system strengthening, this means the World

97. Shakow, *Global Fund and World Bank HIV/AIDS Program.*

Bank, which has technical expertise as well as closer, more collaborative relationships with developing-country governments. For private-sector delivery systems, this means the private sector itself. In this area, the organization might consider encouraging the practice of NGO-bidding for the provision of health-care services and the administration of programs, rather than delivering those services or administering programs itself. This was done successfully in a pilot program in postconflict Cambodia[98] and more recently in Afghanistan.[99] Through such decentralization, grounded in evidence-based research, WHO member states can lessen the principal–agent problems experienced during the organization's half-century history.[100]

Focusing on WHO's Comparative Advantages

WHO has certain comparative advantages over other health organizations, including its roles as advocate, or "global cheerleader"; standard setter; technical adviser; and mediator. As an advocate, WHO and the U.N. can help raise awareness about and thereby generate funding for developing-world health concerns. As a standard setter, WHO (and the U.N. more generally) benefits from what Gavin Yamey calls "near universal representation" with its 193 members having equal voting power. Although this can make consensus difficult, when consensus is achieved, it carries much influence and under some circumstances (such as health regulations on quarantine), much power.

WHO can also act as a convener, bringing together experts in committees

---

98. The pilot program in Cambodia found that districts in which health services were contracted out to NGOs "consistently outperformed" both control districts and contract-in districts on the predefined indicators of health-care delivery coverage. Indu Bhushan, Sheryl Keller, and Brad Schwartz, "Achieving the Twin Objectives of Efficiency and Equity: Contracting Health Services in Cambodia," (Asian Development Bank Economics and Research Department Policy Brief 6, March 2002), at www.adb.org/Documents/EDRC/Policy_Briefs/PB006.pdf (accessed December 8, 2008).

99. Natasha Palmer, Lesley Strong, Abdul Wali, and Egbert Sondorp, "Contracting Out Health Services in Fragile States," *BMJ* 332, no. 7543 (March 25, 2006): 718–21, at http://bmj.bmjjournals.com/cgi/content/full/332/7543/718 (accessed December 8, 2008).

100. Decentralization and greater local-level ownership is often proposed as a solution to information and incentive problems in the public-sector provision of health-care service. Still, the success of decentralization relies on the institutional capacity of the country where reforms are implemented. Limin Wang, "Health Sector Reforms," chap. 2 in *Analyzing the Distributional Impact of Reforms*, vol. 2, ed. Aline Coudouel and Stefano Paternostro (Washington, DC: World Bank, 2006), at http://siteresources.worldbank.org/INTPSIA/Resources/490023-1120845825946/3622-02_Ch02.pdf (accessed December 8, 2008).

to help to set "norms and standards in advising countries on their implementation at global, regional, national, and local levels."[101] Yet WHO and
its member states need to guard carefully against adopting overambitious
strategies, such as the Health for All effort.

With the proliferation of financing and implementing health agencies,
WHO can also act as a technical adviser and mediator, "engaging new constituencies, such as academies of science . . . by clearly communicating priorities for developing global public goods" where the private sector is
genuinely failing to address health concerns.[102] WHO can also act as a
trusted forum for tracking clinical and public health data. Specifically, if
WHO notes a rise in drug-resistant malaria in a country (reported by the
country or an implementing aid agency and verified by WHO's independent staff), it can advise implementing agencies to switch strategies from
first-line to second-line malarial drugs.[103] Most Western countries will trust
data provided by the United States and other governments, but other countries will oppose such government data for political reasons.

However, even this role need not be WHO specific. For example, the
International Society for Infectious Diseases' Program for Monitoring
Emerging Diseases is a global electronic reporting system for outbreaks of
emerging infectious diseases and toxins. The Global Public Health Intelligence Network, an Internet-based early-warning system developed and
managed by the Public Health Agency of Canada, gathers and disseminates
relevant information on disease outbreaks, infectious diseases, contami-
nated food and water, bioterrorism and exposure to chemical and radionu-
clear agents, and natural disasters. It also monitors issues related to the
safety of products, drugs, and medical devices.

Member states should carefully assess WHO's activities and initiatives to
ensure that the organization is best suited to implement them, is not duplicating other efforts, and is contributing to resolving the health problems at
hand.

Enhancing the Director General's Authority and Power

As a membership organization, WHO is constrained by the instructions
of its member states. This is to be expected and is often desirable because
the organization should be beholden to its financiers and the beneficiaries

---

101. High-Level Panel on UN System-Wide Coherence, "Delivering as One."

102. Timothy G. Evans, "Health-Related Global Public Goods: Initiatives of the
Rockefeller Foundation," U.N. Development Program, December 6, 2005.

103. Gavin Yamey, "WHO in 2002: Why Does the World Still Need WHO?" *BMJ*
325, no. 7375 (November 30, 2002): 1294–98, at www.bmj.com/cgi/content/
extract/325/7375/1294 (accessed December 8, 2008).

of its programs. However, within the mandates assigned to WHO by its member states, the director general should have the authority necessary to carry out the organization's missions. Strong leadership—clear vision backed up by sufficient authority to compel coordination and prioritize organizational activities—is critical to focus the organization on its core strengths. This is particularly necessary considering the great latitude traditionally enjoyed by WHO's regional offices. A strong leader can also work to distance the politics of the organization from its technical work. Even if the director general fails to deflect political pressure, he or she can "draw attention to the problem and transfer the pressure of politics back to those who would distort the facts or the process."[104]

Throughout WHO's history, the presence of a powerful leader unafraid to dismiss the politically correct status quo has been pivotal to WHO program-specific or organization-wide reform. For example, Arata Kochi appears to have turned around WHO's Global Malaria Program. Appointed director in 2006, Kochi fired at least 20 percent of the staff and bluntly criticized the global antimalaria community: "I said, basically, 'You are stupid,'" Kochi recalled, "'[you are] small and inward-looking and fighting each other.'"[105] Kochi created a new WHO malaria department that would serve as the main technical advisory body to Roll Back Malaria's implementing partners, and publicly castigated forty companies for selling artemisinin monotherapies, which had contributed to increased drug resistance in many countries. He drove the World Health Assembly to pass a resolution committing WHO member states to stop the production and marketing of oral artemisinin therapies.

Implementing reforms in these three areas would result in a leaner WHO: an organization that is more focused on the tasks for which it is uniquely suited and that restricts its other activities to coordinating or supporting other well-funded public, joint public-private, and private activities and organizations. Taken together, this framework would be more efficient, less duplicative, more flexible, and more responsive to health priorities in the developed and developing worlds.

While a more focused WHO would require less funding, the financial demands for addressing international health issues writ broadly is unlikely to decline. Donors need to ensure that their money is used effectively and

---

104. Ruth Levine, "Open Letter to the Incoming Director General of the World Health Organization: Time to Refocus," *BMJ* 333, no. 7576 (November 11, 2006): 1015–17, at www.bmj.com/cgi/content/full/333/7576/1015 (accessed December 8, 2008).

105. Donald G. McNeil Jr., "An Iron Fist Joins the Malaria Wars," *New York Times*, June 27, 2006, at www.nytimes.com/2006/06/27/health/27prof.html (December 8, 2008). For a longer discussion, see Bate, "Rolling Back Malaria."

prioritized appropriately among all the possible actors on the international health stage. Donors should recognize WHO's strengths and weaknesses and demand reform through the World Health Assembly and, if necessary, by leveraging their financial contributions. Ultimately, member states should shift WHO toward a voluntary funding mechanism under which they could demand and pay based on performance. They would not be bound to support politically driven programs that divert WHO from its core priorities.

CONCLUSION

Member-state-driven organizations like WHO no longer dominate the international health arena. That realm is increasingly being filled by well-financed national health programs, private NGOs, businesses, and foundations focused on specific initiatives. Often they are better financed, placed, staffed, and equipped to handle many of the missions that WHO has assumed over the past six decades.

WHO has a role to play, but it would do well to *nosce te ipsum* (know thyself) and acknowledge its weaknesses, divest itself of inappropriate programs, identify its areas of comparative advantage, and move forward playing a focused role. Its current condition is the end product of an ambitious mandate and a half-century of mission creep. Its reformed role as advocate, or global cheerleader; standard setter; technical adviser; and mediator should be based on evidence, anchored in integrity, and not swayed by political considerations. It should help to focus and leverage the large influx of bilateral and private aid by highlighting successful health initiatives and criticizing failures. Its budget should be refocused to fit this new mission and shifted toward voluntary funding to provide member states with a more effective feedback mechanism.

Conclusion

The United Nations

Neither Irrelevant nor Indispensable

Brett D. Schaefer

Considering America's prominent role in creating the United Nations and the noble aims of the organization, it is little wonder that the U.N. has considerable latent support among the American people. Numerous U.S. presidential administrations, private organizations, and individual Americans have struggled mightily to make the U.N. a more effective agent in preventing conflict and advancing worldwide respect for and observance of human rights and fundamental freedoms. Since the U.N.'s founding, the United States has been its largest financial supporter out of faith in its purposes, currently providing 22 percent and 26 percent of the assessed regular and peacekeeping budgets of U.N. and similar contributions to many of its affiliated organizations. In addition, the United States provides voluntary contributions to many U.N. organizations. Total U.S. contributions to the U.N. exceed $4 billion annually.[1]

---

1. The State Department reported that the United States contributed about $3 billion to the U.N. in 2004, but this excluded contributions by many other parts of the federal government that provide funds to the U.N. In 2006, the Office of Management and Budget (OMB) calculated that U.S. contributions to the entire U.N. system totaled $4.1 billion in 2004 and $5.3 billion in 2005—substantially larger sums than previously estimated. The OMB transferred responsibility for producing the report to the State Department for subsequent years. The State Department reported U.S. contributions of $4.5 billion in 2006 and $4.2 billion in 2007, implausibly indicating that the United States had reduced its U.N. contribution for two successive years despite rapid growth in U.N. budgets over that period. The department provided no explanation for the lower reported contributions. U.S. Department of State, Bureau of Public Affairs, "U.S. Participation in the United

Despite its strong political and financial support, active participation, and influential position as a permanent member of the U.N. Security Council, the United States has often been disappointed by the U.N.'s inability to take decisive action to promote and advance peace and security and its founding principles. During the organization's first forty years, this ineffectiveness was blamed, with some justification, on Cold War politics. The rivalry between the Soviet Union and the United States, with each using its vetoes in the U.N. Security Council to block actions that might benefit the other, often relegated the United Nations to a political, military, and economic backwater.

However, more recent U.N. failings have no such excuse. Since the end of the Cold War, U.N. peacekeepers failed to impose a credible government in Somalia, have been captured and held hostage in Sierra Leone, stood aside as genocide and other atrocities were committed in Rwanda and Srebrenica, and preyed on those whom they were asked to protect in the Democratic Republic of the Congo and in many other countries. Fraud and mismanagement involving billions of dollars went unchecked in the Oil-for-Food Program for Iraq and continue in U.N. procurement. Investigation and condemnation of human rights abuses are uneven throughout the U.N. system, with countries such as Israel singled out for harsh criticism, while China, Cuba, and other habitual human rights abusers escape serious scrutiny. Efforts to address global problems such as proliferation of weapons of mass destruction, terrorism, and human trafficking have been weak, ineffectual, or counterproductive.

As a result, Americans today hold a conflicted view of the United Nations. Some polls show that most Americans support the United Nations, while other polls reveal a majority who have little confidence that the U.N. is an effective or well-managed institution worthy of U.S. support.[2] These results indicate American support for the ideals of the U.N. and

Nations: Financial Contributions," September 8, 2005; U.S. Office of Management and Budget, "Report on US Contributions to the United Nations System," July 31, 2006, at http://coburn.senate.gov/ffm/index.cfm?FuseAction = Files.View&FileStore _id = 4d8e1af8-452e-4030-bd5a-6e0bdf9fbedb (accessed January 27, 2009); and Tom Coburn, "U.S. Contributions to the U.N. System Are Over $5.3 Billion," Subcommittee on Federal Financial Management, Government Information, and International Security, Committee on Homeland Security and Government Affairs, U.S. Senate, August 1, 2006, at http://coburn.senate.gov/ffm/index.cfm?FuseAction = OversightAction.View&ContentRecord_id = cb1276da-802a-23ad-4f6e-9b71d30d 4064 (accessed January 27, 2009). State Department reports for 2006 and 2007 are unpublished, but available on request.

2. For instance, a 2006 poll by Public Opinion Strategies showed that a majority of Americans had a favorable image of the United Nations and that 78 percent of registered voters believed "it is in America's best interest to actively support the United Nations." By contrast, a poll conducted a month earlier by Luntz Maslansky

a desire to see the organization effectively advance its founding principles, as well as bitter disappointment in the reality.

President Barack Obama mirrored this inconsistency after the November 2008 election, when he declared the United Nations to be both "an indispensable and imperfect forum."[3] Based on its track record of the past six decades, few would argue that the U.N. is perfect. On the contrary, considering its many failings, calling the U.N. "imperfect" is putting it kindly.

THE "INDISPENSABLE" U.N.

The more interesting—and debatable—part of President Obama's statement is his assertion that the U.N. is indispensable. This statement is frequently uttered by self-interested proponents of the U.N., such as U.N. secretary-general Ban Ki-moon, his predecessor Kofi Annan, and others whose livelihoods and goals depend on the U.N. Indeed, the notion that "global problems require global solutions and global resources"[4] and that the U.N. should spearhead such efforts has become so deeply ingrained in international discourse that individuals often unthinkingly repeat variations of this cliché[5] when discussing any of a host of international issues.

Strategic Research concluded: "A majority of Americans (57%) now believe the United Nations should be scrapped and replaced if it cannot be reformed and made more effective." Mark Leon Goldberg, "New Poll: Americans Support the UN," UN Dispatch, October 23, 2006, at www.undispatch.com/archives/2006/10/new_poll _americ.php (accessed January 27, 2009); and PR Newswire, "Available Americans Grade the U.N.: 'Get It Together or Get Out,'" September 11, 2006, at www.prnews wire.com/cgi-bin/stories.pl ? ACCT = 104&STORY = /www/story/09-11-2006/00044 30011 (accessed January 27, 2009).

3. Barack Obama, "Obama National Security Team Announcement," *New York Times*, December 1, 2008, at www.nytimes.com/2008/12/01/us/politics/01text -obama.html (accessed January 27, 2009).

4. Paul Wolfowitz, "Opening Address by the President of the World Bank Group," in International Monetary Fund, *Summary Proceedings of the Sixtieth Annual Meeting of the Board of Governors*, September 19–20, 2006, p. 22, at www.imf.org/ external/pubs/ft/summary/60/summary60.pdf (accessed January 27, 2009).

5. For example, Ban Ki-moon said: "In this new world, the challenges are increasingly those of collaboration, not confrontation. Nations can no longer protect their interests, or advance the wellbeing of their people, without the partnership of the rest." Ban Ki-moon, "Our Power Lies in Unity," *Guardian*, September 23, 2008, at www.guardian.co.uk/commentisfree/2008/sep/23/unitednations.development (accessed January 27, 2009). Javier Solana said: "There are many things in the world that will have to be changed. My core message to you, to the American People and to the citizens of Europe is that we have to try to do this together. . . . The stakes are very high and we have to formulate a common agenda. And what is more important: to implement it together . . . the global financial crisis . . . is a global problem

The popularity of the sentiment is understandable. After all, should not global problems be addressed by all nations? And what better place to discuss and resolve these problems than the United Nations where nearly every nation is represented? As individuals such as U.N. secretary-general Ban repeatedly assure us, "Global problems demand global solutions. And the United Nations is, truly, the world's only global institution."[6]

There are numerous examples of global problems that could be effectively addressed if a global consensus could be reached. However, achieving such beneficent consensus in the U.N. is elusive, to say the least. For instance, the U.N. Charter includes the lack of respect for human rights among the global problems that it seeks to address. Yet the U.N. regrettably includes among its membership regimes that brutally repress their citizens and refuse to grant them the right to choose their own governments. Their number includes China, which has approximately 20 percent of the world's population and a repressive government with a well-established record of denying its citizens basic human rights and fundamental freedoms. With such a membership, the U.N. is an inherently poor standard-bearer for freedom and human rights.

No compelling reason dictates that multilateral action to advance human rights should be the exclusive purview of the United Nations. Indeed, the failure to observe human rights, while a concern for those who wish universal observance of human rights and fundamental freedoms, is primarily a domestic matter. It does not require a global response; it simply requires abusive governments to observe and protect human rights. Other nations can encourage such policies, but they cannot impose those changes short of using force via sanctions or invasion. Based on past experiences with situations in Burma, Cuba, Iraq, Iran, Sudan, Zimbabwe, and many other

---

and therefore requires a global solution." Javier Solana, summary of remarks to the European Parliament Foreign Affairs Committee and the Chairs of the Foreign Affairs and Defence Committees of the National Parliaments, November 5, 2008, at www.consilium.europa.eu/ueDocs/cms_Data/docs/pressdata/EN/discours/1038 02.pdf (accessed January 27, 2009). Former U.N. Assembly president Srgjan Kerim said: "To promote effective multilateralism, to find global solutions to global problems, it is incumbent upon all of us to bolster the authority and international standing of this Assembly." Srgjan Kerim, quoted in press release, "Strengthened General Assembly Needed 'to Find Global Solutions to Global Problems' President Says, As Revitalization of Work Debated," U.N. General Assembly, November 26, 2007, at www.un.org/News/Press/docs/2007/ga10662.doc.htm (accessed January 27, 2009).

6. UN News Center, "UN Best-Placed to Tackle Global Problems in Today's World—Ban Ki-moon," July 26, 2007, at www.un.org/apps/news/story.asp?News ID = 23345 (accessed January 27, 2009).

countries, nations proposing such actions would likely find their efforts unwelcome at the U.N.

Moreover, some purportedly global problems are clearly not global or may in practice be better addressed through selective participation. Including nations with little at stake or minimal ability to effect a solution to a problem—which is the default process in the U.N.—can impede international action. Such was clearly the case with the Kyoto Protocol. Why should landlocked nations be considered essential parties to the Law of the Sea Treaty? Or nations with no outer space capabilities strongly influence deliberations of the U.N. Committee on the Peaceful Uses of Outer Space by constituting an overwhelming majority of its sixty-nine members?

The term "indispensable" implies dire consequences if support for the U.N. is lacking, but, as explained in the chapters of this book, unconditional support for the U.N. also has consequences. When the U.N. assumes tasks and responsibilities that it is poorly positioned to carry out effectively, the result can be worse than inaction. It can result in genocide, as in the extreme cases of Rwanda and Darfur where the international community mistakenly believed that the U.N. could address the situations. It can result in diplomatic dead ends, such as the Kyoto Protocol, that are pursued for years to little effect. It can shield human rights violators from scrutiny, while other nations are excoriated for far less. By its inaction, it can provide cover for states, such as Iran and North Korea, to acquire nuclear weapons or proliferate weapons of mass destruction. It can encourage countries to adopt economic policies that retard their growth and cause untold suffering. The problem with the belief that the U.N. is an indispensable body of first resort is that it encourages increasing intervention by the U.N. and its affiliated bodies into matters that they lack expertise, authority, or capacity to address effectively.

However, the problems plaguing the U.N. system do not necessitate condemning all its programs, funds, bodies, and activities. In many cases, the problems and issues with international implications merit U.S. engagement and cooperation with the U.N. and its affiliated bodies. Some global problems are undeniably being addressed through the U.N. and its related bodies or by multilateral action under a U.N. mandate. Indeed, in many chapters of this book, the authors acknowledge and identify numerous instances where the U.N. is serving or could serve useful functions—albeit with more limited and focused missions and mandates.

Among other functions, the U.N. often serves as a useful forum for multilateral meetings and discussions to address shared concerns. Peacekeeping operations, humanitarian missions, and political missions such as election monitoring are often more politically acceptable under the U.N. flag than as unilateral or multilateral efforts outside of the United Nations. In an excellent series of case studies, Greg Mills and Terrence McNamee show that

U.N. peacekeeping operations are best used in limited circumstances but that they can be effective within those parameters.

Similarly, the authors have identified numerous useful, often critical, activities conducted by the U.N. and its affiliated organizations. For instance, Roger Bate and Karen Porter note that the World Health Organization's international nature and universal membership may justify its continuing some of its activities even if "other public and private actors might perform some of these roles more efficiently."

Multilateral cooperation through international organizations such as the U.N. and affiliated bodies can be tremendously useful. However, it is wrong and counterproductive to assume that, because the U.N. is useful in some areas, all its activities are useful or that the useless or counterproductive activities are an inevitable and acceptable cost of the useful activities.

U.N. MISSION CREEP

Indeed, working separately, the authors identified a problem common to the U.N. in all the international issues discussed in their chapters: the U.N.'s unfortunate tendency to involve itself in activities which it lacks the competence or ability to resolve or address effectively. Regardless of whether this expansion is unplanned or by design, the authors lay out convincing cases that the U.N. has assumed, surreptitiously or at the behest of the member states, an agenda that often grossly outstrips its authority and capabilities. Based on their experience and research, they have analyzed fundamental activities of the U.N. system in international law, peace and security, human rights, environmental issues, disarmament, and other matters and found them wanting.

In some cases, the U.N. system is flawed and desperately needs to be focused and streamlined, but it could still serve a useful function if reformed. In her chapter on the U.N. and trade, Daniella Markheim points to the evolution of the United Nations Conference on Trade and Development (UNCTAD) from ideological opposition to free markets and trade to a more pragmatic advocacy of developing country interests within the context of a more liberal globalized economy. She concludes that if UNCTAD is refocused on helping developing countries more quickly embrace open markets and if other parts of the U.N. system are streamlined to eliminate activities that overlap or duplicate UNCTAD's mandate, UNCTAD can serve as a valuable complement to the World Trade Organization.

Another problem is a general lack of accountability and responsibility in the U.N. system. For instance, Bate and Porter point out that the international health arena is more crowded than ever. U.S. initiatives, such as the President's Emergency Plan for AIDS Relief (PEPFAR), and private entities, such as the Bill and Melinda Gates Foundation, are growing increasingly influential and better equipped to handle tasks traditionally assigned to the World Health Organization (WHO). They recommend that WHO "focus on roles in which it enjoys a comparative advantage . . . and divest responsibilities not directly related to these roles."

In his chapter, Ambassador Terry Miller identifies the critical failure of the U.N. in development: its commitment to a failed ideological approach that is hostile to free markets and serves to encourage polices that undermine economic growth. Moreover, he notes that duplication and overlapping mandates among U.N. organizations undermine efforts to identify who is responsible for various projects or activities and reduce accountability for results. In such circumstances, success has a thousand fathers, while failure is an orphan.

The need for clear lines of responsibility and metrics for measuring success in the U.N. is overwhelming. As Ambassador John Bolton outlines in the foreword, a system of voluntary funding for the U.N. would help to force various U.N. bodies to more clearly identify their unique contributions in order to garner financial support.

ALTERNATIVE AVENUES

In some cases, the authors conclude that the U.N. or its affiliated bodies are not the best option to perform the tasks assigned to them by member states. For instance, Christopher Horner points out the many drawbacks in using a universal membership organization such as the U.N. to address environmental problems, even if they are global in scope. In Horner's opinion, limited, focused processes such as the original U.S.-led Asia–Pacific Partnership on Clean Development and Climate have proven superior to the U.N. template for addressing "global warming" because they are less vulnerable to manipulation by third parties and thus more likely to achieve their objectives.

Baker Spring similarly sees most U.N. arms control and disarmament activities as counterproductive and, in some cases, harmful to international peace and security. According to Spring, the U.N.'s arms control and disarmament processes increasingly focus on the goal of disarmament divorced from accountability. Worse, the U.N. has demonstrated a troubling tendency to "avoid confronting the arms buildups of forces for repression." The combination necessitates "a series of changes to return the focus of international arms control and disarmament efforts to states that have a direct, vested interest in negotiating realistic, effective, and verifiable agreements."

In our chapter on the U.N. and human rights, Steven Groves and I conclude that the United Nations is uniquely unsuited to the task of promoting human rights and confronting nations that violate the basic rights of their citizens because it includes those nations as member states in good standing. Experience, most recently with the gravely disappointing U.N. Human Rights Council, clearly shows that these nations can and do cripple the organization's ability to undertake these tasks in a balanced and consistent manner. We recommend reducing U.N. human rights activities and creating an alternative body composed of states that demonstrably support human rights and fundamental freedoms.

CIVIL SOCIETY AND NGOS

Several authors highlight a related problem of incorporating the voices of civil society and nongovernmental organizations (NGOs) into the work of multilateral organizations. These groups perform vital work by promoting and publicizing the opinions, needs, and sufferings of individuals living under repressive and totalitarian governments. The information that they provide should be taken into account by multilateral organizations.

However, NGOs and civil society groups must never be granted a status that is superior or equal to sovereign states in international organizations. The vast majority of NGOs represent narrow interests supported by slivers of national populations. They typically do not reflect national constituencies. Often, they go through the U.N. to advance their agendas precisely because they lack domestic support for their causes. Susan Yoshihara, Baker Spring, and Christopher Horner offer examples of instances in which NGOs have secured unwarranted influence in the U.N. system to advance radical agendas that do not have broad-based support.

While an inclusive process should take the opinions of civil society and NGOs into account, their role should be appropriately circumscribed, and they should not be granted equal status with democratic governments that, through free and fair elections, represent the will of their citizens.

GLOBALIZATION OF DOMESTIC ISSUES

Finally, the authors frequently express concern about the U.N. tendency, often with the encouragement of member states, to move beyond the limited role established in its Charter, which prohibits the organization from interfering in the domestic affairs of member states. The trend of elevating what are traditionally domestic policy concerns or multilateral issues involving a handful of nations to the global arena is proliferating in both scope and frequency.

Examples abound of formerly domestic issues that the U.N. and sympathetic governments and nongovernmental organizations now consider "global." Recent years have seen attempts at international interventions on issues as large as regulating national economies to reduce greenhouse gas emissions and asserting legal jurisdiction over individuals whose governments are deemed unable to govern or simply delinquent to issues as small as criticizing governments for celebrating Mother's Day or deciding which bed nets governments should buy.

As Lee Casey, David Rivkin, and Susan Yoshihara discuss in their chapters, the means of intervention are becoming progressively more intrusive and expansive in asserting political agendas in legal guise as new international norms, necessitating a careful reevaluation of U.S. engagement with international legal bodies and participation in international negotiations for treaties, conventions, and other binding legal instruments. Casey and Rivkin warn:

> The United States must make clear in all its international dealings and particularly in its interactions with the U.N. bureaucracy and other member states that it respects the law of nations, but that it also continues to reserve to itself the right to interpret and apply that law on its own account. It must act consistently with this position in the formulation and implementation of American foreign policy and should urge other states to maintain the same position.

PROTECTING U.S. INTERESTS

Because of the U.N.'s potential both to advance U.S. interests and to create mischief, U.S. policymakers must take the United Nations seriously. Most nations extend enormous respect and credibility to the United Nations and its affiliated bodies. Doubtlessly, some governments do so out of an altruistic desire to bolster the "global community," but most nations support the U.N. because it serves their interests. Some nations seek to use the organization as a counterweight to the United States and as a means to frustrate policies that they oppose. Other nations, particularly small or less influential ones, see it as a way to promote their policies and priorities that otherwise might be ignored. Some see it as a cost-effective means for leveraging international funding and attention to causes that they deem important. Other nations use it as a vehicle for advancing policy agendas that would have little traction in strictly state-to-state negotiations, but have drawn strong support from nongovernmental organizations and international bureaucrats in the U.N. system. Examples of all these agendas are sprinkled throughout this book.

Regardless of the reasons, most nations do value the United Nations. If the United States is to protect its interests and advance its priorities, it must continue to take the lead in addressing the many problems plaguing the U.N. system. However, the Obama administration and subsequent administrations should not base this process on the assumption that the organization is indispensable.

As Kim Holmes explains, the United States must be pragmatic in its approach to multilateral engagement. The United States, like any other nation, should first identify its objective and then determine if going to the U.N. is the best option for achieving it. A number of U.N. technical agencies and specialized bodies and activities are effective and serve U.S. interests, and the United States should support them. Others are hindered by policies, practices, and mandates that squander resources; the United States should seek to reform and refocus them on their core missions.

International cooperation is often critically important to U.S. interests, and the U.N. and its affiliated organizations can play a vital role. Failing to demand that these activities are undertaken effectively and efficiently does a disservice to the U.N.'s mandate and fails to respect the American people, whose tax dollars underwrite a large share of the U.N.'s activities. The U.S. government needs to ensure that every agency and body in the U.N. system is operating in a transparent, accountable, and well-managed manner. As only one nation among 192 U.N. member states, the United States is generally not in a position to impose reforms to advance these objectives. As such, it has an obligation to use its position as the largest financier of the U.N. to press for key reforms.

If the United States is to engage in multilateral forums, negotiations, and initiatives that support rather than undermine its interests, it must fundamentally reevaluate and reshape its relationship with other governments and international bodies, particularly the United Nations. Obstructionism and intransigence in the U.N. continue to impede its effectiveness in addressing the entire range of its responsibilities. The United States must seek to address this problem.

However, this does not mean that the United States should support or participate in all U.N. bodies simply because they exist. If a U.N. body has proven irrelevant, hopelessly flawed, or antithetical to U.S. interests, the United States should not reward its poor performance with U.S. financial support or participation, which would lend it unwarranted prestige and credibility. To the extent necessary, the United States should observe and report on proceedings in such bodies, but it should end formal participation, stating clearly its reasons and the changes that would lead to a resumption of U.S. participation. The United States followed such a policy to positive effect with the International Labor Organization in the 1970s and UNESCO in the 1980s.

All countries should be wary of unquestioning support for supranational organizations such as the U.N. The U.N. itself replaced the League of Nations when the League proved incapable and ineffectual. If the U.N. proved irretrievably flawed or incapable of promoting cooperative action among its member states to preserve international peace and security and of advancing human rights and fundamental freedoms, nations would be foolish not to consider fundamentally reforming it.

If the U.N. or its affiliated bodies prove too resistant to reform, the United States should not shy away from proposing and pursuing alternatives. To his credit, early in his presidential campaign, President Obama praised actions to circumvent the U.N. when they addressed issues of critical importance:

> Stalin's obstruction created stalemate in the United Nations, but the United States was not deterred. American presidents created new institutions, like NATO, and encouraged others, including the European Economic Community, to advance the principles and mandate of the U.N. Charter.[7]

This welcome observation demonstrates an understanding that it is the tasks and charges placed before the U.N. that really matter. The organization itself, while possessing intrinsic value as a universal forum, is far less significant than the purposes for which it was created.

The United States must be flexible in its approaches to international cooperation. If the United States and other nations operate only through the U.N., they hand the spoilers the means to frustrate their efforts. Multilateralism is a tool, not an end in itself. The United States should be open to working through the U.N. and other international organizations to address joint concerns, but the United States must not allow solutions to be held hostage by an irrational adherence to past practice or theoretical jurisdictions.

Such flexibility has proven useful in the past. When the International Atomic Energy Agency and the Security Council were not being assertive enough in curtailing proliferation of weapons of mass destruction, the United States and like-minded allies established the successful Proliferation Security Initiative to fill the gap. While the Kyoto Protocol floundered, the George W. Bush administration pursued actions through the Major Economies Process on Energy Security and Climate Change, the Asia–Pacific Partnership on Clean Development and Climate, and the annual G-8 meetings with states that had the most at stake and were capable of acting to address the issue. To address security concerns, America and its allies intervened or initiated the use of force in the former Republic of Yugosla-

---

7. Barack Obama, "The United States and the United Nations," *Congressional Record* (September 25, 2007): S12046.

via, Iraq, and other places without the express permission of the U.N. Security Council.

These types of alternatives will rise and fall based on their success, effectiveness, and seriousness. A body or initiative that confronts its responsibilities with due deliberation and a willingness to act will draw the interest, participation, and respect of nations that are equally committed to advancing that agenda. The successful alternatives will starkly contrast with those instances in which the U.N. system has proven ineffective.

Obviously, a failed initiative would engender little support and should be abandoned or reexamined to see if it could be fixed. This is appropriate and should apply as much to the U.N. and its affiliated bodies as it does to non-U.N. efforts, such as the Community of Democracies, that have failed to live up to expectations.

RETHINKING THE INTERNATIONAL SYSTEM

The extensive work by the chapter authors leads to the conclusion that the United Nations system remains seriously flawed and is in desperate need of reform. The United Nations is suffering from confused purposes and competing interests among the member states, which make it an unreliable means of addressing threats to international peace and security, a misguided advisor on development and economic growth, a limited venue for resolving international problems, and an uneven and unfair arbiter of human rights. The U.N. has also proven susceptible with distressing frequency to mismanagement, ineffective practices, and politically driven efforts to undermine effective action.

It is time to rethink and reshape U.S. engagement with the United Nations so that it better serves both U.S. interests and the organization's own stated purposes. The United States should continue to lead the international community by working through the U.N. when it can be effective, but it should also lead in establishing alternative mechanisms, coalitions, partnerships, alliances, and organizations to act when the U.N. proves unable or unwilling.

Such a process does not necessitate abolishing the United Nations or even making significant change in some cases. Indeed, parts of the U.N. system are well worth preserving. However, most of the U.N. suffers from mission creep and a lack of focus on those tasks in which it provides unique contributions. These problems all too often undermine effective action to resolve international problems and urgently need to be addressed.

Each year, the need for reform becomes more important as more and more issues central to U.S. interests are placed on the U.N. docket. If the United States is to benefit from the U.N., it must lead an effort to remove redundancy of mandates in the U.N., establish clear lines of authority and responsibility, and improve transparency and accountability. It must also seek to improve U.N. responsiveness to the demands of its major donors by introducing competition into the U.N. system by moving more budgets to voluntary funding.

Critically, the United States must be willing to push for competition with the U.N. itself. As President Ronald Reagan observed in his 1985 address to the U.N. General Assembly:

> The vision of the U.N. Charter—to spare succeeding generations this scourge of war—remains real. It still stirs our soul and warms our hearts, but it also demands of us a realism that is rock hard, clear-eyed, steady, and sure—a realism that understands the nations of the United Nations are not united.[8]

The United States should not and must not permit the U.N. to become the means for constraining the efforts by the United States and other nations to secure a more stable and peaceful world, advance fundamental human rights, and improve the health and living standards of people in both developed and developing countries. As it has in the past, the United States needs to explore new organizations and alternative approaches when the existing ones fail.

The recommendations in this volume are a guide to resolving the U.N. conundrum. They provide a sound basis for judging where and when to pursue actions within the U.N. and when to consider alternatives. They draw critical lessons and identify principles to ensure that the capabilities and potential of the United Nations and other international organizations are appropriately and adequately incorporated into U.S. policy decisions without unduly infringing on national sovereignty or impeding a nation's right to defend its interests. Such an approach is critically important not only for nations like the United States that are understandably concerned about such matters, but also for the U.N. and its efforts to address international problems large and small.

---

8. Ronald Reagan, address to the U.N. General Assembly, October 24, 1985, at www.reagan.utexas.edu/archives/speeches/1985/102485a.htm (accessed January 27, 2009).

Index

1503 procedure, 142, 142n22, 156
3 by 5 Initiative (HIV), 312–313, 315

abortion, 150, 177, 183, 188–192, 197–199, 223, 227
ACABQ. *See* Advisory Committee on Administrative and Budgetary Questions
accountability, xv, xxi–xxii, xxv–xxvi, 19, 194n71, 330–331, 337; in arms control and disarmament, 264, 274–275; in development work, 210, 230, 234–235, 250, 254–255; in health programs, 303, 305–306, 330–331; in human rights decisions, 163; and the One U.N. program, 229; in peacekeeping operations, 89–92; need for, xxi–xxii, xxv, 2; and NGOs, 163, 204; problems with, 13, 29, 34, 88, 124, 202, 292, 303; and treaty bodies, 202; and voluntary funding, 23, 124, 205, 274
acquired immune deficiency syndrome, 227, 295, 309, 310, 315. *See also* Global Fund to Fight AIDS, Tuberculosis and Malaria; human immunodeficiency virus; President's Emergency Plan for AIDS Relief; United Nations Joint Program on HIV/AIDS

ad hoc courts, 14, 32, 49–54, 272n15; authority, 50, 52; considered for Darfur, 14; distinguished from the Nuremburg tribunal, 51; precedential value of, 52. *See also* tribunals.
Advisory Committee on Administrative and Budgetary Questions, 218, 221–223, 224n33
Affordable Medicines Facility for Malaria, 318
Afghanistan, xx, 57, 58n3, 59, 64, 84, 89, 198, 321
Africa, 59, 62, 78, 83, 91n67, 92, 160, 208; biotech restrictions, 102; development issues, 207, 255, 299–300; disarmament, pacification, demobilization, and repatriation (DDR), 81, 83; Economic Commission for Africa, 255; Economic Community of West African States, 89; and health, 191, 199, 208, 297, 298–300, 309, 311–315, 318; malaria, 297, 298n19, 305; Maputo Plan of Action, 199; and the OIC, 155; peacekeeping and peacebuilding operations, 58–63, 66, 69, 77, 82–83, 92; seats on Human Rights Council, 155; Tswalu Protocol, 82. *See also* African Union; Congo; Darfur; Rwanda; United State Africa Command; and Zimbabwe

About the Contributors

Economist **Roger Bate**, PhD, is the Legatum Fellow in Global Prosperity at the American Enterprise Institute, where he writes on international health policy in Africa and the performance and effectiveness of international organizations and development policy initiatives. His writings have appeared in the *Wall Street Journal*, *Financial Times*, *Lancet*, *British Medical Journal*, and others.

John R. Bolton is a senior fellow at the American Enterprise Institute, where his portfolio includes foreign policy and international organizations. He served as the U.S. permanent representative to the United Nations from August 2005 until December 2006.

Lee A. Casey is a partner in the Washington, D.C., office of Baker & Hostetler LLP. He is an expert in international and constitutional law and served at the Justice Department during the administrations of Ronald Reagan and George H. W. Bush.

Edwin J. Feulner, PhD, is president of The Heritage Foundation. He has served as a member of the bipartisan Task Force on the United Nations, which was organized by the United States Institute of Peace as mandated by the U.S. Congress.

Steven Groves is the Bernard and Barbara Lomas Fellow in the Margaret Thatcher Center for Freedom at The Heritage Foundation. Prior to joining Heritage, Groves served as senior counsel to the U.S. Senate Permanent Subcommittee on Investigations, and played a lead role in the subcommittee's investigation into the United Nations Oil-for-Food scandal. Prior to that, Groves practiced law at Boies, Schiller & Flexner LLP and served as an assistant attorney general for the State of Florida. Groves received a law degree from Ohio Northern University College of Law in 1995 and a degree in history from Florida State University in 1992.

Kim R. Holmes, PhD, is vice president for foreign and defense policy studies and director of the Kathryn and Shelby Cullom Davis Institute for International Studies at The Heritage Foundation. He served as assistant secretary of state for international organization affairs in the first term of President George W. Bush, with responsibility for advancing U.S. interests and policies at the United Nations and forty-six other international organizations. He a member of the Council on Foreign Relations, and the author of *Liberty's Best Hope: American Leadership for the 21st Century* (2008).

Christopher C. Horner, an attorney and senior fellow at the Competitive Enterprise Institute, is author of *Red Hot Lies: How Global Warming Alarmists Use Threats, Fraud, and Deception to Keep You Misinformed* (2008) and *The Politically Incorrect Guide to Global Warming and Environmentalism* (2007). He has testified before the U.S. Senate and written extensively on a wide range of treaty issues.

Daniella Markheim is Jay Van Andel Senior Trade Policy Analyst in the Center for International Trade and Economics at The Heritage Foundation, where she specializes in international trade and monetary theory, comparative economic systems, and international financial management. She worked seven years in the economics division at Joint Warfare Analysis Center, with the last four as senior economist and project leader. She has served as a board member for the Society of Government Economists and as a consultant to the World Bank, where she designed and built a database for a study of economic productivity in Eastern Europe.

Terence McNamee, PhD, is director of publications at the Royal United Services Institute for Defence and Security Studies, based in London. He has worked on a number of peacebuilding initiatives in fragile states, particularly in Africa. He is the editor of *War Without Consequences: Iraq's Insurgency and the Spectre of Strategic Defeat* (2008).

Ambassador Terry Miller is director of the Center for International Trade and Economics at The Heritage Foundation. Prior to joining The Heritage Foundation, he had a distinguished career as a diplomat and public servant, most recently serving as U.S. ambassador to the United Nations Economic and Social Council.

Greg Mills, PhD, directs the Johannesburg-based Brenthurst Foundation, established by the Oppenheimer family to strengthen African economic performance. He served during 2006 as head of the "Prism" strategic analysis cell and special adviser to the commander of the International Security Assistance Force (IX), based in Kabul, and from January 2008 to August 2008 was seconded to the government of Rwanda as strategic adviser to the president. He currently also serves as a member of the Danish prime minister's Africa Commission. From 1996 to 2005 he was national director of the South African Institute of International Affairs.

Karen Porter is a research assistant at the American Enterprise Institute, where she is a regular contributor to AEI's Health Policy Outlook series. Her articles on development, international organizations, and foreign aid have appeared on the *American* online.

David B. Rivkin Jr. is a partner in the Washington, D.C., office of Baker & Hostetler LLP. He is an expert in international and constitutional law and served at the Justice Department, the White House counsel's office, and the office of the vice president during the administrations of Ronald Reagan and George H. W. Bush.

Brett D. Schaefer is Jay Kingham Fellow in International Regulatory Affairs in the Margaret Thatcher Center for Freedom at The Heritage Foundation. He has testified before Congress and written extensively on a wide range of United Nations issues. From March 2003 to March 2004, he worked at the Pentagon as an assistant for international criminal court policy and served in 2005 as an expert on the bipartisan Task Force on the United Nations, which was organized by the United States Institute of Peace as mandated by the U.S. Congress.

Baker Spring is F. M. Kirby Research Fellow in National Security Policy in the Douglas and Sarah Allison Center for Foreign Policy Studies, a division of the Kathryn and Shelby Cullom Davis Institute for International Studies, at The Heritage Foundation. He served as legislative assistant to Senator David Karnes (R-NE) during the Senate's consideration of the 1987 Intermediate-Range Nuclear Forces (INF) Treaty with the Soviet Union.

Susan Yoshihara, PhD, is vice president for research at Catholic Family & Human Rights Institute (C-FAM) and director of the International Organizations Research Group. Since 2006 she has participated in major international social policy negotiations as a leader in civil society coalitions, including the negotiations for the U.N. Convention on the Rights of Persons with Disabilities and the annual Commission on the Status of Women. A retired U.S. naval aviator, she taught international relations at the Naval War College, and worked on international trade issues as a White House fellow. She writes frequently on human rights, humanitarianism, and intervention.